SINICIZATION AND THE RISE OF CHINA

China's rise and civilizational processes of Sinicization suggest that a recombination of the new with the old, rather than a total rupture with or return to the past, is China's likely future. In both space and time, civilizations offer the broadest context for world politics. Civilizational politics is of particular salience in China. Reification of civilizations into simple categories such as 'East' and 'West' is widespread in everyday politics and common in policy and academic writings. This book's emphasis on Sinicization as a specific civilizational process counters political and intellectual shortcuts and corrects the mistakes to which they often lead. Sinicization illustrates that, like other civilizations, China has always been open to variegated social and political processes that have brought together many different kinds of people, adhering to very different kinds of practices. This book tries to avoid the reifications and celebrations that mark much of the contemporary public debate about China's rise. It highlights instead complex processes and political practices that avoid easy shortcuts in bridging East and West. The analytical perspectives of this book are laid out in Peter Katzenstein's opening and concluding chapters. They are explored in six outstanding case studies, written by widely known authors who inquire into questions of security, political economy, and culture.

Featuring an exceptional line-up and representing a diversity of theoretical views within one integrative perspective, this work will be of interest to all scholars and students of China, Asia, international relations, sociology, and political science.

Peter J. Katzenstein is the Walter S. Carpenter, Jr. Professor of International Studies at Cornell University, USA. His work addresses issues of political economy, security, and culture in world politics.

WITHDRAWN
UTSA LIBRARIES

SINICIZATION AND THE RISE OF CHINA

Civilizational processes beyond East and West

Edited by
Peter J. Katzenstein

London and New York

First published 2012
by Routledge
2 Park Square, Milton Park, Abingdon, Oxon OX14 4RN

Simultaneously published in the USA and Canada
by Routledge
711 Third Avenue, New York, NY 10017

Routledge is an imprint of the Taylor & Francis Group, an informa business

© 2012 editorial and selected matter, Peter J. Katzenstein; individual contributions, the contributors.

The right of Peter J. Katzenstein to be identified as editor of this work has been asserted by him in accordance with the Copyright, Designs and Patents Act 1988.

All rights reserved. No part of this book may be reprinted or reproduced or utilized in any form or by any electronic, mechanical, or other means, now known or hereafter invented, including photocopying and recording, or in any information storage or retrieval system, without permission in writing from the publishers.

Trademark notice: Product or corporate names may be trademarks or registered trademarks, and are used only for identification and explanation without intent to infringe.

British Library Cataloguing in Publication Data
A catalogue record for this book is available from the British Library

Library of Congress Cataloging in Publication Data
Sinicization and the rise of China : civilizational processes beyond East and West / edited by Peter J. Katzenstein.
    p. cm.
  "Simultaneously published in the USA and Canada"—T.p. verso.
  Includes bibliographical references and index.
    ISBN 978-0-415-80953-5 (hbk.) — ISBN 978-0-415-80952-8 (pbk.) — ISBN 978-0-203-12706-3 (ebook) 1. Sinicization. 2. East and West. 3. Civilization—Chinese influences. 4. China—Civilization—1949–1976. 5. China—Civilization—1976-2002. 6. China—Civilization—2002- 7. China—Relations. 8. Economic development—China. 9. Social change—China. I. Katzenstein, Peter J.
  DS779.23.S56 2012
  951.05–dc23   2011034894

ISBN 13: 978-0-415-80953-5 (hbk)
ISBN 13: 978-0-415-80952-8 (pbk)
ISBN 13: 978-0-203-12706-3 (ebk)

Typeset in Bembo
by Cenveo Publisher Services

Printed and bound in Great Britain by
CPI Antony Rowe, Chippenham, Wiltshire

To the memory of
S.N. Eisenstadt (1923–2010) and
Samuel P. Huntington (1927–2008)

CONTENTS

List of Contributors   *ix*
Preface   *xi*

1 China's rise: rupture, return, or recombination?   1
   Peter J. Katzenstein

PART I   **39**

2 Reimagining the frontier: patterns of Sinicization and the emergence of new thinking about China's territorial periphery   41
   Allen Carlson

3 One China, two worlds: Taiwan and China's quest for identity and security   65
   Xu Xin

PART II   **97**

4 Compressed development, flexible practices, and multiple traditions in China's rise   99
   Tianbiao Zhu

5 The rise of China and its implications for East Asia   120
   Takashi Shiraishi

PART III   151

6 Cultural Sinicization in four diasporic lives   153
   Chih-yu Shih

7 Becoming "Chinese" in Southeast Asia   175
   Caroline S. Hau

PART IV   207

8 Sinicization in comparative perspective   209
   Peter J. Katzenstein

   References   *242*
   Index   *280*

CONTRIBUTORS

Allen Carlson is an associate professor in Cornell University's Government Department. He is also the author of *Unifying China, Integrating with the World* (2005) and the co-editor of *Contemporary Chinese Politics* (2010).

Caroline S. Hau is an associate professor at the Center for Southeast Asian Studies, Kyoto University. Her most recent book is *Traveling Nation-Makers: Transnational Flows and Movements in the Making of Modern Southeast Asia*, co-edited with Kasian Tejapira.

Peter J. Katzenstein is the Walter S. Carpenter, Jr. Professor of International Studies at Cornell University. His work addresses issues of political economy, security, and culture in world politics.

Chih-yu Shih teaches cultural studies, China studies, and political psychology at National Taiwan University. He publishes on Chinese ethnic politics, socialist reform, village democracy, foreign policy, and Asianism, among other subjects, and edits *Asian Ethnicity*. He is currently working on comparative epistemology of China Studies.

Takashi Shiraishi is president of the National Graduate Institute for Policy Studies as well as the Institute of Developing Economies Japan External Trade Promotion Organization. He is also an executive member of the Council for Science and Technology Policy, Cabinet Office.

Xu Xin is an adjunct associate professor in the Government Department and director of the China and Asia-Pacific Studies Program at Cornell University.

His areas of interest include Chinese foreign policy, East Asian security politics, and the Taiwan issue.

Tianbiao Zhu is an associate professor in the School of Government at Peking University, where he currently serves as Associate Dean. His teaching and research interests include international and comparative political economy and the political economy of development.

PREFACE

This book is part of a trilogy exploring civilizations in world politics. The first volume, *Civilizations in World Politics: plural and pluralist perspectives* (2010), developed a particular conceptual approach stressing the plurality and pluralism of civilizations and applied it to six major civilizations. Two follow-on volumes explore civilizational processes and identities in greater detail. Situated in a broader comparative perspective, *Sinicization and the Rise of China: civilizational processes beyond East and West* (2012) inquires into Sinicization during the era of China's peaceful rise. With particular attention to the problematic relationship between liberalism and race, *Anglo-America and Its Discontents: civilizational identities beyond West and East* (2012) analyzes the evolution of civilizational identities of Anglo-America. Drawing on *Civilizations in World Politics*, the conceptual foundation of the trilogy is restated in the largely identical first section of the concluding chapters of volumes 2 and 3. The two subtitles of these volumes convey the central message of both books: we need to move beyond sharp distinctions between East and West.

The intellectual origins of this project lie in the twists and turns of my research and teaching during the last two decades. In the 1990s I tried to understand better the importance of norms and identities in world politics. Addressing general theories of international relations in one book, I applied the approach to Japanese security in another. In the last decade I have also thought some about regionalism and regionalization in world politics. I have remained unsatisfied with how I posed and sought to address the issue of regional identities in East Asia and Western Europe. The history of maps offers vivid illustrations of how regional identities evolve and how the world is being reimagined. Regional borders and meanings remain forever open to political debate and conflict. In both ways, regions resemble civilizations. The language of civilizational politics, I hope, offers a compelling way of capturing that kind of politics.

Indeed, the civilizational level of analysis could be added easily to conventional theories of international relations. This trilogy seeks to better specify the cultural context of world politics, focusing on Sinicization and Anglo-America as examples of complex processes and contested identities normally subsumed under the rubrics of globalization and internationalization. Even though they refer to different objects, for the most part these two concepts are used interchangeably. Globalization describes processes that transcend time and compress space, with novel and transformative effects for world politics. Internationalization refers to processes of territorially based exchanges across national borders, reflecting basic continuities in the evolution of the international state system. Globalization favors convergence around common standards as well as a variety of local adaptations to global change. Internationalization permits continued national differences in national practices. In this view, contemporary world politics is marked by a mixture of transformative global and incremental international effects that shape and reshape the international system.

A focus on civilizational processes and identities invites us to move from a generic to a more specific characterization of global and international contexts that illuminates the distinctive characteristics of intercivilizational engagements and encounters, as well as occasional civilizational clashes. Contextual specificity is a complement to rather than a substitute for international relations theory. Our theories tell us a number of things at a level of generality that is unhelpful for understanding or engaging the world. This trilogy does not seek to develop precise implications of the civilizational turn for the theoretical debate in international relations. It is an exercise in pattern recognition rather than in the specification of particular puzzles and scope conditions, or the articulation of alternative explanations and indicators helpful for quantitative analysis. My hope is to illuminate the broad contours of world politics and thus to create novel perspectives that invite more probing and precise inquiries by others.

Ever since the publication of Samuel Huntington's famous 1993 article in *Foreign Affairs*, his clash of civilization thesis has been required reading in the large introduction to International Relations that I regularly teach at Cornell. That article has remained a perennial student favorite and is typically included among the top three of the close to 50 readings that I assign. A decade ago when the impact of religion on world politics became one of my research interests, I encountered Shmuel Eisenstadt's concept of multiple modernities, in some ways an antidote and in other ways a complement to Huntington's analysis. Finally, a few years ago I developed a new course on American foreign policy. In preparing a new set of lectures I became reacquainted with the broad corpus of Huntington's writings on America and recognized both its affinity to Louis Hartz's views and its consistency with Huntington's civilizational writing. I also learned that Eisenstadt's concept of multiple modernities had a close cousin in Rogers Smith's powerful, multiple-tradition critique of Hartz's (and Huntington's) view of America's liberal tradition. America, and some of its kin countries, I concluded, could be viewed quite profitably through lenses that differed from those deployed by my realist and liberal friends and colleagues. America is not only the most powerful state in the international system and the leading capitalist democracy in global markets; it is also a civilization in its own right.

What is true of any book is also true of this trilogy – it remains unfinished. If the initial spur for this project was Huntington's cultural realism, at the end the limits of liberal internationalism became my central concern. Like cultural realists, liberals continue to adhere to by now outdated aspects of a nineteenth-century Eurocentric model of world politics. Then as now, the civilized or advanced countries set the standards for the uncivilized or developing ones. My engagement with liberal theory and practice forced me to think specifically about the racial dimension of world politics. Born at the end of World War II in Nazi Germany and liberated by US soldiers, many of whom had sacrificed their lives so that I could live freely, this was a topic fraught with intimations of the Holocaust from which I had shied away for a long time. Furthermore, my deep admiration of and attraction to the United States had made me gloss over the problematic and ungainly aspects of a country that had adopted me with so much generosity and that I had come to embrace so fully.

Even though their politeness made them downplay the fact in the presence of an American-German *gaijin*, over many years I learned from my colleagues in East Asia that they considered race to be a salient factor for any serious analysis of world politics. I realized early on that my American colleagues who studied international relations were either uninterested in or openly hostile to inquiries into the relation between liberalism and race. Arguably they live in a society that continues to bear the very visible and ugly scars of a never forgotten racism; but for the most part they regard this to be a non-issue in the era of multiculturalism and human rights. Liberal theorists reformulate Wilsonianism to make this basic policy approach relevant to our times. Alternatively, realist critics of Woodrow Wilson seek to diminish his far-reaching impact on world politics by characterizing him as an unrealistic idealist. Neither spends even a passing moment to reflect on the significance that as a man of the South, Wilson the liberal was also a racist. I thus conclude the trilogy by reflecting on the similarities and differences between the global reach of Anglo-America and Islam; inquiring into the limits of international liberalism; and searching for historical analogies that can help us grasp more fully the movement to what I call "polymorphic globalism." Although that globalism contains within it close links to liberalism, it goes further to deal with a humanity larger and more diverse than that of the West or Anglo-America.

I eventually found my interest in civilizational analysis being met with more than a healthy dose of skepticism by various audiences. Those interested in the cultural terrain of the modern world in particular showed a visceral aversion to the concept of civilization, overladen for that audience by the connotations of Eurocentric racism. While they were often sympathetic to the main parts of my argument, their most persistent question was, "why bother with this concept?" Would it not be better to rely on a different and less contaminated conceptual language? Eventually I prepared two answers to that question. First, I would offer my critics a wager. They should do a content analysis of a reasonable sample of the front page of any number of newspapers, count the times their personal or favorite research project was mentioned, and compare that symbol count to the invocation of the concepts of "East" and "West." To date nobody has taken me up on my offer. I remain confident that common language use shows these civilizational concepts to be ubiquitous. Second, I would mention the reading preferences of Cornell undergraduates referred to above. On both scores I think it is important for scholars to engage public discourse on its own terms rather than to hide behind neologisms or disregard the opinions of their students.

I got a different reaction from scholars of international relations. Realists would simply shrug their shoulders. Typically uninterested in the cultural aspects of world politics, they are convinced that Huntington has been proven wrong decisively. Clashes occur for the most part within rather than between civilizations. That reaction overlooks Huntington's most enduring contribution – to alert us to the fact that, with the end of the Cold War, the cultural context of international relations had undergone a fundamental change. Liberals had a very hard time accepting that the insistence on universal standards of good governance rooted in liberal principles had a deep and troubling affinity with nineteenth-century civilizational analysis, as I argue, and that international liberalism is not sufficiently capacious to encompass the full normative reach of the emerging world order.

With its focus on processes of Sinicization, this volume explores the substantive political importance of China's rise on questions of security, economy, and culture. It does so from the perspective of process and mechanism analysis, which has gained increasing support in the social sciences. International relations theory often favors structural models. Since most structures are slow moving processes, there may be some advantage in analyzing carefully processes such as Sinicization. This book looks at civilizational processes from the perspective of political practices – actions and discourses – without unnecessarily committing itself to an a priori choice of one over the other. Specialists in international relations accustomed to thinking in terms of structures and strategies may find some of this conceptual language unfamiliar and challenging. Drawing on a broader perspective from the social sciences and humanities, it is quite natural for scholars of civilizations.

My ideas for *Sinicization and the Rise of China* were greatly influenced by my longstanding interest in East Asia. Over many years Mary, my life's love and partner, provided intellectual nourishment (and Indian meals) to help me along. An East Asia Institute fellowship permitted me to travel throughout East Asia in April 2008 and offer a preliminary paper for seminar discussions convened in Seoul, Taipei, Tokyo, Shanghai, and Beijing. I thank the Institute and all seminar participants for giving me this fabulous opportunity and so many good ideas and advice at the outset of this project. An authors' workshop convened at Peking University in January 2010 and a larger conference at the same venue in March 2011 were welcome occasions for the discussion of preliminary, analytical outlines and well-developed draft papers that my colleagues in this project and I had prepared. I would like to thank Professors Tianbiao Zhu and Wei-ming Tu for hosting the two meetings and for providing partial financial support. Most of the costs of those meetings were borne by Cornell's Walter S. Carpenter, Jr. Professorship.

I would like to acknowledge with enormous gratitude the generous financial support that I received in 2009–10 from the Louise and John Steffens Founders' Circle Membership at the Institute of Advanced Studies in Princeton. The year was crucial for giving me the quiet and uninterrupted time to refine the arguments I advance in the trilogy and to do a large amount of reading in literatures that led me in many different directions, with unexpected findings along the way.

Finally, I would like to thank my co-authors, who were already or have now become close companions and friends. I have learned much more from them than I can convey either here or in the acknowledgments to my chapters. Their many ideas and suggestions, their comments on my paper drafts, and their own papers all deepened and sharpened enormously my understanding of the subjects discussed in these two books and, more generally, many aspects of world politics that I had not understood well or thought about at all. The pleasure of working together was deep and intense, and I shall miss our conversations as we, Melville's wandering seafarer Ishmael, set our sails once again, on the lookout for new cargos and new companions. Both books reminded me once again that the process of creating new knowledge is deliciously social *and* solitary.

I dedicate this book to the memory of Shmuel Eisenstadt and Sam Huntington, two great scholars of civilizations from whom I learned many lessons, and one in particular: civilized disagreement is the salt of a scholar's life.

Peter J. Katzenstein
Ithaca, N.Y.
July 2011

1

CHINA'S RISE

Rupture, return, or recombination?[1]

Peter J. Katzenstein

All states that have experienced the flush moment of their rise in recent decades have had to accommodate to rapid disappointment. In the 1970s and 1980s, Germany and Japan were briefly intoxicated by the prospect that they might provide the institutional models other states would emulate. The United States has lived the same dream for a much longer period of time. Yet, American hopes were dashed by a failed foreign policy strategy adopted in the early months of the first George W. Bush presidency, followed by a disastrous meltdown of its unregulated financial system in the waning months of the second. Talk of the German model was quickly dashed as the country faced a painful decade of structural adjustment in the 1980s, was weighed down by the costs of unification in the 1990s, and needed much of the first decade of this century to recalibrate its political economy. Significantly, Germany's strong performance during and after the financial crisis of 2008 has not revived such talk. America's, Germany's, and Japan's overblown aspirations were disappointed; and so may be China's.[2] And just as the fears of the new Japan, Germany, and even the United States were excessive, so probably will be the fears of China. Rates of change in contemporary world politics, and the unintended consequences of many of these changes, defy the simple, straight-line projections of both optimists and pessimists.

The case of Japan a few decades ago is of immediate relevance for understanding contemporary China's ascent.[3] In the 1970s and 1980s the Japanese sun was rising visibly, both in world affairs and on book covers. Japan's new technological prowess powered its commercial expansion and its rise to a novel, civilian great power status. The realignment of currency values in 1985 underlined the fact that Japan had become America's major creditor and Asia's major investor. Japanese-style industrial policy was refashioned to create a region-wide infrastructure designed to benefit both Japan and its Asian partners.[4] Japan's power was not encased in formal institutions but rested instead in decentralized network structures.[5] Its exciting take-off and trajectory appeared to create enough draft to pull along the rest of Asia. But suddenly Japan stopped in midair, as its real estate and financial bubbles burst simultaneously. Just as its partner countries were changing their sense of self and their aspirations, so was Japan. Networks realigned, with new nodes emerging, old ones refurbishing, and some connections being broken altogether. Rather than providing a model for others to follow, Asia's regional development moved beyond Japan.[6] This does not mean that Japan fell off a cliff. Far from it. After two decades of economic stagnation, Japan's per capita income is about $42,000, compared to $47,000 for the United States and $4,300 for China.[7] Asia, however, was not revolving around the Japanese sun. Japanization processes were multi- rather than unidirectional. Japanization did not mean only, as the Japanese had expected, making Asia more like Japan. It also meant making Japan more like Asia and the larger world beyond. Understandably, at both human and political levels, disappointment followed in the wake of failed expectations that had rested on an incomplete understanding of power.

Often referred to in China as revival or rejuvenation, China's rise and processes of Sinicization are best analyzed with an understanding of the concept of power that includes all of its dimensions. Michael Barnett and Raymond Duvall have insisted that the behavioral effects of power which are directly targeted and exercised in specific and observable ways are important but do not exhaust the full panoply of power. Equally important are the non-behavioral effects of power that are indirectly targeted and are exercised in diffuse and not readily observable ways.[8] China's rise includes both the invisible and non-behavioral as well as the visible and behavioral dimensions of power. Recombination rather than rupture or return is China's likely future.

Power is closely linked to politics. Civilizational politics is a matter of concern primarily for intellectual and political elites. In both space and time, it offers the broadest social context and worldview. The breadth of civilizational attachments is politically highly salient, especially in China.[9] This is not to deny that other and often more powerful identities are nested within civilizational identities. Historically, national identities tended to crystallize on the peripheries of civilizations, illustrated by Vietnam, Korea, and Japan in their relations to China; England and Germany in their relations to France; and Spain in its relations to Islam.[10] In an era of mass politics, nationalism provides for most people the most powerful collective identity, reflected in what Ernest Renan has called plebiscites of everyday practice. Furthermore, nationalism embeds other identities, among them local, professional, and personal ones. For their own political benefits and purposes, governments typically seek to mold civilizational and other types of identities.

Reification of numerous civilizations into simple categories such as East and West is widespread in everyday politics and common in policy and academic writings. Through the concept of Sinicization and an emphasis on process, I seek to counter these political and intellectual shortcuts and correct the mistakes to which they can lead. Acknowledging the importance of complex processes, the contributors to this book – and, I assume, many of its readers – remain divided on whether or not these processes invoke, touch on, and alter irreducibly different core values that distinguish "Self" from "Other." I argue here that a recognition of complex processes and an insistence on the existence of core values are two aspects of the same political dynamic. Creating the belief in the existence of uniform, crystallized, core values and practices is a political project that reduces uncertainty in a world of change. Change can lead to a degree of individual and collective insecurity and a politics of threat and fear that elicits a political and intellectual response – simplification through the creation of misleading binaries. Conditions of uncertainty and change and the search for stability are thus politically closely linked. What the authors of this volume do agree on is that Sinicization exists and that it is politically consequential for policy and practice. At the point of origin, over the course of civilizational evolution, and at whatever point of destiny we choose to impute to history, civilizations have always been open to variegated social and political processes that have brought together many different kinds of peoples adhering to very different kinds of practices. In the language of Martin Bernal, Athena has always been brown, not black or white.[11] The insistence on the openness of Sinic (or Han) civilization or their unique role in bridging otherwise unbridgeable civilizational divides are common arguments that are not unique to China.

In the past, China was at the center of a Sinocentric order that encompassed large parts of East Asia and the surrounding seas. In cultural affairs, this Sinocentric order distinguished among insiders (civilized people, who belonged to it); outsiders (beasts, who did not); and an intermediary group (barbarians, who might become civilized through continuous interaction with the civilization's center). Pervasive female, juvenile, or historical metaphors often crop up as legitimizing the Confucian, Christian, and Communist civilizational projects that have been applied to China's cultural peripheries.[12] In economic affairs, this order recorded astounding accomplishments and distinctive practices, such as tributary trade, that helped to define interstate relations in a regional hierarchy. In security affairs the Sinocentric order remained remarkably peaceful for long stretches of time, especially toward the South and East – although it was always open to challenge, particularly when the power of the center broke down. The specific cultural, economic, and security models and practices of the Sinic world were never fixed but forever contested and changing.

Today China's physical and demographic size, its economic growth, and its government's determination to enhance national unity and shape broader political outcomes in world politics make it understandable why many Chinese and foreign observers alike focus on the central Chinese state and impute unity and legitimacy to it. As is true of others, China's civilization provides a complex context for political action that is marked by multiple traditions and dynamic processes of Sinicization. Sinic civilization does not act. And examining Sinicization is different from making a case for it. This book seeks to avoid the reifications and celebrations that mark much of the contemporary public debate about China's rise. It aims instead to open the subject to scholarly inquiry from a perspective that highlights complex processes and avoids easy shortcuts.

Widely acknowledged as an issue of prime importance, China's rise now elicits starkly different reactions from those of the past.[13] Unqualified economic admiration exists side by side with ominous political warnings. The potential for high economic growth and large profits in China's enormous domestic market, we are told, is stabilizing a global political economy that weakened dramatically during the financial crisis induced by America's unregulated financial system in 2008. Alternatively, economic growth is occurring in a country that is fated to become a serious political rival and perhaps a deadly military challenge to the United States – if not today, then tomorrow, or the day after. Such optimistic and pessimistic views permeate not only journalistic writings and policy debates but also the more detached scholarship on what William Callahan has dubbed "the pessoptimist" nation.[14]

This chapter reviews rupture, return, and recombination as three lenses through which to view China's rise, analyzes in general terms China's civilizational identities and processes, examines more specifically the cultural, economic, and security aspects of China's rise, and concludes with a discussion of recombination in terms of Sinicization.

Return, rupture, and recombination in China's rise

Martin Jacques makes the contemporary case for China's "return" to the past.[15] In his sweeping analysis, China will soon rule the world again, as the rise of the Middle Kingdom brings an end to the Western world. For a few decades we may see a transition, as globalization fractures into a world of regional blocs with different currencies and spheres of influences; but thereafter, China will rule and the world will be Easternized as it turns hierarchical, illiberal, and statist. With American power fading quickly, China will step ahead of both the rest and the West. As China rises to economic preeminence – measured in aggregate rather than per capita income – military, political, and cultural power will flow to Beijing. In the return of a Pax Sinica, now on a global scale, the renminbi will become the world's reserve currency. Shanghai will replace New York and London as the world's center of financial power. Mandarin will replace English as the global language. People will celebrate the great discoverer He Zheng rather than Christopher Columbus; the Chinese Renaissance and polymath Kuo Shen rather than the Italian Renaissance and Leonardo da Vinci; and Confucius and Mencius rather than Plato and Aristotle. Jacques' analysis is a simple straight-line projection. Some macro-historians have provided indirect support for this view. In their frontal assaults on Eurocentrism, John Hobson and Andre Gunder Frank, for example, suggest that China will soon regain its ability to set the international agenda by itself rather than merely reacting to others.[16] In brief, the future is about to restore China to its ancient position of global preeminence.[17]

This view is implausible. Many sociologists and historians have in recent decades taken a less unilinear view of the longue durée of Chinese history.[18] Without denying the importance of China's central position in the old order, this perspective emphasizes the growth of intra-regional trade, migration, capital and money flows both before and after the encounter with the European powers and America.[19] Asia's regional industrialization was greatly influenced by trade and other economic exchanges between China and Japan. Neither country imported technology or organizational forms wholesale; and neither country attempted to catch up with the West on its own. Japan's industrialization took advantage of the far-flung Chinese merchant networks spanning most of Asia, and Chinese competition was crucial for the technological upgrading of Japanese industry during the interwar period, when East Asia was the only region in the world that was able to sustain active trading. Similarly, China's nationalist government adopted its industrialization policies pressured by Japan in competitive markets and through power politics.[20] Put in a broader historical perspective, this research has established the importance of China and Asia for an informed understanding of the evolution of global capitalism and the West without insisting on China's global dominance. As Paul Cohen reminds us, we gain little by adopting one-sided, unilinear Western or Sinocentric views.[21]

A casual stroll through airport bookshops will yield a large number of books looking at China with breathless adulation and arguing the case for "rupture."[22] These books see in China's economic ascent nothing less than a dramatic break in world affairs, especially the economic affairs of Asia-Pacific. They tend to offer vivid reportages, often written by seasoned observers, whose descriptions point to only one conclusion: China's rise constitutes a fundamental break in the economic affairs of China and the world. China is the epicenter of an economic revolution that is transforming East Asia and the global economy.

History suggests otherwise. Although declining, China's economic importance for East Asian and global markets was substantial throughout the nineteenth and twentieth centuries.[23] The treaty port system provided not only an opening to the West but also a simultaneous gateway to Asia, and on an unprecedented scale. In contrast to their Western competitors, Asian exporters of opium, cotton yarn, and sundries were penetrating deep into China's interior. Trade patterns changed after 1912 as the economic links of China's interior with the rest of Asia weakened, in part because of internal disruptions and in part because of a reorientation of Western traders toward littoral China. Furthermore, in the wake of Western imperialism, East Asian and specifically Chinese merchants exploited the economic opportunities that Western imperialism had brought. Drawing on their expertise and entrepreneurship, they were able to further Chinese and Asian economic development. A broader historical perspective is a good antidote to the inclination of impatient journalists to recognize historical ruptures in a specific decade, especially the one they are covering in their writings.

"Recombination" offers a third perspective on China's rise. Writing in the realist-liberal mainstream, scholars such as Tom Christensen, Avery Goldstein, John Ikenberry, Qingguo Jia, Iain Johnston, Robert Ross, David Shambaugh, Jisi Wang, and many others too numerous to list assume that China is rising in the existing Western state system of 1648, currently shaped by American primacy.[24]

With their focus on the asynchronic patterns of modernization rather than the system of 1648, China's global and Marxist historians, Edward Wang argues, share a similar, Western-centered or Eurocentric view. China's rise may be smooth and cooperative or contentious and conflictual. But it will occur in an order not of China's making. This is an assumption that both Chinese and Western scholars of international relations are beginning to question.[25] Three examples illustrate the range of debate. Yaqing Qin disagrees with Barry Buzan, whose analysis of the primary institutions of international society is taxonomic and static rather than relational and processual. Buzan thus overlooks, Qin argues, the changing character of China and international institutions and the possibility, indeed probability, of peaceful transformative change.[26] Naazneen Barma and her co-authors detect empirical trends suggesting that China is not rising in and contained by a US-centered liberal international order. Instead, they see trends suggesting that China is evolving into a world without the West and may be building an international system very different from the one portrayed by liberal scholars such as John Ikenberry, who argues that the Western order is persisting and growing stronger while American power is waning.[27] Finally, William Callahan examines critically Tingyang Zhao's elaboration of the concept of All-under-heaven (*tianxia*) and its proclivity for confronting the problem of "otherness" through conversion or conquest rather than conversation or negotiation. Callahan argues that All-under-heaven represents little more than an updated version of hierarchical governance by a newly empowered China. Offering his own criticisms of Zhao's work, Feng Zhang argues that Callahan is misreading it.[28]

The relative merits of the various arguments in these debates matter; more importantly, all of them agree on the premise that China's rise should make us pose foundational questions about the nature of the international order that conventional analyses typically take for granted or neglect altogether. International relations scholars like Xuetong Yan are looking to China's past for new ideas.[29] And historians who have embraced global history as a way to build connections between China's and other countries' seemingly divergent historical trajectories, Gale Stokes writes, "focus on encounters and comparisons rather than on hegemony and dominance."[30] In this view, and mine, history neither ends nor repeats itself. China's rise is neither a rupture with nor a return to history. Instead, in China's rise we can recognize the recombination of old and new patterns and components. They provide the rhyme for Chinese history.

The empirical case studies in this book illustrate the importance of recombination. Allen Carlson analyzes in Chapter 2 China's approach to its interior borders. China experienced a real rupture at the end of the Qing dynasty in 1912, generating extensive discussion and eventual adoption of the conceptual language of Westphalian territoriality. After 1949 the concept of territorial sovereignty was hardened further by policies that established regional autonomy and national minorities as unquestioned attributes of the People's Republic of China (PRC). New voices, Carlson argues, are in recent years breaking the silence that for half a century has surrounded a more flexible, traditional discourse. The reconsideration of past approaches to territoriality interacts with the import of new concepts embedded in a discourse on human security that challenges the traditional Westphalian security paradigm. Conceptual moves that seek to promote regime legitimacy, social stability, and national unity are thus recalibrating Chinese discourse and eventually, perhaps, Chinese practice. In Chapter 3, Xu Xin argues that rupture in the form of an unprovoked Chinese attack on Taiwan remains unthinkable; and given Taiwan's democratization, any future extension of the civilizational bonds between Taiwan and China – to include political unity – would make a return to China's imperial past irrelevant. Instead, China's reunification is best captured by the concept of recombination and the dialectical aspects of Sinicization processes that reflect both the constraints and the opportunities that Westphalian and Sinic ideologies create for political leaders in Beijing and Taipei.

Tianbiao Zhu points in Chapter 4 to deeply engrained practices of flexible production and flexible politics that make the concept of rupture inapplicable to China's economic rise. The same is true of the notion of return, as traditional values and practices recombine with new ones, illustrated by the contemporary role that state, capital, and foreign investment play in China's compressed development. Takashi Shiraishi agrees in Chapter 5, insisting that in a regional and global perspective China's economic rise is best captured as a process of recombination. The larger political and economic structures, both in Asia and globally, in which China is rising continue to be US-centered. This makes the categories of rupture and return inapplicable. Chih-yu Shih's discussion in Chapter 6 focuses on four individual scholars and reaches the same conclusion. In their biographies and scholarship, these scholars neither ruptured their relations with their home states nor returned to China's fold. Instead, they were always recombining their own identities and China's social image, paying heed to their and their audiences' interests. Finally, in Chapter 7 Caroline Hau's analysis centers on the claim that no one institution or agent, not even rising China, has been able to establish itself as the sole, authoritative cultural arbiter of what constitutes "China" in its various dimensions. Here, as in the other case chapters, the evidence does not support alternative notions of rupture or return. Recombination is the only game in town.

Food offers a good illustration of the civilizational processes of recombination that flow from West to East, and East to West.[31] In the nineteenth century, lavish banquet diplomacy shaped European and American elite views, which differed greatly from the perception of Chinese food as unhealthy and unsanitary, especially among Europeans living in China. The diffusion of Chinese cuisine in the United States was closely related to patterns of discrimination that pushed Chinese immigrants into service industries, such as restaurants and laundries, thus reinforcing further the feminized image of Chinese in American popular culture. Unavailability of crucial ingredients made Chinese cooks develop chop suey as a dish suitable for American taste buds; American work life, particularly the rising employment of women and a growing demand for takeout food, helped spread Chinese cuisine; and greater familiarity with China spurred the rise of the regional cuisines of Beijing, Shanghai, Sichuan, and Hunan.

The history of the fortune cookie illustrates the back and forth that characterizes civilizational processes more generally.[32] In the nineteenth century, fortune cookies were a Japanese invention. Nobody then thought about marketing them. In the 1920s and 1930s, American-Chinese would go to Japanese confectionery stores in California to buy Japanese fortune cookies. Japanese cookies became fully Chinese in the 1940s, most likely because of the internment of American-Japanese after Pearl Harbor. Japanese-run shops were closed or relocated, and the little scraps of wisdom were now written in English rather than Japanese. By the 1940s, fortune cookies were common in San Francisco and southern California, enjoyed especially by GIs on leave who soon demanded them nationwide. By 1946, "Chinese fortune tea cakes," as they were then called, were removed from the Office of Price Administration control list. Fortune cookies found their way into American restaurants and later to restaurants in Europe and all over the world – except for China. Sinicization works like the history of fortune cookies. Full of unintended consequences and historical twists and turns, it reflects diverse practices spanning East and West.

Sinicization and China

Civilizational processes and identities

Norbert Elias has focused our attention on civilizing processes, specifically on the adoption of polite manners by a European aristocracy that had once been unmannered and uncouth.[33] As is true of domestic affairs, in our globe-spanning, contemporary civilization of modernity, civilizational processes yield contingent outcomes. Social groups and states that draw sharp boundaries between Self and Other seek to cement their power and prestige. Claiming civilizational superiority as a condition is a political tool. It has little to do with civilizational processes, which are mutable and can be reversed. When power differentials are very great between a favored in-group and a disfavored out-group, it becomes normal for people to think of the power differential as immutable. This was true in the nineteenth century, when European states were thought to have set *the* standard of civilization, thus providing justification for Europe's rule over much of the rest of the world.[34] But when power differentials shift, as is evidently the case now between China, its Asian neighbors, the United States and Europe, our attention shifts away from supposedly unchanged civilizational conditions to variable civilizational processes.

These processes have a Janus face. One side describes the process of remaking a civilizational "Other" to be more like the civilizational "Self," either through total assimilation or by making "Other" conform more closely to dominant civilizational practices. The other side describes the process by which "Other," through appropriating aspects of "Self," exerts its own effects on the civilizational center. The first process is typically conceived of by the civilizational center as reaching outward; the second typically refers to the practices of actors located in various civilizational peripheries or in another civilization. Rather than a set of practices forced on others, as in theories of cultural imperialism, civilizational processes often reflect self-chosen practices; both typically occur simultaneously. At one extreme, as Jonathan Zeitlin argues for the specific case of Americanization, is simple diffusion of best civilizational practices that do not alter the center in any way. At the other extreme are self-reflective peripheral actors who recombine and absorb the center's civilizational influences into effective ensembles of interdependent elements.[35] Profoundly interactive, these multi-sited and multidirectional processes can have positive and negative consequences for both civilizational center and periphery.

In its broadest sense, Sinicization means making the world suitable to China and the Chinese. The creation of comfortable milieus extends beyond the world of states to include all of society; it involves both government policy and social practice.[36] Like other civilizational processes, such as Japanization and Indianization discussed in Chapter 8, Sinicization is affected by the rise and decline of civilizational states, polities, or empires. Civilizational processes, however, do not simply radiate in one direction, outward, from one center, as is widely assumed. Instead, Sinicization is a non-linear, multi-sited, and multidirectional set of processes. It is interactive and can involve both practices and discourses that change the identities of Self and Other. It can be reinforcing as in re-Sinicization, and reversible as in de-Sinicization. Although rupture, return, and recombination are all possible outcomes of particular Sinicization processes, in the aggregate, this book argues, they sum to recombination.

These characteristics are at the center of the empirical chapters of this book. In Chapter 2 Allen Carlson emphasizes the non-linear and multi-sitedness of Sinicization, as the political center of Sinic civilization seeks to stabilize the borderlands of its geographic periphery. The ebb and flow of political discourses centers on interactions and the reversible and reinforcing features of Sinicization. The contemporary debates that are the main focus of the chapter have a direct relevance for policy. Xu Xin stresses in Chapter 3 how Taiwan's loss, return, re-separation, and prospect of pending reunification illustrate different currents of deeply interactive processes of de- and re-Sinicization that have resisted simple control by either Beijing or Taipei. Sinicization captures the tensions between the impulse of China's modern nationalism and of the preservation of its multiple civilizational traditions. Those tensions reflect a complex, non-linear, and contested politics that occurs in numerous sites and spreads in many directions. Tianbiao Zhu shows in Chapter 4 that China's multiple economic traditions are non-linear, multi-sited, and multidirectional as they vary between political centralization and economic closure, and political decentralization and economic opening. These traditions are deeply interactive with newly emerging ideas and practices, illustrated by the recombination of state and foreign capital in China's economic rise. And they can lead to the simultaneous occurrence of de-Sinicization (as in the combination of central planning with late development that undercut the tradition of flexible politics and production) and re-Sinicization (as in the economic reforms adopted in the process of compressed development that offer a permissive environment for the flourishing of flexible policies and multiple forms of property rights). Takashi Shiraishi's arguments in Chapter 5 establish that creating a milieu in which China can operate comfortably is a world apart from remaking Asia in China's own image. Furthermore, economic Sinicization is remaking China. Chinese state corporations, for example, learn from their deals with partners operating in countries that have institutionalized elite circulation, greater competition, and deep connections with the global economy. Similarly, Chih-yu Shih and Caroline Hau stress in Chapters 6 and 7 how the individual lives of four scholars and the process of imbuing China and Chineseness with changing meaning in Southeast Asia are described accurately, in discourse and practice, by the interactive, non-linear, multidirectional, multi-sited, reversible, and reinforcing features that make Sinicization such a complex set of processes.

China

David Kang's analysis of the relations between China and its nomadic neighbors to the north, as well as its Sinicized neighbors to the east and south, provides a good illustration of the complexity of Chinese identities.[37] From this perspective it makes little sense to speak of China as a unitary actor and of the oriental critique in the singular.[38] For example, Henry Kissinger's insistence is unpersuasive that all Chinese strategists think like players of the game Go (*wei qi*) while Western strategists think like chess players. Kissinger imputes a deeply crystallized unity of purpose to the Chinese avoidance of encirclement and the Western preference for head-on clashes. Chinese strategy does not produce only strategic flexibility, and chess is not a game invented by the West.[39]

China is plural not only in its origin but throughout its history.[40] Conflicts over relative gains between China and the nomads were exacerbated by the nomads' evident lack of interest in adhering to China's civilizational standards. A chasm of identities and practices separated the two, generating an almost permanent state of war. In contrast, convergence on one civilizational standard shared by China and its neighbors to the south and east helped generate prolonged peace. Despite this mixed historical record, today the Chinese notion of all-embracing unity (*da yitong*) is normally uncontested by adherents of China's various intellectual traditions.[41] It is a core value that has significant consequences for how Chinese view the world and conduct their foreign policy. Occasional dissents point to the fact that the time of division in Chinese history was longer than the time of unity. But such dissents typically fall on deaf ears. Instead, a deep-rooted Sinocentric worldview persists as "a myth backed up at different times by realities of varying degree, sometimes approaching nil."[42]

Confucianism offers a tradition for China that has proven sufficiently plastic and contested to accommodate China's internal disagreements.[43] Discarded as an imperial institution since the middle of the nineteenth century and hollowed out as a political ideology, the relevance of various incarnations of New Confucianism is now seen to lie in its humanism. Widely thought to have been a major factor for many of China's ills during the last two centuries, in recent years the Chinese government has vigorously revived Confucianism. This ideology operates on the basis of hierarchical, reciprocal, and morally based values. The political qualities that supposedly flow from these values – wisdom, morality, generosity, obligation to respect the interests of others – are now extolled as assets, not liabilities.

The ethical and religious concerns of Confucian humanism, Weiming Tu argues, remain relevant in the quest to address contemporary China's pressing problems.[44] For Tu, cultural China focuses on the meaning of being Chinese.[45] It is not a geopolitical, linguistic, or ethnic concept. Instead, cultural China is defined by transnational relationships in Greater China and the fluid borders separating civilization from barbarism.[46] Tu posits that Greater China comprises three distinct cultural worlds: first, the four states or quasi-states populated largely by ethnic Chinese – mainland China, Taiwan, Hong Kong, and Singapore; second, the diaspora of overseas Chinese living in Northeast and Southeast Asia, the United States, and throughout the world; and third, individuals who are trying to understand China intellectually and interpret it to their own national communities. Cultural China emerges from the dialogues within and between these different Chinese worlds, with the erstwhile peripheries of the second and third Chinese world now in the unaccustomed role of civilizing China's first world. Put differently, for Tu transnational intellectual and cultural networks trump established state and national identities. Confucianism is not an essential attribute of Chineseness, rooted in an empire, polity, or modern nation state. It is instead a cultural resource mobilized primarily on the periphery of transnational Chinese networks.

Furthermore, inside mainland China, the tradition of Confucianism is complemented by and competing with alternative traditions of Daoism, Buddhism, Islam, Christianity, popular religion, atheism, and secularism. Outside of China, in the Sinocentric sphere of cultural influence, contested and contestable traditions of Confucianism can also be found in Japan, Korea, and Vietnam. Tu's analysis of civilizational dialogues agrees with Eisenstadt on the persistence of cultural pluralism in a broader civilization of modernity that encompasses all Axial Age civilizations.[47] Avoiding the stipulation of any cultural essences, Tu focuses attention on civilizational dialogues and processes. This formulation concurs with William Callahan's insistence on the existence of transnationalism inside Greater China as the unstable product of contingent relations reflecting day-to-day practices.[48]

Confucian traditions are also applicable to the economic rise of industrial East Asia.[49] The economic importance of the overseas Chinese and Chinese transnationalism has been widely noted as a critically important aspect of the economic rise of East Asia.[50] Tu's analysis does not differentiate clearly among the values, habits, and institutions that mark the culture of Greater China. It does, however, underline the importance of their joint impact. That said, in Confucianism, strong government, meritocracy, high trust politics, and enduring familial and social relations are all important values that are expressed in routinized behavior. And just as East Asian capitalism is dynamic and evolving, so is economic Confucianism.[51]

Indeed, China's economic success may become more attractive to other parts of the world in the future. A "Beijing consensus" – authoritarian politics and capitalist competition – offers, at least in theory, an alternative to the "Washington consensus" – market economies and democratic government.[52]

Confucian consensual values at home and a stipulated Beijing consensus abroad are the political constructions of two of China's many traditions, propelling China's many centers of power to a broad range of experimentation with pragmatic accommodation to unanticipated change. Contemporary Chinese discussions stress the prevalence of multiple traditions including new Right and new Left; Pearl River Delta Capitalism and what Mark Leonard calls Yellow River Capitalism; markets and rights as central aspects of the reform period; justice and equality as part of the Mao Zedong era; and many versions of Confucianism over the centuries. These traditions sometimes conflict and sometimes converge.[53] Put differently, China's rise is built on a distinctive foundation that is grounded in and supportive of Eisenstadt's notion of "multiple modernities," Zhiyuan Cui's concept of "alternative modernities," Nonini and Ong's concept of "Chinese transnationalism," Martin's notion of "contested modernities," and Collins's notion of "competing zones of prestige."[54]

Sinicization[55]

Today's Sinicization recombines old with new elements and is evolving differently in different domains. A long, complex, and unending process, historically Sinicization refers to the eventual assimilation by Han civilization of non-Han people who have entered the Chinese realm.[56] Although the PRC has reemerged on the international stage after a long period of national humiliation, marginalization, and isolation, to date its civilizational impulses remain relatively vague and undefined. Viewed against the background of the changing political fortunes of different strata of overseas Chinese living in the various states of Southeast Asia and beyond, Sinicization is a highly variegated set of social processes.[57] During the last two decades, the emergence of a region-wide consumer society in the major East Asian metropolitan areas has become an undeniable fact of life. Upper- and upper-middle class Chinese are making choices, for example about their preferred use of mother tongue (such as Mandarin, Cantonese, or Hokkien) and about the education they prefer for their children – Hong Kong and Singapore for better high school training in English and Mandarin, Britain and the USA for college and professional education. Indeed, Takashi Shiraishi goes as far as to call the appearance of "Anglo-Chinese" (Chinese of whatever nationality who are fluent in English and comfortable with Anglo-American norms and practices) the most important of the many momentous changes that are transforming Southeast Asia.[58] Sinicization will leave the social make-up of Southeast Asian societies heterogeneous and polyglot.

Contemporary and past Sinicization processes share a fundamental similarity. It is true that today, as in the past, the Chinese state at times seeks to impose its heavy hand on provinces that adhere to beliefs and practices that differ greatly from those of the center, as in today's Tibet and Xinjiang. Most of the time, however, Sinicization is not flowing only in one direction and creating sameness. It is instead a network which permits traffic to flow in many directions and which leaves ample space for persistently heterogeneous social and political practices. The case of the Manchus is instructive. While Ping-Ti Ho and Evelyn Rawski disagree on the definition, application, and importance of Sinicization, both agree that the Manchu rulers in the Qing dynasty made vital contributions to creating and consolidating a multiethnic empire unprecedented in Chinese history. The Manchus thus laid the foundation for contemporary China to emerge as a modern, multinational state.[59] While they accepted the Confucian canon as the foundation for state ideology, the civil service entrance examination, and many policy decrees, the Manchus also emphasized that their "Manchu virtues" gave them a superior position to represent Chineseness.[60]

Indeed the imperial image consisted of much more than Han influences. The Manchus conquered the Ming dynasty with a multiethnic force that included Manchus, Mongols, and Chinese living in Northeast Asia, outside of Ming borders. The key to success was combining Sinicization with the shrewd ability to differentiate and engaging, at the same time, in empire building among the non-Han peoples south of the Yangtze River. The Qing concept of universal emperorship was predicated on the assumption that the Qing would rule over different peoples with distinct cultural identities. According to Rawski, Sinicization – or, more accurately, Hanization – was a program applied most effectively to ethnic minorities living in the South and Southwest of the Qing empire.[61] Han Chinese literati who played a central role at the Qing court had to share power with a separate conqueror elite, banner nobles, and imperial kinsmen (of Manchu, Mongol, or Han descent) that existed parallel to and often superimposed on top of the imperial bureaucracy.[62] This was reflected both in the administrative structures the court imposed on the "outer" non-Han and "inner" Han domains of the empire, and in the disagreements on vital matters of policy, such as China's stance at the outset of the Opium War. Being Manchu and becoming Chinese turned out to be a false dichotomy.[63] During the Qing dynasty the Sinicization of Han blended with Northeast Asian political elements. Falling well short of total assimilation, as Tibet and Xinjiang illustrate, the process was one of give and take.[64]

This convergence of acculturation and differentiation in the process of Sinicization holds more generally.[65] Often, though not always, writes Wang Gungwu, Sinicization "was not associated with coercion and the need to dominate."[66] Instead, typically it was a spontaneous process that included both the provision of institutional models and practices worth emulating and the capacity to appropriate from abroad both religious–philosophical ideas (such as Buddhism) and aspects of material culture (such as technology). With China's economic ascent, the material balance of power is shifting; and so is the ratio between receiving and giving in contemporary processes of Sinicization.[67]

China's rise and global culture

For many centuries, China was more than a vast market and a powerful state; it was also a civilizational polity endowed with a strong sense of self, reflected in specific practices and values. Whether China experienced the same historical break in the sixth century BCE as did other Axial Age civilizations remains a matter of scholarly controversy.[68] Uncontroversial, however, is the statement that for centuries the Sinocentric world was one of the world's great civilizations. Its cultural influence radiated outward. At the same time, it assimilated foreign elements and conquerors. Then as now, civilizational empires, polities, states, and processes cannot be captured adequately by the reification of categories such as "East" and "West." They are instead institutionalized social orders formed around more tightly integrated nation states and more encompassing diverse transnational communities. China's civilizational identity does not trump national identity. Rather, it is a broader social identity that is of political relevance and that contains national, ethnic, and other identities. The contested nature of these identities and their forever changing boundaries depend on the quality, intensity, and homogeneity of social interactions.[69]

Contemporary China's rise is clearly evident in cultural affairs. Increasingly, Chinese leaders, analysts, and scholars tend to focus on China's social power – as expressed, for example, in public diplomacy and popular culture.[70] In contrast to the traditional Sinocentric order, the social dimensions of power that once created a sense of regional order in East Asia appear to be largely absent. There is little evidence suggesting that contemporary China is returning to that older world. Furthermore, today's globalizing world is knit together by information technologies with diffuse and indirect effects. And there is no evidence indicating that China's rise is making it participate more actively than before in this new cultural domain. Recombination rather than return or rupture is the concept that best captures the cultural dimension of China's rise.

Since 2004, the Chinese government has put in place an initiative to more effectively deploy what it regards to be China's appeal, through public diplomacy, the opening of cultural centers, and increased language training. While across Southeast Asia American cultural centers run by the State Department's United States Information Service have closed their doors, since the 1990s China has been expanding its public diplomatic presence. Compared to the Voice of America's 19 hours, by 2004 China Radio International was broadcasting in English 24 hours a day. In July 2010 China's Xinhua News Agency launched an English language TV service, CNC World, which offers global coverage and broadcasts 24 hours. It is countered not by an American government-run entity, but by the private CNN-International channel.[71] Specific initiatives in public diplomacy seek to convey China's peaceful intentions. Museum exhibits celebrating the 600th anniversary of Chinese discoverer He Zheng are one example. His voyages explored Asia, the Middle East, and Africa; yet he never conquered foreign territories.[72] Recently a government-owned film and TV investment group put down $30 million and hired Antoine Fuqua, a well-known director, to produce a China-friendly historical romance movie. Hollywood is also doing its part: In the recent disaster movie *2012* the Chinese save the human race by building the next generation of enormous and technologically advanced boats.[73] Furthermore, since 2004, the Chinese government has moved quickly to set up a growing number of Confucius Institutes abroad, language schools affiliated with foreign institutions that aim at promoting Mandarin as one of Asia's leading languages. China is also increasing the number of Chinese language teachers working abroad, primarily in Southeast Asia.[74] Although the figures are impossible to verify, China's Education Ministry claims that 40 million people were learning Chinese worldwide in 2004 and predicted that this number would more than double by 2010.[75]

Student exchanges also illustrate the growth of China's attraction. Chinese universities reportedly enrolled 260,000 foreign students in 2010, compared to 195,000 in 2007, 120,000 in 2004, 36,000 in 1994, 8,000 in 1984, and less than 1,000 in 1960.[76] In Cambodia, students now have the opportunity to attend Chinese-language schools that receive funding from the Chinese government. Good students are then eligible for scholarships for advanced study at Chinese universities.[77] The turnaround in Indonesia is also striking. In 2003, 2,563 Indonesian students received visas to attend Chinese universities, compared to 1,333 who went to study in the United States, down from 6,250 in 2000. The 9/11 attacks had a large impact on the sharp decline of the American figures. But the rise in the Chinese figures points also to underlying long-term change. Singapore's government now sends as many of its best students on scholarships to China as to the USA and Britain. For the professional middle class in Southeast Asia, the option of Chinese universities has emerged as an attractive alternative, at less than 10 percent of the cost, to sending their children to study in the United States.[78]

These cultural initiatives are notable. They show the government seeking to portray China in an attractive light. But it is less clear that they show China commanding social or soft power. Chinese initiatives are largely targeted and direct, and seek to operate peacefully and through economic incentives. In recent years, politicians and pundits everywhere have been eager to appropriate the concept of soft power. It has "nice" connotations – fuzzy, modern, and humane – highly desirable attributes in an often violent and cruel world. Indeed, the adoption of the soft power terminology by Chinese officials and pundits recalls Japan of the 1990s. China has quickly learned how to use its economic and diplomatic power softly.[79] Prudent these strategies may be. But they do not indicate that, as of now, China has social power operating indirectly and in a diffuse manner.[80] As Chih-yu Shih and Caroline Hau show in Chapters 6 and 7, this argument presumes what is very much in doubt: that China is endowed with the capacity to claim authoritatively what is, and what is not, Chinese. Their chapters demonstrate that at individual and group levels processes of Sinicization are social; they are open to unexpected innovations; and they resist state control.

The evolution of popular culture in East Asia offers another example that points to the limited cultural effect of the PRC. Films, music, and TV originating from parts of the Chinese world have spread throughout Southeast Asia in recent years. However, Hong Kong with its movie industries and "Canto-pop" and Taiwan with the Meteor Garden television series and boybands F4 or 5566 have lost some of their appeal, while American Internet and regular Chinese television have gained in fickle markets.[81] Chinese moviemakers have received much international acclaim for films such as *Crouching Tiger, Hidden Dragon*, which grossed more income than any other foreign language film in the American market. But inside China their movies are banned, though readily available as pirated DVDs. Domestic political restrictions and censorship do not only constrain China's room of maneuver in the movie industry. The restrictions that Chinese censors impose on the Internet are deeply antithetical to how especially the young lead their lives all over the world. China's bristling response to regular foreign criticism of its policy is not conducive to spreading its power softly. Heavy-handed political control in China's cultural policy abroad can misfire badly, as illustrated by its hostile reaction to the awarding of the 2010 Nobel Peace Prize to civil rights activist Xiaobo Liu and its unsuccessful campaign to have all countries boycott the ceremony. Organized by a few nationalist scholars, the staging of an alternative Confucius Peace Prize ceremony in Beijing was a public embarrassment, which the hand-picked Taiwanese prize winner chose not to attend.

The meaning of being Chinese, Weiming Tu points out, lies at the very center of cultural China.[82] And since China has always been an open empire,[83] Chineseness is explicitly defined by transnational relations in Greater China.[84] China is an integral part of a global system of "brain circulation" rather than brain gain or drain. Many of the returning scientists and businesspeople are playing leading roles in China's rise.[85] Transnational networks of intellectuals now complement and interact with established ethnic and national nodes of identities. In the spring of 2008, the pro- and anti-Chinese demonstrations that accompanied the global parade of the Olympic torch tracked the far-flung existence of the Chinese diaspora in all parts of the world. These transnational networks are always in flux as they recombine old with new elements.

How many Chinese live abroad is not really known. The figure may well run as high as 35 million at the outset of the twenty-first century, up from about 20 million in the early 1980s.[86] Substantial Chinese communities can now be found not just in Southeast Asia, but also in Africa and Latin America. Chinese migrants are changing the ethnic composition of northern Burma and Vietnam.[87] South Korea estimates that it has about one million illegal Chinese immigrants,[88] a number that is most likely modest compared to figures for Japan, the European Union (EU), and the United States. Since the early 1990s, China has rebuilt its contacts with the associations of ethnic Chinese, especially in Southeast Asia. Chinese Buddhist associations network across Asia and are as active as various Christian ministries. And throughout Southeast Asia, ethnic Chinese, who traditionally have stayed clear of politics, now avow their Chinese heritage.[89] In Southeast Asia, many of the once resolutely anti-Communist and anti-Beijing younger overseas Chinese are beginning to shift some of their views. When anti-Chinese sentiments in the region recede, overseas Chinese feel freer to adopt a more positive attitude toward China.[90] Chih-yu Shih shows in Chapter 6 that individual calculations and motivations are driven by a complex confluence of factors that are related to individual life histories, conditions in host countries, and developments in China. And Caroline Hau argues in Chapter 7 that it is the overseas Chinese, rather than the Chinese government, who are driving shifts in attitudes.

On cultural issues, China is trying to use its social power with no more than limited success. Since social power depends substantially upon the reactions of others, it is not something that a government can simply claim on its own. The rapidity of China's ascent has created a wide gap between its own self-image as a fragile regional power, and external perceptions of China as a robust global giant. In its foreign policy, China seeks to bridge that gap by evoking four dominant national images – peace-loving nation, victim of foreign aggression, anti-hegemonic force in world politics, and developing country.[91] The government hopes that these images will generate support for the "Beijing consensus" (marked by the practice of institutionalized experimentation, the aspiration for social equality, and the reliance on high-tech defense) as an international rival to the increasingly discredited "Washington consensus" (marked by ideological commitment to market principles, willingness to tolerate inequality to maximize growth, and assertive power projection).[92] In contrast to the Washington consensus, the Beijing consensus espouses the principle of strict non-intervention and adheres to an economic and social definition of the concept of human rights that excludes the duty to protect civilian lives. To date, evidence of a Beijing consensus rests largely on journalists' assertions of its existence.

China's cultural attraction faces inherent limitations. Democratization, good governance, honesty in government, responsible environmental policies, cultural autonomy, protection of economic and social rights of workers, and a functioning judiciary are deeply problematic issues that tend to undercut the appeal of Chinese values and norms, and that serve as warning signals to other countries not to admire too much everything Chinese.[93] A recent study concludes that public opinion in Asia and the United States is "somewhat" or "very" uncomfortable with the idea that China will become the leader of Asia. Across various categories of social power, "China's rise looks far from complete."[94]

Yet as a country that is experiencing more rapid change than any other, China may have one great advantage. Its greatest appeal lies in the excitement of an unprecedented process of self-invention. In the language of advertising, China is a white brand onto which the world can project its hopes and fears.[95] While it may sound far-fetched to American ears, there exists a family resemblance between China's white brand and the American Dream. Full of internal contradictions, like the American Dream, China's white brand is empty and leaves boundless space to the human imagination. That may be its greatest attraction for mass publics that are looking for a ray of hope in their often difficult lives; and it feeds the imagination of those (writers of spy novels among them) who give voice to our darkest fears.[96] New Confucianism, like Liberalism, may be little more than an official creed, a reified concept deployed by politicians who lack a vision of their own. In this view, it is the vacuity of that Beijing vision rather than its crystallization that offers a spur to the human imagination. If true, then China might eventually be able to deploy a social power it now lacks. But that is in the future. For now, a relative absence of China's social power makes recombination rather than rupture or return the concept that best captures China's cultural rise.

China's rise in the world economy

The same is true of the economic sphere. Throughout the world, China's rise is viewed foremost in economic terms. Economic globalization and domestic reforms have set China on a path marked by annual growth rates of about 10 percent for the last three decades. The sharply increasing size of China's economy has profound consequences for its Asian neighbors as well as the global economy. Many businesspeople and journalists see China's rise as a deep rupture in the world economy, especially when viewed against the broader experience of East Asia's recent past and India's imminent future. In this view China is creating something radically new – for itself, for Asia, and for the world. I argue instead that old and new elements are recombining to make China a large and dynamic economy that is structurally very open to the world.[97]

China's economy is marked by variable relations between capitalism and the state on the one hand, and market economies that trade over long distances on the other.[98] Variable relations between capitalism and the state are central to an understanding of the change from state socialism to market capitalism in contemporary China. And market economies, often linked by long-distance trade, are central to understanding the important role the overseas Chinese communities continue to play in China's economic rise. The two factors converge today in the structure of a Chinese economy that is distinctly open, measured in terms of trade and foreign investment, compared to the relatively closed developmental state capitalism that characterized Japan, South Korea, and, to a lesser extent, the states of Southeast Asia during the last generation. To give but one example, Apple's cheapest iPad model costs $499 and is "made in China." What precisely does this label mean? Apple makes a gross profit of $270 on costs of $229. Of the cost component, $219 is for components imported from around the world, including, prominently, Taiwan, Korea, Japan, and the USA. Chinese "labor" costs amount to $10.[99] For sure, China will rapidly move up the value chain in coming decades, as Tianbiao Zhu shows in his analysis of compressed development in Chapter 4. But for many advanced products China is, in terms of profits, a relatively small part in a global assembly line with values accruing largely outside of China.

Asia has long been viewed as an inert region that was incapable of generating either technological or institutional change from within. While the last half-century belies that notion, so, it now turns out, do the nineteenth and early twentieth centuries. Under the impact of the West, Asian economies proved to be highly adaptable. For an even longer period, economic historians now insist, East Asia had developed as predominantly rural economies that produced growth with efficiency, but along a path that differed from the West. Asia's industrious revolution exhausted its potential only in the first half of the nineteenth century. In contrast, the industrial revolution revealed its explosive potential in the century's second half. Many historians tended to pay attention primarily to events in individual countries that experienced trade and currency rivalries, diplomatic tensions, clashes between imperialism and nationalism, and war. They largely missed the dynamic gains from region-wide intra-Asian trade and the intra-regional technology transfers that had shaped Asia's regional economic developments for centuries.

Thus, Asia's "economic miracle" after World War II, and now China's economic rise, are both parts of one coherent economic narrative that dates back at least 150 years and perhaps much longer.[100] In that narrative, the choices of Chinese merchants and manufacturers are much more central than the traditional economic history has been willing to acknowledge. China's trade links with the world economy and its Asian neighbors in the eighteenth and nineteenth centuries were of great importance and survived the onslaught of the West. Specifically, Chinese networks accommodated British banking and the massive inflow of silver into China between the sixteenth and eighteenth centuries, preceding the outflow of silver to pay for opium in the nineteenth century and the loss of sovereignty in the wake of China's military defeat in the Opium War. These historical precursors are relevant to the financial aspects of contemporary China's economic rise. Inter-Asian financial links have grown tighter, while China has accumulated massive dollar reserves. Then and now, China and Asia have been fully integrated into the world economy. China's contemporary economic rise and East Asia's emerging economic order thus reveal important historical continuities.[101] Such continuities are evident also in other aspects of China's economic history. Well into the twentieth century, Western colonialism in East Asia took advantage of enduring and powerful Chinese networks as the economic foundation for building new connections. And after 1945, Japan's commercial expansion into East and Southeast Asia was in many ways both supported by and in rivalry with those networks, as Takashi Shiraishi argues in Chapter 5.

Overseas Chinese were very helpful to China's economic rise, especially in the 1980s and 1990s. The very term "overseas Chinese" is a convenient shorthand, not a suggestion that a cohesive bloc of ethnic Chinese is waiting to be reunited with the motherland. Overseas Chinese communities are not usefully defined in terms that presume the existence of immutable notions of collective identity yielding a distinctive type of capitalism.[102] Instead, native place and inherited dialect provide a powerful basis for informal ties. The communities of overseas Chinese are not what C. Wright Mills in the 1950s referred to as a "power elite" in the American context, marked by extensive interlocking business links shaping decisively the political and economic future of their societies.[103] Although close, their relationship to the state has been subservient. Only in Singapore have overseas Chinese played an autonomous role. Divided by class, length of stay, generation, and identity, they have faced formidable impediments to collective action. But the sharing of a common language and historical experience offer an undeniable stimulus for Taiwanese businesspeople in Asia and for Southeast Asian Chinese dealing with Taiwan. Specifically, large Taiwanese companies have organized around loose groupings of small- and medium-sized producers of components of various products.[104] And Southeast Asian governments have encouraged overseas Chinese to vigorously pursue new market opportunities in China. These ties lie behind the investment flows that Tianbiao Zhu discusses in Chapter 4.

Since the late 1970s, China has attracted perhaps as much as half a trillion dollars in foreign investment, about ten times the total foreign investment that Japan has received since 1945. Between 1985 and 1995, about two thirds of realized foreign investment in China is estimated to have come from domestic Chinese sources using Hong Kong to circumvent domestic taxes, and one third from foreign investors. Since 1995 this proportion is widely believed to have reversed itself. Of the 250 billion dollars in total foreign investments, perhaps as much as half has come from Taiwan, and additional undetected large amounts of funds have flown into China from Southeast Asia, including Singapore, Hong Kong, and Indonesia.[105] Overseas Chinese provided capital to cover the start-up costs of Chinese investment projects; especially small- and medium-size firms were interested in short-term deals.[106] China's diaspora never regarded China's economic rise as a platform for peaceful reunification with the motherland. But it did intensify existing trade links and create new ones.[107] Overseas Chinese have provided China with an opportunity to take advantage of their privileged access to trade opportunities, technological know-how, investment capital, management expertise, and marketing skills. Conversely, China's economic rise provided ethnic Chinese operating in Southeast Asia with an opportunity to compete better with foreign multinational corporations, both in emerging Chinese markets and globally.[108]

In the last decade the role of the overseas Chinese has become less central, as China's growing private sector and its modernizing state-owned enterprises, assisted by large multinational corporations, have turned to Asian and world markets with less need for any intermediation. The reconfiguration of industrial networks shows China's increasingly important role in Asian-Pacific trade relations.[109] China exports capital to the USA and Europe. Chinese entrepreneurs, often using Hong Kong or Singapore as a platform, are fashioning global strategies of direct foreign investment. Acting like national champions, state-owned enterprises are acting on a global scale, through mergers and acquisitions in some markets and through joint ventures in others. And since China's accession to the World Trade Organization (WTO) in 2001, political elites are focusing on new strategies of bilateralism on questions of trade and investment. These are a complement and political hedge rather than a substitute for multilateral arrangements that occasionally threaten to become too intrusive into domestic institutional practices and too destabilizing of entrenched political alliances.[110]

While the underlying structures that connect China and the world economy are not new, the speed of China's economic rise is. This does not signify a return to an age-old pattern of a world economy dominated by China. China's economic rise is, rather, built on firm historical foundations that are open to new developments. Past institutional arrangements and the links that have connected China to East Asia and the world beyond are vital to understanding China's contemporary economic practices.[111] The economic size and openness of China's economy and the network structures through which it has been linked to other Asian economies and global markets are variable. Furthermore, due to shifts in competitive advantage and migration flows, these networks are dense, and their nodes are forever changing. While its relative size will surely increase, it is unlikely that China will any time soon again account for a third of the global economy, as it did at the beginning of the nineteenth century.[112] Furthermore, as Tianbiao Zhu shows in his discussion of flexibility in Chapter 4, China's economy is structurally incomparably more open than it ever was in the past, due to its own policy choices and the liberalizing global economy in which it has found itself after the onset of economic reforms in 1979. Informal and market-driven tie-ups rather than formal institutions are defining the rise of China in Asian and world markets. As has been true before, and enriched by new elements, the evolution of Chinese capitalism is not only a domestic but also a regional and global phenomenon. In sum, China's rise in the last three decades does not constitute a fundamental rupture in or return to the economic history of China and East Asia. Instead, the significant changes that are reshaping the political economies of East Asia and the world are best analyzed in terms of the recombination of old and new elements.

China's rise and international security

The same is true for questions of security.[113] Much of the contemporary American discussion looks at China's rise as posing a potential security threat that is unavoidable. In the view of "offensive realists," before long this will lead to a deep rupture with the existing balance of power. "Defensive realists" view China's rise instead as politically manageable, but always operating under the looming threat of systemic rupture. Still other analysts view current developments as returning Asia and China to a Sinocentric world of bandwagoning that has experienced long periods of relative stability and peace. I argue here for the recombination of old and new elements in China's security policy and East Asia's institutionalized security order. Specifically, the US–Japan alliance arrangement greatly constrains tendencies toward balancing and bandwagoning. This security order reduces uncertainty for all East Asian states. It also affects the grand strategies of China and the United States. In its absence, the case for potentially large-scale change, either through unchecked balancing or bandwagoning, would be more plausible, and with it the possibility of historical rupture or return.

China's rise has direct implications for Asian security. Japan, India, and the United States are all directly affected by China's increasing military capabilities, as are all of China's neighbors. For now, the United States maintains a substantial lead in East Asia and an overwhelming one globally. But China has closed the gap, especially in East Asia, much faster than anyone predicted only a couple of decades ago. High economic growth rates enable the Chinese government to push ahead with a far-reaching modernization of its military, which many of America's allies in the region – Japan, South Korea, Thailand, and the Philippines – simply cannot or do not want to match. The build-up of its ballistic missile forces for a potential conflict with Taiwan is one widely noted development. Others, including the modernization of China's naval capabilities, various weapons systems such as cruise missiles, and a rapid push into space, are of similar importance in closing the military gap with Japan. Asia's growing economic dependence on China rounds out a picture of a potentially serious challenge to the accustomed role the USA has played in East Asia. In the future, American allies will be increasingly constrained to endanger their political relations with a country on which they have become economically so dependent.

Policymakers and scholars ponder the consequences of China becoming either the primary power in East Asia or, more dramatically, eventually ascending to a position of global power rivaling that of the United States.[114] From this perspective, China's rise will lead to fundamental political and military ruptures. Furthermore, the intensity of nationalist sentiments and painful historical memories give this account an emotional resonance that marks contemporary Sino-Japanese relations in particular. Indeed, had it not been for the attacks of 9/11 and the American invasion and occupation of Iraq, China might well have become the overriding focus of the foreign policy of the Bush administration. Long before, American conservatives and neo-conservatives had fastened on China as posing the most likely long-term strategic threat to American primacy. With economic power shifting toward China in the long term, the United States might have to confront China, perhaps sooner rather than later. Similar views were heard during the growing rivalries between Britain and Germany in the late nineteenth century, and Germany and Russia on the eve of World War I.

Developed in the 1990s, "China threat" theory became a subject of extended debate in the United States.[115] In a matter of only a few decades, threat theorists argued, China will have a world class military that will have outpaced the military power of Japan and will pose a serious regional, and eventually global, challenge to the United States. Furthermore, according to this view, the combustible issue of Taiwan will remain a thorn in China's side that could be used as a pretext for war at any time – by a strong government flexing its muscles in an assertive nationalist move, by a weak one in need of shoring up its lack of legitimacy through populist appeals, or in periods of regime transition.

"Offensive" realists are united in their sparse, materialist view of the world that sees rupture as inevitable – with China moving unavoidably into a position of regional primacy in East Asia and probably into a global challenge to, and quite possibly war with, the United States. If war were to come, it would be instigated either by a revisionist China or by a United States unwilling to countenance the rise of a regional rival in East Asia.[116] Other conservative foreign policy specialists argue in strict analogy with Europe; A.J.P. Taylor's writings on the struggle between Britain and Germany over the mastery of Europe, for example, remind

Aaron Friedberg of "the struggle for mastery in Asia."[117] From this perspective, China's peaceful strategy of engaging its neighbors in a number of multilateral venues, such as the ASEAN Plus Three (Association of Southeast Asian Nations Plus China, Japan, and South Korea) initiative, the Shanghai Cooperation Organization, or early moves toward an East Asian Community, is only a thinly veiled attempt to drive the United States out of Asia.[118]

Scholars embracing a more historical perspective and holding to realist views that differ from offensive realism develop alternative analyses.[119] Ruizhuang Zhang, for example, insists that offensive realism overlooks significant weaknesses in China's economic rise.[120] And Xuetong Yan argues that Chinese history illustrates the inherent limitations of the preferred strategy of offensive realists: 2,000 years ago the Chinese philosopher Zi Xun thought that morality made the true kingdom system (*wang*) superior to and more stable than international hegemony (*ba*).[121] In the period of the warring states, one strategy was to make friends with a distant ally to attack one's neighbor from two sides, thus seeking an unending string of military victories in a strategy of territorial expansion. An alternative strategy was to form alliances with one's neighbors, seeking friendship and amity and domination through hegemonic rule. The first strategy is no longer viable in an era dominated by nuclear weapons and excessive costs of occupying and holding foreign territory. Only alliances hold forth the promise of long-term success.[122]

"Defensive" and "neoclassical" realists offer additional arguments that undermine the case for inevitable rupture. Multiple factors may exercise moderating influences on Chinese policy.[123] While rapid shifts in material capabilities intensify security competition, such competition does not necessarily lead to war. Geography and nuclear weapons, for example, make territorial conquest more difficult now than it was in nineteenth-century Europe.[124] The memory of China's century of humiliation does not only instill nationalism; it also imposes a culture of self-restraint, to avoid acting like the bully that the Chinese experienced in the Western powers. Confucian values that counsel against imposing one's values reinforce such historical memories.[125] Furthermore, material capabilities are filtered by perceptions and misperceptions of intentions that have diverse roots. Nothing in any of these conditions suggests that military conflict is inevitable.

A second and very different line of argument highlights the possibility that China's rise actually signifies a return to the Sinocentric security order in East Asia. In this view, China's rise as a military power and East Asia's evolving security order are built on distinctive historical foundations.[126] After the fall of the Ming Dynasty, China lacked what distinguished Europe: intensive region-wide military competition coupled with extensive global geographical expansion.[127] Admittedly, China was beset by civil and frontier wars. The frontier wars of the Qing dynasty – military alliances with the Eastern Mongols, extermination of the Western Mongols, conquest of Xinjiang, and the securing of formal suzerainty over Tibet – made for a substantial territorial expansion that aimed at the pacification of the periphery and the creation of a viable buffer zone against always possible invasions from Inner Asia. Still, in comparison to Europe, China and substantial parts of East Asia were at relative peace with one another for almost 300 years, bracketed by two Japanese invasions (Korea in 1592–98, Taiwan in 1894–95).[128] While in East Asia the number of countries and their boundaries have remained largely the same over many centuries, in Europe the number of states shrank from about 500 in 1500 to about 20 in 1900.[129]

It is significant that China and the other East Asian states did not exploit the opportunities they had to compete with one another in building overseas empires. Instead, as was true of Japan and China in the seventeenth century, competition focused on domestic development. Compared to the global expansion of the European settler dominions and colonial empires, China's conquests were modest, circumscribed by a defensive orientation, and lacking the systematic effort to extract resources. International trade was a much more important source of wealth and power for European states than for China. Admiral He Zheng's seven great voyages (1405–33) revealed a level of seafaring technology that was far superior to what Portuguese and Spanish discoverers could muster a century later. But the economic burden of these expeditions was considered too great given pressing domestic needs. Investment in canals and protection of the northern borders expanded greatly the size of China's national market. Control of foreign sea-lanes was simply less important. Instead, China perfected a system of tributary trade. It was symbolic, not extractive. In economic terms, tributary trade tended to benefit the vassal state more than it did China's imperial court. Symbolically, it helped to organize a cultural order that centered on China.

Why this moderation in China's foreign orientation, and why this comparative peacefulness of East Asia's state system?[130] One answer lies in East Asia's characteristic imbalance of power. Because of China's size, hierarchy and bandwagoning rather than equality and balancing, as in Europe, characterized the international relations of East Asia.[131] This is the core claim of David Kang's bold argument.[132] Kang holds that China's meteoric rise is recreating the structural conditions for regional hierarchy, peace, and stability in East Asia. Although this is a structural argument, since Kang concedes the existence of other causal factors, the outcome is not preordained. Yet it remains true that prior to the intrusion of the Western powers at the beginning of the nineteenth century, for long periods East Asia's international relations had been remarkably peaceful and stable. And China's foreign policy had been remarkably accommodating to the needs and demands of secondary states. Independent or suzerain states evolved political practices in a regional system that mixed the principle of formal hierarchy with informal equality. As long as the formal script of hierarchical relations between the primary and secondary states was observed, China saw little reason to intervene in the domestic affairs or foreign policies of its nominally subordinated "vassal" states – a sharp contrast to the European pattern of formal equality, informal hierarchy, and almost uninterrupted war.[133] Viewed from a Sino, rather than a Euro/American-centric perspective, it is thus significant that detailed statistical analyses of balance of power behavior in different world regions lead Scott Bennett and Allan

Stam to the conclusion that there exists "no support for the argument that [Asian] behavior will converge on that of Europe. In fact, all of the regions outside of Europe appear to diverge from the European pattern [of classical balance of power]."[134]

Finally, there is the case of recombination of new and old elements. It points to novel elements in East Asia's security system, some of which intensify security competition (such as the potential for strong nationalism and memory politics), some of which attenuate such competition (such as the US role in Asia's security arrangements as a stabilizing force because it acts as an offshore balancer), and some of which are indeterminate (such as Russia's role in East Asia and the vagaries in the domestic politics of various countries). The dynamics of security cooperation in the ASEAN Regional Forum (ARF) and a variety of Track 2 and 3 Dialogues belie the notion of a return to the world of bandwagoning. A lot of balancing behavior is clearly occurring. But in many instances, balancing occurs in a gradually evolving set of multilateral institutional arrangements. China's growing confidence in the stability of its security environment during the last two decades has made it accept multilateral security institutions as important elements of its national security strategy. Established in 2001, the Shanghai Cooperation Organization (SCO) illustrates this broader trend.[135]

In their analyses of China's border policies toward the North and its Taiwan policy toward the South, Allen Carlson in Chapter 2 and Xu Xin in Chapter 3 elaborate on the case for recombination. With particular attention to embryonic, recent changes away from China's strict insistence on its territorial integrity by some influential intellectuals, Carlson's analysis focuses on shifting discourses and border policies. Xu Xin reviews traditional Sinocentric and modern Westphalian approaches to diplomacy and recognizes in China's Taiwan diplomacy an overlay of both.

The most durable element in East Asia's institutionalized security order that permits partial innovations in Chinese diplomacy is the bilateral US–Japan security treaty. Without that treaty, East Asian security affairs would be less predictable and probably more volatile. The alliance operates in two ways. It affects the USA and Japan very directly. But it also has a large indirect effect on every state in the region. In a period of China's ascent, the alliance helps to reduce the uncertainty in the regional security environment in which China and its neighbors operate. Although the Chinese leadership would never admit to it in public, rather than worrying about Japan's return to an autonomous foreign policy and a possibly serious attempt at rearmament, China can take some comfort from a structurally integrated and controlled Japanese military in East Asia's security order. At times, Japan has wanted to play the broker between Asia and the West, seeking good relations with both. At other times, it has adhered to the policy of playing the part of Britain in East Asia, an island nation that seeks a special relationship with the United States. In both of these roles, Japan is anchored deeply in its security arrangement with the United States. For China, the one serious threat of the US–Japan alliance would arise in the eventuality of a Taiwan crisis. Yet in the past, strong American support of China's determined opposition to any unilateral change in the status quo across the Taiwan Strait has offered sufficient reassurance for China to continue to adhere to its grand strategy of accommodation. Furthermore, Taiwan's Presidential and Parliamentary elections of 2008 and the passage of the Economic Cooperation Framework in 2010 have sharply reduced the political fear of a military conflagration brought about by the Taiwanese independence movement; future elections and leadership successions, however, could easily increase cross-Strait tensions once again.

Based on the regional security order anchored in the US–Japan alliance, the Chinese and the United States governments are both acting like status quo powers. Both are hedging their bets. For now, they aim at engagement (the United States) and domestic development (China) and hold in reserve a strategy of explicit balancing (the United States) and regional primacy (China). The presence of the United States as East Asia's preeminent power complicates but will not stop China's rise. But it makes that rise occur in an institutionalized environment that itself has shaped indirectly how China conceives of its own security needs. Chinese strategy prizes international accommodation and accords priority to domestic growth and development over international assertiveness – except on the issues of Taiwan's independence and Tibet's autonomy, both of which it regards as strictly domestic issues. American strategy is reflected in the persistent policy of engagement that has sought to strengthen China during the last three decades, and to make it a more powerful and responsible power in world politics. China is defending strictly the principle of national sovereignty, thus resisting what it regards as America's overbearing, unilateral power on a number of international issues. And it embraces Asian multilateralism as a alternative to what it considers worrisome bilateral initiatives of the United States in Asia. Hedging to some extent contradicts the two grand strategies of China and the United States without, to date, seriously undermining them.[136]

Thanks to an existing security order centered on the US–Japan security treaty, East Asian governments and populations accept rather than fear China's rise. For them, a strong China is better than a weak one. If forced to choose, many East Asian states might well prefer China to Japan as Asia's leader. Every state in East Asia wishes to have good relations with the United States; none wishes to be caught in a conflict between China and the United States; and most are reluctant to participate in a US-led effort to contain or balance Chinese power for one simple reason: historically, East Asia has been primed for political and military imbalance, not balance.[137] The consolidation of the postcolonial states in Southeast Asia, the rapid transformation of Vietnam, the growing dependence of South Korea and Japan on Chinese markets, and the absence of Japanese attempts to define its role as a regional leader in Asia all point to a future in which China's rise will occur in the existing security order, thus combining old with new elements. The upshot of this discussion is clear: recombination rather than rupture or return best captures China's rise in Asia's security order.

Sinicization as recombination

Across cultural, economic, and security domains, China's rise is recombining rather than rupturing existing relationships or returning to its past. In cultural affairs, the civilizational legacy of China and the existence of communities of overseas Chinese favor the projection of social power, however ineffectual it may be, and weaken political forces demanding the pursuit of hard realpolitik. Communities of overseas Chinese have opened China's economy to an extraordinary degree to external influence, extending a longstanding tradition that the liberalization of the international economy during the last half-century has reinforced. Finally, China's rise as a military and political power in East Asia is occurring within the context of an existing security order centering on the US–Japan alliance. In sum, recombination, not rupture or return, is an accurate description of political developments attending China's rise.

The concept of Sinicization can make us think more precisely about the recombination of old and new elements in China's rise. Sinicization processes are constituted by historical and spontaneous interactions of individuals, societies, and states, with each intentionally and unintentionally affecting the other. Elias studied civilizing processes in European domestic politics, on questions of social manners and the restraint of aristocratic aggression. His style of analysis is also applicable to international affairs outside of Europe. It was after all the European society of states that superseded the Confucian order in East Asia, as China's standard of civilization concerning international trade, diplomacy, and law came to reflect the dominant European standard of civilization, codified in treaty law and subsequently also in European writings on customary law.[138]

In contrast to the nineteenth century, today there exists no longer a single standard. Instead, multiple standards are sustained by multiple civilizational processes. Sinicization is a two-way street that connects Chinese individuals, Chinese society, and the Chinese state to the world. It also serves as a conduit for developments in the world that are affecting China. China's domestic actors are involved in a process of dizzying multiplication and diversification, as economic and social change transform a simpler domestic structure into a more complex one. This more complex structure is composed of global, international, transnational, national, provincial, and local arenas of power. Some aspects of Sinicization overlap with global and international processes. They capture elements of integration that Max Weber called "rationalization" and that have now created common standards for a global market civilization.[139] At the same time, Sinicization contains elements of differentiation that are distinctive of China's civilizational polity. China, for example, has acceded to the widely subscribed norm of international arbitration in commercial disputes. But Chinese corporations and the Chinese government insist that arbitration boards meet in Beijing, Hong Kong, or Singapore rather than in London, Zurich, or New York.[140] Today's Sinicization is not remaking East Asia in the image of China. Instead, it combines old with new elements as it evolves along different trajectories in East Asia. In brief, Sinicization captures conceptually the sum total of processes that yield recombination rather than rupture or return.

As the case studies in Chapters 2–7 illustrate, Sinicization refers to multiple practices yielding multiple standards. For example, China's sheer size creates novel and very different economic opportunities and security threats for East Asia. Economic opportunities abound in markets that are growing rapidly and in populations that are skilled, adaptable, and hardworking. At the same time, new threats arise in the form of organized crime in gambling and prostitution, drug trafficking, the smuggling of migrants, piracy, and new environmental hazards. Cultural processes and practices intersect with historical memories that are creating their own political dynamic. This is of course true for Sino-Japanese disputes over the treatment of Japanese aggression in the 1930s and 1940s in Japanese history textbooks. Such memories also surface in other diplomatic relations, as they did, for example, in 2004 in the relations between China and South Korea. That dispute centered on the Koguryo kingdom (37 BCE to 668 CE) as either the forerunner of the Korean nation or a Chinese vassal state. In brief, Sinicization summarizes the recombination of old and new processes and practices culled from the cultural, economic, and security domains of China's rise. For strictly illustrative purposes, I offer here three brief examples of recombination in the domains of culture, economy, and security.

First is the resurrection of New Confucianism as a state ideology. This development speaks directly to the issue of China's cultural power.[141] In the recent past, Confucianism was blamed for many of China's ills in the last two centuries. In an attempt to bolster its legitimacy, in recent years the Chinese government has attempted to revive Confucianism as a hierarchical, reciprocal, and morally based value system. The qualities that flow from these values – wisdom, morality, generosity, obligation to respect the interests of others – are now extolled as highly conducive to economic growth and political stability, resonating with similar arguments made earlier in Japan and Singapore. Confucian values are invoked deliberately in the hope of filling the spiritual vacuum left after the demise of Communism. In promoting the idea of a "harmonious society" that bolsters the position of the Communist Party, the Chinese government now seeks support from a political thinker it reviled not long ago. Like all intellectual traditions, New Confucianism recombines older components that government officials introduce to fit a new context. Under siege by the challenges posed by the West, earlier versions of Confucianism were either hollowed out or eliminated altogether. In its new incarnation, the relevance of New Confucianism is now said to lie in its humanism. Without any explanation, a 31-foot bronze statue was unveiled near Tianamen Square in front of Beijing's National Museum in January 2011, catty-corner from the iconic portrait of Mao Zedong. Under cover of darkness, again without any explanation, it suddenly disappeared four months later, an indication of dueling political traditions inside the Chinese government.[142]

New Confucianism seeks to fill a spiritual and legitimacy void in the domain of culture. This is no easy task. In a head-on collision between Hollywood's blockbuster movie *Avatar* and a clumsy though lavishly produced and well-advertised Chinese production of *Confucius*, the future beat the past by about 3:1.[143] The Chinese government, however, remains committed to elevating China's cultural profile abroad. The first Confucius Institute conference was convened in the Great Hall of the People in 2006, attended by representatives from 35 countries. President Hu Jintao and Prime Minister Wen Jiabao thus have hitched their vision of a "harmonious" society to a symbol and tradition reviled only a few decades ago. As an international brand, Confucianism offers a pacifist, familial metaphor that reassures. Following in the footsteps of the British Council, the Alliance Française, and the German Goethe Institutes, the Chinese government is committed to founding a large number of Confucius language institutes abroad. In the first two years, between 2004 and 2006, 75 such institutes reportedly were opened, with very different records of activity and achievement. By the end of 2010, there reportedly existed 322 such institutes in 96 countries.[144] Rather than operating under the strict control of an understaffed Education Ministry, this network of institutes has grown, often through local initiatives and with uncertain levels of funding, and typically in close interaction with foreign partners. Cultural joint ventures, co-sponsorship and co-funding with host institutions, are an important reason for the successful start of this initiative. Adaptability to local demand is high, as there is no set curriculum that must be followed. This pattern agrees with the broad conclusions that Chih-yu Shih and Caroline Hau reach in Chapters 6 and 7. Both point to the inability of any one actor, including the Chinese government, to define authoritatively what it means to be Chinese. Instead, processes of definition or redefinition are dispersed among individuals and groups located in many different social and geographical places. Whatever the shortfall in public diplomacy, their chapters concur on the importance of persuasion, imitation, and adaptation.

When Chinese preferences and the preferences of others are shared, China's cultural power can be amplified. One aspect of China's international trade in particular is germane to a discussion of social power.[145] International economic exchange, especially between large and small economies, can shape domestic politics indirectly. Over time, coalitions that gain from these exchanges will form and defend their interests in maintaining good relations with the larger economy and thus help shape the definition of the national interest that informs foreign policy choices. Takashi Shiraishi shows in Chapter 5 how this political logic operates in parts of Southeast Asia that are not well integrated into the global economy. This realignment of economic and social interests affects not only firms but also sectors, regions, coalitions, and, at times, entire polities. China's economic rise brings into play this "influence effect," especially in intra-Asian trade. All Asian states thus have growing stakes in a prosperous Chinese economy. Public opinion surveys and foreign trade dependence data support this view.[146]

The economic importance of the overseas Chinese and economic transnationalism offers an "alternative modernity" to an exclusively territorially centered national economy.[147] Tianbiao Zhu and Takashi Shiraishi refer in Chapters 4 and 5 to the importance of the horizontal, border-spanning dimension of processes of Sinicization. China's economy has important transnational ties and a distinctive degree of economic openness. Indeed, Chinese capitalism is not merely a domestic phenomenon but also an integral part of the world economy.[148] Chinese merchant capitalism has developed along a very different trajectory from Japanese industrial capitalism. The conventional comparison of Japanese success and Chinese failure at the beginning of the twentieth century is too simple. Success is often defined implicitly, in terms of output in highly concentrated heavy industries and the successful pursuit of military objectives by centralized states. Such a definition overlooks a radically different pattern of Chinese economic development, marked by reliance on light industry, medium- and small-sized family-owned, extensively networked firms covering large geographic areas and economic sectors, and decentralized or weak states. In contrast to Japan, Chinese capitalism was integrated early into the world economy. Even today, Hong Kong, Singapore, and Taiwan, as well as concentrations of communities of overseas Chinese elsewhere, exemplify this road to modern capitalism.

Security studies offer a third example. In line with the emphasis on the rediscovery and overlay of traditional Chinese and contemporary Westphalian modes of diplomacy that Allen Carlson and Xu Xin develop in Chapters 2 and 3, Canrong Jin has pointed to China's "multifaceted diplomacy" as part of a grand strategy that subsumes traditional great power diplomacy.[149] Chinese diplomacy focuses not only on the major powers, but also on its neighbors and less developed countries in other parts of the world, including Africa and Latin America. Many Chinese diplomatic initiatives focus on concrete social, cultural, economic, and environmental issues. China's multifaceted diplomacy includes summits, top-leader meetings, bilateral exchanges, multilateralism, and forum diplomacy. This turn in Chinese diplomacy is often cited as evidence that China has softened its international stance. Some go as far as to suggest that with the American turn toward unilateralism after 9/11, besides the EU, China has become the most ardent defender of the institution of multilateralism, the greatest diplomatic innovation of the United States after the end of World War II. Perhaps.

The empirical record, however, supports a different view. There exist significant differences among the various multilateral fora in which China is involved. Some are conventional multilateral institutions in which the various members participate on relatively equal terms, such as ASEAN or the ARF. Some have been convened by other countries, with China joining as an active participant. The Latin American Forum, for example, is a Singaporean initiative seeking to strengthen the cooperation between East Asia and Latin America; China is an active participant that initiates and sponsors various activities. The Pacific Island Forum resulted from a New Zealand initiative. China has established a dialogue relationship with it, in part because after 2000 the Chinese government was intent in various multilateral institutions on fending off a diplomatic offensive by Taiwan's independence-seeking government.

But China is also involved in some multilateral fora which it set up as the founding member. Here, China is the clear leader, agenda setter, and, at times, major donor. It holds a central position and orchestrates the bilateral discussions, consultations, and negotiations between itself and each of the other members. Typically, collective agreements can be presented at summit or ministerial meetings only after these bilateral meetings have been concluded successfully. The Chinese government tends to describe these fora as win-win, multilateral institutions that embody the five principles of peaceful coexistence. In practice, they strengthen China's economic, security, and political ties with member states, enhance China's influence in the region, and provide China with more support at larger international gatherings and at the United Nations (UN). The main examples of this kind of multilateral forum diplomacy date back no further than the late 1990s and include the Shanghai Cooperation Organization (SCO), the Forum on China–Africa Cooperation (FOCAC), the Forum on Cooperation between China and Arab States, and the China–Pacific Islands Countries Economic and Development Cooperation Forum. Reflecting neither conventional bilateral nor multilateral institutions, China's forum diplomacy is a genuine innovation that draws on some of China's longstanding and well-tested political practices, calibrating them with the novel situation in world politics that China's rise is creating. Africa offers a laboratory for multilateralism with a Chinese face.[150]

China's cultural, economic, and military rise is best captured by the concept of recombination rather than rupture or return. Recombination captures China's emergent realities better than the stipulation of overarching structures or general trends. One such structure is "Chimerica," a monster hybrid of China's massive industrial exports feeding American overconsumption, accounting together for a third of global output and two-fifths of economic growth between 1998 and 2007.[151] Similarly, experts such as Martin Wolfe talk of "the great convergence" in income between East and West, a reversal from the great divergence that occurred in the nineteenth and twentieth centuries.[152] Explicating China's rise in three different domains suggests one conclusion. China's rise can easily mislead us to think of a simple linear trend. Yet unitary and additive constructs or arguments offer limited insight and do little to advance our understanding. Instead, we should inquire into Sinicization and investigate the processes, policies, and practices that accompany China's rise. They do not yield either rupture or return but point instead to recombination of old and new elements as *the* defining aspect of China's rise.

Notes

1 This chapter was first written as a discussion paper (Katzenstein 2008) for the East Asia Institute, which supported my month-long trip throughout East Asia in April 2008. I would like to thank Allen Carlson, David Kang, Richard Samuels, Mark Selden, and Takashi Shiraishi for their insightful comments on the project proposal; Allen Carlson, William Callahan, Jian Chen, Yuhan Chu, Sherm Cochran, Zhiyuan Cui, Peter Gourevitch, Takeshi Hamashita, Carol Hau, Qingguo Jia, Wendy Leutert, Victor Nee, T.J. Pempel, Yaqing Qin, Richard Samuels, Mark Selden, Chih-yu Shih, Takashi Shiraishi, Eric Tagliacozzo, Akio Takahara, Yi-feng Tao, Xu Xin, Tingyang Zhao, and Tianbiao Zhu for their insightful comments and criticisms of various drafts; and all of the participants in the EAI expert seminars sponsored by the East Asia Institute that convened

in Seoul, Taipei, Tokyo, Shanghai, and Beijing in April 2008 for their helpful comments. Hong Duan summarized for me the content of Zhengyi Wang's 2007 article. I have also benefitted enormously from subsequent criticisms of various drafts by participants at workshops convened at Peking University in January 2010 and March 2011; from extensive written critiques by Martin Bernal, Gregory Noble, Miles Kahler, David Leheny and Tingyang Zhao; from the many comments, criticisms, and suggestions of my co-authors in this project; from the anonymous reviewers of the book manuscript; and from Mary Katzenstein who subjected the penultimate draft to close scrutiny and provided careful criticisms that helped me greatly to improve it further. For their invaluable research assistance I am indebted to Emma Clarke, Elisa Charbonnel, and Jill Lyon. Sarah Tarrow helped smooth my prose. For all the good advice and friendly criticisms that I received, and did not heed, my stubbornness and intellectual obtuseness must be blamed. Finally, I would like to acknowledge with enormous gratitude the generous financial support that I received in 2009–10 from the Louise and John Steffens Founders' Circle Membership at the Institute of Advanced Studies in Princeton.
2 *The Economist* 2010a; Pan 2010a, b; Cheng 2010; Zhou 2010; Leonard 2008, 133.
3 Lohr 2011; *The Economist* 2010c.
4 Hatch 2010.
5 Katzenstein and Shiraishi 1997.
6 Katzenstein and Shiraishi 2006.
7 Lohr 2011, 1, 6.
8 Barnett and Duvall 2006. They exclude consideration of effects that produce action through mutual agreement or interactions in which one actor persuades another to alter voluntarily and freely her beliefs, interests, and actions. Hence, in their understandings, and in mine, the exercise of power always entails constraints and incentives.
9 Jacques 2009, 196–7.
10 I would like to thank Martin Bernal for pointing this out to me.
11 Bernal 1987.
12 Harrell 1995, 16, 18.
13 Spence 1998. In the opinion of American political scientists, during the next ten years China's rise (40 percent) ranks only slightly behind two other leading issues, international terrorism (50 percent) and proliferation of weapons of mass destruction (45 percent). Two-thirds think that China and East Asia will be the strategically most important region for American foreign policy twenty years hence. See Maliniak, Oakes, Peterson, and Tierny 2007, 2. For American elite views, see Pew Research Center 2009. For American public opinion, see Tao and Page 2010, and Page and Tao 2010. For Chinese public opinion of American power, see Zhang 2005. Because the concept of "peaceful rise" raised possible objections in a variety of domestic and foreign quarters, it was soon replaced in official Chinese discourse by "peaceful development." I am adhering to the conventional American terminology of "China's [peaceful] rise." Of the 25 articles published on China in *Foreign Affairs* in the odd-numbered years between 2001 and 2009, the explicit or implicit reference in the titles to "China's rise" outnumbered other concepts by a ratio of 3:1; for book reviews, that ratio was more than 10:1.
14 Callahan 2010; Foot and Walter 2011; Zhang 2011; Womack 2010a, 2010b; Sheng 2010; Yan 2010, 2006, 2001; Wang 2010; Beeson 2009; Jacques 2009; Tsunekawa 2009b; Institute of International Strategic and Development Studies 2009; Cheng 2010; Feng 2009; Ross and Zhu 2008; Kastner 2008; Callahan 2007; Glaser and Medeiros 2007; Tammen and Kugler 2006; Zheng 2005a, 2005b; Goldstein 2005; Suettinger 2004; Kokubun and Wang 2004; Brown et al. 2000.
15 Jacques 2009, 363–413.
16 Hobson 2004; Frank 1998.
17 *The Economist* 2009, 84.
18 Wong 1997; Pomeranz 2000; Arrighi 2007; Arrighi, Hamashita, and Selden 2003; Stokes 2001; Hobson 2004.

19 Latham and Kawakatsu 2006; Sugiyama and Grove 2001; Sugihara 2005b.
20 Sugihara 2005a, 2–3, 4–13.
21 Cohen 1996.
22 Overholt 1993; Kynge 2006; Shenkar 2006; McGregor 2006; Engardio 2007.
23 Sugihara 2005b.
24 Rosecrance and Guoliang 2009; Christensen 2009; Goldstein 2005; Johnston 1995, 2008; Johnston and Ross 1999; Ikenberry 2008a; Jia 2009; Shambaugh 2005a; Wang 2005.
25 Ren 2008; Wang, Yiwei 2002; Lynch 2009; Song 2001.
26 Qin 2010; Buzan 2010; see also Tong 2006.
27 Barma et al. 2009; Ikenberry 2008a, 2011a, 2011b.
28 Zhao 2006, 2009a; Callahan 2008; Tong 2006; Zhang 2010b.
29 Yan 2011.
30 Stokes 2001, 2. See also Wang 2010, 279–81, 283–8; Morris 2010; Hui 2006; Wong, R. Bin 2003; Goldstone 2003; Duchesne 2001/02, 2003; Alam 2003; Pomeranz 2000; Frank 1998; Wong 1997.
31 Roberts 2002.
32 Lee 2008a, 2008b; Ono 2007a, 2007b. See also Mintz 2009.
33 Elias 2000, 1978; Linklater 2011, 154–93; Katzenstein 2010b, 20–2.
34 Gong 1984; Barth and Osterhammel 2005.
35 Zeitlin 2000, 16–17.
36 Wolfers 1962, 67–80.
37 Kang 2010b. See also Pijl 2010, 2007.
38 Tai 1989, 11.
39 Kissinger 2011.
40 Holcombe 2001.
41 Xu 2009, 51.
42 Yang 1968, 20.
43 Bell and Chaibong 2003; Makeham 2003; Bakar and Nai 1997; Woodside 2006.
44 My analysis of Weiming Tu's writings is based in part on Duan 2007.
45 Tu 1994a.
46 Ong and Nonini 1997b; Callahan 2004.
47 Tu 2000, 2002.
48 Callahan 2004, xx.
49 Tu 1991; Duan 2007, 4–11.
50 Ong and Nonini 1997b; Katzenstein 2000a, 2000b, 2005.
51 Fukuyama 1995, 84–6.
52 Ramo 2004.
53 Leonard 2008, 15–16, 28–32, 35, 119.
54 Leonard 2008, 14; Ong and Nonini 1997b; Jacques 2009, 140–5; Collins 1998; 2004.
55 I would like to thank Jian Chen for his helpful comments on this section.
56 Rawski 1996, 842; Ho 1998, 150–2.
57 Shiraishi 2006.
58 Personal correspondence, May 2007.
59 Ho 1998; Rawski 1996.
60 Kuhn 1990, 66–72.
61 Rawski 1996, 831, 835.
62 Bartlett 1991, 25–6.
63 Ho 1998, 125.
64 Elliott 2001, xiv.
65 Osterhammel 2005, 376–81.
66 Wang 1984, 9.
67 Ho 1998, 150–2.
68 Schwartz 1975; Eisenstadt 1986.
69 Huang 2002, 222; Deutsch 1966.

70 Vyas 2011; Hunter 2009; Li 2008a; Wuthnow 2008; Ding 2008b; Yu 2007; Cheung 2006. On the discussion of the various dimensions of power, see Barnett and Duvall 2006.
71 Perlez 2004.
72 Kurlantzick 2006, 3.
73 Totten 2011.
74 Jain and Groot 2006.
75 Bezlova 2006; French 2006.
76 Sharma 2011; Wang and Ma 2008, 2. According to official Chinese statistics between 1979 and 2007, China sent 1.6 million students and scholars abroad, with half a million returning to China. See Zweig and Han 2010, 89. Martin Bernal, personal communication, 14 April 2011.
77 Kurlantzick 2006, 3–4; Nye 2005.
78 Perlez 2004.
79 Zakaria 2006.
80 The data on student exchange, however, point to an important potential source of future social power. David Shambaugh (2005a, 2), for one, quoting Joseph Nye (2004, 2), argues that, in contrast to Japan, China is currently lacking many of the elements of soft and social power attraction – such as philosophies or ideologies, popular or high culture, sports, fashion, or role models. Two decades earlier, Japan's rise illustrated for Nye 1990, 168 the very same point.
81 Cheow 2004.
82 Tu 2000, 2002.
83 Hansen 2000.
84 Ong and Nonini 1997b; Callahan 2004, xx.
85 Zweig and Han 2010. See also Zweig 2002, 161–210.
86 Hunter n.d., 6.
87 Kurlantzick 2006, 4.
88 Hunter n.d., 7.
89 Kurlantzick 2006, 3–4; Hunter, n.d., 7.
90 Cheow 2004, 2.
91 Wang, Hongying 2003, 70; Ramo 2007.
92 Ramo 2004.
93 Rachman 2007; Yang 2010.
94 Chicago Council on Global Affairs 2008, 5.
95 Ramo 2007.
96 *The Economist* 2010a, 41; Berenson 2009.
97 Any economic analysis must be qualified by a number of different data problems that stem from the fact that the Chinese economy is in transition to a market economy and that conversion into official exchange rates or Purchasing Power Parity (PPP) rates can create troublesome technical issues. Chinese economic statistics are of variable and at times dubious quality, as *The Economist* (2008) reports. Furthermore, past recalculations of China's GDP by the World Bank, sharply upward in 1993 and sharply downward in 2007, raised many questions about the Bank's research methodology. The 1993 calculation of about $1.5 trillion (roughly the midpoint between the low estimates of $300 billion and the high estimates of $3 trillion that had been used by economists before) overnight catapulted China into the ranks of a large East Asian economic power. The World Bank's 2007 recalculation of Chinese GDP reduced China's economic size overnight by 40 percent, from $8.9 to $5.3 trillion, with hardly a political ripple as Albert Keidel (2007) notes. Maddison and Wu (2008, 19) take exception with both official Chinese and World Bank figures, including with the Bank's 2007 downwards revision. Their estimate of $7.3 trillion falls between the official Chinese figure of $9.2 trillion and the Bank's revised estimate of $5.3. For different reasons, Lester Thurow (2007) also has raised questions about a possible overestimation of China's GDP figures; in private conversation (29 April 2008), Professor Shulong Chu argued that current Chinese economic

statistics underreport the size of China's GDP for various technical and political reasons. Looking ahead, forecasts for the year 2030 vary between a Chinese economy 2.5 times as large or half as large as the American economy, with much resting, among others, on guesses about the future of the exchange rate of the dollar and the renminbi. There exists, however, general agreement that on a per capita basis China ranks today somewhere around the midpoint of the 230 economies for which we have data, with a per capita income roughly one tenth of Japan and the United States. Furthermore, Mark Selden and Jieh-min Wu (2011) document that poverty remains a widespread problem, that China's migrant workers enjoy no social protections and are economically exploited, and that economic inequality between urban and rural China and different social strata is strikingly high and growing rapidly. In terms of productivity, China lags far behind the United States and its East Asian partners. Foreign firms dominate the high end of manufacturing production and exports. China's foreign trade dependence was an astonishing 67 percent of GDP in 2006 before dropping back to 44 percent, far outstripping that of the United States (28 percent) and Japan (31 percent). And at market exchange rates, rather than purchasing power parity, Asia and China continue to lag behind Europe: Asia's 31 percent share in 2009 was only 3 percent above its 1995 figure as *The Economist* (2010b) reports, reflecting the fact that China's economic rise has largely been cancelled out by Japan's decline. Furthermore, in a few decades China will confront the challenge of an aging society that will be much more serious and severe than is Japan's today. It is difficult to come to an overall assessment of these various facts and trends. At a minimum, the image of an unstoppable Chinese economic juggernaut is often based on a partial analysis that abstracts from many imponderables, including the character of China's future political regime.

98 Hung 2009.
99 Selden 2011.
100 Arrighi, Hamashita, and Selden 2003; World Bank 1993.
101 Hamashita 2008, 1997; Selden and Grove 2008.
102 Callahan 2003.
103 Gomez and Hsiao 2001a, 2–3, 5–7, 11–12, 33.
104 Gomez and Benton 2004, 6.
105 Interviews, Tianjin and Beijing, March–April 2006.
106 Gomez and Benton 2004, 8; Katzenstein 2005, 60–9.
107 Kumagai 2007; Rauch and Trindade 2002.
108 Gomez and Hsiao 2001b, 2004; Ong and Nonini 1997b; Naughton 1997; Weidenbaum and Hughes 1996; Dædalus 1991.
109 Kuwamori and Okamoto 2007.
110 Private conversations with Mi Ji, Jing Tao, and Zhengyi Wang, Beijing, 26–27 April 2008.
111 Hamilton 2006a and Wang 1997.
112 Maddison 2006, 261.
113 Xu Xin 2008; Goldstein 2005; Zheng 2005a, 2005b; Economy and Oksenberg 1999; Johnston and Ross 1999. For reasons of space only, this discussion leaves unexamined issues of societal insecurity such as the environment, migration, organized crime, terrorism, and an aging population. All of these "new" security issues arguably also point to recombination rather than rupture or return.
114 Fishman 2005.
115 Roy 1994, 1996; Shambaugh 1996; Goldstein 1997/98; Bernstein and Munro 1997; Mearsheimer 2001; Broomfield 2003; Gries 2005; Ravenhill 2006; Callahan 2007.
116 Mearsheimer 2006; Kirshner 2010.
117 Friedberg 2000.
118 Offensive realism offers a materialist account of the security consequences of China's rise. Since systemic balance of power arguments can never specify the direction of the balance (for which one needs to rely on sub-systemic features of politics), looking to the "China threat" as a factor that determines the direction of balancing is politically

expedient but theoretically unconvincing. The concept of threat refers to ideational phenomena, specifically the relationship between Self and Other, as Johnston (2004) and others argue. Invoking threat is quite compelling if the move toward a constructivist argument is acknowledged explicitly. But most adherents of "offensive realism" deny that their analysis has anything to do with ideas. Threats emerge naturally and deterministically from capabilities. This is an exceedingly implausible view if it is held implicitly. If held explicitly, it leads to the kind of analytical eclecticism that most offensive realists seek to avoid, as it requires sacrifices in the theoretical parsimony they cherish. In addition, it should be noted that offensive realists offer an argument that talks about "tendency to war" without committing to when such a war might occur. What looks like a determinist argument in its analytical formulation turns out to be indeterminate in application. See, for example, John Mearsheimer's lecture "Can China Rise Peacefully?" (Cornell University, Government Department, 29 March 2007), and Mearsheimer 2006.
119 Kaufman, Little, and Wohlforth 2007.
120 Zhang 2008.
121 Yan, Xuetong 2011, 2008, 2006. See also Wei 2006.
122 Xuetong Yan, private conversation, Beijing, 27 April 2008.
123 Christensen 2006, 2009; Kirshner 2008; Fravel 2008.
124 Goldstein 2005.
125 Xinbo Wu, private conversation, Shanghai, 23 April 2008.
126 This rich literature grapples with the risk of distilling Chinese and European history into sharply different molds, such as universal empire in the case of China and balance of power in the case of Europe. China's long history, however, is simply too varied. In the distant past, for example, as Hui (2005) shows, Qin's unification of the ancient Chinese system replaced balancing strategies in a multipolar system that resembled European feudalism with counterbalancing (divide-and-rule and divide-and-conquer) domination in a unipolar system. Self-strengthening reforms in the process of state formation (such as the rationalization of national taxation and establishment of more meritocratic administrations, as well as the introduction of universal military conscription) overrode the logic of balancing. Wei (2006) makes a compelling case that neorealism needs to broaden its focus beyond balancing to bandwagoning and withdrawing, and has to go beyond the anarchic structure of the international system to include other variables. Zhang (2009 and 2010a) argues against the misspecifications of the concepts of tributary trade and hierarchy in the analysis of Chinese history. Yuan-Kang Wang (2001, 2002, 2011) shows that power politics, as characterized by structural realism rather than cultural realism, best explains twenty cases involving Chinese military policy making during the Northern Song (960–1127), Southern Song (1127–1279), and Ming dynasties (1368–1644). Alastair I. Johnston (1995) disagrees. (See also Lantis 2002; Yong 1999.) He finds that rather than following the dictates of structural realism, or expressing Confucian pacifism, China's strategic culture during the Ming dynasty especially along the empire's northern border was characterized by a war-prone stance permitting the ready use of military power. The alternative Confucian–Mencian strategic culture centered on notions of internal rectification and virtue. Johnston argues that it may have served a number of purposes, such as justifying immoral behavior with appeals to moral imperatives, making instrumental use of symbolic language to delegitimate alternative strategies, or providing psychological reassurance to individuals shocked by their own behavior. But it did not guide China's national security strategy. All of these studies suggest that no one model is likely to capture the variability in China's history; different variants of realism all find some support in China's rich historical record.
127 Arrighi 2008, 2007; Kang 2005, 2010a.
128 Relative peace between states actually lasted 500 years, since during the 200 years preceding 1592 China was at war only once, during the 1406–28 invasion of Vietnam to restore the Tran dynasty. This is not to deny an enormous amount of domestic

violence and bloodshed in Asia including peasant uprisings in the late Ming dynasty; the chaotic rise of the Tokugawa; the Manchu conquest of China; incessant revolts in Vietnam during the Le dynasty; religious persecutions of Buddhists and Christians; and many rebellions in nineteenth century China, most famously the horrible bloodshed of the Taiping uprising.

129 Kaufman 1997, 176.
130 I neglect here a discussion of China's strategic culture that considers how ideas and events matter in bringing about foreign policy change as exemplified by Legro (2007). China's experiences, doctrines, and practices are as broad, or broader, than those of the United States with its multiple and contested foreign policy traditions. If structural and cultural variants of realism can find support in China's historical record, so can variants of Confucianism and idealism. In the view of John Fairbank (1968, 1974) (see also Mancall 1984; Zhang 2009), China's most successful and widely acclaimed foreign policy has been non-violence. China relied primarily on diplomatic maneuvering, cultural attraction, tributary trade, and other non-coercive means. Parts of Fairbank's argument resonate with Kang's (2010b) scholarship, which I summarize below. But as an independent argument it simply does not accord with some of the careful empirical research done well after Fairbank ceased publishing. For example, Alastair Johnston (1996) shows that China's relatively hard realpolitik strategic culture survived Maoist China for a while, despite a sharp reduction in the threat that China's external environment posed, and despite China's incorporation into international economic institutions. Johnston's finding does not only undercut the historical sweep of Fairbank's analysis. It also contradicts the different systemic arguments advanced by realists and liberals who point to the forever destabilizing effects of threat and stabilizing effects of international institution. Since the 1990s, however, there has been a remarkable shift in Chinese foreign policy toward greater accommodation, which Johnston (2008) also documents and analyzes. Based on carefully assembled evidence illuminating different micro-processes of socialization – mimicking, social influence, and persuasion – Johnston concludes that on questions of security today, hard realpolitik no longer trumps soft *idealpolitik* at all times.
131 Hierarchy refers here to regional relations that are organized around a dominant state, rooted in material powers as well as in shared expectations and norms governing the conduct of both primary and secondary states. Crucially, all states understand that the primary state has different rights and responsibilities than do all other states in the region.
132 Kang 2010b, 2007, 2005, 2004, 2003/04, 2003. See also Huntington 1996, 229–38; Cha 1998.
133 Mongolia and Tibet were two notable exceptions.
134 Bennett and Stam 2003, 193–4.
135 Johnston 2008; Leonard 2008, 83–114.
136 Christensen 2006, 110–22.
137 Japan and India, however, are both interested in and wary of engaging in a balance of power politics to contain China.
138 Gong 1985, 172; 1984.
139 Bowden and Seabrooke 2006.
140 Xingping Jia, private conversation, Beijing, 26 April 2008.
141 Bell and Chaibong 2003; Makeham 2003; Cha 2003.
142 Jacobs 2011.
143 LaFraniere 2010.
144 Paradise 2009.
145 Hirschman 1980/1945; Kirshner 2008; Abdelal and Kirshner 1999/2000. Also relevant, and more frequently cited than the indirect influence effect, is the direct coercion effect.
146 Yang, Jiemian 2007; Yang, Ying 2007; Huang and Ding 2006; Gill and Huang 2006.
147 Ong and Nonini 1997b; Duan 2007, 4–11.

148 Hamilton 1996.
149 Professor Jin discussed China's Forum Diplomacy in a public lecture delivered at Cornell University, 17 October 2007. Hong Duan and Jing Tao helped me gather some of the empirical material I rely on here.
150 Leonard 2008, 99–104, 109–14, 118–20.
151 Ferguson and Schularick 2009.
152 Wolfe 2011a, 2011b; Pomeranz 2000; Elvin 1973.

PART I

2
REIMAGINING THE FRONTIER

Patterns of Sinicization and the emergence of new thinking about China's territorial periphery

Allen Carlson

This chapter examines the recent unexpected emergence of new Chinese considerations of how to conceptualize and govern the frontier (*bianjiang*) of the People's Republic of China (PRC), defined as the regions near the state's territorial limits and their inhabitants. For China, this issue encompasses both the PRC's borders and its approach to the minority nationalities (*shaoshu minzu*) that live near them. The chapter first places this trend within a broader context by reviewing the fluid manner in which such terrain was previously conceived and ruled. While avoiding oversimplification, it finds a qualitative difference between the relative ease with which the spatial limits of imperial China shifted, and the much more persevering approach of the contemporary period. More specifically, the chapter then observes that following the establishment of the PRC the elasticity and vibrancy of the past was replaced by silence and rigidity on frontier issues. Finally, it describes the starkly contrasting conceptual practices and policy prescriptions for *bianjiang* that have recently been articulated within the emerging Chinese discussion. It places a particular emphasis on the three divergent approaches to frontier-related issues that Chinese elites have developed since 2005.

First, proponents of "frontier studies" (*bianjiangxue*) – led by Ma Dazheng, the "father" of this field of study – have built on their previous work and sought to revive traditional concepts of such regions, while at the same time expressing a deep attachment to the modern spatial norms of sovereignty. In so doing, Ma has endorsed Beijing's current intransigent approach to governing these areas. In contrast, a handful of scholars, especially Yu Xiaofeng and Xu Lili, leading figures in China's nascent field of non-traditional security (*feichuantong anquan*), have proposed a reorientation of Chinese thinking around the concept of frontier security (*biananxue*) and indirectly called for a wide-ranging renovation of the way in which Beijing rules the territorial periphery and those residing in it. Finally, Ma Rong, a Peking University sociologist, has directly challenged both schools of thought by questioning the dual theoretical foundations (regional autonomy and the nationality classification system) of the PRC's stance on establishing control over frontier regions, and heretically pushed for a dismantling of these core aspects of current Chinese policies. Although each of these two latter approaches lays out unorthodox stances to the PRC's frontier, neither questions the current shape of China. Yet, at the same time, in simply suggesting a reformulation of the manner in which China administers such spaces, this new work is unprecedented within recent Chinese discussions of both territory and nationality.

The chapter explains past shifts within the Chinese approach to frontiers – and the current growth of such divergent Chinese approaches to *bianjiang* – with reference to the concept of Sinicization, understood as openness to not only geographic, but also temporal border-crossing. I first argue that the relative mutability within the dynastic Chinese approach to frontiers was produced by, and an exemplar of, Sinicization. Throughout most of this period, a rhetorical space existed that allowed for the flow of both ideas and people across China's territorial periphery, accompanied by an ongoing attempt to discipline and define such a region. This characteristic was not always a constant over the thousands of years of recorded Chinese history; however imperial boundaries tended to possess a degree of impermanence that contrasts with the staticity found in more recent times. Indeed, by the midpoint of the last century, the wholesale importation of ideas about the impermeability of political borders, in the form of the Chinese embrace of the Westphalian concept of sovereignty, stifled such a pattern of exchange across imagined political boundaries and eventually replaced it with an inert understanding of the territorial limits of modern China.

The pervasive silence about *bianjiang* that then predominated during the first three decades after the establishment of the PRC was only partially broken in the late 1970s, when Deng Xiaoping's emphasis on pragmatic policies created a sliver of ambiguity within Beijing's approach to China's territorial periphery. However, this limited aperture remained largely unexplored until the security situation within such regions shifted following the collapse of the Soviet Union. It only became truly active over the last several years, in the wake of two broad developments. First, the PRC's perceived "rise" as a major player within the international system provided a further impetus for the expansion of Chinese thinking about what "shape" China should take absent previously existing material constraints. Second, such confidence on the world stage has been paired with looming concerns about preserving domestic security and social stability, particularly in China's territorial periphery. This trend was punctuated by the short-lived March 2008 protests in Tibet and the summer 2009 surge of unrest in Xinjiang. While neither of these events seriously challenged Chinese rule in either region, they provided a catalyst for the acceleration of new thinking about how Beijing should go about holding on to such regions. This pairing of confidence and sensitivity has opened up a new rhetorical space for reconsidering how to govern and administer China's frontier.

Within this unexpected set of discussions about *bianjiang*, differences stem from two factors. First, each of the main contributors to it has synthesized components of China's past and current international role in distinct ways. In brief, those writing about *bianjiang* have all reached back into China's long historical record in search of dynastic formulas for envisioning and governing the interior periphery, in hopes of discovering previously overlooked points of intellectual resonance with China's current situation. The past has then been revisited and reimagined in the service of the present in a way that is intended to help make China's place in the current international order more apposite. Alongside this attention to history, contributors have incorporated contrasting ideas about territory that originated outside the "Chinese" context in order to create new approaches to the territorial limits of the PRC. Such experimentation with old norms and newly imported concepts has produced the rather public, and divisive, debate about *bianjiang* now taking shape in China.

A brief consideration of the past – from diversity and debate to convergence and silence

China's *bianjiang* is in one sense simply a geographic zone, one whose location has shifted over time along with the waxing and waning of dynastic power. It generally consists of the region that runs from the Tibetan plateau through the arid reaches of Xinjiang, and across the frigid northern steppe to the forests of Heilongjiang. Historically, frequent conquests of these areas by imperial forces were often followed by the garrisoning of dynastic troops in remote border outposts. Yet, subjugation of the borderlands was not achieved by force alone; collaboration with frontier peoples and accommodation of cultural and linguistic differences were also commonly employed as those at the center struggled to establish their rule over such varied terrain.

Conventional wisdom has it that different dynasties gravitated toward one or the other of these frameworks for governing the territorial periphery. For example, the Yuan and Qing are most often associated with the extensive frontier military campaigns that were carried out throughout both dynasties. In contrast, the Ming is linked to the construction through its northern borderlands of what became known as the Great Wall. The Tang dynasty is then juxtaposed with these other periods as one of great cosmopolitanism and commercial as well as cultural engagement with those polities located along the periphery. However, as dominant as such perceptions are, a closer examination of each empire's handling of border relations quickly reveals an often acute awareness of conditions in peripheral regions and the employment of diverse policies in those regions. Throughout this period even questions of who had the right to rule the empire were largely unsettled. The point of this observation is not to overstate the pliability of dynastic borders. Rather, it is to call attention to both the extent to which the location of such lines often changed, and, more importantly, the degree to which imperial territory was thought of as being (at least in theory) unbound and unlimited (even if in practice it was often fractured and conscribed). Or, as Arthur Waldron commented in his renowned study of Ming defense policies, "Dynasty after dynasty has faced the question of where China should end, because for most of her history China's northern frontier has not been walled, but quite open. Since no Great Wall has ever supplied a ready-made boundary for them, each dynasty has had to define for itself where its political sway would end. Far from agreeing on a single line, they have made a great variety of choices."[1]

These variegated approaches at times led to the successful pacification of borderlands; but such triumphs were usually temporary as new challenges arose, and the status quo rarely held for long. Not surprisingly, the issue of how to manage these regions became a frequent point of contention within the imperial center. Moreover, as Alexander Woodside noted, "It was not just the borderlands whose boundaries were shifting and negotiable; it was also the boundaries of what the political centre itself was supposed to be or to mean."[2] In the same vein, Sinicization in history has been non-linear and multidirectional. In conceptualizing and defending the geographic periphery of the empire, politics thus created the space for the definition of what it meant to be Chinese and the limits of the empire.

As China was drawn into the western international system during the second half of the Qing empire, and torn asunder by a combination of internal upheaval and foreign occupation, elites in the dynastic center began to strive to preserve their polities' place in the world through developing new definitions of China – in part through their conceptualization of its territorial limits. Against such a backdrop, debates over managing the borderlands became all the more acute and divisive. Indeed, as Peter Purdue observed, "The story of the eighteenth-century Qing Empire is of an effort to seal off this ambiguous threatening frontier experience once and for all by incorporating it within the fixed boundaries of a distinctly defined space, and by drawing lines that clearly demarcated separate cultures."[3]

Within this context, Chinese thinking about territory underwent a deep and rapid change as the concept of sovereignty quickly attracted significant attention in Chinese intellectual circles. The concept had distinctly foreign origins (the term came to China from its original European context via a process of transplantation that included a Japanese interlude), and it ran counter to core aspects of indigenous Chinese approaches to territory. Indeed, whereas it had been relatively commonplace over the course of dynastic Chinese history to treat peripheral regions of the empire as fluid zones, sovereignty (and its attendant concepts of national unity, territorial integrity, and non-interference) contained little, if any, room for such nebulous spaces. Polities in a sovereign world order are imagined to be contiguous and discrete entities (even if the system of international politics often failed to live up to such visions): where one ends, another begins, with no distance between them.

Despite such sources of potential dissonance, attachment to the sovereign world order achieved hegemonic status in China by the final years of the Qing (and especially during the Republican and Nationalist Eras) – in the process radically reversing the directional pattern of Sinicization that had long dominated in the region. More specifically, for most of China's dynastic history the empire was considered to be at the center. Even if weakened, occupied by those thought to be nomadic interlopers, open to the importation of new religious beliefs (such as Islam or Buddhism) or oceanic trade, the dynasty – and more specifically the imperial capital – stood at the core of Asia. Thus, China's rulers had been able to see themselves as occupying a symbolic world in which the capital possessed a superior normative value, even if the practice of Chinese diplomacy rarely matched such symbolism. In contrast, during the final years of the Qing, Chinese elites were preoccupied with the painful reality that their polity was peripheral within the expanding Westphalian international order. China, then, was no longer the center, but rather a pole; if it was to survive, it was imperative to adjust to this new system. The appeal of such a concept was obvious: it could provide a normative buffer against the further erosion of Chinese territory. A sovereign China, rather than a dynastic one, would no longer be subjected to the humiliation of encroachment upon its territorial possessions.

Yet, the turn to sovereignty initially did little to prevent territorial losses, as few in the international community recognized Chinese claims to sovereign independence and many, particularly Japan, viewed the collapsing Qing empire and its successors as ripe for military conquest. For the purposes of this chapter it is then also important to note that the elite Chinese rush to embrace sovereignty simply reversed the direction of Sinicization, but did not stop it. Indeed, to the extent that Sinicization is considered to encompass the flow of ideas into (not only out of) China, the intellectual ferment of this period may be seen as exemplifying a new pattern of this process. As "old" ideas about territorial organization were jettisoned, the search for an intellectual blueprint for the articulation of a coherent vision of the shape and meaning of "China" drove the importation of "new" concepts across its borders. In this sense, sovereignty's rise in China was not intended to erase the past, but rather to provide a foundation for the continuation and survival of the Chinese polity within a new, and potentially lethal, international order. This process brought about intellectual ferment and discussion: what shape would China take within an international system that dictated that each member should have clearly demarcated territorial boundaries? Thus, during this period, Sinicization was highly interactive and displayed reinforcing and reversible tendencies.

As the necessity of this adjustment took root within China toward the end of the 1800s, differences grew among elites over how to specifically conceptualize and protect a sovereign "China" on the world stage. Such disagreements played out in an ongoing series of intellectual debates about China's territorial expanse, who should be considered Chinese, and which groups should then fall under the rule of the modern Chinese state. For example, was Mongolia a part of China? Did Tibetans have the right to pursue independence? Was Xinjiang a sovereign entity? Would China be a Han nation alone? What relationship should pertain between the Han majority and the races and ethnic groups of the frontier region? All of these questions were posed, more were asked, and sharply contrasting answers were forwarded.

As fluid as this situation was through the 1940s, such pluralism came to an abrupt end following the establishment of the PRC. While signs of rupture were already pronounced in the later years of the Republic of China's rule on the mainland, the break with past approaches to imagining and governing Chinese territory reached its apex only after the creation of the new Chinese state in 1949.[4] It was during this period that the debates of the preceding decades were definitively replaced by a mono-cultural intellectual environment and static policies. The narrowing of the Chinese approach to peripheral regions stemmed from a combination of two factors. First, as Mao and the Chinese Communist Party (CCP) consolidated their power within China, the need to placate those living in frontier areas with formulas for granting them extensive political rights was lessened. Second, fears of foreign invasion and encirclement led to the militarization of border spaces (first through their "peaceful liberation" and then via prolonged stationing of military forces).

These dual developments made protecting China's territorial periphery into a core issue of preserving national security and promoting national interest. Within such a rubric, there was little, if any, discursive room for considering any alternative imagining of the borderlands' relationship to the center. As a result, beginning in the 1950s, references to both borderlands and frontiers quickly disappeared from official statements and even from most unofficial publications. Or, as Michel Oksenberg succinctly noted in one of his final publications, the "set of arrangements that were viable in the past, rooted in another system of interstate relations, cannot be recreated in today's international system. In that sense, the concept of sovereignty and its associated ideas are confining."[5]

This development was then formally entrenched through the imposition of a pair of rigid orthodoxies for thinking about the territorial extent of China and the status of those who resided there. On one side, the system of identification for each of the nationalities (*minzu*) of the PRC was established. While questions relating to the creation of such a structure – and the identification of which groups within China were deserving of the nationality moniker – generated intense interest in the early 1950s among China's nascent anthropological community, such intellectual tumult was short-lived. It was then replaced over the course of the decade by an entrenchment of the now well-known classification of 56 such groups (led by the Han nationality [*hanzu*]), along with 55 "minority nationalities" (*shaoshu minzu*).[6]

This scheme created lines between those who were designated as citizens of the PRC (while giving some acknowledgment to their cultural and linguistic differences), and those who were foreign. Alongside this categorization of China's population was promulgated the system of autonomous regions (*zizhiqu*), establishing a set of guidelines for governing such areas through acknowledging internal diversity within the PRC without ceding any ground on what had become the untouchable issues of protecting the territorial integrity and national security of China.[7]

The enshrinement of the minority nationality framework and the regional autonomy construct then completed the rupture with the past. Once these interlocking stances attained an authoritative status within the PRC, they effectively erased all vestiges of the former elasticity in thinking and policy making toward the periphery. It was as if the Great Wall – which Waldron insightfully identified as being more mythical than real through much of modern Chinese history – had finally been erected, forming an impermeable boundary between China and the rest of the world.

The shift in emphasis in frontier policies under Deng, and the new debates of the last decade

The tightness of the discursive straitjacket surrounding the discussion of China's *bianjiang* was partially relieved during the 1980s by two major developments. First, following Deng Xiaoping's ascendency in the late 1970s, Beijing began to experiment with more pragmatic approaches to border-related issues. This move began with the implementation of new policies that provided more space for local cultural practices, religious beliefs, and languages, all of which had been categorized as anti-revolutionary activities during Mao's Cultural Revolution. Initially piecemeal and tentative, these reforms then garnered more substance, gaining official legal standing in 1984 via a modest revision of the regional autonomy law originally passed in 1954. They took further root later in the decade, as Beijing continued to expand the space for minorities to govern themselves (albeit always within the limits of supporting the national unity and territorial integrity of the PRC). On the heels of such trends, the collapse of the Soviet Union at the start of the 1990s meant that for the first time since the establishment of the PRC, Beijing no longer faced a substantial military threat along its inner Asian periphery. The first shifts introduced a degree of flexibility into a policy arena that had become incredibly ossified as the Maoist era progressed, while the second alleviated underlying existential fears of vulnerability to foreign invasion in these regions (even as it heightened sensitivity within China to challenges to national unity, an awareness that became more acute over time).[8]

In the wake of such tectonic changes, an even greater degree of latitude emerged during the 1990s within China's approach to its territorial periphery. During this period, Beijing began to experiment with the utilization of regional multilateral forums to cope with transnational challenges to Chinese rule in this region. Prior to this juncture, China had eschewed such institutions in dealing with the difficulties it was facing in Central Asia. Starting in 1996 with Beijing's active participation in establishing the Shanghai Five, followed by its promotion of its successor organization the Shanghai Cooperation Organization (created in 2001), China made this multilateral forum a core part of its approach to both Xinjiang and the region. China's leaders also started to allow for the commercialization of ethnic relations and the promotion of "ethnic tourism" in other segments of this contested terrain. Minority regions that had previously been celebrated for the diversity they added to the PRC's population were now featured as appealing destinations for both international and domestic travelers. Tibet, Xinjiang, and especially Yunnan were each touted as exotic locales that would provide visitors with glimpses of ancient cultures, colorful rituals, and appealing cuisines.

However, acceptance of diversity was not the sole hallmark of Chinese policies in frontier areas. On the contrary, throughout this period Beijing moved to clamp down on dissent in these regions. Such moves resonated with the harsher, more assimilative policies of the Maoist era, and signaled that while Beijing might be willing to experiment with new approaches to governing the interior periphery, it would brook no challenge to its rule in such regions. For example, the series of demonstrations against China's presence in Tibet, which rocked Lhasa between 1987 and 1989, predictably resulted in the imposition of martial law in the region, followed in the 1990s by an ongoing military presence and recurring rounds of detentions, monitoring of public spaces, and efforts to cull the monastic population of any remaining supporters of the Dalai Lama. At the same time, the 1990 Baren "riot" and the 1997 Yili "uprising" in Xinjiang led to an escalation of Beijing's coercive efforts to weed out would-be supporters of East Turkistan independence, a campaign that, as in Tibet, produced a series of charges by international observers of human rights abuses in the region.

In sum, over the course of the 1980s and 1990s Beijing's policies began to move beyond the narrow restrictions that had grown out of the mutually reinforcing prominence given to protecting sovereignty and securing the nation during the early years of the PRC. Yet, there was at first no sign of an accompanying change in Chinese thinking about these contested areas. On the contrary, through the 1990s, the silence of the preceding decades continued to reign.[9] Or, more accurately stated, within the trickle of new publications dedicated to borderlands, minorities, and other related issues, a uniformity of opinion prevailed. The majority of commentary in such outlets consisted of little more than the repetition of official statements about the sanctity of Chinese sovereignty and the inviolability of its territorial boundaries. This tendency was only breached by the occasional inclusion of opinions that were even more intractable than Beijing's own, and by a greater attention to historical detail than was to be found in official statements. In other words, the frontier remained a dead end within the Chinese imagination in much the same way that it had since the early years of the PRC.[10]

While it is premature to assert that Chinese elites are now entering a new era of far-reaching dialogue about the nature of this space, a new set of discussions have begun to take shape in recent years, as noted in the introduction. This trend is evident within the universe of Chinese academic journals, where the term *bianjiang* received only limited attention through the 1990s. For example, during this period a keyword search for all articles in the comprehensive CNKI database with *bianjiang* in their title revealed no more than 100 pieces on the frontier published in China in any given year. In contrast, using the same search criteria it was discovered that in 2003 this number jumped to 147 articles, and by 2006 nearing 200 annual publications (a surge that was sustained through 2009).[11] Moreover, an initial examination of these articles revealed that the number of publications carrying such work had also expanded during the last ten years. Whereas in the first few years covered in the content analysis such articles tended to be found only in a handful of journals dedicated specifically to the geographic history of the frontier (*bianjiang shidi*), much of the recent work has appeared in other outlets, including journals that generally focus on minority affairs, national defense and security, and even cultural studies.

The underlying conditions for this rise in interest in *bianjiang* are located in the ongoing emphasis within China on implementing new economic policies in peripheral regions, and the now longstanding removal of external security threats within these areas. As noted above, as early as the first part of the 1990s, such dual developments created an opening for a new discussion of territory, illustrating the reversibility of Sinicization. However, there was over a ten-year lag between the emergence of such trends and the current surge of writing about border-related issues within China. In other words, pragmatism and a new local external security dynamic were insufficient to reignite the earlier Chinese fascination with frontiers. This shift only occurred over the last five years, as Chinese elites began to make sense of an additional set of contrasting developments. On the one hand, they came to the realization that, for the first time since the end of the Qing, China might no longer be in a reactive, even passive position on the international stage. In other words, China's rise, however potentially fragile and contingent, meant that Chinese elites could once more consider how the world might be shaped, and China defined, in a manner that was more amenable to China and the Chinese. On the other hand, elites were also confronted with mounting signs of stress within Beijing's existing policies for governing the territorial periphery. Concern with maintaining stability initially grew with reference to the Chinese interior (as official reports of persistent, if relatively low level, social protest in these areas became increasingly common). However, it was only in the latter half of the decade that such worries, as they applied to the territorial periphery specifically, became more acute. Indeed, they were directly aggravated in 2008 with the eruption of protests against Chinese rule first in Tibet and then in Xinjiang in July of 2009. While these expressions of discontent were quickly and relatively easily silenced, their occurrence raised a host of difficult issues for China's leaders and policy elites. In short, the Chinese establishment was confronted with the question of how to square the accumulation of international prestige and influence with the persistence of pervasive, if not regime threatening, challenges at home. More directly, how would, and should, a rising China deal with what seemed to be still unresolved issues of national unity and territorial integrity?[12]

Such a combustible pairing of confidence and concern created the discursive space for experimentation with two new sets of concepts related to frontiers. First, ideas grounded in contrasting interpretations of China's history began to attract a great deal of attention in Chinese intellectual circles. While the resuscitation of the *tianxia tixi* concept[13] has attracted the most notice outside China and is reflective of the Chinese self-assurance on the world stage, in elite work on the frontier, where such poise is mixed with a degree of apprehension, it has also stimulated interest in dynastic approaches to preserving long-lasting control over China's territorial periphery. Second, during this same period, Chinese foreign policy elites began exploring a variety of ostensibly "foreign" concepts about the manner in which the contemporary international system should be organized, and how such ideas might be utilized to develop new approaches to China's contested territorial periphery. More specifically, some contributors to the new Chinese work on frontiers drew directly on the new "western" literature that explores the ambiguity between Westphalian concepts of territory and global patterns of integration. Such exogenous thinking was then applied to China's own situation in the service of the existing territorial status quo, albeit with the intention of challenging existing orthodoxies about how to govern frontier areas. In concert, these two trends (the openings to the past and to the outside world) then created the intellectual conditions within which a new consideration of the frontier could take root and flourish.

The emergence of new Chinese thinking about the frontier encompasses three main strands of thought, which are exemplified in the writing of Ma Dazheng, Yu Xiaofeng and Xu Lili, and Ma Rong. These approaches are unified in that they remain deeply attached to the concept of sovereignty and national unity that came to dominate Chinese thinking about territory over a century ago. They also all seek to reconceptualize how the periphery is understood, and how it should be governed. Yet, at the same time, they differ sharply about how their purveyors make use of China's history of frontier relations, and the extent to and manner in which they deploy newly imported ideas about such terrain.

Ma Dazheng and the rise of modern Chinese frontier studies

Among the scholars discussed in this chapter, Ma Dazheng is the only one who has been directly charged by Beijing to focus on territorial issues, as indicated by his role in the development of the Chinese Academy of Social Science's Borderland History and Geography Center (*Bianjiang Shidi Yanjiu Zhongxin*), which he directed through much of the 1990s. In addition, Ma was a prominent figure in the rewriting of the Koguryo history related to China's Northeast Project, work that stirred nationalist sentiments on the Korean Peninsula.[14] In light of this assignment, it is not surprising that Ma's approach to *bianjiang* neatly aligns with the manner in which China's leaders have articulated their stance on defending the PRC's territory. In other words, his is an orthodox, authoritative voice. Yet, at the same time, Ma has grounded his analysis of contemporary frontier-related issues upon a conviction that the problems now facing the PRC are not new, but rather stand as the most recent manifestation of difficulties that Chinese emperors confronted in the past. For Ma, if any fault is to be found in Beijing's current approach to this region, it lies in a lack of understanding and appreciation of this convoluted past. Past dynasties had experimented with a plethora of different approaches to managing outlying lands, and there was much to be learned within the record of the successes and failures of such enterprises. Ma's challenge is then to demonstrate this relevance of history. While his vision of how this may be accomplished does not transgress spatial boundaries between China and the outside world, it does promote a degree of temporal elasticity within Chinese thinking about the Asian interior.

At a basic level, this turn was led by Ma's attempt to lend substance to the term "frontier" that resided within his center's own name. A recent example of this focus can be found in a 2004 article that was featured on the main page of the *Bianjiang Shidi Yanjiu Zhongxin*'s website through the fall of 2009. The piece began with the observation that, while the meaning of China's frontiers has changed over time, such a region has always been understood in line with the principle of promoting the development of a "multi-national country" (*duominzu guojia*) and protecting "China's unity" (*zhongguo tongyi*). Within this context, the idea of China's frontiers should be understood quite broadly. More specifically, to begin with, this region encompasses "the area near a country's border." However, such a description was insufficient, as the exceedingly complicated historical, military, economic, and cultural trends that have unfolded within such areas have made their relationship with the political center relatively fluid and nebulous. Indeed, the statement noted that the *bianjiang*'s location, and its role within Chinese history, had not been adequately studied by either contemporary Chinese scholars or leaders. It expressed concern that misperceptions about China's frontiers have persisted and that, all too frequently, policies implemented to stabilize the situation in such regions have proven to be ineffectual. The article thus saw it as the central goal of all students of *bianjiangxue* to treat the frontier as "an entirely independent and complete research subject. In so doing it is possible to directly assist in the development of this region."[15]

For Ma, successfully carrying out such a task required researchers in China to reconsider how previous Chinese polities had successfully managed their borderlands. In so advocating, the senior scholar repeatedly emphasized that the examination of history was not intended to challenge the regional autonomy and minority nationality systems that currently grounded Beijing's approach to the territorial periphery. On the contrary, strengthening such structures could be accomplished through a greater awareness of the lessons of the past. History was then more relevant to the present situation within China's territorial periphery than was commonly realized; oversight of such a fact stood in the way of the development of more effective policy formulation and implementation.

This emphasis arguably constitutes a particular pattern of Sinicization in which boundary transgression hinges more upon temporal flexibility than upon openness to the importation, or exportation, of ideas about China's place in the world. As noted above, imperial China did not exist in a system of sovereign states; therefore, exploring how China's previous rulers had placated borderlands and preserved dynastic unity implicitly raised the question of how modern Chinese interpretations of Westphalian organizing principles might be adjusted or revised in a manner that is more in accord with an older, pre-existing, Chinese world order. In making the past come alive, Ma implicitly raised the possibility of easing the restrictions that have limited Chinese thinking about territory since the 1950s – even as he methodically pledged to uphold such limitations through an allegiance to the principles of national sovereignty and territorial integrity.

An unwavering commitment to this search forms the intellectual core of what Ma defined as the field of "frontier studies" (*bianjiangxue*), a research approach that predates Ma, but whose growth within contemporary China he has both promoted and chronicled. Indeed, a self-awareness of field development runs through Ma's publications. Thus, over the last decade he has published a series of articles that identify three high tides within the modern study of governing China's frontiers, the first occurring at the end of the 1800s, the second lasting from the 1920s through the 1940s, and the third starting in the 1980s.

While Ma's consideration of the two earlier periods of development of frontier studies has been extensive and informative, his identification of the defining characteristics and challenges within the current wave of research are most relevant to the issues considered in this chapter. On this front, Ma has most consistently emphasized the ongoing importance of historical lessons for the current management of the Chinese frontier. More specifically, in a 2003 article, he observed that in order to address the difficulties China faces along its territorial periphery during the twenty-first century, it is imperative for those working in the field of frontier studies to focus on the crucial question of how to "synthesize" (*jiehe*) history and current "reality" (*xianshi*).[16] While Ma expressed concerns in this piece about how successful Chinese scholars had been at this task, in a subsequent publication he struck a more optimistic tone. Indeed, he took special note of the fact that frontier studies had finally "broken through" (*tupo*) the tendency to only examine the narrow issue of boundaries (*bianjie*), while at the same time expanding beyond the limits of "historical geography" (*shidi*).[17]

Ma attributed this progress to what he viewed as the field's attachment to a series of rigid principles, and a self-awareness of its subservient relationship to the Chinese state. He argued that it is essential for frontier studies in China to remain guided by Marxist ideology, but also grounded in a patriotic embrace of national unity, cooperation among ethnic groups, and the promotion of frontier stability. Ma then hastened to add that further development of *bianjiangxue* would require scholars to pay even more attention to dynastic China's handling of frontier-related issues. More directly, he subsequently observed that if Chinese scholars and leaders "do not understand frontier history, this will make it impossible to clearly recognize the difficulties" that exist in frontier regions, "and even less possible to institute (*zhiding*) correct policies (*zhengque de zhengce*). ... The scientific development of frontier studies thus requires research into how the past relates to the present and future."[18]

This emphasis on the relevance of the past to China's present has also emerged as an increasingly visible component within the work of other scholars in China who have contributed to the field of *bianjiangxue*. Some of this scholarship focuses on the topic of frontier governance (*zhili*), arguing that valuable insight into current difficulties in China's frontier regions could be gained by paying greater attention to the manner in which various Chinese dynasties had managed this aspect of political life. For example, Zhou Ping, of Yunnan Daxue, one of China's leading institutes for studying minorities, recently wrote in the influential *Zhengzhi Yanjiu* that Beijing's approach to the territorial periphery had been overly influenced by an attachment to the modern concepts of nationality (*minzu*) and nationality policies (*minzu zhengce*), rather than the historically more successful frame which he designated as "frontier issues" (*bianjiang wenti*). As a result, despite Beijing's relative successes in developing the geographic interior, it "had no specialized direction for the strategic development and construction of the frontier."[19] Alongside Zhou's work, others scholars have contended that the key to advancing the field of *bianjiangxue* is to be found in a reinvigoration of an area of study categorized as borderland political studies (*bianzhengxue*). More specifically, Duan Jinsheng recently noted that such an approach, which had flourished prior to the establishment of the PRC, had fallen out of favor over the last sixty years and was now primarily pursued by academics in Taiwan (not those on the mainland). While Duan then listed the resulting ill-effects upon the accumulation of a deeper understanding of conditions within China's territorial periphery, he took particular note of how acute such concerns have become in recent years, as difficulties in such regions appear to have grown.[20]

Each of these scholars, following Ma's example, is intent upon demonstrating the relevance of China's past to Beijing's current challenges along its territorial interior. In general, the proponents of *bianjiangxue* find that while Chinese emperors did not use the same vocabulary as China's modern leaders, they did allow for a significant degree of autonomy and acknowledged the differences among peoples within their dynasties. Work in this field, though, has been published by scholars with intimate ties to the existing order (especially in the case of Ma Dazheng), and thus has rarely strayed far from Beijing's official stance. For the proponents of *bianjiangxue*, bringing the lessons of history into the present does not create a pressing need for Beijing to radically alter the way in which it currently administers such terrain, but rather may enable China's leaders to even more effectively govern the still restive Chinese frontier.

Yu Xiaofeng and Xu Lili, and the promotion of non-traditional security and frontier security in China

Alongside Ma Dazheng, a handful of scholars in China have recently begun to advocate for the development of a new approach to territory, mainly that of "border security studies" (*biananxue*). While the name of this field differs by only a single character from *bianjiangxue*, and does resonate with historical frames for studying such regions, the nascent discipline contrasts quite sharply with Ma's more established research framework. The work does not directly step on any of the foundational aspects of current policy; but it also does not dwell upon the supposed successes of the existing order. Instead, it pays more attention to the conceptual blind spots and practical shortcomings in the existing Chinese approach to the frontier. Indeed, although *biananxue* remains tethered to Beijing's official stance of promoting national unity and territorial integrity along the PRC's borders, the methods that it advocates contain a broad, if largely implicit, critique of the manner in which China's leaders have operated in such regions. Whereas Ma Dazheng's writing generally lauded the policies of national autonomy and minority nationalities, similar praise within the work of those proposing the development of *biananxue* in China is difficult, if not impossible, to find.

The intellectual derivation of *biananxue* is also quite distinctive. Rather than putting historical considerations in a primary position within the field, its conceptual foundation grows out of a consideration of how recent theoretical debates in the international sphere about the changing nature of security, and concepts of territoriality, might be extended to China's current frontier challenges. The past is not eschewed by those writing about *biananxue*, but rather is only to be considered within the framework provided by the importation of exogenous ideas about the manner in which the structure of international politics may be changing. *Biananxue* is thus a clear example of how Chinese elites have grappled with the seemingly expanding paradox that exists within the current international system, between the territorial divisions imposed by Westphalian sovereignty and the forces that are so prominent within globalization. The promotion in today's China of such an approach to thinking about *bianjiang* constitutes a significant opening of the Chinese territorial discourse. Moreover, it represents a return to a pattern of Sinicization in regards to the conceptualization of political space that was last visible in China during the first half of the last century.

The external grounding of the field of "border security" stems from its origins in the expanding Chinese discussion of *feichuantong anquan*, or non-traditional security (NTS) – a concept that was largely absent from Chinese discussions of national defense until the turn of the century but which has, over the past ten years, become a growing area of concern in China. For example, as I have documented elsewhere, during this period many of China's major foreign policy research institutes established NTS research programs. This trend was led by Wang Yizhou's Institute of World Economics and Politics (*Shijie Jinqji yu Zhengzhi Yanjiusuo*), coupled with a multi-year research project on NTS at the State Council's Institute of Contemporary International Relations (*Xiandai Guoji Guanxi Yanjiusuo*), and given added weight in 2006 with the establishment of China's first NTS research center, the Center for Non-Traditional Security and Peaceful Development Studies (*Feichuantong Anquan yu Heping Fazhan Yanjiu Zhongxin*) located at Zhejiang University.

Despite notable differences in application of the NTS construct to China, all of those Chinese scholars who have written about it have agreed that the concept itself is imported. More specifically, Chinese analysts unanimously acknowledge that the NTS concept grew out of discussions that began in Europe via the rise of the so-called Copenhagen School and debates about human security (*ren de anquan*) and the concept of securitization (*anquanhua*).[21] Tellingly, some security elites have fixated on the term's foreign (*guowai de*) and Western (*xifang de*) origins, raising questions about the extent to which the concept may constitute a cloaked attempt by the "West" to promote its hegemonic status and undermine China's security by cleverly directing the attention of China's leaders away from real, traditional security concerns. However, such dissenters have, to date, been outnumbered by those who have argued that attention to such a non-indigenous set of ideas about security is warranted, due to the degree that they appear to accurately reflect the newly emergent challenges China faces within an increasingly interdependent international system. Or as Liu Weiqiang, a scholar at Nanjing University's Public Administration Department, recently wrote, it is imperative "not to underestimate" (*bu ke digu*) the influence of the challenge NTS issues pose to China's peaceful development.[22] Wang Yizhou, one of the earliest Chinese proponents of developing NTS in China, then argued that it was essential for Chinese students of NTS to develop "new concepts and ideologies," especially by considering how to more accurately categorize the relationship between traditional security and NTS.[23]

Such calls have been followed by a wave of NTS-related publications within China. Yet, only very recently have a handful of Chinese scholars, for the first time, attempted to extend the NTS discussion to the specific issue of securing China's contested territorial frontiers. This move has been led by Yu Xiaofeng, director of the aforementioned NTS research center at Zhejiang University, and Xu Lili of Lanzhou University. Their first published work in this regard appeared in the influential *Minzu Yanjiu* and began with a detailed tracing of the origins of NTS concepts on the world stage. More specifically, Xu and Yu approvingly took note of the UN's first promotion of the term in the 1960s, followed by its development in a series of UN reports during the 1980s and 1990s, as well as its theoretical maturation in the work of Barry Buzan. The article then observed that scholars such as Wang Yong and Wang Yizhou had begun to introduce the term into China in the mid-1990s; since then, it has been featured in an expanding series of articles by Chinese foreign policy elites.

The choice to lead their article off with such a literature review might appear at first glance to be rather mundane, as it follows commonly accepted standards for academic writing in the fields of security studies and international relations. Yet, when juxtaposed with the more inward- and backward-looking approach that predominates within Ma Dazheng's *bianjiangxue*, its significance grows. In taking such a turn, Xu and Yu clearly located the foundations of their analysis within the international sphere.

Xu and Yu's article then deployed the NTS concept in an attempt to move the Chinese discussion of *bianjiang* away from the conventional frames of protecting sovereignty and repelling military threats, toward a more subjective set of issues including cultural traditions, psychological traits, normative values, and identities. Such a shift, they posited, would allow for the development of a deeper understanding of cultural difference in frontier regions. Indeed, the authors then artfully, and possibly with an eye toward political expediency, formed a bridge to both Chinese history and current orthodox language, noting that such connections may ideally create the space to transform "the entire world into a multicultural (*duoyangxing wenhua*), harmonious yet different (*he er bu tong*) village" and promote a "harmonious order" (*he xie you zhi*) among humanity.[24] Two factors appear relevant to framing this intellectual move. First, it carves out an orthodox foundation for what might otherwise be categorized as a heretical set of arguments. Second, it subtly distorts the normative vision of the Copenhagen School approach to security studies, as the importation of NTS thinking is not designed to create a new rhetorical space for freeing or liberating those in such regions, but rather to guide the development of more effective policies to govern them.

This being the case, Xu and Yu argued that such a research framework allowed for the development of more accurate identification of China's primary challenges within its "frontier nationality regions" (*bianjiang minzu diqu*). The authors then dutifully catalogued the scope of such difficulties. Their list in this regard began with the relatively predictable issues of countering the persistence of the so-called "three evils" (terrorism, splittism, religious fundamentalism), but continued into a more unexpected survey of the intractability of problems in frontier regions related to ecological security, resource development, transborder nationalities, and migration into minority nationality regions by other nationalities. This catalogue of challenges then concluded with a stunning admission regarding the fragility of "national identity" (*guojia rentong*) in frontier regions. More specifically, Xu and Yu acknowledged that while older generations of frontier nationalities had a stronger sense of national identity than they did of their specific nationality, some within the younger generation had experienced a weakening of their sense of belonging to the nation (*guojia rentong yishi danhua*).

Tellingly, Xu and Yu contended that none of these issues tended to be visible within conventional Chinese approaches to either security or frontier studies. Moreover, they argued that the threats that each posed to Beijing's rule over the periphery were amplified by the fact that the issues do not stand as discrete obstacles, but rather were interconnected, and thus even more intractable than they first appeared. Yet, as potentially disheartening as such an observation may appear to be, the co-authors concluded on a hopeful note: simply by realizing such "interrelatedness," Beijing could take a major step toward solving these difficulties. More specifically, only when the Chinese government was able to utilize an NTS approach to come to terms with the actual situation in frontier regions – particularly the complex identity politics at play – would it be possible for Beijing to "really solve the issues" (*zhenzheng jiejue wenti*) that have persisted in such places.[25]

In a companion piece that was published in the Journal of Zhejiang University, Xu and Yu then embraced the *biananxue* label for their evolving approach to studying China's territorial periphery, giving more extensive consideration to the manner in which such a research framework may open up a new vantage point for studying China's historic approach to such a region. They noted,

> The normative foundation of frontier security is human security....the concept of human security surpasses the limits of traditional sovereignty and high politics, it allows one to get to the issue of the human security (*ren de anquan*) within the relations between nationalities of different beliefs and cultures and seek out the foundation of common interests between such groups....Therefore, the foundational principle of "frontier security" is derived from the idea

of "human security" and implies that attaining security in a frontier region must place a priority on the individual rather than the group.[26]

Ma Rong and culturalizing the frontier

While Xu and Yu's criticism of Beijing's approach to the territorial periphery extended well beyond that forwarded by Ma Dazheng, it pales in comparison to the arguments made by Ma Rong, who over the last several years has directly challenged core aspects of how China has attempted to deal with its contested frontier regions. In this regard, Ma Rong has redirected attention away from the question of territorial boundaries toward the more nebulous issue of how to think about the people who reside within frontier regions, and has done so through focusing his work upon the concept of nationality as it applies to China's territorial periphery. This move was hinted at in Xu and Yu's work, but never fully developed. In contrast, it is central to Ma's theorizing about the frontier; in underscoring such issues, he became the first contemporary Chinese scholar to reinvigorate the divisive debates over the frontier that had been so prominent throughout earlier Chinese history, and he rapidly achieved a level of notoriety within Chinese elite circles.

As with Xu and Yu's *biananxue*, Ma Rong's thinking about frontiers is built upon theoretical debates that are exogenous to the current Chinese intellectual scene. More specifically, his work is steeped in references to the literature in western sociology relating to nationalism, ethnicity, and multiculturalism (but does not extend to recent political science work on ethnic conflict). Moreover, he charges that the absence of such work within Chinese publications on nationalism and minorities has placed artificial constraints upon the way in which Chinese elites have conceptualized the relationship between the majority Han population and other ethnic groups, as well as hampering the development of more effective policy making. In this sense, Ma is explicitly attempting to import new, "foreign" intellectual concepts into China with the intention of broadening the framework for the contemporary discussion of race and ethnicity and, ultimately, establishing new guidelines for managing Han–minority relations. In this regard, among the three schools of thought considered in this chapter, Ma's pushes furthest toward opening what is nominally China's "internal" domain to exogenous ideas and, as such, to a process of Sinicization that had been largely dormant during the preceding decades.

Ma has articulated his position on these issues in a series of articles published over the course of the last decade. The most widely cited of these was a 2004 piece published in *Beijing Daxue Xuebao*.[27] Ma began the article by underscoring the centrality of ethnic relations to the stability of modern nation states. Indeed, Ma argues, "ethnic relations have become one of the core social issues facing all nations in the twenty-first century."[28] In theorizing such relationships Ma then referenced Wallerstein, Glazer, and Moynihan, rather than Stalin and Mao – thus grounding his work in an intellectual tradition that is quite distinct from those occupied by Ma Dazheng, and even Xu Lili and Yu Xiaofeng.

Ma then painted a starkly contrasting picture between two distinct models for managing ethnic relations that have developed within world politics over time. On the one hand, according to Ma, some states have gravitated toward a policy of "politicizing" (*zhengzhihua*) such relationships, and in the process tended, unintentionally, to make differences on this front more intractable and likely to lead to political fragmentation. On the other hand, Ma found that a "culturalizing" (*wenhuahua*) approach to the same issues (which "treats ethnic relations as cultural interactions") tended to "dilute" contrasting political interests between such groups and promote more harmonious inter-group relations. The intellectual focal point of Ma's writings then resides within a series of attempts to demonstrate the superiority of the "culturalizing" approach over the politicizing one, with the intention of convincing China to follow a path of "depoliticizing" its handling of Han–minority relations. His work articulates a three-fold argument in support of reorienting Chinese policy in the direction of culturalization.

The first tenet of his critical approach to Beijing's orthodox stance on minority issues was primarily historical, arguing that in the past, successive Chinese empires' approach to peripheral peoples had been "culturalizing" in its orientation. Indeed, "culture" was the "core" (*hexin*) of the "traditional Chinese view of ethnic groups." He then contended that such a trait stemmed from a set of overarching Chinese cultural predispositions that valued Confucian sophistication over the backwardness of peripheral barbarians, but also encouraged the development of such peoples through the process of cultural assimilation. Or, as he wrote, "although there were conflicts and wars between the dynasties in the 'core area' and minorities in the peripheries, what characterized interaction between the 'more civilized' and 'less civilized' groups was not mainly animosity and mutual destruction but cultural diffusion and learning."[29] It was this attribute that "enabled the civilized group in the core region to unify and embody the ethnic minorities in periphery areas."[30]

Such an argument would not at first blush seem to be particularly controversial within Chinese intellectual circles, as in recent years Beijing has frequently promoted the "peace"-loving facets of China's past, often in conjunction with the very same references to Confucian traditions that are featured in Ma's own work. Moreover, there is obvious resonance within Ma Rong's turn to history with Ma Dazheng's promotion of *bianjiangxue*. Yet, somewhat surprisingly, this seemingly non-threatening characterization of China's historical approach to frontiers quickly emerged as one of the first points of attack in the wave of criticism that has followed the publication of Ma's arguments. Much of the invective aimed at Ma on this score hinges on the charge that he has vastly oversimplified, and, as a result, distorted the actual historical record. According to Ma's critics, culture may have been "an aspect" of imperial policy, but it was not the sole one. On the contrary, Chinese emperors, at least the successful ones, balanced cultural and political stances in dealing with the periphery, while those who did not lost control of it.

As vociferous as the criticism of Ma's interpretation of the ancient regime was, it paled in comparison to what was generated by the second aspect of his analysis – when he moved from the imperial past to an examination of the genesis of the

PRC's contemporary approach to minority groups (and its implications for current policies). Ma contended that the "culturalizing" approach that China had previously utilized, and that had flourished worldwide, had been eclipsed by a system-wide tendency to politicize inter-ethnic group relations. Moreover, this trend reached its apotheosis in the USSR's failed Stalinist system of formally granting each such group official status, thus cementing its place within the political system. From Ma's perspective, such a system not only hastened the Soviet Union's collapse, but also had a broad influence on China's own approach to its territorial periphery.

More specifically, Ma contended that the imprint of the Soviet model is distinctly visible in Beijing's granting autonomy to minorities within the PRC, and the establishment of preferable treatment for minority groups within China's education system.[31] While he expressed concern about both of these facets of Chinese policy, even more troubling to him was the imprint that Soviet influences had left upon current Chinese terminology about race and ethnicity. Thus, Ma repeatedly argued that the designation of both Han Chinese and other ethnic groups under the category of "nations" (*minzu*) is particularly problematic as it has unintentionally cemented ethnic differences within China and contributed to the rise of tensions among ethnic groups. More directly, Ma argues that Beijing would be well served by replacing the existing orthodoxy of designating China's minority groups as "minority nationalities" with the use of the term "ethnic groups" (*zuqun*). He contends that the *minzu* terminology is confusing when translated into English, and has had wide-ranging, negative, political repercussions within China. Indeed, while Ma concedes that such policies were designed to foster national unity, they paradoxically link "each ethnic minority to a certain geographic area, provide these groups with political status, administrative power in their 'autonomous territory,' and guarantee ethnic minorities the potential to develop at higher speed"; moreover, such policies have "done nothing to resolve the tension" among ethnic groups, "but instead created a more solid base for future separatist movements."[32]

In short, Ma contends that a host of unintended and deleterious effects have arisen out of the choices that were made during the early years of the PRC related to handling the PRC's frontier regions. On the one hand, echoing Dru Gladney's work from a decade before (albeit from a distinctly different normative slant), Ma argues that the creation of the *"minzu"* label elevated and politicized the status of peoples in such areas who had previously existed as little more than loosely affiliated cultural groups into political entities. These nationalities then came to view themselves as possessing distinct political rights not only within the PRC, but also on the international stage. On the other hand, the regional autonomy system wed such inchoate political identities to concrete territorial spaces and thus further underscored the distinctiveness of those living in frontier regions. Implicit in Ma's work, then, is the retrospective charge that absent such policies, the PRC's more problematic minorities might never have emerged as such, and the prospective view that revoking such rules could serve to mitigate the difficulties Beijing faces within some segments of its territorial periphery.

As with his interpretation of China's history, this broadside against the minority nationality system and the regional autonomy framework enraged those who worked on frontiers and minority issues in China. While such consternation is not surprising in light of the centrality of such a scheme to contemporary Chinese thinking about the interior periphery, the vehemence with which it has been expressed is extraordinary (especially in its stark contrast to the usual reserve and caution normally found within the public intellectual discourse about race in China). Within such criticism, Ma is accused of promoting a dangerous stand of analysis with the potential to create greater instability in minority nationality regions, and even to undermine the national unity of the PRC.

Despite such a charge, it is quite clear that Ma's work is not written in a dissident spirit, but rather intended to enumerate a better, more effective way of handling Han–minority relations in China. This prescriptive facet of his writing constitutes the third main component of his work on frontier regions. Ma began his observations by looking outside China in search of examples of more successful approaches to handling ethnic relations. He then lauded the cultural emphasis that contemporary India and the United States have placed upon inter-ethnic relations. In the former country, amazingly in light of the conventional wisdom, Ma observed that despite limited economic development and the vagaries of a weak democratic system, ethnic groups have, albeit not without occasional hostilities, tended to coexist relatively peacefully. In the latter, he celebrated the positive legacy of multiculturalism.[33] Ma then contended that such success stories stand as a sharp rebuke to China's own political turn, while also demonstrating the potential utility of revisiting its own historic emphasis on the same policies. He concluded,

> Although in general ethnic relations in today's China are smooth and cooperative, the differences among ethnic minorities in national identification still remain. The Chinese should learn from their ancestors and their experience for thousands of years in guiding ethnic relations. They also should look to other nations for positive and negative lessons. China might in the future consider changing the direction of managing its ethnic relations from the "politicizing" to the "culturalizing" route. The route of de-politicizing ethnicity might lead China to a new direction, strengthening national identity among ethnic minorities while guaranteeing the prosperity of their cultural traditions.[34]

The suggestion that China might study the American and Indian examples provided even more fodder to Ma's critics. Their anger over such a sacrilegious policy prescription may not be as palpable as that which they expressed over his suggestion that the existing nationality/autonomy system may need to be dismantled; but it was still quite pronounced. Indeed, it was on this front that a number of critics pushed toward directly labeling Ma as traitorous by linking his praise of the US and Indian examples, and suggesting that extending such models to China would have resulted in an even more tumultuous turn of events in Tibet in 2008 and Xinjiang in 2009. In other words, for them, the appropriate response to such demonstrations is to double down on the "political" facets of Chinese policy, to strengthen the foundations of the state, and to repel any arguments that would weaken or undermine such a stance. In this vein, Ma's writing, from his critic's perspective, is particularly dangerous, perhaps even treacherous: it is written as if intended to make China stronger, yet perfidiously sneaks into the discussion of China's territorial frontiers a set of ideas that could undermine such efforts.

The irony of such a charge is that Ma's writings make quite clear his unequivocal support of maintaining the current shape of China. Indeed, there is an element of cultural superiority, perhaps even Han chauvinism in his work that suggests a rather patrimonial, hierarchal interpretation of how the relationship between Han Chinese and Chinese minority groups should be both conceptualized and governed. In this sense, while his writing calls for a radical reorientation of China's approach to frontier issues, such an appeal may not be as progressive as it first appears. Indeed, it is quite possible to interpret it as a conservative, even patrimonial move.

This element in Ma Rong's work stems from his advocacy of stripping political rights from those residing in the periphery. The appeal of such a move stems from the fact that such a system appears to have led to the continuation rather than diminution of contentious politics in many sections of the frontier. To find a direct admission of the failure of such an order within the Chinese elite establishment is unprecedented and, at first glance, promising. Yet it is also apparent within Ma's work that the removal of such a system has the potential to make such groups not safer and more secure, but arguably more vulnerable, unable to use the political tools promised within these structures.

Conclusion

The approaches to *bianjiang* discussed in this chapter are surprisingly diverse and reveal a greater plurality of views within China regarding territory than has so far been acknowledged by students of Chinese security, foreign policy, and minorities. Such a plethora of views is also indicative of an initial opening within Chinese elite circles to both past ideas and foreign concepts that is not often recognized. This tendency reveals a greater prospect for the development of processes of Sinicization, even concerning crucial issues such as territory, than has existed at least since the founding of the PRC over sixty years ago. Yet, at the same time, it is crucial to note that none of those who have so far contributed to the new Chinese consideration of the frontier have questioned any of the most foundational aspects of Beijing's officially sanctioned territorial narrative – mainly, that the sovereignty and national unity of the PRC is above reproach. However, simply by directing attention toward the concept of the frontier, and the place within China of the people who populate such a region, commentators have gone quite a way toward reinterpreting and even, in some cases, stretching various components of this nearly sacrosanct discourse.

This being said, of the three new approaches to *bianjiang* discussed in this chapter, Ma Dazheng's *bianjiangxue* – which is the least innovative and most inward-looking – is the one that continues to dominate mainstream elite thinking about such regions. The main points of emphasis within this field also resonate more closely with the manner in which the PRC continues to govern its frontiers. Consonant with Ma's writing, the minority nationality classification scheme and system of regional autonomy remain firmly entrenched in such regions. In addition, China's leaders to date have given no indication that they are considering dismantling or even modifying this interlocking structure in the years to come.

Moreover, even as China's leaders have shown a limited willingness to more openly acknowledge the historical roots of lingering challenges within these areas, they also exhibit a great deal of confidence in the policy guidelines that have evolved over the course of the reform and opening era. Indeed, throughout most of the last decade, the strategy of augmenting old political structures with new economic incentives, coupled with a degree of flexibility on cultural practices, seemed to have pushed China past the turbulent threats to national unity that had recurrently shaken the PRC since its founding in 1949. As mentioned earlier in this chapter, through 2008, it had been almost twenty years since large-scale anti-Chinese protests had occurred in Tibet. The situation in Xinjiang, while volatile, was also seen as largely stable. Moreover, the situation appeared even more reassuring in other less restive regions of the territorial periphery. Even if economic development lagged and poverty rates surpassed those in most Han nationality regions, political turmoil was limited and the center's control unchallenged. While not perfect, the situation gave few indications of a pressing need to undertake radical reforms and largely appeared to confirm the relative merits of the status quo arguments that predominated within Ma's approach to frontiers.

Yet, the façade of frontier stability was rocked in March 2008 by a short-lived, but geographically dispersed series of demonstrations that began in Lhasa but soon enveloped much of the Tibetan plateau. While this protest movement was effectively contained well before China hosted the Olympics later that summer, the following year brought an outburst of unrest in Xinjiang. Here, too, China's leaders quickly demonstrated the capability to clamp down on the open expression of dissent; but coming so soon after the Tibetan demonstrations, the limited uprising in Urumqi illuminated the potential gulf between the imposition of PRC control over frontier regions and the acceptance of its authority to rule.

While the proliferation of work on *bianjiang* in recent years predated these events, they also gave added impetus to such a development. More specifically, it is clear that in the aftermath of these events the advocates of all three schools of thought featured in this chapter have moved to carefully position their work within the context of the surge in restlessness in China's territorial periphery. For example, in a 2009 online article written following the 2009 Xinjiang demonstrations, both Ma and Yu were interviewed about the event. Ma observed, "Frontier regions are on the frontline of China's national security, and the foundation for reforms, and the platform for China's emergence in the world, the development of frontier regions is directly linked to the ongoing development of China" – therefore, changing the relatively backward state of development in frontier regions is among the most important challenges currently facing Beijing. In contrast, Yu noted that some ministries (*bumen*) do not have a well-developed understanding of the importance of NTS in examining the effectiveness of policies in frontier regions. Moreover, "frontier security is not just about whether or not there are conflicts over borders, if there has been encroachment on territory, or interference in sovereignty, even more important is the psychological stability (*renxin anding*) in frontier regions."[35] In a separate publication, Ma Rong then pushed such observations even further in noting,

> I believe that only when minority "nationalities" in China are transformed into "ethnic groups," the "*minzu*" issue and ethnic tensions can decline. While this challenge to "orthodox" Marxist *minzu* theory has been heavily criticized within China, the freedom of academic discussion in China needs to be improved to enable us to face reality and provide a more scientific base for policy-making.[36]

Realistically, the probability is still remote that even the more tepid of these observations will lead to far-reaching policy changes in the near future. However, the fact that those views have been aired by Chinese elites and within prominent publications within China, especially following the Tibet and Xinjiang demonstrations, should not be taken lightly. On the contrary, such a development is suggestive of a new awareness of the shortcomings of the current approach to governing such regions, and indicative of the growing traction that such views may come to have as the next generation of China's leaders look to move past the current impasse facing the PRC along its *bianjiang*.

Notes

1 Waldron 1990, 9.
2 Woodside 2007, 15.
3 Purdue 2005, 42.
4 See Wachman 2007. For an excellent overview of the study of frontiers through this period, see Leibold 2007. Moreover, it is also important to note that experimentation with these policies can be traced, in limited ways, back to the Qing period as well. This last point stems from an observation made at the Beijing workshop by Chen Jian.
5 Oksenberg 2001, 98.
6 The authoritative, if somewhat dated, account of this development can be found in Gladney 1996.
7 For an extensive treatment of the regional autonomy system, with a particular emphasis on Tibet, see Smith 2008.
8 Please note that I first discussed this trend in 2008 with a Cornell undergraduate, Junrong Koh, while advising him on his senior honor's thesis in our Government Department. Koh's thesis did an excellent job focusing on the autonomy and development themes in official Chinese discourse in Yunnan and Xinjiang.

9 The frontier was, however, an object of fascination in cultural circles, and garnered even more attention in the post-Maoist era. However, as significant as this consideration of the periphery was, it did not extend to elite work on foreign policy, domestic politics, or minority nationalities.
10 For a more thorough discussion of this period, albeit with greater emphasis on sovereignty and self-determination issues in Beijing's Tibet policy, see Carlson 2005.
11 CNKI, China Academic Journals Full-text Database, 1994–2009.
12 I would like to thank numerous participants in the March 2011 Beijing workshop, but especially Iain Johnston, for encouraging me to place greater emphasis on this point than was the case in earlier drafts of this chapter.
13 For overviews of this development, see Bell 2009; Callahan 2008; Carlson 2011.
14 I would like to thank Iain Johnston for calling my attention to this aspect of Ma's career.
15 *Bianjiang Yanjiu Zhongxin*, 2004.
16 Ma 2003.
17 Ma, Dazheng 2007.
18 Ma, Dazheng 2008, 3.
19 Zhou 2008, 72.
20 Duan 2009.
21 Li 2007.
22 Liu 2008.
23 Wang, Yizhou (n.d.). Also please note that these two paragraphs draw directly on Carlson 2010.
24 Xu and Yu 2009b, 35.
25 Xu and Yu 2009b, 43.
26 Xu and Yu 2009a, 15–16.
27 A translation of the article, which was similar if not identical to the original, was published by Ma in 2007. I note which piece I am drawing on through the citations.
28 Ma, Rong 2004, 122–3. Note that Ma's 2007 article uses the term "society" here rather than "nation."
29 Ma, Rong 2007, 203.
30 Ma, Rong 2004, 124.
31 Ma, Rong 2004, 126; and Ma, Rong 2007, 207.
32 Ma, Rong 2007, 214.
33 In contrast, in the context of developing this argument Ma often returned to the negative examples set by the collapse of the Soviet Union under the weight of ethnic differences, and the subsequent implosion of Yugoslavia along the same lines.
34 Ma, Rong 2007, 216; Ma, Rong 2004, 132.
35 Yuan, Tao, and Zhao 2010.
36 Ma 2009.

3
ONE CHINA, TWO WORLDS
Taiwan and China's quest for identity and security[1]

Xu Xin

Sinicization in a broad sense refers to a sociopolitical process of preserving and sustaining Chinese civilization under different historical circumstances. In modern times, Sinicization entails the imperative of Chinese nationalism that strives for China's survival and unity as a sovereign nation state in the international system, through the transformation of Chinese civilization itself. As such, it reifies a confluence of Chinese civilizational and national identities. Inherent in the modern processes of Sinicization, therefore, are the enduring tensions between the past and the present, between continuity and change, and between Chinese identity and foreign influence.

These tensions stand out most conspicuously in the problem of national reunification, which by definition is a process of Sinicization in modern terms – namely, bringing the fragmented parts of Chinese territory into an integrated institutional framework of nation state and constructing Chinese national identity over other alternatives. The tensions are most salient here because national reunification represents a more positive form of Sinicization – "making the world suitable to China and the Chinese"[2] – through changing the unjustified status quo that resulted from China's historical encounter with the West. In this context, no place but Taiwan has made the Chinese more painfully aware that the world is far from suitable to their will and aspirations. Taiwan's loss, return, re-separation, and prospect for pending reunification highlight complex variations and dynamic processes of Sinicization in a dialectical fashion, with re-Sinicization and de-Sinicization as two of its more recent manifestations. In the sixty years' history of the People's Republic of China (PRC), the Taiwan issue has been "a thorn in the side" of China's body politic, which political leaders have vowed and failed to remove. The very existence of this issue has significantly affected China's regime legitimacy, state security, national identity, and international relations. The extent to which this issue remains highly salient and in need of a definitive solution illustrates clearly some of the interactive processes of Sinicization in which Chinese leaders are enmeshed, and through which they seek to achieve their domestic and international goals.

In the modern international system of states, like other divided nations – Germany and Korea in particular – China has had to cope with serious problems of legitimacy, challenged as it was by a rival of the same nationality also claiming state sovereignty. Despite many similarities due to the constraints imposed by external forces, China's reunification problem is much more deeply rooted in its long, continuous civilizational past and much more broadly linked with its widespread, fragile territorial present. The compressed frame of time and space in modern times compels Chinese political and intellectual leaders to think about and act on reunification issues in ways that reflect the collective urge to adopt the framework of modernity and the psychological proclivity to envision policies, as well as strategies, from a long historical perspective.

In terms of China's reunification policy itself, compared to Willy Brandt's concept of "two states, one nation" or Kim Il Sung's proposal for the "Confederal Republic of Koryo," Deng Xiaoping's formula of "one country, two systems" (*yiguo liangzhi*) bears distinct characteristics that blend the Westphalian notion of state sovereignty and the Sinocentric way of dealing with autonomous entities in the periphery. China ("one country" as a continuous civilizational polity) must exist as a united sovereign state (in the Westphalian sense), but in local contexts ("two systems") that accommodate in a flexible fashion a variety of political practices, as illustrated in the case of Hong Kong and Macao. The purposive use of *reunification* instead of *unification* and of *country* rather than *state* in the *yiguo liangzhi* formula is arguably intended to stress a historical source of legitimation for China's unity that is much deeper than a modern source of legitimation based on Westphalian norms. This distinctive combination of the Westphalian paradigm of modernity with Chinese civilizational traditions highlights the in-between character of the Taiwan issue, which reveals highly distinctive features of Chinese reunification and processes of Sinicization, and which is the focus of this inquiry.

This chapter is organized in the following four sections. The first makes a central claim and arguments about an overlay of the Westphalian ideology of sovereignty and territorial state and the Sinic tradition of centralized and differentiated governance in the realm of Chinese reunification. The following three sections present empirical cases of discourse and practices to illustrate how an overlay of Sinic-Western legitimation ideologies unfolds in the areas of diplomacy, cross-Strait relations, and identity politics in compatible or contradictory fashions.

Chinese reunification as dialectics of Sinicization

Chinese reunification is aimed to integrate the separated parts of Chinese territory – the Chinese mainland, Taiwan, Hong Kong, and Macao – into an institutional framework of one Chinese state that blends concepts of a modern nation state and an ancient civilizational polity in distinct local contexts.

Examining a broad range of discourses and practices that center on the Taiwan issue shows that the conception of national reunification is articulated and defined neither monolithically nor linearly, but within a network of contending and changing representations of what China was, is, and should be. National reunification manifests itself as a multiplicity of sociopolitical processes whereby different representations of the nation, informed by both Sinic and Western conceptions of governance and legitimation, contest and negotiate with each other. The objective of building toward one China thus is ideologically premised on a balance of ideas between the Westphalian concept of territorial sovereignty and the Sinic tradition of centralized governance. It is geopolitically contingent on a balance of power between China and the West (American power in particular). In short, processes of achieving reunification generate an overlay of Western and Sinic practices, a political dynamic that I refer to here as dialectical Sinicization. Along these lines, I develop the following three arguments in this chapter.

First, the norms of state sovereignty and territorial integrity motivate and empower state leaders to seek legitimacy through actively pursuing the goal of national reunification — or in the case of Taiwan under Lee Teng-hui and Chen Shui-bian, aggressively pursuing a separate course of Taiwanese nation building. The contest over international recognition constitutes an integral part of state legitimation strategies pursued by both the PRC and Taiwan. Obtaining international recognition would have constitutive effects explicitly on the legal claim to represent China and, by extension, implicitly on the legitimate right to engineer reunification under its rule. The extent to which the norm of sovereignty precludes certain policy practices and solutions that would otherwise be available in the Sinic world — such as accepting less than equal status or allowing ambiguous boundaries — engenders a zero-sum diplomatic warfare between Beijing and Taipei. The de jure one China, once it was institutionalized through diplomatic processes, would give state leaders moral leverage to offset the de facto "two Chinas" or "one China, one Taiwan," but would not be capable of resolving the sovereignty problem altogether.

Second, the Chinese civilizational heritages that bond the Chinese mainland and Taiwan culturally provide another source of legitimation that political leaders may strategically deploy in their competition for legitimacy — mostly to their respective political constituents at home, but also in their negotiations for national reunification. The English term legitimation may refer to *hefaxing*, *zhengdangxing*, or *zhengtong* in the Chinese discursive context; while the first two translations are more or less equivalent to legitimacy in the modern context, *zhengtong* resonates with legitimism in the Chinese historical context. Paradoxically, when Mao carried out socialist and cultural revolution under the guidance of Sinified Marxism-Leninism on the mainland, Chiang promoted re-Sinicization on the island and saw himself as the true heir of Chinese culture; when Jiang and Hu started to reclaim Chinese cultural heritages in their efforts to rebuild a moral order, Lee and Chen resorted to Taiwanization/de-Sinicization through democratization as a new legitimation basis. So cultural one China (civilizational identity) is not necessarily congruent with political one China (national identity). Nevertheless, it remains true that Chinese cultural values and traditional statecrafts still allow considerable latitude for state leaders to deploy a wide range of practices (such as the "Chinese Taipei" model applied to Taiwan's international participation or various non-domestic, non-international mechanisms dealing with actual relations within Greater China). In so doing, they seek to ensure the state legitimacy and security in ways similar to how the rulers of the Sinic world managed the gap between the ideal of "unity of all under heaven" (*tianxia yitong*) and various political realities falling far short of that ideal.

Third, insofar as the issue of unification divides and antagonizes the two sides of the Taiwan Strait, the problem of identity becomes part and parcel of the PRC's and Taiwan's domestic politics and foreign policy. When political leaders on either side use the issue as a legitimation resource, they act under a strong double impulse. They highlight a distinct identity that underlines sharp differences with each other, while emphasizing a shared identity with the international community. In doing so, they seek to legitimize their rule both internally and externally. The contentions about "one China," "two Chinas," "one China, one Taiwan," or "Taiwan independence" are all manifestations of the politics of China's identity. This identity politics is further complicated by the external security of both Taiwan and mainland China in the regional order anchored on American hegemony. Thus the reunification issue provides an interface for multiple players to participate in the processes of making and remaking China. It has a transformative potential to comprise a novel social episteme – "a new set of spatial, metaphysical, and doctrinal constructs"[3] through which the visualization of future China is shaped.

Put briefly, national unification is not simply about the reunification of the nation, but rather marks the site where competing and conflicting representations of China, by both governmental and non-governmental actors across the Taiwan Strait and beyond, confront and negotiate with each other. As Chinese power grows ever stronger, so do Chinese aspirations for national reunification. Against the backdrop of a rising China, this chapter aims to shed light on China's identity and security politics by exploring the Taiwan issue as a dialectical process of Sinicization.

The Westphalian ideology of the territorial state

The Western world emerged with the Treaty of Westphalia of 1648, which established the "territorial state" as the basic unit of international politics, creating the foundation for the international system of states we know today. International boundaries became legal demarcations between states, which thus asserted rightful rule through legal sovereignty. Along with the emergence of the Westphalian system arose nationalism as a dominant political ideology from which states derive their legitimacy. A closer look at this statist and realist doctrine, however, reveals tensions and contradictions.

For neorealist Kenneth Waltz, the state is a unitary actor emerging from and operating in an anarchic international system. Interested only in international outcomes, Waltz is not concerned with state domestic characteristics. The only thing that matters is states' relative power positions, which constitute the structure of anarchy. International anarchy drives all states to pursue security and power. In Waltz's world, balancing power is the basic rule of the game.[4]

David Lake, also a realist, favors instead the classical realist logic, which takes account of domestic politics. The state is not simply a unitary actor. States' officials typically pursue international goals in a domestic context while also pursuing domestic goals in the international system. Here, the key to an understanding of state behavior is the linkage between domestic and international politics.[5] More recently, he further challenges the conventional neorealist view of anarchy, arguing that states exercise authority over one another in *international hierarchies* that vary historically but are still pervasive today.[6]

Another erstwhile realist, Stephen Krasner, has broken with realism in his recent study of sovereignty. For Krasner, instead of the state, the basic unit of analysis is the ruler of the state. In his words, "Rulers, not states – and not the international system – make choices about politics, rules, and institutions."[7] His study of sovereignty highlights the chronic problem of the discrepancy between norm and practice, which he dubs an "organized hypocrisy."[8] However, like Waltz, both Krasner and Lake, as well as all realists and some scholars of other theoretical persuasions, agree on the centrality of territoriality in international politics.

The Sinic ideology of world unity

In sharp contrast to the Westphalian world of territorially fixed, sovereign states, the Sinocentric world was premised on the concept of all under heaven (*tianxia*). It described a hierarchic order centered on the civilizational core state surrounded by differentiated zones. In the Sinic world, the conceptions of political space were ambiguous and fluid. That is, the Sinic system of rule was not entirely territorially defined; it also had non-territorial components and was often cast in universalistic cultural terms. Yet, at the same time, the political space of the core state of Sinic civilization – China (*Zhongguo*) – was delimited and administered in the realpolitik sense.[9] Thus, "cultural and political frontiers need not to be identical."[10]

In the Sinic world, the unity of all under heaven (*tianxia yitong*) was enshrined as a core value of the dominant cultural paradigm. Thus, it provided the defining normative foundation on which legitimate political rule was established and sustained. The drive for unity provided the cultural impulse for China's rulers to seek *universal* preeminence and the rule by virtue (*wang dao*) through a set of *differentiated* institutional arrangements and mechanisms that revolved around the center of Sinic civilization, the Middle Kingdom or the Central Country. In John Fairbank's words, China's unity "is an attribute of Chineseness itself. It springs from a sense of culturalism, something a good deal stronger than mere Western-style nationalism."[11]

In practice, the issue of unity and disunity has been a recurring theme in the course of Chinese civilization. This is illustrated by the opening line of the fourteenth-century historical novel, *Romance of the Three Kingdoms*: "The domain under heaven is bound to unite after long division, and bound to divide after long union."[12] As successive and at times coexisting dynasties rose and fell, uniting fragmented parts into an integrated political order and sustaining such an order posed a central challenge for the rulers of each dynasty. Once a political order in the image of *tianxia* was established or restored, even by former barbarians, the Sinic world continued; and so did civilization. In historical and cultural terms, the dynamics of unification and Sinicization lie at the heart of Chinese civilization.

In his seminal work *The Chinese World Order*, Fairbank and his associates note a significant discrepancy between the idea or myth of *tianxia yitong* and the political reality and practices in China's actual conduct of external relations. The Sinocentric worldview, as Lien-sheng Yang points out, "was a myth backed up at different times by realities of varying degree, sometimes approaching nil."[13] Wang Gungwu echoes this view that "the Chinese ruling groups were able to move back and forth between the assertion of myth and the acceptance of reality so frequently and for so long a time without abandoning this superior view of themselves."[14] While it is important to distinguish myth from reality, or a social reality from a political reality, Yang stresses, both can be influential.[15] According to Fairbank, "the chief problem of China's foreign relations was how to square theory with fact, the ideological claim with the actual practice."[16]

Overlay: the Anglo-Chinese world

At the dawn of the twentieth century, a century-long encounter between the Sinic and Western worlds led to the fall of the Qing dynasty and the rise of Chinese nationalism. The subversion of the *tianxia* system at the hands of Western and Japanese imperialist powers brought about "changes unprecedented in thousands of years" – the profound transformation of Chinese civilization itself. China was forced to enter the modern world wherein Western powers and ideas ruled. Early reformers such as Zhang Zhidong, Zeng Guofan, and Li Hongzhang once hoped that China could meet the Western challenge through self-strengthening based on the idea of "Chinese learning as an essence, Western learning for practical use" (*Zhongxue weiti, Xixue weiyong*). But their endeavors proved futile when China was defeated by and ceded Taiwan to Japan in 1895. In particular, the loss of Taiwan to westernizing Japan, a former member of the Sinocentric system, dealt a knockout blow to the Qing dynasty and played a critical role in awakening Chinese nationalism. As Chinese philosopher Feng Youlan notes, the world of the early twentieth century was as if the China of the warring states period had lasted until this day. This "replay of history" caused enormous suffering to the Chinese; at the heart of the problem, Feng argues, was China's lack of nationalism in confronting the West because the Chinese had long been accustomed to looking at and conceiving of things from the *tianxia* worldview.[17]

Liang Qichao's "Prolegomena to Chinese History" in 1901, as Yu Ying-shih observes, marks the beginning of China's transition from tradition to modernity. Liang admitted that China was no longer the center of world civilization. Now it was Western civilization that dominated the world. However, since China had only recently begun to participate in this Western-dominated world, Liang expected Chinese civilization to play an important role in the centuries to come.[18] Despite Liang's long-term perspective, along with the Republican revolution in 1911, as Prasenjit Duara notes, "the centralizing, statist narrative of History...has become hegemonic in China," and "other modes of figuring the past" have faded out.[19]

Underscoring the defining theme of twentieth-century Chinese history, according to Li Zehou, is the "dual variations of Enlightenment and Salvation."[20] In this context, the "century of humiliation" has been constructed as a powerful legacy. That legacy, or myth as Michael Hunt calls it, "gripped the imagination of three generations of Chinese and stung them into an ever more critical analysis of the international order and Chinese society. The result was an obsession, long sanctioned by official orthodoxy, with expunging all residues of a feudal-imperialist past."[21] China's quest for modernity, identity, and its rightful place in this new world was thus encapsulated in enduring and deeply entangled processes of self-strengthening modernization and nation building which bridged foreign and civil wars, reform and revolution, isolation and opening, disunity and unification.

The Westphalian notion of state-centric territoriality – "disjoint, mutually exclusive, and fixed territoriality" – as John Ruggie argues, "most distinctively defines modernity in international politics."[22] Historically, the Chinese grasped the meaning of sovereignty and territorial integrity through the experience of losing much of both. In this sense, the notion of territorial sovereignty is central to China's search for modernity simply because the "lost territories" or the imposed fragmentation of Chinese territory highlight the "incomplete territoriality" of China in the international system in which sovereign states derive their international legitimacy. Viewed from this vantage point, the objective of integrating the fragmented parts of Chinese territory into an institutional framework of sovereignty and territoriality has been endogenized by all Chinese elites as a core normative value.

In applying Krasner's conceptualization of sovereignty to China, Michel Oksenberg points to the constraining effects of the modern sovereignty norm on the policies through which contemporary elites seek to deal with the issues of Taiwan, Hong Kong, and Tibet.[23] As he argues, "especially the Westphalian notions of territoriality and autonomy and the notion of international recognition as a defining characteristic of nationhood have had a profound impact on the aspirations of all the actors involved"; and "solutions available in the early 1800s are now much more difficult to achieve, while other solutions, inconceivable in the 1800s, have become possible."[24]

Since the Westphalian paradigm has become a driving force in the Chinese quest for modern identity, the obvious question is the extent to which Sinic notions of political space, order, and rule remain relevant. Benjamin Schwartz observes that "the Chinese perception of world order…*was* fundamentally undermined in the twentieth century; we should be extremely skeptical of assertions that assign it great causal weight in explaining present or future Chinese policies."[25] In particular, he stresses pointedly, "The revolutionaries, on the whole, were quite willing to exchange the Chinese universal world order for a strong Chinese nation." Schwartz's argument is partially true in terms of "the triumph of the multistate system" and "conventional national power politics."[26] The distinctiveness of Chinese nationalism, Jin Guantao and Liu Qingfeng note, lies in the separation of the state from the Confucianist moral system and the combination of the state with revolutionary utopia as a new legitimating foundation, which Jin and Liu call neo-Sinocentrism.[27]

The prevalence of Westphalian norms and powers does not and cannot erase the Chinese past even by means of revolution; rather, it only highlights a stark discrepancy between norm and reality under contemporary conditions and intensifies Chinese bitterness at the unpleasant world dominated by the West. This drives home the same chief problem of China's polity: how to square norm with reality, the ideal of unity with the practice of managing disunity. A closer look at China's practices in the domain of sovereignty suggests a more complex picture of China's behavior. Here I find James Watson's observation about imperial China's cultural identity extremely insightful. According to Watson, "orthopraxy (correct practice) reigned over orthodoxy (correct belief) as the principal mean of attaining and maintaining cultural unity" in late imperial China.[28] By orthopraxy, he stresses the role of ritual and importance of "the active participation of people who cooperate (some willingly, some not) to 'construct' a unified culture."[29] Just as orthopraxy was important for the cultural identity and unity of imperial China, as I will show in the three empirical cases below, orthopraxy is also central to constructing the national identity and unity of contemporary China. This is particularly true in terms of the legitimation of the state in the eyes of the national public. Whether willing or unwilling, the cooperation of relevant actors in constructing a unified nation as the state propagates will significantly contribute to China's national identity and unity as long as active participation in standardizing processes (ritual practices) is attained and maintained. In this sense, the Westphalian norms of sovereignty and territoriality must be normally standardized and regularly "performed" in the processes of discourse and practice. As far as China's reunification is concerned, therefore, the principles of "one China," "one country, two systems," and "anti-Taiwan independence" should be more accurately understood as the standardized rites or orthopraxy in terms of the construction of China's identity and unity, and as the consolidation of state legitimacy and security rather than as a simple belief in the Westphalian orthodoxy.

In a broad context, the three "facts" that Schwartz employed to substantiate his argument some forty years ago – "the center of world order now lay outside of China … the doctrine of world order was entirely different from the traditionally Chinese doctrine, and … China actually occupied, at least until recently, an inferior status within this world order"[30] – have become evidently outdated at the dawn of the twenty-first century. As China rises at a phenomenal pace and embraces the arrival of Chinese Renaissance, the center of world economy and politics continues to shift from the Atlantic to the Pacific, and globalization increasingly renders individual nation states incapable of dealing with the issues of governance, development, and ecologic security, it is timely and legitimate to ask what China will do on the global scale and how the Chinese view the rapidly changing world and act on it.

Constructing de jure one China as orthopraxy

In this section, I look at how the PRC has strived for the "sole legal representation" of China and engaged with foreign governments to construct de jure one China as a norm and orthopraxy. To the extent that China's diplomacy revolves around the defining principle of one China (*yige Zhongguo yuanze*), which is underscored by the Westphalian norms of sovereignty and territoriality, the standardization of de jure one China through diplomatic engagement plays a pivotal role in attaining the state's international legitimacy and contributing to the cause of national unity and reunification.

The guidelines for establishing diplomatic relations

Seeking international recognition was one of the major and urgent tasks facing the Chinese Communists on the eve of the founding of New China, only complicated by the unfolding Cold War. When Stalin dispatched Mikoyan to visit Mao in February 1949, Mao expressed his hope that the Soviet Union would be the first to recognize an incoming revolutionary government; at the same time, he told Mikoyan that New China would not be quick to seek diplomatic recognition from Western capitalist countries.[31]

One of the potential dangers that concerned Mao and Stalin in early 1949 was a possible direct American intervention in the ongoing Chinese civil war. To prevent this danger, Stalin advised Mao not to refuse to establish diplomatic relations with the USA and other capitalist countries.[32] Accordingly, the CCP Central Committee decided to consider the question of establishing diplomatic relations with the USA and Britain if they broke their relations with the Kuomingtang (KMT) regime.[33] When the PRC was founded on 1 October 1949, amidst the raging flames of the civil war, Mao Zedong proclaimed:

> This Government is the sole legal government representing all the people of the People's Republic of China. This Government shall establish diplomatic relations with any foreign governments as long as they comply by the principles of equality, reciprocity, and mutual respect for territorial sovereignty.[34]

Driven by their revolutionary mission and nationalist impulses, the Chinese Communists decided to adopt a new name for the country, a new national flag, a new national anthem, a new constitution, and even a new "calendar followed by the majority of the nations of the world."[35] With these novel changes, Mao stated,

> Our nation will, from now on, become a member of the big family of all peace-loving and freedom-loving nations of the world, ... creating *our own civilization* and happiness, while promoting the peace and freedom of the world. Our nation will never again be humiliated. We have stood up....The time when the Chinese were considered *uncivilized* has passed, and we will emerge in the world as a highly *civilized* nation.[36]

For Mao and the Chinese Communists, it was most important that New China make a radical departure from the "century of humiliation." Mao wanted to "set up a new stove" for New China's diplomacy, and to "clean the house before entertaining guests." In the "Directive on Diplomatic Affairs" issued in January 1949, the CCP Central Committee declared: "With no exception we will not recognize any of those embassies, legations, consulates of capitalist countries, as well as the diplomatic establishment and personnel attached to them accredited to the KMT."[37] In his address to the inaugural assembly of the PRC Foreign Ministry in November 1949, Zhou Enlai cited the Empress Cixi of the Qing, Yuan Shikai of the Northern Government, and Chiang Kai-shek of the KMT as examples of "kneeling-down diplomacy" because "all of them were neurotic to imperialism out of fear." As he bluntly put it, "the diplomatic history of China in the past 100 years is a diplomatic history of humiliation."[38]

Aiming at a fresh start in China's foreign relations, Mao saw hope in the prospects for "leaning to one side" – aligning with the Soviet Union and socialist countries. The guidelines for establishing diplomatic relations were thus formulated by differentiating countries into three groups: socialist, nationalist, and capitalist. For socialist countries, China would readily enter into diplomatic relations without negotiation; for nationalist and capitalist countries, diplomatic relations would be established by means of negotiation.[39] Yet for all countries who intended to have diplomatic relations with New China, the explicit and implicit precondition would be the same: they must recognize the PRC as the sole legal government of China, terminate their diplomatic ties with the Republic of China (ROC), and support the PRC membership in the United Nations. This is the one China principle.

Diplomatic war

In a legal sense, the PRC was a new government of the same country, succeeding the ROC which was displaced by means of revolutionary war. As the prospects for liberating the remaining areas controlled by the fleeing KMT forces appeared imminent and inevitable, international recognition would not have become a major issue if not for the outbreak of the Korean War and US re-intervention in the unfinished Chinese civil war in June 1950.

The discredited KMT owed its survival almost entirely to the reversal of Truman's hands-off policy toward the Chinese civil war, declared by Truman himself in January 1950. In June, he ordered the Seventh Fleet to prevent any attack on Taiwan, as well as Taiwan's military operations against the mainland. More significantly, he declared that the future status of Taiwan "must await the restoration of security in the Pacific, a peace settlement with Japan, or consideration by the United Nations."[40]

American re-intervention in the Chinese civil war, non-recognition of the PRC, and declaration of the undermined status of Taiwan not only prevented the Chinese civil war from coming to an end, but also prolonged and complicated the context of the "China representation" issue in international relations as well as crystallizing the US–China confrontation in the next two decades of the Cold War. With US support, the ROC consolidated its rule in Taiwan, averted a diplomatic calamity by securing its membership in the UN and most of its diplomatic relations, and continued to claim legal governance over all of China. Moreover, Chiang even cherished a hope that one day he would launch a counter-attack on the Chinese Communists and return to the mainland.

As the PRC's sovereignty and territorial integrity were contested and its international legitimacy challenged by American and Chiang Kai-shek's joint forces, its diplomacy became an extension and frontier of the Cold War in East Asia, and the Taiwan issue became a central focus of diplomatic war involving Beijing, Taipei, Washington, and essentially all of the actors on the world stage.

In practice, despite its revolutionary rhetoric at times, the PRC undertook its foreign relations and waged this diplomatic war largely within the international framework of Westphalian norms. Seeing those norms as manipulated and distorted by Western hegemonic powers, Chinese leaders advocated and promoted their own interpretations, with an emphasis on the presumption of reciprocity and equality. That is, compliance with the norms of sovereignty, territorial integrity, non-aggression, non-interference, and so on, must be "reciprocal" or "mutual." Mao's insistence on adding "mutual" to the Sino-Soviet alliance treaty of 1950, and Zhou's advocacy of the "five principles of peaceful coexistence" of which the first four include "mutual" as an adjective, are just two examples of the Chinese preferred vision for international relations.[41] The extant and prolonged Taiwan issue has only further motivated the Chinese to aspire to the operation of Westphalian norms to their fullest extent.

Negotiating de jure one China

The US involvement in the unfinished Chinese civil war turned the Taiwan issue into one of geopolitics and regional security. The timing of US intervention in the Taiwan Strait and China's military engagement with American forces in the Korean War compelled Mao to view and handle the Taiwan issue from the broad perspective of China's overall security. In Mao's view, the Taiwan Strait, along with the Korean Peninsula and Indochina, constituted three frontiers along which American military presence and actions posed a direct threat to China's security. When Eisenhower came to office with a decision to withdraw the Seventh Fleet from preventing Taiwan's military operations against the mainland but to continue its mission to protect Taiwan, the tensions were conspicuously aggravated. The result was two crises in the Taiwan Strait in the 1950s, as well as the installation of the China–US Ambassadorial Talks from 1955 to 1970.

Through the two crises, Mao realized the constraints imposed by both superpowers – the United States as China's rival, and the Soviet Union as China's ally. In the first Taiwan Strait crisis of 1954–55, the People's Liberation Army's (PLA) shelling of Jinmen and Mazu did not prevent the USA from further involvement in the Taiwan dispute. On the contrary, the Eisenhower administration imposed more constraints on Beijing's ability to act, both by signing the Mutual Defense Treaty with Taiwan and by threatening to internationalize the Taiwan issue through the UN. In the second crisis of 1958, underneath the confrontation between the two sides of the Taiwan Strait and between the PRC and the USA, there emerged discords between Washington and Taipei on the one hand, and between Beijing and Moscow on the other. Worrying about direct conflict with the PRC, Eisenhower and Dulles tried to persuade Chiang to withdraw troops from Jinmen and Mazu in order to stabilize the situation through "two Chinas" arrangements. Similar discord arose between the PRC and the Soviet Union. As Khrushchev complained to Mao, the shelling of Jinmen and Mazu had created "difficulties for the Soviet Union," and the situation in which the two sides were supported by the two superpowers "created a pre-world war atmosphere." He suggested that Beijing repudiate the use of force against Taiwan, or even let Taiwan have temporary independence.[42]

Not surprisingly, Mao's civil war rival, Chiang Kai-shek, had his own grievances about external constraints. In terms of the indivisibility of Chinese sovereignty, both Mao and Chiang entertained the idea of one China, albeit fighting for whose government was legitimate to represent China. They behaved as if they had formed a united front against the superpowers' attempts at creating "two Chinas" or "one China, one Taiwan." As a result of the second Taiwan Strait crisis, Mao concluded that the status quo was the most realistic policy option under the present conditions. In a Politburo Standing Committee meeting in May 1960, he made clear that Beijing would rather leave Taiwan with Chiang Kai-shek than allow it to fall into the hands of Americans or pro-American politicians. Beijing could afford to wait, and leave the liberation of Taiwan for the next generation to handle. Mao's bottom line: as long as the Taiwan authorities were able to guard Taiwan and prevent it from separating from China, Beijing would not alter the status quo.[43]

Clearly, the US factor was instrumental in shaping this view. As Zhou Enlai explained, "If we go on to liberate Taiwan now, we will engage with American armed forces.... This is the external dimension of the issue. We are confronted with the United States. This has brought about an international dispute."[44] In the prolonged Ambassadorial Talks with the United States, Beijing attempted to overcome this "US factor" in vain. Not until the geostrategic landscape changed to favor the Soviets, causing China and the United States to feel more threatened by growing Soviet power than by each other, did the leaders of the two countries finally come to the negotiation table and start to tackle the Taiwan issue in a serious manner.

Now that Mao and Nixon shared a global vision for containing the Soviet threat, they quickly opened the normalization process, culminating in Nixon's visit to China and the release of the Shanghai communiqué in February 1972. In this first joint communiqué, "the United States acknowledges that all Chinese on either side of the Taiwan Strait maintain there is but one China and Taiwan is a part of China."[45] The start of US–China normalization shocked the world and tipped the regional and global balance of power. But the fact that it took ten years of negotiation, three American presidents, and two generations of Chinese leaders to accomplish normalization testified to the difficulty and complexity of the Taiwan issue.

By the end of 1978, Deng and Carter concluded the normalization negotiations that Mao and Nixon had started. In the joint communiqué released on 1 January 1979,

> The United States of America recognizes the Government of the People's Republic of China as the sole legal Government of China. Within this context, the people of the United States will maintain cultural, commercial, and other unofficial relations with the people of Taiwan.[46]

Although the US made considerable concessions to China, the remaining question of US arms sales to Taiwan and the enactment of the Taiwan Relations Act (TRA) by the US Congress in April 1979 overshadowed the otherwise "normal" state of US–China relations. The TRA, in particular, stipulates that the US decision to establish diplomatic relations with the PRC "rests upon the expectation that the future of Taiwan will be determined by peaceful means" and considers "any effort to determine the future of Taiwan by other than peaceful means … a threat to the peace and security of the Western Pacific area and of grave concern to the United States."[47] Moreover, when Ronald Reagan came to office, he even considered upgrading US–Taiwan relations to the official level.

Alarmed by these signs of retrogression from the normalization agreement on the part of the USA, Deng went as far as threatening to suspend or downgrade China's diplomatic relations with the USA unless the pro-Taiwan trend was contained. As a result, the two governments negotiated another compromise agreement concerning US arms sales to Taiwan – the 8.17 communiqué – in 1982. This third landmark document reaffirms the principles agreed upon by the two sides in the first two communiqués, but adds something new: "The United States…has no intention of infringing on Chinese sovereignty and territorial integrity, or interfering in China's internal affairs, or pursuing a policy of 'two Chinas' or 'one China, one Taiwan.'"[48]

So, even without a satisfactory breakthrough on the real issue of US arms sales, Beijing managed to persuade Washington to move closer discursively and normatively to its version of one China. In the broad context, Beijing's diplomacy finally led to the establishment of "de jure one China" in the 1970s, reified in the PRC's entry into the UN and obtaining diplomatic recognition by a large majority of sovereign states in the world. Insofar as Beijing's one China policy has become an orthopraxy, a ritual has emerged in which the Chinese government routinely reiterates the one China principle in its diplomatic conduct, and foreign governments are frequently requested to reaffirm their one China commitment. In China–US relations, the deployment of the "three communiqués" has been standardized to the extent that they are referenced to address both new and lingering issues and to prevent China–US relations from running off track. The establishment of de jure one China as a norm and orthopraxy has not only significantly empowered the PRC's legitimacy, but also produced normative constraining effects on other countries' behavior when it comes to Taiwan and helped to dampen the unpleasant reality of de facto Taiwan's separation. The remaining question is how to square the reality with the norm.

Practice of sovereignty in a Chinese way

In this section, I survey what may be called the Sinic way of statecraft in the management of core–periphery relations, as most distinctively reified in the idea of "one country, two systems" (*yiguo liangzhi*) that Deng Xiaoping put forth in the era of reform and opening. The defining characteristic of this idea is a combination of symbolic central authority and high-degree local autonomy, which is consistent with the Sinic tradition of indirect rule in China's periphery, albeit wrapped in sovereignty language. Herein lies the practice of sovereignty with Chinese characteristics.[49] Central to this formulation is differentiating the external dimension – unquestioned representation of Chinese sovereignty by the PRC internationally – from the internal dimension – flexible governance within Greater China.

"One country, two systems"

Deng's basic approach to the issue of reunification is embodied in a policy of peaceful reunification according to the *yiguo liangzhi* formula. The strategic shift from the "liberation of Taiwan" to "peaceful reunification" reflects a profound change of the central motif of the CCP platform from sociopolitical revolution to economic construction in China's continuous transformation. Unlike Mao, who believed that war was inevitable and revolution was the theme of the times, Deng viewed peace and development as the prevailing world trends. By late 1978, he succeeded in winning the wide support of elites by rallying the CCP around his tripartite grand strategy – economic development, national reunification, and world peace.

Now that the PRC had secured its status as "the sole legal government of China" internationally, the remaining challenge became how to bring Taiwan back into the embrace of the motherland. Deng wanted to solve the problem by peaceful negotiation on the terms acceptable to all parties. The *yiguo liangzhi* approach, Deng maintained, was of necessity a compromise solution to the conflicting interests of all the parties concerned.[50] It was politically intended to accommodate rather than change the status quo on the assumption that the PRC's representation of one China had been internationally accepted. This formula was designed to ensure one Chinese sovereignty while preserving the two disparate socioeconomic systems as respectively practiced on the mainland and in Taiwan/Hong Kong/Macao; to maintain the PRC as the central government while giving Taiwan/Hong Kong/Macao a high degree of autonomy as accredited to the status of special administrative region (SAR); to centralize official foreign affairs and national defense by the central government while allowing SARs to conduct relevant external affairs; and to exempt SARs from taxation and other duties while giving them ceremonial representations in the central government. The underlying rationale of *yiguo liangzhi* is to stabilize or neutralize the Taiwan issue in China's relations with the outside world, avoiding its unpredictable disruption of Beijing's foremost priority of socioeconomic modernization in a stable and peaceful external environment. In Deng's view, under the framework of *yiguo liangzhi*, integration between the mainland and Taiwan, Hong Kong, and Macao will evolve gradually in a long historical process. In the case of Hong Kong and Macao, Deng designated a fifty-year timeframe; after that time, as he once stressed, there would be no need to change because the mainland and these special administrative regions would already have largely converged.[51] When it comes to Taiwan, Deng and other Chinese leaders have never attached a timetable for reunification unless Taiwan declared independence. Showing infinite patience has been a distinctive feature of Beijing's status quo-oriented approach.

Obviously, the concept of sovereignty unambiguously commands this approach in that the site of *central* government must be the PRC in Beijing, and the status of Taiwan is *local* in both legal and political terms. Yet, the concept of high-degree autonomy assigned to the status of SAR is unique in the whole spectrum of political organization of the modern state in the contemporary world, ranging from federation, confederation, union of states, to commonwealth. Despite a few symbolic representations of state sovereignty at the locus of the central government, SARs may enjoy and exercise higher degrees of autonomy than, for instance, federations in the areas of administration, legislation, and jurisdiction. Whereas Deng insisted that the PLA must be stationed in Hong Kong and Macao after reunification because of their former status as *foreign* colonies, Taiwan would be spared this rule and maintain its own armed forces because of its pre-reunification status as *Chinese* territory.

Given the rather liberal character of this conception, it is intriguing that Chinese leaders in general and Deng in particular have staunchly resisted any alternative concepts – such as federation, which still represents national sovereignty – as an acceptable approach to national reunification. The most-cited arguments are four: (1) the concept of federation is against the Chinese deep tradition of centralized governance; (2) the adoption of a federation would imply the existence of two independent states in the first place; (3) the adoption of a federation would entail the unwarranted change of political organization of the PRC itself; and (4) applying the concept of federation would motivate and embolden Tibetans, Uyghurs, and other ethnic groups to request the same status.

Although all of these arguments are plausible to the extent that they address some real and potential problems facing the PRC, none of them explicitly answers the question of why, then, the conception of special administrative region under *yiguo liangzhi* would have the power to overcome those and other problems while achieving national reunification. More puzzling still, where did Deng's ideas come from?

Sinic governance and statecrafts

In the Sinic world, the seeming uniformity of centralized imperial sovereignty at the apex of the governing structure had typically been mixed and balanced with the diversity of differentiated rules, including direct rule, indirect rule, tributary rule, and equal trading relationships, in outward expanding zones of such a concentric order.[52] In terms of core–periphery relations, according to Qiang Shigong, the Sinic way of governance had historically combined the two forms of statecrafts since the Han: direct control of China's interior through the system of prefectures and counties, and indirect control of China's periphery through a variety of feudal institutions. Describing this tradition as "one country, multiple systems" (*yiguo duozhi*), Qiang argues that Deng's *yiguo liangzhi* is highly consistent with this Sinic tradition.[53]

In my interviews with policy insiders in Beijing, an official from the state security apparatus echoed the view that the policy of *yiguo liangzhi* was consistent with traditional statecrafts deployed to deal with local power holders in imperial China's periphery. But according to another official in the Office of Hong Kong and Macao Affairs, the practice of *yiguo liangzhi* in Hong Kong after its return was "totally new to us" because there were no precedents whatsoever; the only driving factor in their work was to "do whatever it took to avoid turmoil (*bu chushi*)" in Hong Kong. Of course, he added, "we will see to it that the Basic Law of Hong Kong will be followed." The Basic Law itself was crafted according to the concept of *yiguo liangzhi*. The inference we can draw from these contending viewpoints yields an interesting clue to the origin and rationale of Deng's ideas.

One of the traditional statecrafts that was historically deployed in China's periphery was the concept and practice of "loose rein" (*ji mi*). "Loose rein" refers to a set of institutional mechanisms that ensure the symbolic loyalty of local power holders in the periphery without direct intervention from the center. The *ji mi* policy, as Lien-Sheng Yang has surveyed, was "basically one of appeasement," "had a wide range of meanings used in Chinese history," and "could be used either inside or outside of the frontier depending whether China was weak or strong." One concept is *ji mi bu jue* – meaning "keeping under loose rein without severing the relationship"; another is *ji mi bu chen*, also known as *bu zhuanzhi* – meaning "keeping under loose rein without treating [a state of rival status] as a subject," or "not to impose despotic control over them." Both concepts were put into practice in dealing with barbarians in the "wild zone" (*huang fu*) by the Han dynasty. The concept of *ji mi* was further developed and institutionalized throughout the Tang, Song, Ming, and Qing periods, taking the forms of *ji mi fu zhou* ("military and civil prefectures under loose rein"), *ji mi zhou xian* ("prefectures and districts under loose rein"), *tu si* ("local chieftains serving as officials"), and the like. As Yang noted, "Such prefectures and districts under loose rein constituted a frontier prefectural system in name but a frontier feudal system in reality." While the Ming and Qing dynasties attempted to "convert them into regular prefectures and districts" (a process known as *gai tu gui liu*), these efforts "yielded only limited results."[54]

There is little evidence that Mao or Deng directly appropriated *ji mi* policy when outlining *yigang simu* or *yiguo liangzhi*. The actual practices of *ji mi* also historically varied across time and space, with varying degrees of effectiveness and success. Nevertheless, it would also be intellectually insensible to overlook some profound consistencies in terms of governing the center–periphery relationship throughout the course of Chinese history. Recent research by Qiang Shigong reveals a more contemporary origin for *yiguo liangzhi*, which emerged in the CCP's Tibet policy. As early as 1948, Mao started to link the issues of Taiwan, Hong Kong, Macao, and Tibet in his contemplation of China's geopolitical situation. In 1950, he envisioned a peaceful liberation of Tibet policy and set the CCP's Southwest Bureau and the PLA's Southwest Military Region to the task of implementing such a policy. As the first secretary and political commissar of these two units respectively, Deng assumed primary responsibility for this task. Under his supervision, General Zhang Guohua set up a policy institute and recruited a number of prominent sociologists and Tibetologists to investigate the situation in Tibet, study all relevant issues, and make policy recommendations. In May 1950, Deng drafted and submitted to the central leadership the "four principles" for peaceful negotiation with the Tibetan authorities. These principles included expelling American and British imperialists from Tibet, installing ethnic regional autonomy in Tibet after its return to the motherland, preserving Tibet's existing institutions, and exercising religious freedom in Tibet. Taken together, they constituted the core of Mao's further refined Tibet policy, known as the "17 Items." Mao's leadership and Deng's critical role in making and implementing such a policy support an argument that the ideas of *yigang simu* and *yiguo liangzhi* derived from the CCP's peaceful liberation of Tibet policy. As Qiang observes, the CCP's Tibet policy of the 1950s was also largely consistent with the KMT's Tibet policy practiced in the 1930s and with Sinic traditional statecrafts in general.[55]

In this Sinic tradition, the rule of thumb for maintaining an all-embracing unity is to ensure local allegiance by accommodating the local reality, whatever it may be.

Arguably, this Sinic tradition has been further reinforced by Chinese Communist absorption of Leninist hyper-flexibility.⁵⁶ In this sense, the second observation, which implies intuitive pragmatism in the practice of *yiguo liangzhi*, appears complementary with the first – the pragmatic appropriation of historical experience. After all, intuitive or empiricist pragmatism in many ways marks the distinctive way of Deng's rule, as exemplified in his two favorite folk adages: "crossing the river by feeling stones" and "no matter a cat is black or white, as long as it catches mice, it is a good cat."

"Unbundled territoriality" in Greater China and the "Chinese Taipei" model

The *yiguo liangzhi* formula, which was initially intended for Taiwan, has in practice applied first to Hong Kong and then to Macao, with considerable success so far. A close look at Beijing's policy toward these two areas provides another clue to the practice of sovereignty in a distinctive Chinese way.

There are conspicuous contradictions in Beijing's policy and especially in its practice of *yiguo liangzhi*. As Qiang argues, China has claimed to possess sovereignty over Hong Kong and Macao but has not necessarily exercised it in ways that the Western sovereignty theory requires.⁵⁷ When the CCP decided its Hong Kong policy in the early 1950s, Zhou Enlai stressed that the decision of "not taking-over Hong Kong…cannot be judged from a narrow principle of territorial sovereignty."⁵⁸ China did not recognize the status of Hong Kong and Macao as de jure colonies but had to deal with them as de facto colonies; and it did not consider the China–UK and China–Portugal joint communiqués as international treaties but filed these documents to the UN as required for international treaties. Since reunification, residents in Hong Kong and Macao are by law Chinese citizens, but they neither enjoy the same citizen rights nor fulfill the same citizen duties as stipulated by the PRC Constitution; the HKSAR Basic Law and MCSAR Basic Law were enacted by the PRC National People's Congress but are in effect treated as the "mini constitutions" of these two special administrative regions; the PRC Nationality Law accords no recognition of dual citizenship, but in the case of Hong Kong, dual citizenship is allowed. These paradoxes, or the name–reality discrepancies as Qiang puts it, exist because China's legal system concerning the constitution of the state is built upon a set of "names" established in Western political philosophy; any political entity that does not comply with this system would lack de jure legitimacy. Citing Foucault's "blackmail of the Enlightenment," Qiang sees these paradoxes as reflective of the "blackmail" of the Western political theory of modernity onto Chinese political reality. In this context, Chinese politicians and jurists are compelled to craft a set of complex, paradoxical, and innovative legal concepts to counter-effect such a blackmail. The discrepancy between the claim to sovereignty and the exercise of sovereignty, Qiang argues, significantly moves the scope of the Western notion of sovereignty beyond the delimited paradigm of nation states, thus reaching back into the parameter of *tianxia*.⁵⁹

What works for Hong Kong and Macao would work for Taiwan only if Taiwan yielded its own claim to sovereignty. But Taiwan's leaders, from Chiang Ching-kuo, to Lee Teng-hui, to Chen Shui-bian, to Ma Ying-jeou, have all rejected *yiguo liangzhi* as a valid solution from the standpoint of state sovereignty. The public polls periodically undertaken by Taiwan's Mainland Affairs Council also show that the *yiguo liangzhi* arrangements similar to those in Hong Kong and Macao appeal only to a tiny minority of the Taiwanese public.

Despite the seemingly insurmountable problem of sovereignty in the areas of high politics, actual cross-Strait interactions and exchanges have flourished in all areas of low politics under the permissible *yiguo liangzhi* framework, which has far-reaching implications for governance. Take the example of Taiwanese mainland-bound migration. According to Taiwan's statistics, as of December 2010, the cumulative number of Taiwanese visitors to the mainland (in all categories of tourism, business, study, and residence) since the opening of cross-Strait exchange had been 4,464,460 person-times; but the mainland State Tourism Bureau's statistics put that number as high as 60,670,669. The enormous discrepancy, 56,206,209 person-times, according to the Taiwan's Mainland Affairs Council, is accounted for by the different regulations in Taipei and Beijing. Since 2003, Taipei has largely deregulated its restrictions on Taiwanese residents' travel to the mainland – first by granting a multiple-entries-in-three-years permit and then by decontrolling the travel permit application for ordinary citizens. But the mainland authorities stamp every entry of a Taiwan resident traveling to the mainland on his/her travel permit issued by the PRC Ministry of Public Security.[60]

In fact, residents within Greater China may carry one of four different passports depending on where they are from: the PRC passport, PRC Hong Kong SAR passport, PRC Macao SAR passport, or ROC passport (see Figure 3.1). Despite the SARs being de jure and de facto PRC territory, mainland residents are not free to travel there but need a special travel permit; nor are SAR residents, who carry PRC Hong Kong SAR passports or PRC Macao SAR passports, free to travel to the mainland without obtaining a special entry card (Figure 3.2). Taiwan residents must obtain a Beijing-issued "Taiwan Resident Entry & Exit of Mainland Permit"

FIGURE 3.1 Three versions of PRC passport, and ROC passport

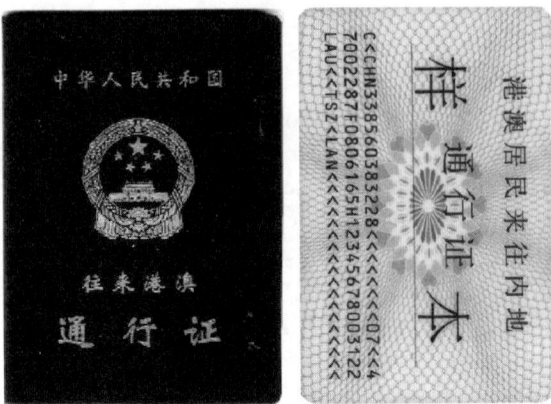

FIGURE 3.2 PRC-issued permits for travel between mainland and HK/Macao

to travel, live, study, or work on the mainland (Figure 3.3, left), while mainland residents must obtain both a PRC-issued "Mainland Resident Entry & Exit of Taiwan Permit" and a ROC-issued "Exit & Entry Permit" to travel to Taiwan (Figure 3.3, center and right).

Further complicating these regulating mechanisms is another set of arrangements for Taiwan and SAR residents to travel between the SARs and Taiwan. In addition, when Taiwan residents are on the mainland, they are not treated as foreigners, nor are they treated as PRC citizens. All of these illustrate a distinctive feature of cross-border movement within Greater China, raising an intriguing question about domestic–international boundaries and the Westphalian concept of territoriality. In fact, when Beijing and Taipei negotiated Taiwan's torch relay route for the Beijing Olympics in 2008, the two sides compromised by defining

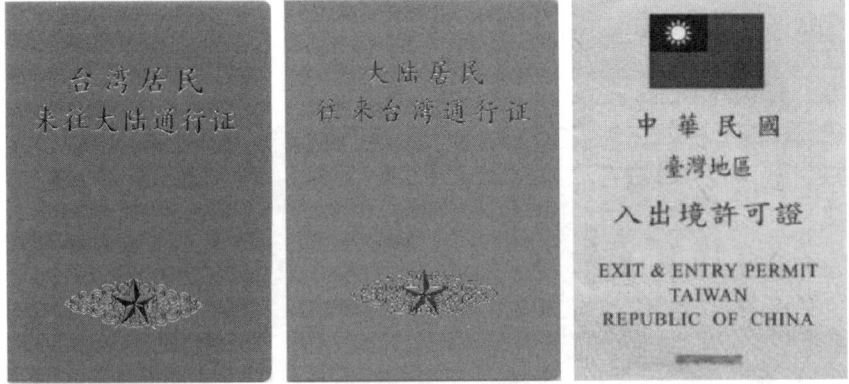

FIGURE 3.3 PRC-issued travel permits for Taiwan residents (*left*) and mainland residents (*center*), and ROC-issued "Exit & Entry Permit" for mainland residents (*right*)

the Taiwan route as "outside of the border" (*jingwai*) – just short of "international" (*guoji*). Beijing then defined the routes of Hong Kong/Macao as *jingwai*, distinguishing them from domestic (*jingnei*) routes but putting them in the same category as Taiwan's. Herein at the functional level we see that the practice of *yiguo liangzhi* makes an internal–external distinction based on exclusive territoriality problematic, and that territorial administration in Greater China possesses the characteristic of "unbundling territoriality."

Furthermore, sovereignty concerns do not always preclude the practice of pragmatism by leaders in Beijing and Taipei concerning Taiwan's participation in international activities. Since 1979, Taiwan has been able to maintain its membership on the International Olympic Committee (1979) under the name "Chinese Taipei," and in the Asian Development Bank (1985) under the name "Taipei, China." It has also obtained memberships in the Asian-Pacific Economic Cooperation (APEC) (1991), the World Trade Organization (WTO) (2002), and the World Health Assembly (WHA) (2009) as "Chinese Taipei" or its variants. The "Chinese Taipei" model, also dubbed the "Olympic model" because of its origin, implies unspecified Chinese sovereignty but allows Taiwan to participate in certain international organizations as a functional entity – be it sports, financial, economic, taxation, or health.

None of these memberships came easily; all entailed painstaking negotiations involving the PRC, Taiwan, and the concerned international organizations. The representatives of the PRC and Taiwan did not negotiate directly with each other but bargained through the brokering of host organizations or host countries when new disputes arose. Although this model seems to resonate with the *yiguo liangzhi* formula and may be understood as its logical extension, the *international* setting of its application still makes it difficult for Chinese leaders to accept. But Deng's principled pragmatism prevailed in the Chinese leadership. For Taiwan's leaders, using anything other than its official name is an even more bitter pill to swallow. But the aspiration for Taiwan's *international* participation is too strong to resist. The fact that these arrangements of "Chinese Taipei" application were negotiated respectively under the Chiang, Lee, Chen, and Ma administrations suggests that pragmatic flexibility may still allow for a compromise solution short of granting Taiwan full sovereignty but the status of a functional entity. As Ma Ying-jeou once said, "Chinese Taipei" is not satisfactory but acceptable.

Overlay of globalization and Chinese renaissance

The identity of China has been intensively contested as much across the Taiwan Strait as within Taiwan. This has occurred due to the divergent historical paths and bifurcating political rules between the Chinese mainland and Taiwan, conditioned on changing geopolitical circumstances. Sinicization finds all its variations here, with re-Sinicization under Chiang's authoritarian rule and de-Sinicization under Lee's and Chen's democratic rule as two of its recent manifestations. In this section, I examine how Taiwan's indigenous democratization has evolved in the form of

Taiwanization and de-Sinicization and thus profoundly challenged the identity of China. That Taiwanization/de-Sinicization coincides with globalization and China rising has only intensified the identity problem on both sides of the Taiwan Strait, sharply highlighted the predicament of Westphalian modernity, and consequently broadened the context of discourse and practices about Sinicization.

The challenge of Taiwanization

Both the CCP and the KMT claim to be true heirs to Sun Yat-sen's Three Principles of the People[61] and thus share the idea of the Chinese nation (*Zhonghua minzu*) as a source of legitimation. Throughout the twentieth century, the two parties had been both allies against Northern warlords and Japanese imperialists and enemies against each other in the civil war. After the Second World War, their failure to work out a common platform for nation building led to a new outbreak of civil war and the defeat of the KMT by Communist forces, which resulted in the relocation of the KMT regime in Taiwan after 1949. Overshadowed by the continuing civil war, Taiwan became a means of legitimation for both the CCP and the KMT, which shared a conviction that the state and nation should be congruent but fought for the legitimate representation of the Chinese nation.[62]

Immediately after the ROC restored Chinese sovereignty over Taiwan in 1945, it launched re-Sinicization on the island through a policy of cultural reconstruction intended to uproot Japanese colonial influence, nurture Chinese nationalism among the Taiwanese, and integrate Taiwan into the Chinese cultural institution.[63] After 1949, Chiang intensified Taiwan's re-Sinicization in order to reconstruct Taiwan, not only as part of China but more importantly as "the model province of opposing communism, recovering the nation" politically, economically, and militarily. The creation of a strong Chinese identity was essential for establishing the KMT's legitimacy.[64]

But the processes of Chiang's re-Sinicization coincided with the ongoing civil war, at the time when the KMT regime was corrupt, oppressive, and unpopular. Its postcolonial rule soon led to the 2.28 Taiwanese uprising in 1947, which was brutally suppressed by KMT forces and followed by an even harsher "reign of white terror" under a state of martial law that lasted from 1948 to 1987. During this period, any anti-KMT activities including the Taiwan independence movement would be repressed under the pretense of countering communist rebellion. Internationally, however, the ROC was labeled by the KMT and Americans as "Free China" on the frontier against "Communist China."

Despite the harsh rule of martial law, the anti-KMT *dangwai* movement never faded away and eventually broke ground with the establishment of the pro-independence Democratic Progressive Party (DPP) in 1986. It is worth mentioning that the ROC's diplomatic debacle – being expelled from the UN in 1971 and de-recognized by the USA in 1979 – considerably weakened the KMT's legitimacy based on Chinese nationalism. Rising to the new challenge, Chiang Ching-kuo launched a series of policy initiatives in 1987 that marked the beginning of democratization in Taiwan. With native Taiwanese Lee Teng-hui succeeding Chiang in 1988, the issue of Taiwan's political status soon surfaced as a focal point of Taiwan's vibrant democratic politics. At the heart of democratization is Taiwanization, which problematizes ethnic relations between mainlanders (*waisheng ren*) and native Taiwanese (*bensheng ren*) within, and the issue of unification vs. independence without.[65] As Lee Teng-hui bluntly puts it:

> For a long time, Taiwanese people was unable to possess their own regime, that is to say, Taiwan had long been "repressed" by alien regimes. Therefore, how to get rid of alien regimes has become the biggest question for Taiwan. Meanwhile, the ethnic issue – whether to identify with China or with Taiwan – must also be clarified and resolved....What is the objective of Taiwan's democratization? Simply put, it is "Taiwan's indigenization."[66]

Lee's political rhetoric seems to resonate with Wei-ming Tu's academic prediction: "If Taiwan (the Republic of China) becomes truly democratic, the question of Taiwan's Chineseness will inevitably become a matter of public debate."[67] In fact, Taiwanization under Lee Teng-hui and de-Sinicization under Chen Shui-bian were aimed at Taiwanese nation building as the antithesis to Chinese reunification. The PRC was of course seen as a "foreign enemy" who harbored a hegemonic ambition to annex Taiwan. In this context, striving for Taiwan's "international space" gained new meaning for Taiwan's identity and became a presupposition for Taiwan's de jure independence.

Alarmed by the Taiwanese nationalist movement, Chinese leaders felt that China's territorial sovereignty was at stake, along with the CCP's legitimacy. For forty years, Mao and Deng had shown infinite patience based on the presumption that Taiwan under the Chiangs remained committed to "one China," no matter how contested its conception. What particularly concerned Beijing was Taiwan's aggressive campaign to expand its "international space" and reenter the UN. For both Beijing and Taipei, international recognition or lack thereof would be crucial to the claim of Taiwan or the ROC on Taiwan to be a sovereign and independent state. Tensions were heightened both across the Taiwan Strait and across the Pacific when the Clinton administration decided to grant Lee Teng-hui a visa for an allegedly private visit to his alma mater Cornell University in June 1995 – which Beijing perceived as a collaborated effort by Taipei and Washington to break the confines of de jure one China. The tension soon slipped into a crisis in March 1996, when the PLA launched missile-firing exercises near Keelung and Kaohsiung, and Clinton dispatched two aircraft carriers to the area of Taiwan. For the first time in twenty years, the Taiwan Strait was again a hot spot in East Asia.

The Taiwan Strait crisis of 1996 ushered in a new era in which Taiwan's identity politics became a driving force in cross-Strait relations as well as in the security politics involving China, the United States, Japan, and other regional actors in East Asia. As the momentum of Taiwan's ethnic democratization carried on continuously, so did the dynamics of popular nationalism on the mainland, which questioned the legitimacy of the CCP squarely from the Chinese nationalist standpoint. When Lee Teng-hui made the so-called "two states" statement in 1999 and pro-independence Chen Shui-bian won the presidential election in 2000, the PRC felt its vital national interest was increasingly under threat. Thus the question of peace and war came to the fore.

All of these events stimulated heated domestic debates on critical issues such as the use of force, possible conflict with the USA, and the implications of war for economic development. With each round of debate, more actors from both inside and outside of the policy establishment – scholars, policy specialists, military analysts, opinion leaders, attentive publics, as well as government officials – took part in the discourse; the process of Taiwan policy making, which had been rendered as a closed, exclusive area of high politics at the discretion of top leaders, was now open to debate in both public and *neibu* (closed) settings. No less significant was the opening of multiple channels of communication and consultation between Chinese officials responsible for Taiwan affairs and foreign officials in key capitals. Furthermore, second and third tracks of diplomacy involving both Chinese and foreign scholars, officials, and other elites became part of an expanding network of Taiwan affairs. On top of these, Chinese leaders engaged in intensive and extensive consultations with their foreign counterparts. The Taiwan issue had for the first time become truly a national and international problem.

The predicament of Westphalian nationalism

Beijing's efforts to contain Taiwan independence through military deterrence and diplomatic isolation have reinforced external constraints on Taiwan. But paradoxically, insofar as the consolidation of China's diplomatic alignment with the "we" community of sovereign states against Taiwan independence highlights the "otherness" of Taiwan's non-sovereign status in the international community, these efforts also seem to alienate Taiwan further from China at the national level – or, put differently, to assist Taiwan independence activists in their de-Sinicization drive as they view the reinforcement of de jure one China as "de-nationalization" of Taiwan.

Discursively, the Taiwanese nationalist movement is poised to challenge Chinese nationalism, Sinocentrism, or the China identity altogether. Lee once articulated the "ideal scenario" in which China would be better off divided into seven or so "fully autonomous" regions, Taiwan included.[68] When he defined cross-Strait relations as "a special state-to-state relationship" (*teshu guo-yu-guo guanxi*) in 1999, the word "state," which was carefully chosen to target the international audience, still implies that Taiwan is part of the Chinese nation but exists as a separate state. When Chen asserted that China and Taiwan are "one country on each side" (*yibian yiguo*) of the Taiwan Strait in 2002, choosing the word "country," which was also intended to target the international audience, pits Taiwan against China as two different nations. In practice, while the DPP bases its legitimacy on Taiwanese nation building, the KMT has also considerably shifted its legitimation basis from the idea of the Chinese nation to the practice of democracy in Taiwan.

The Taiwanization of the ROC poses a fundamental question to the identity of China and prospect for Chinese reunification. The fact that Taiwanese democratization has significantly undermined the legitimacy of Chinese nationalism for reunification highlights increasing incongruence between the state and nation and a predicament of Westphalian ideology of nationalism in the Chinese context. Paradoxically, it takes the threat of Taiwan independence – the most extreme representation of China by "othering" China altogether from a Taiwanese nationalist standpoint – to make other alternative representations of China less illegitimate or even conceivable. With the confluence of all of these competing forces, a relevant question emerges: To what extent has the concept of one China, or the identity of China, been shaped and reshaped by these forces?

In an originally internally circulated article, Taiwan specialist Li Yizhou takes issue with the "established discursive context" in which people conceive and expound their views on Beijing's Taiwan policy. Tracing the establishment of such a context back to the times of Chiang Ching-kuo's reform initiatives in 1987, he refers to the "structural deviation of cognition," which has led to mistaken ideas and constituted the inherent misleading logic and premises for perception and analysis. Consequently, taking Taiwan's consecutive presidential elections since 1996 as an example, he notes that "every time we did what we had to do, every time we got the results contrary to our wishes."[69]

Li's most penetrating critique of Beijing's Taiwan policy is this: for Beijing, the hard-won "absolute advantage" over the issue of one China made it very difficult to accommodate Taiwan outside the confines of "the sole legal government," and the objective of ensuring the status of Taiwan as local government made any other formulations inconceivable. Li attributes the increasingly intensified confrontation between Beijing and Taipei to this "fundamental difference." He argues that only a "major emancipation of the mind" would free China from the entrenched context of "deviated cognition" and enable the Chinese to rise to the challenge.[70] Li's article was written and circulated in a restricted range in 2004, which drew great attention from policy makers and informed Taiwan policy adjustments from 2005 onward. The eventual publication of his article in a leading CCP theory journal in 2009 was arguably intended to stimulate a further emancipation of the mind.

Li's critique appears to have theorized the experimental practices and "new thinking" actively promoted by Wang Daohan, the late chairman of the Association for Relations Across the Taiwan Straits (ARATS), who was entrusted by Jiang Zemin to study Taiwan policy and China–US relations after the Cold War. In order to unbuckle the deeply entrenched identity problem embedded in the Taiwan issue, Wang's various new ideas focus on how to reconcile the reunification ideal with the reality of Taiwan lying outside the PRC's jurisdiction, and the vital interests of China's continued modernization and international integration.[71] Eventually, during his second meeting with his counterpart Koo Chen-fu, the late chairman of Taiwan's Straits Exchange Foundation (SEF) in October 1998, Wang came up with an officially endorsed new interpretation of one China, dubbed the 86-character maxim:

> There is only one China in the world. Taiwan is part of China, not yet reunified as of now. Both sides should make a joint effort, under the one China principle, to confer on reunification through consultations on an equal footing. The sovereignty and territorial integrity of a country brook no division. Discussion on the political status of Taiwan should be carried out under the premise of one China.[72]

Although this new maxim was not fully compatible with some other aspects of Beijing's Taiwan policy[73] and still not readily acceptable to most in Taiwan, it represents a novel discursive exercise intended to overcome the singular predicament of Westphalian ideology. Central to this formulation is the idea of *mutual constitution* of a united China – an ongoing process of building toward one China to which both sides of the Taiwan Strait should be formally committed. This conception entails the idea of *pooled sovereignty* – jointly owned, jointly preserved, jointly exercised sovereignty[74] – and represents an innovative approach to re-establishing legitimacy for Chinese reunification beyond the Westphalian paradigm. In effect, defining one China as an ongoing process of managing disparate polities by acknowledging a commitment to Chinese sovereignty gives rise to a dynamic status quo orientation in cross-Strait relations, averting undue imposition of a definitive solution when conditions for such a solution are not ripe.

New theme of peaceful development

In practice, continuous discursive exercises and policy debates gradually brought about policy changes. Since Hu Jintao took office in 2002, Beijing has made considerable adjustments in its Taiwan policy. Hu's "new deal" culminated in several landmark actions or events in 2005: the adoption of the Anti-Secession Law, the normalization of CCP–KMT relations, and the advance of "peaceful development" as a new defining motif of cross-Strait relations. Through the Anti-Secession Law, the CCP codified its peaceful reunification policy into state law. The use of "anti-secession" rather than "reunification" implies a focus on maintaining the status quo. To win the hearts and minds of the Taiwanese people, the CCP must recalibrate national reunification as a process from which people can actually benefit. While the issue of reunification originated in the civil war, the process of reunification should not be carried on as a continuation of civil war; rather, it should be promoted as a constitutive and transformative process of Chinese Renaissance. In this context, KMT Chairman Lien Chan's ice-breaking visit to the mainland in April 2005 not only symbolized the historic resumption of CCP–KMT ties, but more importantly marked the beginning of a transformation of cross-Strait relations. Lien's meeting with Hu Jintao resulted in the joint communiqué in which the two parties made a common commitment to promote the "peaceful development of cross-Strait relations" based on the '92 consensus, and to create the "future for the Chinese nation."[75]

Since Ma Ying-jeou came to power in 2008, he has adopted a policy of "no unification, no independence, no use of force," endorsing the '92 consensus and the peaceful development theme. He called for diplomatic truce in the hope that that the two sides would not deny each other even if not yet ready to recognize each other. Ma's conciliatory gesture made good chemistry with Hu's new deal. Consequently, cross-Strait relations have been considerably stabilized and improved, as demonstrated in the opening of the "three major links" across the Taiwan Strait in 2008, the establishment of the Economic Cooperative Framework Agreement (ECFA) in 2010, and the signing of fifteen bilateral agreements in nonpolitical areas as of the end of 2010, among others. Moreover, Beijing has loosened its restrictions on Taiwan's international participation. Taiwan has been able to dispatch a high-profile political figure, former vice president Lien Chan, to represent "Chinese Taipei" at APEC annual leaders' meetings and has been granted observer status at WHA in the name of "Chinese Taipei." Ma's call for "diplomatic truce" has also received Beijing's positive, albeit implicit, response: when some of Taiwan's diplomatic allies approached Beijing, they were advised to maintain their diplomatic ties with Taiwan.

Discursively and politically underscoring the breakthrough in cross-Strait relations is the CCP–KMT joint affirmation of the so-called '92 consensus, which was reached between ARATS and SEF in 1992 and paved the way for the historic first Wang–Koo talks in Singapore in 1993. The consensus itself is subject to different interpretations: for the CCP it is the "*one China* consensus" (*yi-Zhong gongshi*); for the KMT it is "one China, *respective interpretations*" (*yi-Zhong gebiao*); and for the DPP it is nonexistent. Nevertheless, in the face of the challenge of the DPP-led Taiwan independence drive, the CCP and the KMT rediscovered an added value in the term "'92 consensus." To prevent cross-Strait relations from sliding into a dead end, a balance must be found between upholding the principle of state sovereignty and managing the reality of disparate governance across the Taiwan Strait.

All of these factors have compelled Chinese leaders to define China's identity and interests from a broader civilizational perspective than a single lens of Westphalian sovereignty and territoriality. As Zheng Bijian argues, China's continuous development, continuous participation in globalization, and continuous efforts to rejuvenate Chinese civilization are just three manifestations of another great transformation of the Chinese nation in the twenty-first century. In this context, a three-*he* grand strategy – seeking *he-ping* (peace) abroad, *he-xie* (harmony) at home, and *he-jie* (reconciliation) across the Taiwan Strait – is what China needs and what China is all about.[76] Zhao Tingyang, in his rediscovery of the *tianxia* system, reminds us that the fundamental point of departure for Chinese politics is not the problem of the state but the problem of the world. He argues that the Chinese *tianxia* worldview would remedy the flaws of the modern statist ideology and would be better capable of addressing problems in the age of globalization.[77] Iain Johnston suggests that the *tianxia* worldview, if it were truthfully held, would permit the status quo in the Taiwan Strait to continue indefinitely.[78]

Herein lies a broader raison d'être for Chinese reunification: an overlay of Westphalian modernist legitimation and Sinic civilizational legitimation, increasingly mediated by globalization and China's reemergence at the center of world affairs. A more relaxed and future-oriented conception of the China identity would be capable of creating a broader political space for the coexistence and co-prosperity of all people across the Taiwan Strait. The prevailing motif of peaceful development in cross-Strait relations marks the beginning of a joint effort to construct and constitute a common future from this broad perspective.

Conclusion

The politics of Chinese reunification as exemplified in the Taiwan issue unfolds as a complicated process of Sinicization largely driven by modernity in Westphalian terms, distinctively tinged with cultural values and statecrafts in Sinic civilization, and increasingly mediated by the transforming forces of China rising and globalization. The historical encounter between Chinese and Western civilizations in modern times evoked Chinese *nationalist* awareness and sense of *national* crisis and catalyzed the transformation of Chinese civilization itself. "The story of modern China," in Lucian Pye's view, "could be described as the efforts by both Chinese and foreigners to squeeze a civilization into the arbitrary, constraining framework of the modern state, an institutional invention that came out of the fragmentation of the West's own civilization."[79] In this sense, the expressive meaning of Chineseness has changed from preserving the unity of *tianxia* in cultural terms to striving for the survival and unity of China as a nation state in the Western-dominated world in nationalist terms. To the extent that the cultural value of unity and unification submerges under the legitimation power of Westphalian modernity and lives on as the "habits of the heart" among Chinese elites, the tension between nationalist impulse and civilizational imperative is central to our understanding of Sinicization in the modern world.

The Taiwan issue presents us with a case of Sinicization in which the identity and representation of China are constantly contested, negotiated, compromised, and redefined by competing forces in and outside of China corresponding to changed circumstances. The manifestations of Taiwan's changed and changing identification as Qing's frontier province, Japanese colony, Chinese nationalists' irredentist trophy and base of re-Sinicization, the frontier of China–US Cold War and grand bargain, the unrealized objective of Mao's liberation, the partner in Deng's economic development, the homeland of Taiwan independence movement, the example of Chinese democracy, the pending business of Chinese reunification, and the ongoing process of Sinic Renaissance are all testimonies to the contested identities of modern China in the world as a living reality. Insofar as political leaders on both sides of the Taiwan Strait seek legitimation from the Westphalian paradigm, they have to live with the disparate reality of incomplete sovereignty and territoriality as a norm and deploy their discourse and practice accordingly in ways that would enhance rather than undermine their competing legitimacy. The establishment of de jure one China coinciding with the changed geopolitical landscape did not lead to a final resolution of the Taiwan issue but only marked the beginning of another round of intensifying identity politics.

Deng's *yiguo liangzhi* initiative was intended to reconcile the reality of disintegrated Chinese polities with the ideal of reunification. Sovereignty in legal terms is needed to distinguish Chinese territory from the rest of the world, but actual boundaries within the Chinese territory, and between different parts of Chinese territory and the outside world, can be kept as flexible and ambiguous as necessary for the sake of political reality. This approach with Chinese characteristics has enabled China to "resume the exercise of sovereignty" over Hong Kong and Macao without disturbing the status quo, and has been an enabling element in the opening and expanding of cross-Strait exchanges in many areas of low politics. Arguably, the practices of *yiguo liangzhi* have given rise to the emergence of "unbundled territory" within Greater China, in which the mainland, the special administrative regions of Hong Kong and Macao, and Taiwan all become constituting and constraining factors in their non-domestic, non-international relations and their respective external connections through multifaceted formal or informal institutional mechanisms.

Yet *yiguo liangzhi* has its limits in resolving the sovereignty and legitimation problem with Taiwan. This is especially true when facing the challenge of a Taiwanese independence movement whose mandate is informed by anti-Chinese Taiwanese nationalism. The confrontation between two divergent nationalisms sets the identity problem in sharp relief, to the extent that the increased chance of war involving great powers highlights the predicament of the Westphalian ideology of statist nationalism. Further complicating the problem is the ongoing transformation of world politics in which China is rapidly rising to great power status and moving into the center of world affairs, while global governance mechanisms have been complementing or substituting for some of the inadequate national government capabilities.

According to Andreas Osiander, nothing akin to what we call the "state" existed before the nineteenth century; the onset of industrialization created the conditions under which the state as we know it could function; and the assumption that the state is timeless, necessary for society, serves as part of its legitimating myth.[80] While China and Western countries took different historical paths to modernity, they both became constitutive parts of the continuous transformation of world politics. As Ruggie notes, some rather profound transformation of international politics may be well underway, so that the modernity in international politics defined by "a particular form of territoriality" is itself in question. The emergence of the "multiperspectival polity" based on "unbundled territoriality," Ruggie argues, is manifest as the "constitutive processes" of transformation that imply the prospects of postmodernity in international politics. In the sense of historical dialectics, the world is moving toward an epoch of "New Medievalism."[81]

The rise of China against the backdrop of the world's transformation has created the conditions for the Chinese to rediscover the value of the Sinic civilizational worldview, as reflected in the reemerging *tianxia* discourse. The great resonance between the postmodernity discourse and the *tianxia* discourse is currently generating a new overlay of globalization and Chinese Renaissance that has only started to inform and shape China's practices in the realm of Chinese reunification. In this context, the prevalence of the peaceful development theme in cross-Strait relations marks a beginning of a new era of negotiating and building toward a common future for all.

Notes

1 I would like to thank Anna Bautista, Allen Carlson, Chen Jian, Sara Friedman, Yinan He, Alastair Iain Johnston, Miles Kahler, Gregory Noble, Jason Oaks, Qin Yaqing, Shih Chih-yu, Yan Xuetong, Zhang Ruizhuang, Zhao Tingyang, and other contributors to this volume for their insightful comments and criticisms on various drafts of this chapter. I am enormously indebted to Peter Katzenstein for his intellectual leadership and guidance throughout the course of this project and beyond.
2 See Katzenstein, Chapter 1 of this book.
3 Ruggie 1993, 173.
4 Waltz 1979.
5 Lake 1988.
6 Lake 2009.
7 Krasner 1999, 7.
8 Krasner 1999.
9 Xu 1993, 370–2; also see Johnston 1995.
10 Yang 1968, 22.
11 Fairbank 1983, 461.
12 The translation is the author's.
13 Yang 1968, 20.
14 Wang 1968, 62.
15 Yang 1968, 22.
16 Fairbank 1968, 2–3.
17 Feng 1985, 213, 222.
18 Yu 1990, 157.
19 Duara 1995, 4, 6.
20 Li 1987, 7–49.
21 Hunt 1996, 9.
22 Ruggie 1993, 174.
23 Macao falls into the same category here.
24 Oksenberg 2001, 87.
25 Schwartz 1968, 284–5.
26 Ibid., 288.
27 Jin and Liu 2009, 243.
28 Watson 1993, 84.
29 Ibid., 82.
30 Schwartz 1968, 286.
31 Shen 2007, 88.
32 Yang 2010, 533.
33 Mao 1978, V, 285.
34 Ibid., VI, 2.
35 Ibid., IX, 302.
36 Ibid., IX, 302–3. Italics added.
37 Chen 2001, 40.

38 PRC Foreign Ministry and Central Documentaries Office 1990, 4–5.
39 Han 1987, 8–14.
40 Clough 1978, 7–8.
41 Chinese scholars of international law have argued that the "five principles of peaceful coexistence" are China's unique and distinctive contribution to international law.
42 Han 1987, 115–16.
43 CCP Taiwan Work Office 1998, 65.
44 PRC Foreign Ministry Diplomatic History Research Office 1993, 107.
45 Ross 1995 (Appendix A), 268.
46 Ibid., 269–70.
47 Ibid. (Appendix B), 274.
48 Ibid. (Appendix A), 271.
49 Deng called *yiguo liangzhi* a "novel thing" of Chinese invention. Deng 1987.
50 Deng 1984.
51 Deng 1987.
52 Hamashita 1997, 123.
53 Qiang 2010, 220–1.
54 Yang 1968, 31–3.
55 Qiang 2010, 159–61.
56 I attribute this point to Iain Johnston.
57 Qiang 2010, 145.
58 Jin 1998, 4.
59 Qiang 2010, 196–7.
60 Executive Yuan Mainland Affairs Council 2011.
61 Three Principles of the People (*Sanmin Zhuyi*) were developed by Sun Yat-sen as a political ideology to make China a free, prosperous, and powerful nation. They are commonly rendered as principles of nationalism, democracy, and socialism.
62 Hughes 1997.
63 Huang 2007, 17, 30, 37.
64 Hughes 1997.
65 Wachman 1994; Rigger 1999.
66 Cited in Shi 2002.
67 Tu 1994b, 10.
68 Lee 1999, 241.
69 Li, Yizhou 2009.
70 Ibid.
71 At one point, Wang was quoted as saying that "One China equals to neither the PRC nor the ROC. Rather, it refers to the mutual constitution of a united China by compatriots from both sides of the Strait; one China is a China not yet reunified, a China that [we] are moving toward." In reference to the English grammar, Wang rejected DPP's interpretation of one China in the past tense and challenged KMT's interpretation in the future tense. He proposed conceiving it as *present progressive*. This unorthodox view, which Wang expressed during his meeting with a veteran KMT politician in November 1997, was quoted in the press only outside of the mainland and caused much controversy within the policy establishment. Zhang 2009.
72 Yan, Anlin 2008.
73 Some of my interlocutors during my interviews in 1998–99 regarded Wang's new thinking as politically irrelevant, pointing out that Wang was a person outside of the establishment (*tizhiwai de ren*). They also revealed that some Politburo members questioned the way in which Wang tried to influence Taiwan policy.
74 Zhang 1998.
75 The CCP–KMT joint communiqué is entitled "Common Aspiration and Prospects for Cross-Strait Peace and Development."
76 Zheng 2005c, 124–5.

77 Zhao 2009b, 76–87.
78 Iain Johnston made this comment at the second workshop on this project at Peking University on 25–26 March 2011.
79 Pye 1990, 58.
80 Osiander 2008.
81 Ruggie 1993, 168–74.

PART II

4

COMPRESSED DEVELOPMENT, FLEXIBLE PRACTICES, AND MULTIPLE TRADITIONS IN CHINA'S RISE

Tianbiao Zhu[1]

China's stunning economic growth since 1979 has been spurred by policies and practices that follow more than one model. China's rise is not the newest incarnation of East Asia's developmental state, following in the footsteps of Japan, South Korea, Taiwan, and Southeast Asia. Nor is China following a liberal model of market capitalism. State power is very much evident in China's rise; but it is the power of flexibility and competitive political relations within the state. Market competition is vibrant; but it is competition that is not based on the rule of law and secure property rights. Instead, I argue, China's rise features a new pattern of compressed development that combines political flexibility with formal policies and informal practices reflecting China's multiple traditions. These multiple traditions are the products of Sinicization processes across time and space. While the other chapters in this volume tend to see Sinicization as "horizontal processes" – that is, the interaction between Chinese civilization and other civilizations – this chapter suggests the existence of "vertical processes" in which Chinese values and practices also interact across time and evolve within the civilization from the past to the present. I argue that China's multiple traditions have been produced by both vertical and horizontal Sinicization processes. As a result, a variety of economic processes of Sinicization will inflect globalization in the same way that Americanization and other civilizational processes have done. The likely outcome will be an economic recalibration and a recalibration of power relations in the global economy rather than economic rupture and systemic transformation.

How China has accomplished so much in so short a time remains a controversial subject. Conventional political economy analysis argues that successful transition from a centrally planned to a market economy has to start with secure private property rights. Yet, during the last three decades China's development has evolved in the context of multiform property rights: even today, private ownership is by no means the dominant form.² Furthermore, China's economic development generates contradictory explanations. For example, some scholars cite economic decentralization as a key factor in China's rapid economic growth.³ Others suggest that it has had no impact whatever.⁴ Still others have pushed the decentralization argument further, to include integration across the Guangdong–Hong Kong border in the south and between the northeast regions of the mainland and Northeast Asia as a key component in China's economic success.⁵

These disagreements and contradictions suggest that we may be well served by adopting a capacious civilizational frame of analysis. Richard Swedberg offers the following definition: "A civilization is a cultural order, to which actors orient themselves and which consists of economic, religious, political, artistic and scientific elements."⁶ People are made in different civilizational contexts, and so are their relationships, on which political, economic, and social organizations are built. In particular, Gary Hamilton argues that the state and economy in Chinese history cannot be understood from theoretical perspectives developed to analyze the state and economy in the West.⁷ For example, concerning the Chinese economy, he notes that "[c]ontracts, property rights, commercial law, and the whole sphere of privileges, rights, and freedom relating to merchants are simply absent in China, while these, in the West, form the very basis of market predictability and continuity."⁸ The organizational characteristics cultivated in civilizational context are the key for Hamilton: while the economy is rule based in the West, it is network based in China. As for the Chinese state, he argues that "political organization in China was not organized as an administrative structure. Instead, the Chinese state is organized as a status hierarchy."⁹ Hamilton's civilizational analysis stresses its dynamic aspects: Chinese values and traditions are not fixed but often interact with other kinds of values and traditions across time and space and therefore evolve constantly.

Thus, we should look not only at organizational characteristics at a given time, but also at both the vertical and horizontal processes of Sinicization that create them – particularly China's evolving multiple traditions. Furthermore, we focus not only on governments' policies but also on people's practices, which contribute to creating and shaping these processes.

With the help of a civilizational frame of analysis, I will discuss compressed development as a new economic trajectory distinctive of China's rise; focus on formal policies and informal practices reflected in China's flexible state; and analyze the private sector and foreign investment flows. Sinicization processes and particularly China's multiple traditions make possible the confluence of these diverse forces and offer hope for the many daunting challenges that await China in the future.

Compressed development

In his analysis of the developmental experiences of Germany and Russia in the late nineteenth century, Alexander Gerschenkron discovered a general tendency that has been observed by many subsequent inquiries into processes of economic development: the later a country starts the process of industrialization, the more organizational power is needed to protect domestic producers against foreign competitors, to mobilize limited capital, and to target those industries that had proved successful for earlier industrializers.[10] First industrializer England relied on firms; later Germany used banks to coordinate its industrialization; subsequently an even more backward Russia turned to the state as the main institution for development. Since 1945 this pattern of late development has persisted, in communist Eastern Europe as well as capitalist East Asia. Communist countries in Eastern Europe pushed organizational power to the extreme in their centrally planned economies. In East Asia, developmental states orchestrated intense cooperation between business and government. In both, the task of the state was similar: large and vertically integrated industrial firms operating in targeted industries pushed forward catch-up industrialization and thus development. Late developers followed a well-marked path and organized human and physical resources to meet specific targets. Institutionalization, standardization, and rule-based bureaucratic operations were their hallmarks. The logic informing late and – in subsequent analyses of East Asia – "late-late" development is compelling. The experience of early developers can serve as a useful guide for latecomers. Unnecessary mistakes can thus be avoided and shortcuts to development sought out. The later a country begins to industrialize, the more its economic power needs to be concentrated.

The acceleration of globalization since the 1980s has greatly altered the economic conditions facing China and other late-late developers. This has given rise to compressed development as a new development paradigm.[11] In compressed development, different stages and sequences of development are collapsed into one single point in time. As a result, developing countries face very different international and domestic conditions than did late developers only a few decades ago. Globalization and attendant technological change create a fragmentation of national patterns of production and are conducive to the organization of cross-national value chains. National economies thus find it difficult to focus solely on national resources and still develop rapidly. Through traditional means such as technical learning and reverse engineering, late developers adopted codified technologies and know-how from foreign producers. In the era of compressed development, late-late developers are fully integrated into the global economy in real-time production systems.

Developing countries thus can find themselves in simultaneously unfolding processes of industrialization and de-industrialization. As the first industrializer, Britain's development unfolded over the span of a century and a half, reversing to de-industrialization in the 1960s. In the cases of South Korea and Taiwan, both began their industrialization in the 1960s, but were well on their way to de-industrialization three decades later. The turning point from industrialization to de-industrialization appears to happen at ever lower levels of gross domestic product (GDP) in the developing world. Thus, different stages and processes of development, which happened sequentially in the era of late development, are now likely to occur simultaneously with compressed development.

Compressed development is inevitable given the ever widening development gap. As developed countries entered the stage of de-industrialization, most developing countries continued to struggle with their large and backward agricultural sectors. But unlike in the era of late development when developing countries would have a single goal of industrialization, developing countries under compressed development no longer need to focus on one goal. To continue industrializing, to directly develop the service sector, or to do both at the same time, are both choices and challenges. Globalization – particularly the accelerating development of new technology, new business models, and new economic activities that increasingly connect people all over the world – has been the main accelerator for compressed development.

Furthermore, traditional, modern, and postmodern values and practices co-evolve in the unfolding process of compressed development. In certain rural areas of a developing country, for example, it is still common for families to arrange their children's marriages; at the same time in the same country, gay couples may have already lived together in major cities. This means that compressed development also has important human and social dimensions. Many developing countries are now facing a "double burden of disease": on the one hand, under-nutrition and communicable diseases usually associated with under-development are still largely present; but on the other hand, over-nutrition and non-communicable diseases, previously limited to the developed world, appear ever more frequently in the developing world as well. In addition, compressed developers are facing a double challenge for education: while building basic education to fulfill the basic needs of development, modern production systems and global value chains exert increasing pressure to secure the educational foundations for advanced knowledge and specialist skills.

Since the 1980s, globalization has set the stage for compressed development in East Asia. Self-contained, national industrialization is no longer the single most important goal of development. Indeed, nationally and vertically integrated production systems are facing strong challenges from global value chains. To gain competitiveness, some parts of those systems have dissolved into horizontal, global production processes. Late development's strong emphasis on heavy industry has gradually given way to multiple sectoral developments. And at the same time, high-tech and service sectors of the economy have become increasingly important. This is a typical result of new global development of information and communications technology, the rapid extension of global value chains into various business activities, and global-scale flows of financial and human resources. Throughout East Asia, the conditions for development thus have shifted profoundly.

China, between 1949 and 1979, was a typical late developer. The central planning system allocated all national resources. Through collectivization in rural areas and nationalization in cities, it extracted most of the agricultural surplus and transferred it to nationalized industrial firms in targeted industries. Prices for industrial products were intentionally set high to extract consumer surplus for industrialization, and the government controlled foreign trade very strictly to shield domestic producers from foreign competition. In short, at the center of the central planning system, the Chinese state organized the economy and carried out catch-up policies.

Then, after 1979, came a fundamentally new and different set of economic reform policies that have allowed China during the last three decades to traverse the path from late development to compressed development. The central planning system has gradually declined in importance. Rather than a single-minded focus on great leaps in industrialization, China is practicing simultaneous development in multiple directions, from heavy industry to multiple sectors, and from state ownership to multiform property rights. From 1978 to 2008, the share of the agricultural sector in total GDP declined from 28.2 to 11.3 percent; the numbers for the industrial sector are 44.1 and 42.9 percent respectively, not much change; and the share of the service sector has increased from 23.9 to 40.1 percent.[12]

Flexible politics

Flexible politics lies at the heart of China's compressed development. And flexible politics results from the specific characteristics of the Chinese state. Shaoguang Wang argues that the Chinese state is marked by a notable lack of capacity.[13] He notes that "[t]he Chinese state is often viewed as a machine whose parts all mesh smoothly. In fact, the system of central control and coordination is largely a sham."[14] Arjan Haan disagrees strongly when he emphasizes, instead, the ability of the central government to both select and enforce policy priorities and to deal with emerging problems.[15] Alvin So shows that the economic role of the Chinese state resembles East Asian developmental states more than Western liberal ones.[16] And Dali Yang argues that Chinese state capacity is altered rather than weak or strong: "the government structure has been reconfigured much more closely along the lines of a regulatory state."[17] Finally, Yi Feng's research alerts us to the risk of viewing state capacities in a static framework.[18] The political capacity of the Chinese state is not fixed. It varies across reform programs and issue domains. Market-oriented reforms tend to reduce, non-market reforms to enhance state capacity. And the extractive capacity of the Chinese state has improved since the 1990s, while its redistributive capacity has not.[19]

The empirical record lends support to some of these arguments. For example, the central government's failure to lower unemployment or to reduce coal production support Wang's claim.[20] While some scholars believe that China's industrial strategy has been induced by globalization,[21] others insist that the core of Chinese industrial development has always been self-reliance.[22] A close examination of China's industrial policy in several key sectors, and of China's recent reform of the economic super-ministry, the National Development and Reform Commission (NDRC), shows that the Chinese state is still far from establishing itself as a reliable regulatory state.²³ And China simply does not look like a developmental state. In Christine Wong's words:

> At present, the capacity of the central government to direct economic and social change is constrained by: the large regional disparities in economic development and human resources; a broken intergovernmental fiscal system that is unable to support national policy implementation; accountability mechanisms that are weak or non-existent throughout the administrative structure, having been severely eroded by long periods of inadequate finance during which local governments and public institutions could not be held accountable for results; an information system that is very weak from disuse; and a bloated bureaucracy where authorities are fragmented, and the transmission of policies and resources are complex and unreliable. Most of all, the government is hobbled throughout the whole administrative apparatus by agents whose (own) revenue hunger dominates decision-making.²⁴

This is not to suggest that arguments concerning specific policy actions are leaning systematically towards one side or the other. During the 1990s, for example, the central government's campaign to downsize local governments often resulted, paradoxically, in expansion rather than reduction of local public employment.²⁵ Yet Kai-yuen Tsui and Youqiang Wang conclude that during the very same decade, the central government regained fiscal control over local governments.²⁶

Most importantly, scholarly controversies and contradictory empirical trends show the primacy of a flexible politics that does not march to only one drum. China does not resemble any successful state we have seen before. It is neither a regulatory nor a developmental state. Jude Howell calls it instead "a polymorphous state that reveals contradictory features of developmentalism and predation, rivalry and unity, autonomy and clientelism, efficiency and inefficiency, across time and space."²⁷ Detailed studies on industrial and technology policy point to China's enduring trait of flexible politics. At the same time, these policies promote a strategy of specialization and comparative advantage and support vertically integrated "national champions."²⁸ They do not yield either a strategy that exploits fully economics of scale and scope, as in South Korea, or one that takes advantage of a network-type economy, as in the Taiwan case.²⁹

Flexible politics requires "policy stretch."³⁰ In compressed development, governments face various challenges on multiple fronts not sequentially but simultaneously. This condition encourages flexible adaptation, experimentation, and improvisation, rather than the fulfillment of planned targets. Here, the comparison with Russia is instructive. In their periods of transition, David Ellerman points to the different reform programs as the main reason for Russian failure and Chinese success.³¹ China's policy stretch and penchant for flexibility was more suited to reform than was Russia's reliance on socially engineered neoliberal reforms. Indeed, Lucian Pye was prescient when he pointed in the late 1980s to exceptional flexibility as the most distinctive feature of Chinese pragmatism:

> [T]he remarkable capacity of the Chinese political culture, more than other political cultures, to be flexible and adaptable, to allow leaders to proclaim policy reversals without apologies, and to insure the equanimity of the public in accepting such reversals and new departures. The history of Chinese politics is one of sudden zigs and zags in announced policies. It is not just that new leaders bring new policies, but the individual leaders have no strong obligations to be consistent.[32]

Political leaders and bureaucrats may well differ in how far they will push flexibility; but they are all experts at bending rules and finding practical solutions. And they are all quick learners. In such an environment, it is difficult for the Chinese state to develop standard bureaucratic operating procedures. Rules are difficult to establish and enforce. Even basic operations of government, such as collecting taxes and data, turn out to be extremely difficult and cumbersome. However, when it faces major economic challenges, the Chinese state typically adapts quickly to new situations, and learns quickly to deploy new tactics and find practical solutions.

China's biggest economic challenge, in the late 1980s and early 1990s, serves as a good example of flexible politics in action. After opening up and decentralizing the economy for a decade, China entered an unstable phase of economic growth. Prior to the initiation of reforms, the government had ruled the economy largely through administrative control. Collectivization in rural and nationalization in urban areas had centralized economic affairs in the hands of the state, which mobilized resources from all areas by administrative orders. The economic reforms initiated after 1978 decentralized economic decision making and thus reduced the resources controlled by the central government. State investment, revenue, and expenditure fell consistently throughout the 1980s. The result was rapid but unstable growth and a weakening of state power. Economic decentralization gave local governments strong incentives to promote locally controlled industrialization, leading to overall rapid economic growth; but the loss of administrative orders as the tool of economic control for the central government meant that this growth was unregulated and not planned at the national level. Redundant and excessive investment overheated the economy, generating both rapid growth and rising inflation, which eventually triggered social and political unrest in 1989. Political recentralization of power and control in 1990 temporarily brought down both growth and inflation. When China recommitted itself to the reform course in 1992, economic instability and inflation quickly returned. However, in the span of only four years, the central government realized that the old tool of administrative orders was no longer appropriate for regulating an increasingly market-oriented economy and quickly learned new tactics of macroeconomic adjustment through fiscal and monetary policy. This approach brought down inflation without diminishing overall economic growth in the 1990s, preventing a similar crisis from recurring. This brief chronology of numerous turnabouts illustrates the remarkable adaptability and learning ability of the Chinese state.

China's fragile financial system and the problem of non-performing bank loans provide a second illustration of flexible politics. At the end of the 1990s, non-performing loans were variously estimated to amount to fully one third of total loans, leading to predictions of a collapse of the Chinese banking sector. In response, the Chinese government transferred more than US$350 billion, about a third of GDP, into the state banking sector. The government also encouraged banks to reform and restructure by offering a mixture of carrots and sticks, adopting laws that allowed them to raise a large amount of capital in domestic and foreign markets on the one hand, and disciplined bank lending practices on the other.[33] These policy moves undertaken in an atmosphere of crisis again illustrated the ability of the Chinese state to adapt flexibly to a major economic challenge. Barry Naughton concurs when he writes:

> The point is not that China has no problems. For certain, China has many serious problems. But the record so far indicates that along with problems, the Chinese system also has the capability to focus policy-making ability and substantial resources on a few of the most serious problems, once they have been able to identify them as problems. ... [o]nce the alarm bells are ringing, the system has an ability to respond and put out fires.[34]

The rapid expansion of China's private sector offers additional opportunities for flexible politics serving the purpose of social control.[35] The government has perfected what Xiaoguang Kang and Heng Han call a system of graduated control of social organizations.[36] Graduated control divides social organizations into different categories, ranked both by their ability to challenge the government and by the value of the public goods they provide. The government represses politically hostile organizations; it turns trade unions into quasi-governmental organs; and it closely supervises religious organizations. Its political flexibility limits the ability of social organizations to challenge state power and also provides these organizations with different levels of support based on the value of the public goods they provide. For example, the government often encourages and supports business and commercial associations as well as official non-governmental organizations (NGOs).

Flexible politics rests on the premise of a Chinese state that is internally differentiated and not a unified actor. Some scholars have used the concept of "fragmented authoritarianism" to describe China's bureaucratic politics,[37] suggesting that policy implementation is a process of redefining policy content by various vertical agencies and spatial regions. "[O]utcomes," Andrew Mertha writes, "are shaped by the incorporation of interests of the implementation agencies into the policy itself."[38] Political flexibility results from the confluence of two apparently contradictory tendencies. For normal problems, binding rules lead to the "fragmentation" of policy implementation at the bottom of the Chinese power hierarchy. In contrast, the country's most serious problems are given priority attention at the top, with high costs for top-down implementation. Put differently, flexible politics yields two patterns. Bureaucratic fragmentation is the day-to-day business of the Chinese state; priority enforcement is reserved for extraordinary challenges given the high associated costs.

The political relations between the center and periphery also provide a good illustration of China's flexible politics. Since the beginning of economic decentralization in the early 1980s, local governments have been of increasing importance for China's economic development. Indeed, decentralization has been one of the key factors in China's economic reform,[39] allowing reform experiments to take place beyond the strongholds of the government's central planning agencies. Naughton characterized this process in China's development as "growing out of the plan."[40] Over time, local governments in China have come to account for more than 70 percent of total government expenditure.[41] Adam Segal and Eric Thun argue that "local governments do not simply try to reproduce and catch up with development efforts initiated by the central government, but are often the actual architects of growth, designing and implementing development policies that are conducive to local institutional frameworks and specific development needs."[42] They go on to point out that even at the local level, there is no "one size fits all" development policy in China: local governments have to pay attention to the specific needs of the industrial sectors that dominate the local economy.[43] In a recent study of infant mortality rates at the provincial level, for example, Hiroko Uchimura and Johannes Jutting argue that provinces that are fiscally more independent from the central government perform better than those that are fiscally more dependent.[44] Decentralization gives local governments more flexibility to find appropriate solutions to local problems. Flexible politics is the crux of both the central government's role in regulating and adjusting central–local relations and the centrality of the private sector's activities for local governments. Policymakers in the central government are keen to retain flexibility in their relations with local governments. Yongnian Zheng notes that "the leadership's priority is to promote economic development rather than to divide power between the center and the provinces and among the provinces. To do so, it has to adjust continuously its relationship with the provinces and mediate the relations among the provinces in accordance with changing circumstances."[45] And in her analysis of central strategies in China's fiscal reforms, Jing Zhan argues that "the central government's agenda-setting power and bargaining tactics allow it to initiate reforms that address the problems, sometimes in experimental, micro steps, before they turn into disasters that threaten the political and economic regime."[46]

In sum, flexible politics has driven China's economic development in the last decades. Using the automobile industry as a case study, Wanwen Qu argues that central and local governments and actors are connected by tight feedback loops.[47] Specific agencies of local governments have supported the development of local automobile industries, in particular the Geely Company. Their efforts were directed explicitly against the stated development strategy of the central government, which sought to encourage the establishment of joint ventures with foreign automakers. When local automobile programs proved to be a success, the central government changed its strategy and endorsed local initiatives. Rule-breaking at the local level and the ability to learn and adjust at the center are key features of China's flexible politics.

Private economy and foreign investment

A vibrant private economy and the influx of a large amount of foreign investment have been at the center of China's economic rise after 1979. Russia's recent history tells us that the declining importance of the central planning system does not always give rise to a vibrant private sector. Differences in the speed of China's and Russia's transformations mattered, but so did the specific nature and context of the private economy and foreign investment.

China's economic gradient runs roughly along a north–south axis. In China's north, state capital continues to dominate the economy. In the middle, township and village enterprises (TVEs) are widespread. In Jiangsu Province, for example, most TVEs are collectively owned enterprises (COEs) with a strong presence of local governments – which were even at times directly involved in running the operations of these enterprises, especially in the 1980s. Further south, in Zhejiang Province, COEs operated largely autonomously from local governments, embedded in a sea of many small private enterprises. Even further south, in Guangdong Province, local governments took a back seat as foreign capital established itself as a dominant economic force. Put boldly, moving from north to south, the presence of the state in the economy weakens, and the role of the private sector grows in importance. Those three provinces are also the richest in China.

However, within the areas in which the private sector dominates, there exist significant differences. In Zhejiang and southern Jiangsu, most COEs and small private enterprises are village- or family-based, located in rural areas. To build up such enterprises often required an entire village or area to contribute financially. Usually these firms produced light consumer goods or industrial parts for domestic producers. Capital accumulation typically relied on kinship ties and extended social networks, which also played a key role in sales. Commerce thus often started with associations and specific localities.

In Guangdong, social networks also played an important role in promoting the development of the private economy. However, these networks were not local or familial but transnational, linking localities to sources of overseas Chinese capital. Before 1997, foreign direct investment (FDI) from overseas Chinese communities (in Hong Kong, Macau, Taiwan, and Southeast Asia) amounted to about 70 percent of total FDI that China received.[48] In the beginning, most of those overseas Chinese investments poured into special economic zones in Guangdong and Fujian Provinces. Later, they spread out to other areas and provinces. Most private enterprises built up with foreign investments were export-oriented. While COEs and small private enterprises in Zhejiang and southern Jiangsu produced for the domestic market in the beginning, private enterprises based on overseas Chinese investments in Guangdong and other places served as the very first link between China and the world market.

Starting in the 1990s, both state capital and the private sector faced new challenges and opportunities. Large state-owned enterprises (SOEs) organized themselves into enterprise groups, hoping to enhance their international competitiveness based on economics of scale. Many large- and medium-sized SOEs formed joint ventures with large foreign companies; small SOEs were simply privatized. Meanwhile, various governments and private actors increased their efforts to attract FDI, as China (normally behind the USA) has become one of the two top FDI receivers in the world. On average, FDI as percentage of GDP in China has been consistently much higher than in its East Asian neighbors during their high growth periods.[49] Some large COEs formed joint ventures based on FDI. Foreign-invested firms have been producing about 40 percent of China's GDP and almost 55 percent of its total trade;[50] in terms of manufactured exports, they accounted for nearly two thirds of China's total.[51] China's rise to the leading exporter of the world was thus powered by foreign investments.

Furthermore, FDI became more evenly distributed across China's coastal areas. Many small private enterprises in these areas joined the production network of international retailers and brand name merchandisers. Since it has massive numbers of small- and medium-sized enterprises, mostly privately owned and located in rural areas, especially in the southeast, China has become a preferred location for these companies. With many small producers, large retailers and brand name merchandisers can use their economic power to drive production costs down by playing one firm off against the others. And in terms of the cost of change, small producers are able to more flexibly accommodate the requests of these big companies than are large producers. Flexible production thus goes hand in hand with small-firm economies, as is true of the private economy in southeastern China.[52]

Cheap labor is a vitally important guarantee for the uninterrupted and growing inflow of FDI and for the adoption of flexible methods of production. Rural migrant workers, experiencing typically harsh work conditions, low pay, and few if any rights, have been the main source of China's international comparative advantage. Since they come from all over China, especially from central and western China, they are both a low-cost basis for foreign investors and a key linkage between coastal and inner China.

Large population and excessive labor supply are certainly one reason for cheap labor, but the Chinese household registration system (*hukou*) also plays a role. The system was originally put in place to divide rural and urban areas and to control the population movement between them under the central planning system. After the reforms began, the *hukou* policy acted to "regulate" the movement of rural migrant workers. In the 1980s, there was a large movement from inner to coastal China, with COEs as the main destination; from the late 1980s, large numbers of rural migrant workers moved into major cities to work in the service sector. Because of the *hukou* system, rural migrant workers have been treated differently from the locals, particularly in their extremely limited access to education, health care, and retirement pensions. For a rural migrant worker, the choice seems to be either to return to where he or she came from, or to accept low wage levels and poor working conditions in order to earn some money. The result is what Mark Selden and Jieh-min Wu called "the incomplete proletarianization of rural migrant workers,"[53] which has played a key role in driving down labor costs in China. Together with a large number of unemployed from state and collective enterprises, rural migrant workers formed a large informal economy from the mid-1990s. In a series of papers, Philip Huang studied this informal economy,[54] arguing that by 2008, workers with little or no security of employment, social benefits, or protection of labor law (his definition of informal economy) have accounted for 182 million, or 60 percent, of the 302 million workforce.[55]

While the formal policy of *hukou* helped to keep labor costs low, the informal practices of local governments contributed to the flourishing of private business and inflow of foreign capital by offering cheap land. In China, peasants only have user rights over land, which is owned by the collectivity; but it is not sufficiently specified how the collectivity is represented and operates. This has led to massive requisitions of land by local governments for development – in particular, the offering of cheap land to attract business and investment. Sales of that requisitioned land have become an important source of local government revenue; one estimate puts it at 37 percent of total village government revenue.[56] The central government has tried to prevent this abuse, trying more than half a million corruption cases and investigating 3,800 government officials between 1999 and 2002.[57] Yet, this practice continues, with an estimated 40–50 million or more peasants having lost their land.[58]

Both cheap labor and cheap land have favored extremely rapid development of China's private economy and foreign investment. Between 1989 and 2006, both the average growth rate of output value and total sales for private enterprises were about 50 percent.[59] According to the most recent comprehensive economic survey done by China's State Statistical Bureau in 2008, the shares of state capital, collective capital, legal entity's capital, individual capital, and foreign investor capital (including those from Hong Kong, Macau, and Taiwan) in total paid-in capital are 33.4, 3.0, 25.5, 22.9, and 15.2 percent, respectively.[60] Parts of the legal entity's capital can also be accounted for as having private and foreign origins. If we also consider the crucial contribution of foreign-invested firms discussed earlier, together these figures show that the private sector comprises about half of the Chinese economy and represents its most dynamic part. Clearly, the informal economy and informal practices have played a pivotal role in China's rapid economic growth. Philip Huang noted:

> What is distinctive to the Chinese system is the very high degree of informality in its actual operation. Such informality exists in any system, but rarely to the extent of the Chinese system. The formal system in China occupies a relatively small proportion of the total national economy, and is often very

much just for looks rather than for real (though perhaps an expression of an ideal for the future): the operative reality at present is primarily informal rather than formal.[61]

It should be noted that China is not only one of the top countries in terms of attracting foreign investment; it has also rapidly become one of the world's largest foreign investors. Since China's adoption of the "going-out" (*zouchuqu*) strategy as its national development policy in 2000 and 2001, the outflow of Chinese capital has been rapid. From 2000 to 2009, the annual growth rate of China's outward foreign investment was an astounding 67 percent. By 2008 China had become the largest foreign investor among developing countries, with its outward foreign investment reaching $56.5 billion a year later. This made China the fifth largest foreign investor in the world (after the USA, Japan, France, and Germany).[62] One estimate puts China into the number one place in 2015 if the annual growth rate can be kept at 30 percent.[63] China's MNCs (multinational corporations) are the extension of the Chinese economy into other parts of the world. For example, the multiple ownership character of the Chinese economy also appears in the formation of China's MNCs.[64]

China's multiple economic and political traditions

The flexible practices of state and economy are rooted in China's past, which is marked by multiple economic and political traditions. Those traditions are reflected in both vertical and horizontal processes of Sinicization. While the interaction between Chinese and other civilizations is shaped and reshaped by traditional values and practices, those values and practices themselves have passed from the past to the present. Over the centuries and millennia of China's history, economic and political developments have centered on alternating swings of centralization and decentralization.

Karl Wittfogel's analysis of oriental despotism, more than any other scholar's, has built an argument around the centralization tendency in Chinese history. He argued that because China's vast arable land of grain production required collective and centralized efforts to prevent floods and to build irrigation system and canals, the rise of a despotic state was inevitable.[65] This was particularly true in northern China, along the Yellow River, the site of early kingdoms and empires. Without exception, the kings and emperors in China's history have endorsed agricultural production as the foundation of the country. However, it is often forgotten that there was also a tendency toward decentralization. Political and economic inventions and interactions along the edge of the empire had a chance to gain strength when empires and kingdoms weakened; at times, indeed, the dynamism of the borderlands helped bring about imperial collapse. Along the northern border, nomads often engaged in military action with the empire, conquering all of China on two occasions (the Yuan dynasty by the Mongol, 1279–1368, and the Qing dynasty by the Manchu, 1644–1911). Along the southeastern coastal areas of the empire, there was often a flourishing of foreign trade and internal commerce, to which we will turn shortly.

In terms of production modes, this centralization and decentralization can be approximately understood by using Hill Gates's idea of the division between "the tributary mode of production" and "petty capitalist mode of production."[66] The former is associated with the centralization tendency and is characterized by the non-market mechanism of surplus extraction, in which imperial officials extracted tribute from peasants in rural areas and directly controlled the production of goods and services in cities. The latter is associated with the decentralization tendency, and features family- and kinship-based organization of business and commodity production for market.

Chinese commerce and petty capitalism date back to the Song dynasty in the tenth century. Ever since Southern Song (1127–1279) established its capital in Linan (today's Hangzhou, the provincial capital of Zhejiang) in the early twelfth century, the Yangtze River delta (today's Shanghai, southern Jiangsu, and Zhejiang) has been among the most prosperous places in China. Family- and kinship-based commercial networks and commodity production played the key role in the wealth accumulation of those areas. From the mid-Ming on (around the turn of the sixteenth century), most widely traded commodities increasingly became differentiated products through brand names and other markers.[67] As argued before, this type of commodity development and small producers fit together perfectly. Thus, family- and kinship-based commercial networks and commodity production continued to flourish, especially in the Yangtze River delta.

Gary Hamilton argues that the organization of economic activity in China today largely follows this pattern.[68] Furthermore, based on previous research on commodity chains and production systems, he points out that with the features of product differentiation, brand name merchandisers, and small producers, this "buyer-driven commodity chain" always has a production end characterized as a "flexible production system." Thus, today's flexible production of China's private economy in response to compressed development has a clear historical origin.

It should be noted that the economic practices of the Yangtze River delta survived even the heydays of the central planning system in the 1950s and 1960s. The private economy in Wenzhou (a region in Zhejiang Province) is a case in point.[69] Despite strong pressure for collectivization, an experiment with private household farming took place in Wenzhou's Yongjia County as early as 1956. Experimentation with private business and petty commodity production became ever more common throughout the pre-reform period. Higher levels of government sent work teams made up of outside cadres, which normally stayed in Wenzhou for short periods. Only during those brief periods were local cadres purged and private local development stopped. But since local cadres were in full agreement on furthering the interest of their local communities, life returned to "normal" after the outsiders had left. Under Mao, the central state could only interrupt, not stop, the development of Wenzhou's private economy.

Wenzhou is not an isolated case under the central planning system; some scholars have also noted the wide spread of TVEs in Jiangsu and Zhejiang during the Cultural Revolution.[70] Peasants were able to take various opportunities to run small businesses and engage in market activities, which "laid more solid foundation for the development of TVEs in Jiangsu and Zhejiang than in other places."[71] Based on that tradition, the private sector flourished after 1979. More importantly, since TVEs were always collectively owned, their survival in those areas did not mean the survival of the private sector. Instead, the private sector and the central planning system worked out a compromise. TVEs were officially not encouraged or even allowed; but since they were not serving private ends, they survived the Cultural Revolution. Today, SOEs and COEs continue to be present in the Chinese economy, reflecting new kinds of compromises under changed conditions – evidence for the multiple traditions of China's economy.

China's opening to the world economy after 1979 is another illustration of its multiple traditions. The growth of a Chinese diaspora outside of mainland China is a historical process that can be traced back to the twelfth century.[72] The trade links between the coastal areas of mainland China and Southeast Asia flourished for many centuries, with the overseas Chinese as the crucial linchpin. Foreign trade revenue was an important source of finance for the Song government.[73] By the end of the Song period, about 100,000 Chinese had already migrated to Southeast Asia, and the number increased to one million in the mid-nineteenth century.[74] Between the Opium War (1839–41) and the mid-twentieth century, China's opening reached new heights, economic links were established with most parts of the world, and Southeast Asia, Europe, and North America, among other places, became destinations for Chinese migrants. One estimate puts 12 million overseas Chinese by the end of this period, creating a solid foundation for the Chinese diaspora we are seeing today.[75] This diaspora has also been helping the outflow of China's foreign investment. In 2008, Asia alone took 71.4 percent of China's total outward FDI stock, and the main receivers are Hong Kong, Singapore, Vietnam, Indonesia, Thailand, South Korea, Macau, and Japan – all inside the Chinese diaspora.[76]

A second tradition points to economic closure. With the idea of agriculture as the foundation of the empire, emperors in Chinese history always had a suspicious attitude towards commerce, especially for foreign trade, fearing it would bring instability. From the late fourteenth century on, China closed its ports to private maritime trading activities, allowing only government-controlled foreign trade. Although the enforcement of this closure policy varied, the Ming (1368–1644) and the Qing were normally regarded as periods of contraction for maritime trade, especially compared with the expansion periods of the Song and the Yuan.[77] In brief, history reveals multiple traditions in China's engagement with the world.

The central planning system built after 1949 was a closed economic system in which foreign trade and investment did not play an important role. During the Cultural Revolution, an overseas connection of any kind could be considered politically suspicious, resulting in almost complete cutoff of China's linkages to the overseas Chinese communities. Since 1979, China has once again rebuilt its linkages. The capital of the Chinese diaspora was the ignition that kick-started Chinese investment and growth. Even after the financial crisis of 1997, many estimates put overseas Chinese investment at or slightly below 50 percent of the total.[78]

Chinese politics is marked by analogous swings between centralization and decentralization. "War making" and "state making" are close cousins, as Charles Tilly famously put it. Periods of state formation typically initiate movements toward bureaucratic centralization.[79] This logic also holds for processes of state formation in early China. Five hundred years of military competition among independent political entities during the Spring and Autumn and the Warring States periods stands as the longest period of decentralization in China's recorded history. When the Qin state emerged as the winner in 221 BCE, the Chinese state with a large standing army, professional bureaucrats, and clear division of labor among various government agencies looked like a centralized set of institutions reminiscent of the state we know today. After this point, long stretches of Chinese history were relatively centralized, stable, and peaceful. This is not to say it has been politically centralized all along. No single dynasty has controlled China uninterruptedly for more than 300 years. During the dynastic changes, there were often wars and separations, the longest separation being close to 170 years. Yet, China has been much more centralized, stable, and peaceful than Europe in the same time frame. David Kang has studied China's foreign relations in the Ming and the Qing (until the mid-nineteenth century), arguing that apart from numerous skirmishes between China and non-state actors along its northern border, the international relations in the Sinic world (including China, Korea, Vietnam, and Japan) and in East Asia have been remarkably peaceful.[80] Only two major wars were fought inside the Sinic world over the span of about five centuries, and about six in all of East Asia, including the Opium War.[81]

Lack of long-term military competition called for a soft governing ideology and a flexible politics. Favoring a more humanistic approach to governance, Confucianism advocated the ideas of benevolent government, loyalty to family and emperor, and a moral society based on governance. Once Confucianism had asserted itself as the governing ideology, politics and governance were widely considered natural. Officials were constrained by Confucian values, which emphasized the moral basis of governance rather than the legal foundation of bureaucratic practice. Lucian Pye notes that "Confucian ideology stressed above all the importance of private morality and public rituals for officials. Individual behavior weighed more heavily than institutional mechanisms or specific public goods."[82] Morality in principle and flexibility in practice have been crucial for the flexible politics we see today.[83] Semi-formal governance by quasi-officials is quite common in today's China. Social disputes at the local level are often resolved by such quasi-officials nominated by communities and endorsed by local governments, practices that date back many centuries.[84]

The above discussion shows that although China was politically centralized for most of its history, in terms of specific governance, it has been very much decentralized due to flexible politics. Of course, this is not to argue that decentralization and flexible politics have persisted throughout history. Between 1949 and 1979, China engaged in late development economic policies with almost exclusive reliance on a central planning system. Both political power and economic decision making were very much centralized, and the political leadership repeatedly created political movements to keep the people in line with the wishes of the Communist Party. Bureaucratic discretion was heavily circumscribed. But even in that period, the power of the central planning system was less than total. For one thing, the system covered less economic ground than in the Soviet Union. By the 1970s, for example, the Chinese system allocated only a maximum of 600 different industrial products; the comparable number for the Soviet Union was 60,000, two orders of magnitude larger.[85] Furthermore, in the vast rural areas, the reach of the state was unavoidably limited. It was quite common for local cadres to act on local needs and interests rather than on policies enunciated by the central government.[86] Finally, since the key characteristic of a moral regime is politicians acting as moral leaders, the Great Leap Forward movement was the beginning of the end of Mao's centralized China.[87]

China's multiple traditions are thus captured by centralizing and decentralizing swings in politics and economics. Those movements reflect both vertical and horizontal processes of Sinicization. Along the vertical line, for example, the petty capitalist mode of production survived in bits and pieces throughout history, reinventing itself again in response to globalization after 1979. Similarly, flexible practices have to face the new situation of compressed development. Along the horizontal line, for example, there were the military interactions between the Chinese empire and nomads and trade links established between China and Southeast Asia. The horizontal processes of Sinicization continue today, for example through capital inflow and outflow, as Takashi Shiraishi discusses in Chapter 5. More importantly, both vertical and horizontal processes of Sinicization constantly overlap. For example, the central planning system may be regarded as a result of horizontal processes of Sinicization in the past; yet as state capital continues to play an important role in the Chinese economy, the values and practices associated with the central planning system have become a part of today's values and practices through the vertical processes of Sinicization. Thus, none of these movements of centralizing and decentralizing swings in politics and economics is mere repetition. There are often new elements of practice and policy that point to the imaginative changes in actor repertoires and new forms of overlay between these traditions. China's multiple traditions are interactive, reinvented, and forever changing.

Challenges for the future

Both vertical and horizontal processes of Sinicization gave rise to multiple economic and political traditions in China, which nurtured flexible practices of the Chinese state and economy and contributed to China's recent economic success in the context of compressed development. This study points to some crucial differences from existing studies. Because most such studies view China through the lens of standard concepts such as late development, property rights, and the developmental state, they generate often contradictory results. I have argued here that these contradictions can be integrated, if not fully resolved, if placed into the perspective of compressed development and the economic and political dialectics that it creates in the era of globalization. With the collapse of distinct development stages and simultaneous and multiple directions of development processes, China's multiform property rights regime suddenly becomes more understandable. And in the context of compressed development, flexible politics appears as a logical strategy to deal with ever more complex economic and social issues.

Today's China faces multiple challenges. Economic and political actors have been doing all they can to stay ahead of multiple and simultaneous developments, and the central government continues to play an important role in managing SOEs and providing direction for China's industrial development. Since 1994 the government has initiated a series of tax reforms to adjust central–local relations, causing many local governments to gradually shift their attention from manufacturing to new service industries. They did so even though the central rather than local governments reaped the largest tax revenues from large-scale industrial production.[88] In 2008, a new Ministry of Industry and Information Technology was set up, linking industrialization to technological innovation, a move that dealt directly with China's growing dependence on global value chains.

Perhaps China's greatest challenge is the country's growing social crisis. Compressed development has always had a social dimension, with the clash of traditional, modern, and post-modern values and practices. Philip Huang has argued that China's economic miracle and social crisis are two sides of the same coin.[89] In order to attract FDI, central and local governments have to keep the cost of land and labor as low as possible. This breeds corruption over land deals, and it spurs social unrest since migrant workers from the countryside are paid very low wages and enjoy neither social benefits nor the protection of China's labor laws. Furthermore, compressed development tends to under-cost and disregard environmental problems, as local governments have no interest in scaring off investors by raising their costs of production. Confronting these challenges, China's policymakers have not been sitting idly by. In October 2006, the Sixth Plenum of the 16th Central Committee of the Chinese Communist Party recognized that China is facing serious social and environmental problems and a growing imbalance between economic and social developments, between urban and rural areas, and among different provinces. The meeting called for the building of a harmonious society to address these problems. In 2008, Ministries for the Environment, Human Resources, and Social Security were created to provide a better focus on environmental and welfare issues. China's top national leaders also made very strong and highly public statements on decreasing social and economic inequalities in early 2011. To date, results of these policy initiatives remain inconclusive.

These challenges are consequences of China's rise. If they create a "threat," it is an internal one for China's compressed development, flexibility politics, and informal practices. Both vertical and horizontal processes of Sinicization, which have contributed greatly to China's recent economic success, point to a strong historical connection for China's rise, making highly implausible the case for a historical rupture brought about by China's rise. At the same time, since those processes are marked by constant interactions of values and practices across time and space, it strains credulity to argue that China could either return to the age of the Middle Kingdom or morph into the economic and political structures and adopt the policies and practices that defined Germany and Japan before World War II. To date, the opportunities and challenges that accompany China's compressed development appear to fully occupy all of the informational and logistical capacities of the Chinese state. And they have created a level of global engagement associated with so many diverse domestic interests and ideas, rooted in China's multiple traditions, that it is difficult to fathom the conditions under which these traditions could congeal to pose one unified international threat. I have argued instead that China's historical evolution has created multiple traditions, which actors continue to reinvent. China's rise will not be a rupture with or return to the past. Rather, it sets the stage for a recombination of old and new elements of Chinese politics and economics. Processes of Sinicization thus are likely to merge China's past, present, and future.

Notes

1 This chapter was written over a span of two years, and many people have made contributions along the way. I would first like to thank the following three groups of people for their thoughtful comments: Peter Katzenstein and all the authors of this volume; the international research team on the concept of compressed development, including D. Hugh Whittaker, Timothy Sturgeon, Mon Han Tsai, and Toshie Okita; and the scholars and students in the 2010 annual conference of the Department of Political Economy at Peking University. I would also like to thank the following individuals for their contributions, suggestions, and help: Steven Balla, Giuseppe Caruso, Jian Chen, Ling Chen, Xi Chen, Miles Kahler, Wendy Leutert, Chen Li, Yang Nie, Greg Noble, Sarah Tarrow, Jiajia Teng, Zhengyi Wang, Nan Xiao, Yongjin Zhang, David Zweig, and the two anonymous reviewers.
2 For a comprehensive review on property rights in China, see Oi and Walder 1999.
3 Montinola, Qian, and Weingast 1996; Feltenstein and Iwata 2005; Zheng 2006.
4 Cai and Treisman 2006.
5 Breslin 2000.
6 Swedberg 2010, 25.
7 Hamilton 2006b, 2010.
8 Hamilton 2006b, 70.
9 Hamilton 2010, 43.
10 Gerschenkron 1962.
11 Whittaker et al. 2010.
12 State Statistical Bureau 2011. Note: The building sector is omitted from the above accounting. Its share in total GDP increased from 3.8 percent in 1978 to 5.7 percent in 2008.
13 Wang, Shaoguang 2003.
14 Ibid., 40.
15 Haan 2010.

16 So 2009.
17 Yang 2003, 46.
18 Feng 2006.
19 Yep 2008.
20 Duckett and Hussain 2008; Wright 2007.
21 Moore 1996 and 2002; Zhang 2003; Zheng 2004.
22 Kerr 2007; Zhu 2007.
23 Pearson 2005; Yeo 2009.
24 Wong 2009, 951.
25 Burns 2003.
26 Tsui and Wang 2004.
27 Howell 2006, 278.
28 Wang 2006.
29 Steinfeld 2004.
30 Whittaker et al. 2010, 458–61.
31 Ellerman 2010.
32 Pye 1988, 81–2.
33 This discussion is based on Naughton 2007a.
34 Ibid., 198.
35 For details, see Pearson 1997, Kennedy 2005, and Tsai 2007.
36 Kang and Han 2008.
37 Lieberthal and Oksenberg 1988; Lieberthal 1992; Mertha 2009a.
38 Mertha 2009a, 996.
39 Shirk 1993.
40 Naughton 1996.
41 Caulfield 2006, 253.
42 Segal and Thun 2001, 558.
43 See also Thun 2006.
44 Uchimura and Jutting 2009.
45 Zheng 2006, 124.
46 Zhan 2009, 462.
47 Qu 2009.
48 Wang 2007, 46.
49 Naughton 2007b, 404.
50 Xing 2010, 310.
51 Whittaker et al. 2010, 451.
52 Hamilton 2006b, 106.
53 Selden and Wu 2011.
54 Huang 2009, 2010, 2011.
55 Huang 2011, 24.
56 Leightner 2010, 347.
57 Ibid.
58 Huang 2011, 17.
59 Zhou and Xie 2008, 65.
60 From the website of the State Statistical Bureau: http://www.stats.gov.cn/tjdt/gjtjjdt/t20091225_402610100.htm, accessed on February 15, 2011. "Paid-in capital" is the capital received from investors when the business is registered, and it shows the nature of the ownership when the business starts.
61 Huang 2011, 21.
62 All above figures come from the following references: Blanchard 2011, 93–4; Lu 2010, 5; MCC 2010, 5–10; Yao and Li 2011, 127.
63 Lu 2010, 5.
64 In 2008, limited liability companies ranked number 1 in terms of foreign investment, ahead of SOEs and privately owned enterprises. See Tian 2011, 380.
65 Wittfogel 1957.

66 Gates 1996.
67 Hamilton 2006b, 109.
68 Ibid., 102–3.
69 Liu 1992.
70 Qi and Chen 2001, 87–8; Ma 2005, 114.
71 Ma 2005, 114.
72 Arrighi et al. 2003; Arrighi 2009.
73 Zhang 2002, 128.
74 Jia and Shi 2007, 99.
75 Ibid.
76 Tian 2011, 380.
77 Arrighi et al. 2003.
78 The fact that investment from Hong Kong and Taiwan dropped to under half of total FDI to mainland China after 2000 may actually not point to a significant decline in ethnic Chinese investment. Such investment, as officially computed, is based on the country of legal origin, such as the USA and Singapore. In any case, one estimate puts Hong Kong's and Taiwan's share at 40 percent of China's total FDI after 2002; 50 percent of total numbers of foreign-invested firms; and 60 percent of total FDI during the entire reform period starting in 1979. See Wang (2007, 46) and Long, Zhao, and Ding (2008, 11).
79 Tilly 1975, 1985, 1992. See also Vu 2010 for a general review of processes of state formation.
80 Kang 2010b.
81 Ibid., 83.
82 Pye 1992, 15.
83 Flexibility alone can easily result in corruption and rent-seeking activity, which serve the personal interests of bureaucrats. Thus, flexibility must go hand in hand with officials' commitment to moral principles. There have been a number of studies suggesting that the CCP has played a key role in disciplining government officials and therefore in limiting corruption (e.g. Shevchenko 2004; Yang 2004; Li and Zhou 2005). Confucian officials have both a sense of superiority over others in society (probably in part due to their status as the most educated group) and a sense of responsibility to serve the empire. They consider themselves as the best people to do the job. Such attitudes come from the Confucian morality of right and wrong. It is this cultural legacy which continues to provide Chinese officials with the concept of "public interest" and the Chinese state with the "will to develop," keys to distinguishing the Chinese flexible state from predatory, rent-seeking states often found elsewhere in the developing world.
84 Huang 2008.
85 Naughton 2007b, 62.
86 Shue 1988.
87 See Shih (1994) for a good discussion on the decline of China's moral regime during the Great Leap Forward.
88 Zhan 2009, 455.
89 Huang 2009, 2010, 2011.

5

THE RISE OF CHINA AND ITS IMPLICATIONS FOR EAST ASIA[1]

Takashi Shiraishi

The sheer size of the Chinese state and economy, and their increasing weight in global and regional affairs, have significant bearing on the behavior of neighboring states and the way in which East and Southeast Asia are organized. "Sinicization" is a useful term for describing the changes in the structures and processes by which states and economies interact in the context of an increasingly important China. These changes are generally beneficial for the Chinese state and for state corporations that move some of their operations abroad. What these players are doing is to create a milieu outside China that is familiar to them so that they can operate more comfortably and perhaps more effectively. Decades ago, Japanese and Americans did the same thing; the difference is that China is a latecomer in a field in which rules and competition are well established in some countries, while remaining in flux in others. Something similar can be said about region making: Chinese players have arrived at the table at a time when ASEAN has been in place for decades, enabling both Americans and Japanese to establish complex relations with these states. China's rise recalibrates power and market relations. It does not rupture or replace them.

In 1980 – a little over a year after Deng Xiaoping's Chinese Communist Party decided on reform and opening – China's economy was valued at $202 billion, or just 19 percent of the Japanese and 7.3 percent of the US economy. Twenty years later, it had a GDP of $1,198 billion, which was 26 percent of the Japanese and 12 percent of the American GDP. By 2010 it had reached $5,879 billion, surpassing Japan's.[2] Trade levels, which were $115 billion in 1990 and $474 billion in 2000, reached $2,207 billion in 2009.[3] This dramatic increase represented a 15 percent annual rise over the 30-year period ending in 2009, when China surpassed Germany as the largest exporter in the world.[4] China's foreign reserve expanded from $166 billion in 2000 to $1,809 billion in 2008, overtaking Japan as the government with the largest foreign reserves in the world.

In the years of its spectacular economic expansion, China's interdependence with the global economy deepened considerably. Its trade dependence increased from 12.5 percent in 1980 to 44.3 percent in 2009, peaking at 67 percent in 2006 before the global financial crisis hit.[5] In the East Asian region, China is the largest trading partner, both in exports and imports, with Japan and South Korea. It is the third largest importer for Indonesia, the Philippines, Thailand, Vietnam, Laos, and Cambodia, and the fourth largest for Singapore. In addition, it is the largest exporter for Myanmar and Vietnam, the second largest for Indonesia, Thailand, and Laos, the third largest for Malaysia and Singapore, and the fourth largest for the Philippines.[6] China's trade with all the ASEAN countries expanded from $35 billion in 2000 (which was 27 percent of Japanese and 26 percent of US trade with ASEAN), to $231 billion in 2008, surpassing Japan to become ASEAN's largest trading partner.[7] China's defense budget has also expanded by more than 10 percent annually since 1991 (when it was $6.2 billion) and reached $70 billion in 2008, while the US Department of Defense estimates that Chinese defense expenditures were $90 billion in 2005 and $140 billion in 2008. It is far less than the US defense budget, which was $529 billion in 2006, but far larger than Japan's, which stood at $44 billion in the same year. The expanding defense budget enabled China to modernize its military, beefing up air and space, naval, and cyber capabilities for its "anti-access" strategy and embarking on the production of aircraft carriers, next-generation jet fighters and missiles, and stealth bombers.[8]

Given China's stunning rise, it is not surprising that many books and essays have been published under such titles as *China's Rise*, *China's Ascent*, *China Rising*, *Power Shift*, *Power Transition*, and even *Pax Sinica*.[9] But power shift in the sense of hegemonic shift has not happened, is not happening, and will not happen for many years to come, if it ever does. By looking at the global context, John Ikenberry,[10] for instance, has persuasively explained why this is true. His basic argument is that global institutions, supported by a broad coalition of states, are already in place; any attempt on China's part to radically transform these institutions is likely to meet with strong resistance from the coalition of states that have a stake in maintaining them. At the same time, there is no denying that the changing distribution of wealth and power caused by the rise of China and other "emerging" countries is transforming the region of East Asia and, more broadly, the world.

How is the region changing with the rise of China? How do states in the region respond to rising China? What are the transnational effects of the rise of China – the flows and movements of people, goods, capital, and firms beyond China's borders? This chapter addresses these questions from three vantage points. First, in light of regional economic development, the end of the Cold War, and the transformation and rise of China, it examines what changes the regional system has undergone over the last three decades. Second, it analyzes the response to a rising China from the perspective of various states in Southeast Asia. Finally, it examines China's economic cooperation, and its transnational political and economic significance and impact in the region. My main focus is on Southeast Asia and

Japan, as this is the area with which I am most familiar. In addition, available research allows scholars to undertake fruitful comparisons across the whole region.

Viewing China's rise and its implications for the regional order from the perspective of Southeast Asia and Japan offers a different picture from that painted by China specialists, who interpret China's rise as a sign of a Sinocentric order in the making.[11] This type of interpretation owes more to ungrounded assumptions of China's centrality than to evidence of actual developments and impact on the ground. International relations specialists tend to examine China's relations with other states in bilateral terms,[12] while security specialists focus on the security implications, mainly from the perspective of power transition.[13] Political economy experts approach China's rise in terms of trade, investment, and regional architecture building.[14] The multi-sited, regional, and cross-disciplinary analysis I advance in this chapter offers a more complex and nuanced understanding of the current developments, showing that East Asian states are in fact not simply engaged in either balancing or bandwagoning with rising China in a realist sense. It reminds us that states do not behave in isolation from other states, and their behavior cannot be understood purely in terms of their dyadic relations with one another. Moreover, state and national interests are not written in stone, but are shaped by domestic politics as well as by the opportunities for and constraints against linkages and alliances posed by the regional system.

The evolution of the regional system

In the concluding chapter of *Network Power: Japan and Asia*, Peter J. Katzenstein and I examined the historical trajectory of the East Asian regional system up to the mid 1990s.[15] Fashioned under American hegemony in the early Cold War years, its organization was informed by two strategic decisions. One strategy was double containment: containing the Soviet Union and communist China on the one hand, while also containing Japan. This was achieved by integrating Japan's military power into the US-led regional security system. The regional hub-and-spokes security system was built on this strategic decision. The other strategy was the fashioning of a triangular trade system of the USA, Japan, and Southeast Asia (and later Taiwan and South Korea). Japanese business wanted to trade with China in the early years of the Cold War. But the USA did not want the containment of China to be undermined. The USA encouraged Japan to go south, eventually leading to the creation of a system of triangular trade among the USA, Japan, and Free Asia (minus Japan).

China was not part of this evolving trade system, but a series of developments in the 1970s prepared the ground for its integration. After China normalized its diplomatic relationship with the USA and Japan in the early 1970s, Deng Xiaoping obtained images of late twentieth century modernity during visits to New York City and Tokyo.[16] From 1978 onwards, China embarked on modernization, initiating its own version of productivity politics – which meant reforming its socialist economy while opening and integrating China with the regional trade system.[17]

China has posted high economic growth rates every year since then. There was a setback in 1989, when the movement for democracy was quashed by the return of conservatives. But with Deng reconfirming his commitment to the country's modernization in 1992, China regained its economic momentum.[18]

Domestic political and economic factors have no doubt been crucial for this transformation. But it was also a product of the politics of integration – part of the invitation for China to develop, as Mark Selden[19] argued – supported by the USA. Regional economic development from the mid 1980s to the late 1990s, which was crucial for East Asian regionalization, also worked for China's transformation and development and led to the integration of China, above all its coastal regions, into the regional economy.

That China successfully transformed itself from socialism to socialist market economy turned out to be crucial for the survival of other socialist states in its vicinity. Both the dynastic party state in North Korea and the military junta in Burma/Myanmar survived while becoming increasingly dependent on China. Vietnam followed in China's footsteps, transforming itself from socialism to socialist market economy through its Doi Moi economic reform. And the region, once bifurcated in the 1950s and 1960s along Communism versus Free Asia ideological lines, became increasingly integrated in economic terms in the 1980s and 1990s.[20]

These developments led to the evolution of an East Asian regional system that is structurally different from the European one. Toward the end of the 1980s, democratic revolutions took place in Eastern Europe, from one country to another, culminating in the collapse of the Berlin Wall, unification of Germany, and disintegration of the Soviet Union. These changes soon led to the North Atlantic Treaty Organization (NATO) expansion as well as the deepening and expansion of European integration and bloody civil wars in the former Yugoslavia in the 1990s.[21] Nothing of this sort took place in East Asia. Democratic transformations did evolve in the 1980s, not in socialist countries but in America's client states such as the Philippines, South Korea, and Taiwan. Although there were democracy movements in China and Burma, no socialist state in East Asia collapsed. Instead, China and Vietnam transformed themselves from socialist party states into socialist market economy party states. Until recently, Myanmar remained under a military junta. And North Korea has survived under a dynastic party state while developing missiles and nuclear bombs, and desperately hoping to cut a deal with the USA.

In the post-Cold War era, China and Vietnam, if not Myanmar and North Korea, have thus come to be integrated into the regional and global economy, while remaining outside the US-led regional security system. This development has created a tension in the regional system that will mount structurally as China rises. Yet, the system has been stable for three reasons. First, the USA has remained engaged in the region, with the US–Japan security alliance, the backbone of the US-led regional security system, redefining its mission not only for Japan's security but also for the region's security and stability. Second, China – its party and state – set economic development as its highest priority, followed Deng Xiaoping's dictum of "hide and bide," and opted to change the regional system from within.

And finally, there emerged a regional political project of building an East Asia community in the wake of the 1997–98 East Asian economic crisis. This happened in part to create a mechanism for regional cooperation, especially in currency, as a hedge to the kind of US intervention that Indonesia, Malaysia, South Korea, and Thailand had experienced; and in part to promote trade and investment in the region in view of the stalling of WTO negotiations and the transformation of the regional triangular trade.[22]

China's emergence as an economic powerhouse was crucial to the change in triangular trade. In the wake of the East Asian economic crisis, Japanese, South Korean, Taiwanese, and other firms reorganized their regional production systems. Producing capital and intermediate goods in their home countries and their production bases in Southeast Asia, they assembled final products in China for export to US and other markets. As a result the triangular trade system, which had consisted of Japan, Asia (minus Japan), and the USA, came to be organized with China, Asia (minus China), and the USA as its three pillars. This change led to the expansion of Chinese exports to the USA and the EU, while the intra-regional trade in capital and intermediate goods expanded between China and the rest of Asia.

The Chinese government also embarked on engaging neighboring states in the wake of the East Asian economic crisis. China normalized its diplomatic relations with its neighbors in two waves: with the USA, Japan, Thailand, Malaysia, and the Philippines in the 1970s, and with Brunei, Indonesia, Singapore, South Korea, and Vietnam in the early 1990s. The Cold War ended just as the USA and its European allies were imposing economic sanctions on China in the wake of the Tiananmen incident. Its diplomatic normalization with East Asian states, as well as the invitation of the Japanese emperor as its state guest, were in part efforts to break free from international isolation.

The 1990s, however, also saw the emergence of two thorny security issues between China and its East Asian neighbors. One concerns Taiwan. Tension between China and Taiwan mounted in the mid 1990s, with the first Taiwanese presidential election. China organized military exercises in Taiwan's vicinity, exerting pressure in the hope of influencing the election outcome. The USA sent aircraft carriers. The USA and Japan also redefined and expanded the mission of their alliance. These developments marked the beginning of China's anti-access strategy.

In addition, there was the issue of territorial disputes with China's neighboring states. China occupied the Paracel Islands in 1974; but it had no physical presence further south until 1988, when its navy took South Johnson Reef. In 1992, China enacted the Law on the Territorial Sea and the Contiguous Zone, in which its "territorial land" was defined to include "the mainland and its offshore islands, Taiwan and the various affiliated islands including Diaoyu Island, Penghu Islands, Dongsha Islands, Xisha Islands, Nansha (Spratly) Islands and other islands." China also embarked on its military modernization and redefined the PLA mission as the maintenance of the maritime environment and defense of maritime interests.[23]

The enactment of the Law on the Territorial Sea and the Contiguous Zone instantly created territorial disputes in the South China Sea between China on the one hand and Vietnam, Brunei, Malaysia, and the Philippines on the other. Vietnam and China scrambled to occupy as many features in the South China Sea as they could in the same year. Tensions mounted between China and Vietnam over oil exploration, prompting ASEAN to issue a declaration of concern urging the parties involved to exercise restraint and settle their disputes peacefully.[24] In 1995, however, while advocating a bilateral approach in settling the disputes, China occupied Mischief Reef, which is claimed by the Philippines.

The ASEAN Regional Forum (ARF) was established in 1994, in part to engage China in a multilateral framework. Initially, China was not an active participant. It did not want the Taiwanese question to be raised there, it chose to deal with territorial disputes in the South China Sea bilaterally, and it did not want its freedom of action to be constrained multilaterally in a framework dominated by the USA and Japan. Toward the end of the 1990s, however, China adopted a new security concept that led to the establishment of the Shanghai Cooperation Organization (SCO) in 2001, and to its multilateral engagement of its neighbors in East Asia. China also became active in creating a framework for East Asian economic cooperation. In 1999 it proposed the institutionalization of financial cooperation with the APT (ASEAN Plus Three) as the framework. China also agreed to hold a summit meeting of China, Japan, and South Korea in the same year and to institutionalize it the following year.

In 2002, China and ASEAN concluded the Framework Agreement on Comprehensive Economic Cooperation and the Joint Declaration on Cooperation in the Field of Nontraditional Security Issues. China and ASEAN also signed the Declaration on the Conduct of Parties in the South China Sea as a guideline for inter-state behavior until agreement could be reached on a more formal code of conduct. The situation in the South China Sea stabilized. In 2003 China signed the Treaty of Amity and Cooperation in Southeast Asia – ASEAN's signature pact of association. In 2004 China and ASEAN upgraded their relations to "enhanced strategic relationship." This took the form of a five-year Plan of Action (2005–10), which included a joint commitment to increase regular high-level bilateral visits, cooperation in the field of non-traditional security, security dialogue, and military exchanges and cooperation.[25] Put differently, China engaged ASEAN in the creation of a free trade area, promoted economic cooperation, and largely succeeded in calming fears of China as a threat.

Against this background, China – its party and state leadership – adopted the policy of building good relations with its neighbors and making them its partners. Here, partnership is understood as both bilateral and multilateral. The APT emerged as a major mechanism for China to address regional issues and to engage ASEAN and other neighboring states in the regional architecture building without US participation.[26] This policy also informed the Chinese approach to Japan. In 1999, China agreed to a summit meeting of China, Japan, and South Korea when the APT summit was held. At President Jiang Zemin's meeting with Prime Minister

Mori Yoshiro in New York, Jiang told Mori that Asia could not develop without Sino-Japanese friendship and cooperation. Prime Minister Zhu Rongji stated in the same year that regional economic cooperation was an important area of collaboration, expressing his hope to promote China's cooperation with Japan in the region of East Asia. On this occasion, Prime Minister Koizumi Junichiro welcomed his statement and called for East Asia community building, appreciated the role China was playing in regional cooperation, and underlined that the rising China offered opportunities – and not a threat – to Japan.

This does not mean that everything proceeded as China hoped. Japan, together with Singapore and Indonesia, proposed the establishment of an East Asia Summit with the ASEAN Plus Six (China, Japan, and South Korea, plus Australia, New Zealand and India) as a counterbalance to the APT. Despite China's protests, Prime Minister Koizumu made annual visits to Yasukuni Shrine for the war dead. The deterioration in the Sino-Japanese relationship manifested itself in anti-Japanese riots and demonstrations in China in 2004 and 2005. This prepared the ground for the rapprochement under President Hu Jintao and Prime Minister Abe Shinzo in 2006, the agreement on the Sino-Japanese strategic relationship of mutual interest, and the participation of Japanese firms in natural gas field development in the East China Sea under President Hu and Prime Minister Fukuda Yasuo in 2007.

China's new policy initiatives, combined with its economic rise, have enhanced its presence in the region. Its trade with its neighbors has been expanding steadily. Its tourists are visiting neighboring countries in ever increasing numbers. It actively promotes economic cooperation in infrastructure developments such as highway construction, power plant building, and power grid construction, especially in the Greater Mekong sub-region (GMS). China's rise no doubt beckons with all the opportunities it offers for neighboring states, industries, firms, and individuals to benefit economically. At the same time, however, China's effort to safeguard its security by developing what it considers a reasonable force structure to deter the USA has created insecurity among neighboring states, especially those states that have territorial disputes with China. China has emerged as a global and regional power in the Group of Twenty and APT. Yet, China has engaged its neighbors in the APT processes in part because the USA is not part of those processes. There is no sign of a change in China's position on what it defines as "core" issues. In fact, the issues defined as such have increased in recent years. All of these manifestations of China's rise bring up questions and concerns relating to whether China pursues exclusive regionalism, whether China is intent on creating a Sinocentric sphere in East Asia, what would be its structure, and whether China envisions a multipolar world in which this Sinocentric regional sphere exists side by side with the US-led sphere and the EU.[27]

Against this backdrop, China's neighbors have come to be increasingly concerned about China's assertiveness. Although China watchers disagree about its causes, the fact remains that China has become assertive in the South and East China Seas. Carl Thayer documents the development in the South China Sea well. Suffice it to note here that China's increasing advances in maritime territorial claims in the South China Sea have led to frictions with Vietnam and the Philippines and made it a source of "serious concern," in the words of Indonesian President Susilo Bambang Yudhoyono. China's National People's Congress decided to create a county-level town in Hainan province, with administrative responsibility over the Paracel and Spratly islands. The Vietnamese government announced that, in 2009 alone, China had seized 33 Vietnamese fishing boats and 433 crew members in the maritime area both states claim. All of the claimant states except Brunei have built structures and garrisoned the features they occupy.[28] Tensions over territorial disputes have also mounted in recent years in the East China Sea between China and Japan, leading to the Japanese government's 2010 decision to enhance its naval and surveillance capabilities in its southwest region and to station troops on small islands there.[29]

The USA has also become more actively re-engaged in East Asia. In his November 2009 speech in Tokyo, President Barack Obama reconfirmed US engagement in East Asia as a Pacific nation. At the July 2010 ARF meeting in Hanoi, US Secretary of State Hillary Clinton stated that the USA, "like every nation, has a national interest in freedom of navigation, open access to Asia's maritime commons. The United States supports a collaborative diplomatic process by all claimants for resolving the various territorial disputes without coercion." When China sent warships to disputed waters and staged massive naval exercises in a show of force, the USA dispatched an aircraft carrier to the South China Sea off Da Nang. And most recently, Clinton, speaking ahead of President Hu Jintao's state visit to the USA, announced that "there is no such thing as a G-2" and reaffirmed the US policy of improving its links with its allies and partners.

A series of developments on the ground have also confirmed US re-engagement in East Asia: the resumption of military exchanges with Indonesia as well as US provision of patrol boats to the newly established Indonesian coast guard; the launch of Vietnam–US defense policy dialogues at the deputy ministerial level; the second US–ASEAN Leaders Meeting; the US agreement to provide India with sensitive missile and civilian nuclear technology; and security policy dialogues at the deputy ministerial level between the USA and the Philippines. It should also be noted that the USA is not only re-engaging with Southeast Asia, but is also more willing than the previous administration to participate through multilateral channels.

The deepening of the US commitment to the Asia-Pacific is also evident in trade. The proposed Trans-Pacific Partnership (TPP) free trade framework originally surfaced in 2006 as a four-nation economic partnership agreement involving Brunei, Chile, New Zealand, and Singapore. The USA, Australia, and Peru expressed their willingness to participate in the new regional trade architecture, embarking on negotiations in 2010 to subscribe to the TPP. As a pathway to achieving a new Asia-Pacific-wide free trade and investment area, the TPP initiative may become as important as, or even more important than, the APT framework advocated by China and the East Asian Summit (EAS) backed by Japan.

The region of East Asia thus finds itself between two superpowers. The global financial crisis has accelerated China's rise, military modernization, and influence in regional affairs. The USA has responded by beefing up its military presence and re-engaging with East Asia. These forces have led to friction in the maritime domain and strategic competition for influence.[30]

The global crisis also provided an opportunity for regional states (as well as firms) to assess the direction of the regional trade system. When the crisis hit in 2008, it was said that East Asia was at a crossroads in shifting its economic growth from the export-oriented economic development model to the domestic demand-led growth model. The US market would remain depressed for quite some time and could not be expected to serve as the engine for East Asian economic growth on the demand side. The Chinese government pumped in a huge amount of money to stimulate domestic demand in the wake of the collapse of Lehman Brothers in 2008. The Chinese economy rode over the crisis in less than a year and came back to the growth path. But it is clear by now that China's domestic demand remains as such: it has not translated into expanding exports from the rest of Asia. China's market for final goods from the rest of Asia remains as small as South Korea's. Its industrial upgrading has led to expansion in the domestic production of intermediate goods at the expense of imports from its neighbors, especially ASEAN countries. This means another transformation for the triangular trade that had developed in the wake of the 1997–98 crisis, wherein China may become more self-sufficient while the USA remains as important a market as in the past.[31]

In regional cooperation, ASEAN insists on its status as the hub in region making, whether through APT or EAS. Interestingly, however, ASEAN decided to expand the EAS to include the USA and Russia, in addition to the previous ASEAN Plus Six. ASEAN has also sought to develop regional security architecture, such as the ARF and more recently the ASEAN Defense Ministers' Meeting Plus (ADMM-Plus) process, which puts ASEAN in a position to set the agenda and to make decisions.[32] Key Southeast Asian states have reacted by adopting self-help measures to shore up their defense capabilities, while aligning themselves with the USA and its allies to pursue hedging strategies as a response to the geopolitical transformation now unfolding in the Asia-Pacific.[33]

Japan has also reaffirmed its alliance with the USA, after Prime Minister Yukio Hatoyama briefly flirted with the idea of an East Asia Community as a way to make the triangular relations among Japan, China, and the USA "equilateral." This is clear from Prime Minister Naoto Kan's January 2011 foreign policy speech in Tokyo, in which he reaffirmed the Japan–US alliance as the cornerstone of Japanese foreign policy, while adding, "At the same time, there are areas in China's strengthening of its national defense in which transparency is somewhat lacking, and we are concerned by its increasingly ambitious maritime activities." Kan did not refer to Hatoyama's East Asian Community initiative.

All of these developments have led to a recent shift in the framework for regional cooperation from East Asia back to the Asia-Pacific. In 1997 the APT started to promote regional cooperation in response to the currency crisis and heavy-handed

US intervention, evolving as a major mechanism for regional cooperation while keeping the USA out. Now, however, China's assertiveness has caused concern for many states in the region – especially those that have territorial disputes with China – leading them to align themselves with the USA and its allies while expanding the framework for regional cooperation back to the Asia-Pacific, of which the USA is a part.

This may change if China redefines its position on territorial sovereignty issues. Though this is not the place to examine why China puts such importance on territorial sovereignty, one wonders whether tranquility in the South and East China Seas is more important to its long-term national interest than is its sovereignty over the maritime sphere. As Carl Thayer sensibly points out, China has much to gain through joint development of maritime natural resources, and much to lose through continued confrontation with ASEAN, not to mention the USA and Japan.[34] For now, however, tension has mounted between the regional security and the regional trade systems, not only as China becomes more assertive in territorial issues, but also because it briefly deployed trade (the export of rare earth) as a foreign policy instrument to impose its will on Japan in a territorial sovereignty issue. As tension has mounted, US allies as well as some others have aligned themselves with the USA, while engaging China multilaterally and seizing opportunities offered by China for economic gains. China, on its part, promotes economic and trade cooperation in order to break what it calls containment. This underlines the fact that China's rise is mainly economic. The states in its vicinity certainly want to gain from its economic rise, but as soon as they feel threatened by China, they align themselves with the USA and its allies. The regional framework for cooperation is flexible enough to swing back and forth between East Asia, where the USA is excluded, and the Asia-Pacific, where it is included. East Asian regionalism has been shaped by a history of small and middle powers having to negotiate between at least two great powers.[35] The regional system, despite its inherent structural tension, has much staying power in the region of East Asia/Asia Pacific.

Comparing individual state behaviors

The previous section examined the significance of China's rise in the evolution of the regional system in East Asia, arguing that although China's rise does not threaten the long-term staying power of the regional system, its economic emergence has made China a major trading partner for all the states in the region. China's rise has also transformed the triangular trade system and encouraged East Asia's heads of states, prime ministers, and ministers to visit China far more often than, say, in the 1990s. Bilateral economic and political relations between China and all the neighboring states are clearly expanding significantly.

The question is how states in this region have handled their relations with China, and how to account for their behaviors. International relations experts tend to employ words such as soft-balancing, limited alignment, and hedging, as well as accommodation and bandwagoning (the last two of which are off the mark);

but these descriptions are too blunt to capture their behavior in any nuanced way, and do not have explanatory power. The same is true of simplistic notions of Sinicization which assume that influence radiates only outward from a China that is rising and remaking the East Asian milieu in its own image. What follows is an attempt to describe and analyze the behavior of Thailand, Indonesia, Vietnam, and Myanmar comparatively in light of the positions they occupy in the regional system, their embeddedness in the regional and global economy, and their domestic political structures.

Thailand

With its capital of Bangkok, Thailand serves as a major hub in mainland Southeast Asia. It is a hub that links maritime Asia with the mainland world of Cambodia, Laos, Vietnam, and Myanmar. It is a hub to link with Kunming in China's Yunnan Province through the north–south highway via Laos, and with Da Nang through the east–west highway via Laos and Cambodia. And it will be a hub to link with Saigon and Phnom Penh to the east and the port city of Dawei in Myanmar to the west through the south–south highway now under construction.

Thailand is a long-standing US ally. It co-hosts Cobra Gold which, first conducted in 1982 bilaterally with the USA, has evolved into the largest multilateral military exercise in the region. However, Thailand refuses to allow US weapons stockpiling in its territory, while in recent years conducting regular joint military exercises with China.[36] Thailand has no territorial disputes with China. Its major security threat comes from the domestic insurgency in South Thailand. The country's status as a major hub in mainland Southeast Asia also makes it vulnerable to transnational crimes such as trafficking in weapons, drugs, and human beings. Thai political elites also worry about Myanmar because of its plan to develop missiles and nuclear weapons with North Korean assistance, and Myanmar's inherent political fragility.

The Thai economy is fully embedded in the regional and global economy, with its trade dependence of 107 percent in 2009. Thai trade with China has expanded as China's economy grew: Sino-Thai trade in Thai trade increased from 4.7 percent in 2000 to 11.6 percent in 2009, while Thai–Japanese and Thai–US trade declined from 19.5 and 16.7 percent in 2000, to 14.3 and 8.8 percent in 2009, respectively. Sino-Thai trade expansion is more pronounced in the area of exports. Thai exports to China as a proportion of total Thai exports increased from 4.1 percent in 2000 to 8.3 percent in 2005 to 10.6 percent in 2009, while Thai exports to the USA declined from 21.3 percent in 2000 to 15.4 percent in 2005 to 10.9 percent in 2009. In the meantime, Thai trade with the three ASEAN countries of Singapore, Malaysia, and Indonesia has remained steady, 13.3 percent in 2000 and 13.9 percent in 2009, while its trade with Vietnam has increased in recent years. In short, Thailand, with industrial clusters in metropolitan Bangkok, is deeply integrated in the regional production network. It has no need to worry about its dependence on China, because the expansion of its trade with China almost automatically leads to similar expansion with Taiwan, South Korea, and ASEAN countries. Trade with Japan and the USA has declined, but this represents a more balanced and diversified trade structure.

Thai domestic politics is built on its geopolitical and geoeconomic position. Its social and regional divisions – between Bangkok urban middle classes on the one hand, and peasants and farmers in the north and northeast on the other – are now increasingly felt because of the rising expectations of the less privileged. There is broad consensus across pro- and anti-Thaksin political forces that the purpose of politics is economic growth to create jobs, reduce poverty, and improve the standard of living. This explains Thai promiscuousness in free trade agreements (FTAs) and economic partnership agreements in recent years. After all, Thais have little to lose in promoting trade and investment liberalization bilaterally and multilaterally. This explains, for instance, Prime Minister Thaksin Shinawatra's selection of tourism, automotive industry, and agribusiness as the engines of Thai economic development, and his promotion of free trade and economic partnership agreements with China, Japan, and others. The number of Chinese tourists visiting Thailand has increased enormously. China's expanding middle classes promise to be a fast expanding market for Thai agribusiness. As a site of the Japanese FDI-led industrial clusters in Southeast Asia, Thaksin envisioned Bangkok as Asia's Detroit, which would serve as a major hub in the production network of machinery and automotives in East Asia.

China has been instrumental in making Thailand a hub in the region. Thailand obtained concessions to export agricultural products at the start of negotiations for an ASEAN–China free trade agreement. China is an active partner in the GMS development and wants to make it a model for the future China–ASEAN free trade area. And Prime Minister Wen Jiabao in 2005 encouraged Chinese business to participate in the economic development in the GMS countries.[37]

In sum, Thailand welcomes the rise of China. It has promoted trade with China. It has encouraged Chinese tourists to visit Thailand. It worked closely with China (as well as the Asian Development Bank (ADB) and Japan) in the GMS development and the ASEAN–China FTA. A long-term US ally, it has no territorial dispute with China, and it is very well integrated into the regional and the global economy. Being a hub in mainland Southeast Asia, it is in a position to gain from the rising China without any serious concern for risks that this may entail.

Indonesia

Following the collapse of the authoritarian state in the midst of the 1997–98 economic crisis, as well as three parliamentary and two presidential elections, Indonesia has emerged as a stable democracy in recent years. It has overcome the risk of disintegration with the return of peace in Aceh and has succeeded in containing the jihadist threat. The politics of productivity has come to be embraced by the middle class, who now dominate local and national politics, as the Indonesian economy is back on the growth path and as social divisions along ethnic and religious lines are contained locally through radical decentralization and democratization.[38] With experiences and memories of the transition from Suharto's authoritarian politics to the current democratic politics of productivity, a new broad-based consensus has emerged with national unity, integrity, and economic growth as major planks, despite the country's fissiparous party politics.

Indonesia officially maintains a foreign policy of non-alignment. During the Cold War years, however, it was aligned with the USA and Japan when Suharto was in power. More recently, it has begun to reconnect with those two countries in light of China's assertiveness, although it has also actively established strategic partnerships with China, India, Australia, and South Korea. In the case of Japan, this is simply a return to a longtime de facto ally. As the largest market for Indonesian exports, Japan has been Indonesia's closest trading partner since Suharto's era, and it has provided assistance to Indonesia under Sukarno, under Suharto, and in the post-Suharto years.

US–Indonesia relations are more complicated. The relationship deteriorated in the post-Cold War years because of human rights abuses under Suharto, culminating in US sanctions in the wake of the referendum in East Timor and the violent destruction of Dili in 1999. In recent years, however, there has been a dramatic rapprochement. Secretary of State Condoleezza Rice talked about strategic partnership during an Indonesian visit in 2006, and military cooperation and arms sales were resumed. Secretary of State Hillary Clinton visited Indonesia on her first official trip to Asia in 2009. In 2010 the Secretary of Defense resumed the International Military Education and Training (IMET) program with Indonesia's Army Special Forces, the symbol of human rights abuses under Suharto, fully restoring military exchanges between the USA and Indonesia. In the same year, Clinton and her Indonesian counterpart inaugurated the US–Indonesia Joint Commission and issued a Plan of Action to implement the strategic partnership.[39] Indonesia's security policy has been built on assumptions of a US-led regional security system and ongoing US military presence in Asia. Indonesia has not invested heavily in defense, either under Suharto or in the post-Suharto years, and it has only recently started to embark on building "minimum defense capabilities."

Indonesia does not make any territorial claims in the Spratly or Paracel islands, but China's claims to the South China Sea overlap with the Natuna Island's Exclusive Economic Zone (EEZ), an area known to be rich in oil and gas as well as marine resources.[40] A showdown took place there in 2010, between an Indonesian patrol vessel trying to seize Chinese boats engaged in illegal fishing and an armed Chinese patrol vessel that was protecting them. Indonesia lodged a letter with the UN Secretary General declaring China's maritime claims to be illegal under international law. China's assertiveness in the South China Sea as well as Indonesia's territorial disputes with Malaysia, combined with its concern for territorial integrity, maritime security (especially in such areas as the Malacca, Sunda, and Lombok straits), and marine and natural resources in its EEZ led the government under Yudhoyono to embark on building its military, particularly its minimum defense capabilities for maritime security.[41] Although China's recent assertiveness is a source of serious concern, Indonesia is intent on creating a "dynamic equilibrium" in the region and focuses on the long-term strategic implications of China's economic ascent for regional architecture and the purpose and intentions of its military modernization. As President Yudhoyono once said, Indonesia welcomes the rising China, but expects it to play the game by the rules that all agree upon, not by those that China imposes on others.[42]

Indonesia is not as well integrated in the regional and global economy as Thailand is. Its trade dependence was 58 percent in 2000 (in the wake of the 1997–98 economic crisis) and 39.5 percent in 2009 (in the midst of the global financial crisis). Indonesia's trade with China has expanded five times from 2000 to 2009, with China's share in Indonesia's total exports increasing from 4.5 percent in 2000 to 7.6 percent in 2009, and in its total imports from 6 percent in 2000 to 12.8 percent in 2009. But Indonesia has also become part of the regional production network, and its trade with the three ASEAN countries of Singapore, Malaysia, and Thailand expanded from 16.3 percent in 2000 to 27 percent in 2009. Indonesia, like Thailand, does not need to worry very much about becoming too dependent on China.

However, Indonesia does differ from Thailand in one important respect: where Bangkok Sino-Thai middle classes have become an important part of Thai elites, Indonesia's business elite remains divided along ethnic lines between Chinese Indonesians and Pribumi Indonesians. Sino-Indonesian economic cooperation may complicate this ethnic division. We will look at China's economic cooperation more closely in the following section. A quick look shows that President Hu Jintao visited Indonesia in 2005, along with approximately 200 businesspeople who attended a business summit that the Indonesian government had organized on the occasion. Hu and Yudhoyono agreed to expand bilateral trade between Indonesia and China from $14 billion in 2005 to $20 billion in 2008, and to increase investment to $10 billion.[43] Two months later, Yudhoyono visited China and witnessed the signing of economic cooperation agreements worth $7.5 billion for the construction of power plants, railways, oil refineries, and toll roads, as well as the development of an oil palm plantation of 1–2 million hectares. A month later, Vice President Jusuf Kalla's visit resulted in agreements on infrastructural developments worth $4.9 billion. Kalla returned to China in 2006 to conclude an agreement with Chinese firms on a "crash program" of building thermal power plants.

Three features stand out in Sino-Indonesian economic cooperation. First, infrastructural development, especially the construction of power plants, occupies a central place. Second, Sino-Indonesian economic cooperation projects involve Suharto's former cronies. The most salient case in point is the oil palm plantation project in Kalimantan, a joint venture of Chinese state corporation CITIC and Sino-Indonesian business group Sinar Mas, with $500 million in loans from the China Development Bank. Sinar Mas prospered under Suharto, but went bust in the 1997–98 economic crisis. It is now back in business as a partner of Chinese state corporations. And third, although Sino-Indonesian economic cooperation included defense industries, then Indonesian Defense Minister Yuwono Sudarsono pointedly denied its political significance, stating that it did not indicate any shift in its alignment with the USA and adding that Indonesia was willing to cooperate with any state for its military build-up.

In sum, Indonesia, located at a geographical remove from China, is well integrated into the regional and global economy and aligned with Japan and the USA. It sees itself as a power in the region, as confirmed by its G20 membership. Indonesia is active in establishing strategic partnerships with all the powers in the region – the USA, Japan, India, Australia, South Korea, and China – and is intent on building its minimum defense capabilities in maritime security. It welcomes its expanding trade with China for its own politics of productivity. But Indonesian businesses are competing with – and losing to – Chinese businesses in global markets. The ethnic divide among its business elites between ethnic Chinese and Pribumi remains, and may be complicated by murky business deals in Sino-Indonesian economic cooperation projects.

Vietnam

Despite the loss of its most important ally, the Soviet Union, Vietnam has successfully transformed itself from a socialist party state into a socialist market economy party state. Since 1988, it has defined peace and economic development as the foremost strategic objectives for its survival, pursuing economic development and trade and investment promotion for regime stability and legitimacy.[44] Vietnam's foreign policy approach is predicated on this national strategy, with a focus on maintaining peaceful external environments (and solving its territorial disputes with China by peaceful means), opening its economy, diversifying its external relations, integrating with the global economy, and promoting international cooperation.[45]

The Vietnamese economy expanded at 7.25 percent annually from 2000 to 2009, and its per capita income increased from $402 in 2000 to $1,068 in 2009.[46] Its trade dependence surpassed 100 percent in 2001 and has stayed above 130 percent since 2005. As its trade with ASEAN countries stands at 10 percent in exports (to Singapore, Malaysia, and the Philippines) and 18.8 percent in imports (from Singapore, Malaysia, and Thailand), it is now well integrated in the regional production network, with final products destined for the USA and Japan.[47] Vietnam has succeeded in diversifying its trade and no longer needs to fear becoming too economically dependent on China.

How Vietnam handles its external relations can best be understood if we look at the actions of its party and state leadership in 2006, in the wake of the Vietnam Communist Party congress. Nong Duc Manh, who was reelected as Party Secretary, visited China and concluded an economic and technical cooperation agreement with his Chinese counterpart. On the other hand, Nguyen Tan Dung, who was elected as prime minister, visited Japan, signed a joint statement to build a strategic partnership for peace and prosperity in Asia, and agreed to initiate negotiations for a Japan–Vietnam economic partnership.[48] Foreign visits of Vietnamese party and state leaders underline the same point: in 2008–9, President Nong Duc Manh visited China and Japan once each, while Nguyen Tan Dung visited China three times, Japan twice, and the USA once.

Vietnam's deft handling of foreign policy has been rewarding. It has emerged as a major destination for Japanese FDIs at a time when Japanese firms, increasingly worried about their exposure to China risk, are choosing Vietnam as an alternative site for their factories. Vietnam has also become Japan's largest Official Development Assistance (ODA) recipient, with funding for strategic infrastructural projects such as a high-speed train system and a nuclear power plant. Vietnam–US relations have also improved in the 2000s. Its economic relationship was enhanced with the signing of a bilateral trade agreement in 2001 and Vietnam's accession to the WTO in 2007. Prime Minister Nguyen Tan Dung's visit followed in 2008, when President George W. Bush declared the USA's "positive, growing friendship [and] mutual respect" for Vietnam and pledged "support for Vietnam's national sovereignty, security, and territorial integrity." The 2010 US Quadrennial Defense Review stated that Vietnam was a country with which the USA sought to build a "new comprehensive partnership," and the Deputy Assistant Secretary of Defense and the Vietnamese Deputy Defense Minister held the first formal defense dialogue in the same year.[49]

China has loomed large in recent developments in Vietnam–Japan and Vietnam–US relations because of its proximity, size, and rising economic power, combined with the history of invasions and punitive actions. Since the 1990 Sino-Vietnamese summit in Chengdu and the comprehensive political settlement of the Cambodian conflict a year later, Vietnam and China have established a semblance of normalcy in their relationship. But the fundamental problem of asymmetry haunting Vietnam will never go away,[50] despite its efforts at soft-balancing.

Vietnam has tended its relationship with China since the diplomatic normalization in 1991, regarding China as a "good friend, good comrade, good partner and good neighbor" and upgrading its relationship to a partnership in comprehensive strategic cooperation. Agreements were signed on land borders, and the two countries agreed upon high-level talks to define maritime borders with the goal of making the South China Sea "the sea of peace, friendship, and development." At the same time, Vietnam worked successfully to expand the EAS to include the USA and Russia, raised the issue of the code of conduct in the South China Sea at the 2010 ARF meeting, and decided to build a navy shipyard in Da Nang with Russian assistance, to be made available to navy ships, submarines, and aircraft carriers from all states.

In sum, integration into the regional and global economy and political soft-balancing inform Vietnam's external strategy. It is not a US ally, and it still views as a threat the enemy forces that are "abusing democratic freedom, freedom of religion and human rights" to undermine its party state regime. But it also sees its disputes with China in the South China Sea as a risk to its territorial integrity.[51]

Soft-balancing is a way to deal with the asymmetries that haunt it. At the same time, its party state regime stakes its survival on Vietnam's economic development and the expansion of its trade with the external world. Deepening its integration with the regional production network makes Vietnam less dependent on China, while economic cooperation with Japan allows it to build infrastructure such as railway systems, highways, and nuclear power plants.

Myanmar[52]

The military junta that took over the Burmese state in 1988 – blatantly dismissing the popular mandate given to Aung San Suu Kyi's National League for Democracy in the 1990 election and renaming their state "Myanmar" – remained in power for over twenty years. But the establishment of a new government under Thein Sein in 2011 has seen a number of important changes in Myanmar's domestic and foreign policies. The USA and EU have imposed economic and military sanctions on Myanmar, while ASEAN made Myanmar a member and engaged it in the hope that peer pressure will eventually pave the way for political reform. But neither economic sanctions nor strategic engagement succeeded in democratizing Myanmar under Than Shwe. The junta equated itself with the government, and the government with the national state. It saw the US and EU calls for regime change as a national threat,[53] and the US dispatch of an aircraft carrier to Myanmar's territorial waters for disaster relief in 2008 was taken as evidence of that threat. Recent years also witnessed increasingly closer ties between Myanmar and China. This started in 1989 with the visit to China of Than Shwe, then the Myanmar Armed Forces (MAF) deputy chief of staff, and was followed by the signing of a military assistance agreement worth $1.2 billion in 1990.

US and EU economic sanctions, which practically banned FDI from the USA, EU, and Japan, kept Myanmar economically stagnant and isolated from the regional and global economy. Myanmar's per capita income has remained low. Yet its economic stagnation has not translated into social and political crisis. Koichi Fujita's findings are useful to understanding why this is the case.[54] First, although Myanmar's per capita income is even lower than those of Laos, Cambodia, and Bangladesh, Burmese eat and drink as well as Khmers and Laotians and better than Bangladeshis. Second, Myanmar's poor infrastructure in electricity, water, roads, and housing, as well as its international isolation, has made class differences less apparent. People in the upper 20 percent income group eat better than those in the bottom 20 percent, but the differences in their lifestyles are not that distinguishable. Lower income people, for their part, have not developed inflated expectations. These findings in part explain political stability in Myanmar and the junta's staying power.

While China has provided assistance to Myanmar over many years, it acted to deepen its political and economic ties with the junta. Between March 2009 and April 2011, four of the nine members of the Politburo Standing Committee visited Myanmar: Politburo member Li Changchun in March 2009, Vice President Xi Jinping in December 2009, Premier Wen Jiabao in June 2010, and Chairman of the Chinese People's Political Consultative Conference Jia Qinglin in April 2011. During former State Peace and Development Council (SPDC) Chairman Than Shwe's visit to China in September 2010, Chinese leaders pledged major economic and technical assistance to aid Myanmar's development. When Wen Jiabao visited Myanmar, he met with Than Shwe and concluded the agreement on the Myanmar–China oil and gas pipeline construction from Sittwe on Myanmar's west coast to Kunming in China's Yunnan Province. Than Shwe no doubt extracted many concessions from his Chinese counterparts for that construction. Myanmar's oil and gas as well as its hydropower resources are a top focus for China. Once completed, the oil and gas pipelines will boost China's access to crude oil from Africa and the Middle East, and are expected to make China the largest consumer of Myanmar's natural gas by 2013.

The strategic partnership between Myanmar and China is built on China's provision of credit facilities, concessional loans, plant exports, infrastructural development, and military assistance in the name of cooperation. Yet, China is not Myanmar's largest trade partner. Myanmar is economically isolated, and business with its three neighbors of Thailand, China, and India comprises more than 65 percent of its total trade. China is the largest exporter to Myanmar. But Myanmar's largest export market has been Thailand, at 46.4 percent of its total exports in 2009.[55] This is because the first gas pipeline was built from Myanmar to Thailand, and the bulk of its gas is exported to Thailand. In addition, the junta welcomed economic cooperation with Thailand. For instance, Thai Prime Minister Abhisit Vejjajiva visited Myanmar in 2010, meeting with Than Shwe and Prime Minister Thein Sein to agree on projects worth $58 billion, including the construction of port facilities in Dawei, a highway from Bangkok to Dawei, power plants, and industrial estates.

Myanmar has also cultivated its ties with India. In 2006, India's army, navy, and air force commanders visited Myanmar. Myanmar's navy sent a corvette to participate in an Indian-led joint naval exercise in 2006, the first time the navy had participated in an international military exercise. Myanmar also invited Indian navy officers to the Coco islands in the Andaman Sea to show that there was no Chinese PLA radar facility there. More recently, former SPDC Chairman Than Shwe's visit to India from 25–29 July 2010 – his first since 2004 – showcased the two countries' stronger bilateral ties. During the visit, India and Myanmar signed pacts in areas including information sharing, science and technology, and mutual legal assistance in criminal matters. The Indian government pledged $10 million for the purchase of modern agricultural equipment, and India's EXIM bank promised a $60 million line of credit for railway projects. After the visit, Indian state-owned energy companies announced $1.3 billion in planned investment for gas and pipeline projects in Myanmar.

Subject to US-led economic sanctions, isolated economically, and with little political legitimacy domestically, the junta survived in Myanmar because people eat reasonably well, society remains poor but peaceful, the state can earn hard currency by exporting natural gas, and its neighbors provide resources in the name of economic cooperation. China may provide the most assistance to Myanmar and protect it politically in international arenas, but Myanmar is not dependent on China economically and is far from a client state of China, even as some of its areas – notably the Kachin and Shan States that share the border with China – have close economic links with China's Yunnan Province. Thailand remains the largest trading partner with Myanmar because of the junta's decision to build its first gas export pipeline to Thailand. Although a second pipeline is now under construction for gas export to China, the junta organized its first ever joint military exercise with India during the negotiations on its construction. One can easily imagine the building of a third pipeline to link with India. But the new government under Thein Sein has shown signs that it is redefining the purpose of national politics in terms of the politics of economic growth. Myanmar is gearing itself toward deeper integration into the regional and global economy, and is avoiding overdependence on China, as shown in its recent suspension of a huge hydropower dam project funded by Chinese state corporations.

Regional mosaic

It should be clear by now that the state behaviors of Thailand, Indonesia, Vietnam, and Myanmar in the face of the rising China are far more complex than such terms as limited alignment, soft-balancing, engagement, and hedging, let alone accommodation and bandwagoning, can capture. The same is true for conceptualizations that view Sinicization processes as simple, unilinear extensions of Chinese processes and practices. These states' behavior can be better understood in terms of the position they occupy in the regional system and their domestic politics. A long-term US ally without any territorial dispute with China, well integrated in the regional and global economy and well positioned to gain from China's economic expansion, Thailand under productivity politics happily welcomes China's rise. Further south, with a long history of alignment with Japan and the USA, increasingly better integrated in the regional production network, but with legacies of ethnic division among its business elites and rich in natural resources, Indonesia under productivity politics approaches the rising China cautiously. With a long shared border and history of territorial disputes with China, increasingly alarmed by China's assertiveness in the South China Sea, and by now well integrated in the global and regional economy, Vietnam with authoritarian productivity politics welcomes the economic opportunities China offers, but hedges its risk by aligning with Japan in strategic infrastructural development and with the USA in security. And finally, threatened by US-led sanctions, isolated economically, but rich in gas and oil resources, the Myanmar junta had depended for its survival on strategically using its gas exports as a foreign policy instrument to extract aid from China, while cultivating its ties with Thailand and more recently with India. Recent attempts at reform indicate that the Myanmar government has redefined the purpose of its national politics by opting for a politics of economic growth (a politics shared by most of the countries in the region) that has, in turn, spurred the state's efforts to deepen its integration into the regional and global economy as well as use ASEAN as a leverage for its foreign policy. This move also entails lessening its overdependence on China and doing the necessary "homework" to get Americans to lift their economic sanctions. In sum, there is no doubt that ASEAN states welcome the economic opportunities the rising China offers; but they do their best to maintain their freedom of action under conditions imposed by their domestic politics as well as their positions in the regional system. The Myanmar case suggests, in fact, the extent to which an ASEAN state will redefine itself to fit in the current regional system rather than remain outside it.

While it is sometimes said that Japan is the only exception to the bandwagoning and accommodation among China's neighboring states, closer examination again reveals a more complex reality. Japan is a major ally of the USA, and the US–Japan alliance constitutes the backbone of the US-led regional security system. Yet, Japan's trade with China has surpassed that with the USA. Its economy is deeply embedded in the triangular trade structure of China, East Asia minus China (but including Japan), and the USA. Japan therefore does not engage China solely from a bilateral perspective. The Japanese government formulates its China policy within a regional framework, and with the behaviors of other states in that system in mind.

Japanese policymakers work on the assumption that the rise of China (and India) and the relative decline of Japan and the USA will lead to the redistribution of wealth and power in this region, with inevitable impact on the political and economic order. They also assume that these same processes will most likely deepen economic interdependence both regionally and globally. These assumptions shape Japan's policy of maintaining the US–Japan security alliance, keep the USA engaged in the region, deepen regional and global economic interdependence, and promote norm making in the name of an East Asia community building.

This kind of thinking has informed Japan's regional policy over the past ten years, even though emphasis may shift from one administration to another. It should not come as a surprise, then, that Japan under Prime Minister Yukio Hatoyama has explicitly opted for recalibrating the US–Japan alliance while promoting East Asia community building, in part as a way to engage China in a regional multilateral framework. This did not mean a radical departure from Japan's foreign policy in any substantial way, although its political naïveté annoyed foreign policy experts. It is useful to remember that Junichiro Koizumi called for a Japan–ASEAN economic partnership agreement in 2002 as the first step toward East Asia community building. And more recently, Japan is actively involved in the swing of the pendulum back from East Asia to the Asia-Pacific as a framework for regional cooperation. As we saw earlier, Prime Minister Kan's foreign policy speech in January 2011 lent credence to this recent development.

From the discussion above, we can identify three salient factors in shaping states' behavior in this region: position in the US-led security system; degree of embeddedness in the regional and global economy; and achievement of a national consensus on the purpose of politics (productivity politics). None of these factors can be discussed independently of each other.

First, whether an East Asian state is part of, or aligned with, the US-led regional security system is crucial in shaping state security policy with regard to China. As a longtime US ally, Thailand happily engages China. Indonesia, long aligned with Japan and the USA, now wants to strengthen its security ties with both states. Vietnam is consciously cultivating ties with Japan and the USA as a counterweight to China. Myanmar, for now, is threatened by the USA and relies on China for security, while trying its best to lessen its dependence on China by cultivating ties with India.

Second, the degree to which an East Asian state is integrated into the regional and global economy is crucial in shaping that state's trade and economic cooperation policy with regard to China. The cases of Thailand and Indonesia illustrate that the more integrated Southeast Asian countries are into the global and regional economy, the less dependent they are on China, and the more freedom they have to pursue economic cooperation with China without fear of overdependence. Vietnam has succeeded in integrating itself into the regional production system, while Myanmar, for now, remains isolated and relies on energy exports as an instrument of foreign policy.

And finally, the ability of a country's political players to achieve a national consensus on the question of what the purpose of politics is or should be is crucial to state identity and the objectives that the state pursues on the international front. Thai, Indonesian, and Vietnamese politics are predicated on the assumption that economic performance decides the fates of incumbents in Thailand and Indonesia and shores up the legitimacy of the party state in Vietnam. This politics of productivity[56] views the economic rise of China as a welcome opportunity for economic and trade cooperation. In the case of Indonesia, however, such cooperation may be complicated by the problematical position of the Chinese Indonesians in the Indonesian body politic. The fact that Myanmar's political elites are concerned mainly with regime survival means that China's economic cooperation with Myanmar works differently from its cooperation with other neighboring countries. The junta-led Myanmar state itself benefits from this cooperation without the benefits accruing to the society at large, although the new government may face domestic pressure to deliver economic development to boost its legitimacy and popularity.

Transnational effects of China's economic cooperation

The rise of China has transnational effects, as flows and movements of its people, capital, goods, and firms over its borders shape its neighbors' political economies, societies, and cultures. For example, the rise of middle classes in southern China has led to the expansion of jasmine rice production in Thailand.[57] More Sino-Thais are sending their children to Chinese-language schools to learn standard Chinese. The increase of Chinese tourists in Thailand may lead to the creation of

Chinese-language quarters in Bangkok red-light districts, located side by side with Japanese- and English-language quarters. These are all examples of the transnational effects of the rising China.

This chapter, however, looks at the transnational effects of China's economic and trade cooperation for a simple reason. As discussed earlier, China's rise is primarily economic: the most important instrument China can and does deploy to make its leaders' foreign visits successful is its economic and trade cooperation.[58] Through these tools China provides export credits, concessional loans, investments, grants, technical assistance, and even labor for real estate development, building presidential palaces and fertilizer plants, infrastructural projects such as power plants, power grids, highways, bridges, port facilities, and other development projects. I am not interested in assessing their usefulness. Whether useful or not, they have the potential to change the parameters by which states and their leaders define their national interests in this region. Transnational effects here mean this possibility.

Along with the expansion and diversification of its trade and investment, China's economic cooperation has undergone important changes since the 1990s. China started to provide economic and military assistance to Myanmar, Thailand, Vietnam, and other Southeast Asian countries toward the end of the 1990s as part of its neighborhood diplomacy. More recently, it has deployed its economic cooperation as an instrument for natural resources procurement.[59] Its mode of assistance has also undergone change. Joint ventures emerged as an important vehicle for project implementation in the 1980s, in which state corporations and state banks became important players in the 1990s. But now, economic cooperation often means business collaboration in joint ventures in which trade and trade finance, investment, and official assistance (grant and concessional loans) are fused indistinguishably.[60]

It is not surprising, then, that China's state corporations are expanding their business beyond China's borders in the form of economic cooperation, mobilizing export credit facilities, state concessionary loans, and grants for that purpose. Projects of strategic significance, such as the construction of oil and gas pipelines from Myanmar to China, are handled directly by the party and state leadership, as seen in the fact that all the Chinese leaders visiting Myanmar in 2006–10 – Hu Jintao, Wen Jiabao, Xi Jinping, and Li Keqiang – raised it with Than Shwe. In cases of less strategic significance, however, state corporations and banks do business in a milieu in which transnational politico-business alliances of China's party and state officials, state banks and corporations, and their political and business counterparts team up across borders.

Myanmar provides us with good examples. As we saw earlier, Than Shwe visited China in 2003, met with Jiang Zemin and Hu Jintao, and was awarded special credit facilities of $200 million at a time when the total official development assistance from the Organization for Economic Cooperation and Development (OECD) countries amounted to $80 million.[61] Projects thus funded included the construction of power plants and communication facilities. China's investments, on the other hand, focused on oil and gas development. Its investments in Myanmar in 1989–2004 were small, no more than $190 million in 25 cases, which constituted a mere 2.5 percent of the total foreign direct investment of $7.75 billion in the same years. But 14 of 25 cases were in oil and gas development, with a total investment of $160 million.[62] This pattern, it seems, continues today: power plants and other infrastructural projects are implemented as part of China's economic cooperation, while China's state corporations invest in oil and gas and other natural resource-related projects. Thus, CNOOC signed an agreement with the Myanmar government in 2004 for oil and gas exploration in Rakhine State. PetroChina signed an agreement to purchase natural gas from Myanmar in 2005. The plan to build a gas pipeline through Rakhine State to Kunming was raised on this occasion, together with the construction of highways and port facilities.[63] The Myanmar government understood the strategic importance of oil and gas pipelines for China. It also knew that China needed natural resources for its development, and accordingly, it used oil and gas exports to obtain as many concessions as possible.

Against this backdrop, China and Myanmar concluded a series of agreements to build power plants. Myanmar's largest hydropower plant, the Shweli River I Power Station, was constructed under a build–operate–transfer agreement by the Chinese company Huaneng, has an installed capacity of 600 MW, and has boosted Myanmar's hydropower capacity by nearly one third. The project is reported to have cost $440 million. All five of China's state-owned power companies are investing in Myanmar's hydropower sector, and Huaneng has already signed a Memorandum of Understanding (MOU) with the Myanmar government for construction of the Shweli II facility.[64] Data in 2005 also show that Chinese power companies built five plants in 2000–5 with a total power generation capacity of 525 MW, and that six more power plants were under construction with a total capacity of 1,469 MW. With the completion of these projects, Myanmar's power generation capacity is expected to expand from 1,710 MW (as of 2005) to 3,170 MW; the share of power generated by the Chinese-made power plants would increase from 32.5 percent to 60 percent of the total capacity. Myanmar media reports tell us that the 280-MW Ponron hydroelectric power plant built by the Yunnan Machinery Export and Import Corporation cost $800 million, while the 790-MW Yeywa hydroelectric power plant built by CITIC cost $1.35 billion. This suggests that the entire power plant project with a power generation capacity of 2,000 MW implemented in economic cooperation with China is estimated to cost over $4 billion. To put it simply, China's state power companies have gone beyond Sino-Myanmar borders to control Myanmar hydropower resources, making the northern part of Myanmar a part of the Chinese economy.

Something similar but more transparent has happened in China's economic cooperation with Laos. Chinese foreign direct investment in Laos from 1990 to 2006 amounted to $877 million for 236 projects. The Laotian ministry of planning and investment also tells us that firms from 22 different countries invested $971 million in 2006–7, of which Chinese firms invested $496 million. In terms of industrial sectors, Chinese firms invested in 46 out of 140 projects in the mining sector as of August 2006. It is safe to conclude that Chinese firms are major investors in Laos, and that their investment is pronounced in the mining sector.

On China's investment strategy and risk management, we can find a good example in the case of a cement plant project. The funds were provided by the Chinese government to the Laotian government in the form of loans of $177 million – $131 million in concessional loans provided by the Chinese government and $46 million in commercial loans from a Chinese bank – for the construction of a cement plant, a cement sack factory, and coal mining as a package. The Laotian government loaned 40 percent of these funds to a Laotian state corporation and 60 percent to Yichang International Economic and Technical Corporation (YIETC). In short, the Chinese government provided funds, most of them on a concessional basis, to a Chinese firm via the Laotian government as a two-step loan for cement production and coal mining.[65]

An even more politically problematic example is a Vientiane new town development project. To host the Asian games in 2009, the Laotian government obtained loans from a Chinese state bank and contracted with a Chinese state corporation to build a stadium on a plot of land the Laotian government provided for the project. It was also incorporated into a comprehensive "new town development project," the signing of which was witnessed by President Hu Jintao during his visit to Laos in 2006. Modeled after the Suzhou industrial estate development project, the plan was to build a new town of residential, commercial, service, and other areas in suburban Vientiane. The Laotian government agreed to provide 1,600 hectares of land for the project and awarded the right to develop the land over fifty years to a Laotian–Chinese joint venture in which three Chinese state corporations own 95 percent of the stock, while a Laotian state company controls 5 percent.

Why was the construction of a stadium coupled with the development of a new town in suburban Vientiane? A Chinese state bank provides funds for the construction of a stadium, which the Laotian government has to pay back in due course. But the stadium cannot generate any cash income for loan repayment. Herein lies the answer. The Laotian government will share the profit commensurate with the land value it provided for the project – 5 percent – for the repayment of loans, while Chinese state corporations have obtained a large plot of land in suburban Vientiane for real estate development. The announcement of the scheme created a commotion in the Laotian parliament. It was rumored that the new town development project was meant to be a new "Chinatown" development project because tens of thousands of Chinese, both legal and illegal, were living in Laos. The Laotian government backed down, scaled down the development project from 1,600 hectares to 200 hectares, and denied the "Chinatown" rumor.[66]

The cases we examined above in Myanmar and Laos show that China's politico-business alliances, which now dominate its political economy, have gone transnational beyond its borders. Chinese businesses, backed by the mainland government and party officials, are teaming up with local (that is, Burmese and Laotian) politicians and their business cronies. We can speak to some extent of a partial

"Sinicization" of the political economic systems in countries like Myanmar and Laos, which are not very well integrated in the regional and global economy, and whose politics are dominated by the military elite in Myanmar and party cadres in Laos. These are also countries in which Chinese corporations face little or no competition from either local or non-Chinese transnational firms. By partial Sinicization, we mean the exporting from China of a model of business–state alliance that has worked in China over the past two decades and that underpins China's economic cooperation. This model incorporates local players in Myanmar and Laos to create a community of interests that has come to shape the parameters by which the two countries' political elites define their national/state interests. Here, the issue is not one of "collusion" and "corruption," but a question of whether a model that works in China can flourish in neighboring political–economic milieus. In this sense, China's economic cooperation in less regionally and globally integrated countries works differently – and has different effects – than in relation to countries such as Thailand and Indonesia, which are better integrated in the regional and global economy and which have a procedural democracy that promotes the regular turnover of political elites.

Indonesia provides a good case study.[67] As we saw earlier, President Hu Jintao visited and concluded a strategic partnership agreement with Indonesia in 2005. Indonesia's Vice President Jusuf Kalla followed up with a visit to China in 2006, signing an economic cooperation agreement with the Chinese government for the construction of thermal power plants to be completed before the 2009 presidential election, now publicly known as the "crash program." The program did not proceed as scheduled, and most of the power plants remain to be built as of the end of 2009. The question is why it went wrong.

The episode started in 2005 when it was projected that Indonesia, especially Java, would face a serious power shortage in a few years if the Indonesian economy continued to grow as expected. Vice President Jusuf Kalla decided to build power plants with a total capacity of 10,000 MW. He chose to work with the Chinese government for their construction because Chinese state corporations, he said, could provide the plants at a rate that was 30 percent cheaper than their Japanese, European, and American counterparts. The agreement Kalla signed with the Chinese government in 2006 did not require the Indonesian government to provide guarantees for the loans awarded by China's state banks. On the assumption that the entire project's financing would be provided by China, the Indonesian Electric Power Agency invited tenders without Indonesian government loan guarantees; but in the absence of such guarantees, Japanese, European, and US heavy machinery makers did not apply. As a result, all but one of the project contracts were awarded to Chinese state corporations. Once the financing negotiations started, however, Chinese state banks demanded an Indonesian government guarantee, which was extended at Jusuf Kalla's instruction. The Bank of China (BOC) and China Export Import Bank (CEXIM), as consortium leaders, signed loan agreements with the Indonesian government with the insurance provided by Sinosure (China Export and Credit Insurance Corporation) in 2008.

All of the non-Chinese banks were shut out of the project financing because they did not meet the conditions required by Sinosure. The Chinese consortium leaders also demanded a higher interest rate than the Chinese government had initially suggested: over 10 percent on a par with a buyer's credit, because of risk premium, instead of 3–3.5 percent on a par with concessional loans provided by OECD Development Assistance Committee (DAC) member countries. After the collapse of Lehman Brothers, Chinese consortiums again demanded the increase in interest rate, leading President Yudhoyono to instruct the finance minister to review the entire project finance agreement with the Chinese consortiums and look for ways to raise funds domestically. It was also rumored that Chinese plant makers colluded in offering tenders and that they demanded the price increase by 30 percent, thus annulling the price advantage Jusuf Kalla had counted on.

When the program was announced, the total power generation capacity of the Java–Bali power grid was 23,000 MW. Kalla's enormous program envisioned building an additional 7,000 MW of power generation. This included nine projects with the total power generation capacity of 7,145 MW at an estimated cost of $5.9 billion. Two projects were funded by CEXIM, while BOC served as the consortium leader for six projects and another project funded by a Malaysian bank. The contracts for eight Chinese bank-funded projects went to Chinese plant makers, all state corporations (CMC, CNTIC, CMEC, CHD, Sinomach, Chengda, and ZEPC).

Business experts believe that the interest rate for the power plant projects was jacked up because Chinese state banks and insurance firms, inexperienced in international project finance, overestimated the risk premium.[68] They also believe that Japanese, European, and US makers would have offered tenders if the Indonesian government loan guarantee had been in place from the beginning. Indonesia's power plant business had been dominated by Japanese firms since the 1980s, and this was the first time Chinese plant makers had cornered the market. Crucial to this success was their link-up with a powerful Indonesian political ally (Vice President Jusuf Kalla) and the fact that other players – Japanese, European, and US – did not know the Chinese game plan. But this may not happen again, and if China – the government, state banks, insurance firms, and plant manufacturers, that is – plays the same game, other governments, banks, and manufacturers will demand that China play the game by rules that all players agree on.

An instructive example of the potential political fallout of China's economic cooperation is a scandal in the Philippines involving then-President Gloria Macapagal-Arroyo's husband, rival Filipino political elites, and mainland Chinese business corporations. In April 2007, the Philippine government signed a deal with mainland Chinese firm Zhong Xing Telecommunications Equipment (ZTE) to build a National Broadband Network at a total cost of $330 million. About two months later, a newspaper columnist published an exposé of Commission on Elections Chairman Benjamin Abalos's connections with the ZTE deal. Jose de Venecia III, son of the former House Speaker and a major stockholder in the Amsterdam Holdings, Inc., a rival firm that had placed a bid for the project, revealed that First Gentleman Mike Arroyo had told him to "back off" the deal. One of the consultants/liaisons involved in the deal, a Chinese-Filipino named Rodolfo "Jun" Lozada, was abducted by unidentified men, and only the media attention sparked by his wife's public appeal saved him from possible "salvaging" (extrajudicial execution). Lozada blew the whistle on the deal, exposing the web of connections between the ZTE Corporation and the Arroyo family that had led to substantial "overhead" padding of the $330 million deal.

This episode not only exposed the intense competition among Filipino political elite families, but rendered mainland Chinese firms vulnerable to the domestic politics of the country in which they were doing business. The fact that the rival political family of the de Venecias also had connections with another mainland Chinese firm headed by a "princeling" (that is, a child of high-ranking Communist cadres who goes into business by using his or her familial political connections) – in this case no less than Chinese president Hu Jintao's son Hu Haifeng – was largely overlooked by the media, which focused on then President Arroyo's husband. Criticism quickly took on a racial slant as ZTE Corporation came under criticism for fomenting "Chinese corruption," with Senator Miriam Defensor-Santiago accusing China of having "invented corruption."[69] Public anger, however, was directed mainly at the Filipino political elites and their collusion. This case illustrates the potential for Chinese transnational political–business alliances with Southeast Asian counterparts to become the targets of popular critique as well as objects of elite internecine struggles in Southeast Asia.

Conclusion

It should be clear by now that hegemonic shift is not happening anytime soon, that a Sinocentric order is not in the making, and that states in China's vicinity are doing their best to maintain their freedom of action. These states are seizing opportunities offered by rising China to gain economically but hedging their political and security risk by aligning themselves with whatever outside powers are available, in particular the USA. Crucial to explaining their individual behaviors are the positions they occupy in the regional security system, the degree of their embeddedness in the regional and global economy, and the achieving of national consensus on the purpose of their politics.

Yet, the transnational effects of China's rise may change the parameters by which some states define their national interests and thus structurally transform the bases for their behavior. This may happen in Myanmar and Laos, where political elites and business cronies can become wedded with the political economic system transplanted from China and thus may no longer be able to define their interests independent of China. But it is hard to imagine this happening in countries that are better integrated with the regional and global economy, where other governments and firms can demand China play the game by rules all players agree on, and where non-Chinese firms are more likely to compete with Chinese corporations. In countries with a more dynamic system for elite circulation, it is difficult for Chinese firms to establish stable politico-business alliances that would endure over time and reshape the political economy of those countries. All of this suggests that the regional system will remain, with its own structural tension between its security system and its trade system; that norm building (relating to the creation of common rules and codes of conduct) will become more important; and that the future for the regional system very much depends on what roles China and its people want to play regionally and globally, and what kind of Chinese political and business elites emerge in the process of socialization.

Like their Japanese and American counterparts, Chinese state and non-state actors are attempting to create a milieu in which they can operate more comfortably and effectively. This is what region-wide Sinicization is all about. China's economic cooperation – the principal instrument of its engagement with its neighbors – has reorganized the political–economic structures in some countries but not in others. Specifically, its brand of bureaucratic capitalism is making deep inroads into certain sectors of the economy and parts of the state in Myanmar and Laos. These are parts of Southeast Asia that to date have not yet been fully exposed to the global economy. In other states, such as Thailand or Vietnam, for different reasons, Chinese influence has remained more circumscribed. At the same time, China's growing influence in Asia has been undeniable. This is illustrated by its promotion of the East Asia Community, which excludes the USA. Furthermore, the Chinese state has succeeded to an important extent in making its presence felt and voice heard in other settings such as the ASEAN Plus processes. These instances illustrate the significance of Sinicization. Yet none of these changes are portending a transformation of the structures of power in the regional and global political economy. Rather than replacing them, China is rising in established structures of power. Sinicization describes that process of recalibration.

Notes

1 I would like to thank Michael Kahler, Wendy Leutert, Gregory Noble, and Peter J. Katzenstein for their substantial comments and suggestions on this chapter and Sarah Tarrow for her editing. I thank my partner, Caroline Sy Hau, for her comments and suggestions as well as her support and encouragement. Research for this chapter was in part funded by the Japan Society for the Promotion of Science research grant (21401011) on "The Rise of China and the Political and Social Transformation of Southeast Asia: International, Transnational and National Perspectives."
2 Sekai Keizai no Neta Cho 2010.
3 Asian Development Bank 2010a.
4 Yabuki 2010, 244–7.
5 JETRO 2010a.
6 Asian Development Bank 2010a.
7 ASEAN–Japan Centre 2011.
8 Amako and Mifune 2010, 7; Kang 2007.
9 See, for instance, Tsugami 2003; Bert 2003; Deng and Wang 2005; Sutter 2005; Shambaugh 2005b; Kang 2007; Keller and Rawski 2007; Ross and Zhu 2008; Li, Rex 2009; Tsunekawa 2009a; Amako and Mifune 2010.
10 Ikenberry 2008b.

11 See for instance Kang 2007; Amako and Mifune 2010. For a more balanced analysis, see Shambaugh 2005b.
12 See, for instance, Saw, Sheng, and Chin 2005; Lam, Ganesan, and Durkop 2010.
13 See, for instance, Ross and Zhu 2008, which has several excellent essays.
14 See, for instance, Keller and Rawski 2007, especially Brandt, Rawski, and Zhu 2007 and Frost 2007.
15 Katzenstein and Shiraishi 1997.
16 Miyamoto 2010, 82–3. This is one of the most insightful books on Japan–China relations published in Japanese in recent years. The author served as ambassador to China from 2006 to 2010.
17 Shambaugh 2005b, 1.
18 Shiraishi and Hau 2010, 28.
19 Selden 1997.
20 Shiraishi and Hau 2010, 34–5.
21 Ibid., 26–7.
22 Pempel 2010.
23 Takahara 2009.
24 Thayer 2010, 31.
25 Ibid., 20.
26 Takahara 2009; Thayer 2010, 22.
27 Amako 2010, 10–11; Thayer 2010, 3.
28 Thayer 2010, 32–3.
29 Boeisho 2010.
30 Thayer 2010, 12.
31 Maruya 2010.
32 Thayer 2010, 30. ASEAN defense ministers met for the first time in 2006 to start the process of institutionalizing defense cooperation on a regular basis. The third ADMM, held in Thailand in 2009, adopted the Joint Declaration on Strengthening ASEAN Defense Establishments to Meet the Challenges of Non-Traditional Security Threats. ASEAN held its first ADMM-Plus meeting in Hanoi in 2010 with the participation of defense ministers from eight of their dialogue partners, which included among others Australia, China, Japan, and the USA. Thayer 2010, 25–6.
33 Thayer 2010, 12.
34 Ibid., 337.
35 Acharya 2009.
36 Kubota 2011.
37 Amako and Mifune 2010, 31.
38 Shiraishi 2010a.
39 Murphy 2010, 375–6; Thayer 2010, 44.
40 Murphy 2010, 378.
41 Rizal 2009, 12.
42 Interview with the author, 4 December 2010, Bogor, Indonesia.
43 Trade reached $18.3 billion in 2007 and $45 billion in 2008.
44 Nguyen 2010, 123.
45 Ibid., 129.
46 JETRO 2010b.
47 Asian Development Bank 2010a.
48 Ajia Keizai Kenkyusho 2007, 222–4.
49 Brown 2010, 333.
50 Ibid., 334.
51 Nguyen 2010, 124–5.
52 I thank Wendy Leutert for her substantial comments on this sub-section.
53 Tin 2010, 138–9.
54 Fujita 2008.
55 Asian Development Bank 2010b.

56 Maier 1978.
57 Miyata 2011.
58 This point is borne out by Wen Jiabao's and Hu Jintao's recent foreign visits. Prime Minister Wen Jiabao visited India in December 2010 and agreed with his Indian counterpart to expand bilateral trade to $100 billion by 2015, along with the establishment of strategic economic dialogue for economic cooperation. In his visit to Pakistan, Prime Minister Wen agreed with his Pakistani counterpart to expand bilateral trade to $15 billion by 2012 and witnessed business deals amounting to $20 billion. During President Hu Jintao's visit to the USA in January 2011, the Chinese government made business deals worth $45 billion, including 200 Boeing aircrafts.
59 Ito 2007, 4.
60 Ibid., 5, 155–6.
61 The total official development assistance of OECD member countries amounted to $68, $89, $79, and $83 million in 2000, 2001, 2002, and 2003 respectively. Ida 2007, 162.
62 Ida 2007, 162–3.
63 Ibid., 18.
64 I thank Wendy Leutert for this information.
65 Hara, Souknilanh, and Yamada 2011.
66 This project reminds us of the local government loan platforms that have emerged as the main engine of local government-initiated development projects in China in recent years. Enterprises obtain loans from state banks for real estate and property developments on land made available by local governments. Satoru Shibata (2011, 156) estimates that the state banks loaned out 3.8 trillion yuan to those platforms in 2009 alone. The new town development project shows that this platform model of real estate development business is taking place in Laos, involving both Laotian and Chinese actors. It is important not to confuse this model with crony capitalism, in which political elites and politically connected private-sector business elites obtain rent through politically rigged business practices. The model can be better understood as an evolving Chinese political economy whose "business model" – a brand of bureaucratic capitalism – is being transplanted in Laos.
67 The case below is based on Komiya 2009.
68 CEXIM was established in 1994, Sinosure in 2001.
69 Uy 2007.

PART III

PART III

6

CULTURAL SINICIZATION IN FOUR DIASPORIC LIVES

Chih-yu Shih

The meaning of the concept of Sinicization is complicated, multidimensional, and contested. It refers to conceptions of Self and Other that are typically deeply intertwined. The practices it represents, discursive and otherwise, can signify either the broadening or the narrowing of social and cultural distances. Many of the developments that are currently shaping the contemporary world – such as globalization, capitalism, nationalism, and multiculturalism – provide the context in which China encounters and engages both East and West, often but not always in what one might call Anglo-China. The lives and scholarship of the four individuals examined in this chapter represent clearly the complexity of these processes.

Sinicization in its various guises, involving Self and Other, is about influence and interaction among people as much as states;[1] the Chinese and their self-understanding as much as China and its sphere of influence;[2] and China and its diaspora conceived of beyond the category of territorial China.[3] Moreover, Sinicization focuses our attention on those mediating between China and the world. Consumers of goods made in China, Taiwanese pro-independence advocates, Chinese villagers fighting for rights, and indigenous Chinese loyal to Southeast Asian states can all act as cultural brokers involved in processes of encounter, engagement, and clash between different civilizational complexes.[4] Sinicization is a concept that summarizes important processes leading to self-discovery and self-interpretation. Without it, the economic, security, and political dimensions of Sinicization are devoid of meaning. In this chapter, I focus attention on four well-known academics whose lives and works display clearly the importance of processes of Sinicization and of Anglo-China.

Specifically, I track the identities and associated practices of four Asian diasporic academics – John Wong, Chung Tan, Samuel Kim, and Akira Iriye – who generally present their scholarship on China's economy, politics, history, and culture in English. Their careers and intellectual evolution, and the simplifications and complexifications in their work, offer us a window into their understanding of identities and practices in the perceived Sinic world constituted by the Chinese. Their careers are not representative in any way. But they do illustrate well the possibilities that structures provide for self-reflexive agents to make meaningful choices and thus to shape, at least to some extent, their environments, without ever fully determining them. Writing outside of China and for an English-speaking audience, these four academics illustrate with particular clarity the liminal positions they occupy between China and Asia and between East and West. Their lives and work thus illustrate Sinicization as a set of multidirectional, multi-sited, discursive processes, including variants of de-, re-, and self-Sinicization. In short, Sinicization presupposes agency and the appropriation and re-appropriation of Chinese phenomena by Chinese and non-Chinese agents, for their self- and group-interested use in an Anglo-Chinese world.

These four academics illustrate in their lives a variety of geographical, linguistic, as well as temporal possibilities, illustrating the multi-sited and multidirectional character of Sinicization. They were born into different Asian communities – Korea, China, Hong Kong, and Japan. They lived and worked in different countries – the United States, Singapore, and India. And while they read and wrote for the most part in English, their occasional reliance on other languages teaches us that Sinicization does not have to proceed in either Chinese or English.[5] Rather, the use of third languages can be a statement of who one is, from where one comes, and where one is heading.[6] In brief, Sinicization reveals, in one person, the existence of multiple cultural–geographical selves. Later in their careers, all four experienced a rising concern over their home countries, often reflected in the shift, undertaken consciously and rationally, of their academic and political agendas and frequency of visits. This fact is a healthy antidote to the common preconception that structures are all-determining and that Sinicization is a unilinear process that radiates from China outward. As these four individual lives show, nothing could be further from the truth.

Even far-reaching views that seek to associate China with very specific images, such as "rise," "all under heaven," or "Chinese characteristics," represent choices, not inevitabilities. The lives and works of these four academics contradict any such notion. If one insists on the nation state as the only viable civilizational actor in world politics, Huntingtonian clashes of civilizations may have some plausibility. Academics living and working in transnational careers, however, have been free to choose practices unrelated, even resistant to the constraints and opportunities that nation states provide.[7] Promotion or denial of Chinese distinctiveness always involves choices. Thus, no view on China can be politically neutral. Sinicization is unavoidably shaped and impacted by conceptions of identity and political practice.

This does not mean that actors have full control over their scholarship on China or over the self-identifications that implicitly or explicitly inform their perspectives. None of the four academics could control either the larger forces that prompted their civilizational encounters, or the liminal positions they held.[8]

Their choice of language, for example, would not go unnoticed by one community or the other. Home and host countries posed structural constraints simply because they differed from one another. Any narrative strategy about China could not help but activate those differences. Yet, meaningful choices persisted, including both choosing sides and avoiding the choosing of sides. Structural determinacy thus fails to remove the capacity for strategic indeterminacy.

Discursive analysis shows that these four academics consciously manage their liminal positions through the discursive and practical aspects of their scholarship: Kim's synthetic analysis, Iriye's centrist mediation, Tan's geo-civilizational critique, and Wong's scientific Chineseness. In their work on China, we see at least two common puzzles that call for answers. How do they place themselves in the perceived Sinic world constituted by the Chinese: does China belong to an identical or a different ontological order? How do they want China to be evaluated: should China conform to a Western standard expressed in values that are claimed to be universal? Kim's and Iriye's professional affiliations in the United States seem to push for a universalist prescription for China's place in the world; the peripheral relationship between Kim's and Wong's homes on the one hand, and China on the other, pushes instead for a shared ontological identity. By contrast, freed from both American affiliation and a sense of belonging to the periphery, Tan has a different and more innocent sense of China. Given the constraining civilizational positions in which they found themselves and the empowering cultural resources at their disposal, each of the four scholars has to decide, discursively, professionally, as well as personally, how to formulate their own identity strategy and style.

Two diasporic dimensions of Asian scholars' views on China

Peter Katzenstein argues in Chapter 1 that the processes of Sinicization that accompany the rise of China have triggered a recombination of, rather than a rupture with, established patterns and practices.[9] Although Sinicization is not just a territorial expansion of influence, recombination is more visible in areas located close to China's territorial state. It proceeds in the mind rather than through territorial changes.[10] Sinicization is thus composed of processes of increasing mutual self-knowledge as well as increasing knowledge about China. Since one needs to make sense of China's rise and its implications for one's relationship with China, the understanding of China is intimately tied to self-understanding. Mutual constitution is normally invoked as an abstract category and is rarely itself analyzed as I do here.

The responses of Asian diasporas outside Asia can offer valuable insights into the multidirectional character of processes of Sinicization. Mutual constitution is central for Asian diasporic scholars, who usually take on identities addressing their relationships with China and the country of origin or residence. Their home and host countries are important geo-cultural contexts for Sinicization at the micro level. However, the designation of home country is often a complicated matter, since in many cases a person may have lived in many different places; home identity is a complex and situational choice, complicated further when it involves territorial China: self-identity can then become a matter of the periphery or the center.

More specifically, the cultural dimension of Sinicization invites us to answer two questions: how does one view China? and how does one think that others view China? The two answers focus, respectively, on identity and image. A comparison of each of the four possibilities thus generated permits me to make some conjectures about processes of Sinicization. Cultural Sinicization concerns discourses, and how these discourses emerge from a specific social and cultural context. Since individuals make strategic choices, their decision to move in one direction or another is never simple or neat. Illustrating a key feature of Sinicization, the interaction between individual strategy and a larger conjuncture are unavoidable.

I am not arguing that the background of these four scholars is sufficient for characterizing their thematic choices. I show instead that their choices are well grounded, without precluding that other choices might have been possible. In short, background gives meaning to texts, and so do recollections in subsequent years. I rely on a comparison of their writings as well as interviews to accomplish two tasks: to gather evidence that their intellectual position can be traced to a larger context *and* that their position always rests on meaningful choices. Methodologically, this means that scholarly texts on China or Asia and their reinterpretations at a later career stage, expressed in interviews, represent equally meaningful possibilities of understanding individual choices, each illustrating a decision to adapt to or resist social contexts – understood here either as agreeing with or dissenting from conventional views of China rising. The open-ended character of Sinicization is richer if we shift between rather than seek to reconcile texts, interviews, and life histories. The meaning of Sinicization, I argue, cannot be determined in advance. Sinicization proceeds through the mechanisms of encounter or engagement at the collective level and choice at the individual level. In brief, Sinicization is made possible through mutual constitution of China, China scholar, and China scholarship.

Asian diasporas have generally experienced an identity dilemma involving home and host country.[11] On issues involving their home country, members of the Asian diaspora should think and act like fellow citizens in the host country. At the same time, they need a home country that enjoys respect in their host country so as to reduce the anxiety that their status as a diaspora might become a liability. The worst case occurs when the host and the home country are in conflict. Were it to involve a serious conflict, the rise of China could put Asian diasporic scholars under the scrutiny of colleagues and readers,[12] who would interpret their views of China as revealing their choice between home and host country.

The identity strategy of diasporic scholars and the social image of China they portray in their scholarly writings are connected.[13] First, they need to decide if China should be evaluated by the often universal standards accepted in the host country. These standards typically concern democracy, human rights, capitalism, and peace. Second, if these norms are not applicable, then they need to make sure the other norms are intelligible to the host country. In brief, diasporic scholars incur social costs for any analysis that gives the impression that China does not have to conform to widely accepted norms. By no means do diasporic scholars have to agree with the mainstream view of the host country; but invoking a cause larger than China is essential to demonstrating independent scholarship to the audience in the host country.

In brief, the authors' portrayal of China involves questions of personal identity and social image. Identity concerns itself with the type of home country, image with the type of host country. If the home country used to be peripheral in the Sinocentric world, the need to differentiate from China should be comparatively weak on questions of identity; if equivalent in status, that need should be stronger. Diasporic Korean scholars, for example, should be less interested than diasporic Japanese in differentiating China from their respective home countries. Analogously, if the host country is a Western state, the expectation that China should conform to specific and allegedly universal norms should be relatively strong; if not, it should be weaker. Thus, the Chinese diaspora living in North America or Western Europe would probably be more attuned to China's failure to abide by the norms of liberal democracy.

Mutual constitution of self-knowledge and knowledge about China thus involves personal identity and social image, with self-knowledge telling the actor how to view China, and knowledge of others about China telling the actor how China is viewed. The actor's conception of the rise of China thus involves his or her judgments on questions of both identity and image. To understand how individual judgments are embedded in a scholar's background, I rely on interviews with four Asian China experts, all teaching outside of their countries of birth: Samuel Kim (an "idealistic" Korean living in the USA), Akira Iriye (a "defeated" Japanese also living in the USA), Chung Tan (a "betraying" Chinese living in India) and John Wong (an "objective" Hong Kong China watcher living in Singapore). Note that these individuals are not samples as defined conventionally. Rather, like any other individual, each of these four is treated as a bundle of possibilities of placing the self in larger social contexts. In short, I study these individuals because they illustrate the range of individual choices and because I know and like them. I construct Table 6.1 based on my reading of their work rather than on any abstract principles.

I argue that their different conceptions of China reflect both their diasporic social positions and hybrid cultural bearings, and their specific choices about their identities. Multidirectional Sinicization processes expand the China discourse in ways determined partly by individual biography and partly by individual choice.

Originally from Japan – which is relatively equal to China in status – but living in the United States, Akira Iriye sees China as different and ready to conform. Iriye's position is in line with, as well as different from, that of Hidemi Suganami. Born in Soviet-occupied Korea, which is peripheral to China, and now living in the United States, Samuel Kim views China as similar and ready to conform. Kim's views are in line with and also different from David Kang's Sinocentric analysis.

TABLE 6.1 Diasporic perspectives on China: contexts and choices

Self-identity / Social image	China is identical (home country in a subordinate position)	China is different (home country in an equal position)
China should conform (host country in the West)	Synthesis/Sinocentrism Samuel Kim/David Kang	Centrism/solidarism Akira Iriye/Hidemi Suganami
China need not conform (host country not in the West)	Statism/nationalism John Wong/Yongnian Zheng	Civilization/ commonwealth Chung Tan/Wang Gungwu

John Wong came originally from peripheral Hong Kong and lives in Singapore. He sees China as quite similar to other states and does not insist that China should conform to the universal standards defined by others. Wong's view is in line with as well as different from Yongnian Zheng's nationalism metaphor. Chung Tan originally came from China and lived in India before his retirement. He sees China as different from other states and sees no need for China to conform to the norms propounded by others. Tan's views both agree with and differ from Wang Gungwu's commonwealth metaphor.

Akira Iriye[14]

A diasporic Japanese on China

Iriye calls himself a centrist, placing himself between the United States, Japan, and China. Committed to individual diplomacy, he points in his scholarship to possible avenues to accommodate seemingly irreconcilable positions. Arguing that culture offers such an avenue since the love of culture is universal, he uses music as the quintessential example. Iriye does not attempt to mediate through consensus building. Rather, he seeks to breed confidence in a universal humanity that transcends mundane conflicts of interest. His scholarship expresses the view that conflict among states takes place over superficial issues that are based on ignorance. A deeper sharing of common values is made possible by redirecting attention away from political and economic, and toward cultural issues. Other than reducing enmity, Iriye does not want to change anyone else's position. He resorts to simple facts and logics that may have limited theoretical appeal, insisting on the simplicity of a universal human spirit. Iriye's self-described "centrist" scholarship avoids controversial issues in an effort to reduce the salience of existing and at times bitter policy disputes.

Iriye is therefore more ready than many of his Japanese colleagues to sympathize with China's nationalist mood, rooted in deeply felt grievances caused by the violence Japan inflicted on China during World War II. However, Iriye's scholarship on Japan shows no sign of placing blame for its past policies.[15] For him, misunderstanding is the root of all problems, with cultural exchange the only avenue to resolution. China is an important place to begin retrieving universal humanity. If Japan and the USA are to achieve genuine peace, he argues, then East and West must come together, specifically through the building of an integrated and unified Asian Community;[16] this would require the reconciliation of China and Japan. To achieve that end, Iriye's scholarship does not advocate a change in or transformation of China. History shows how misunderstandings have emerged. And history shows why China possesses a character different from Japan and quite legitimately adheres to policies informed by China's own interests. Understanding and respecting China in the context of the historical evolution of its policy choices is the first step to bridging the gap that separates China from its opponents. China's rise is a phenomenon of globalization, not a threat or disruption to it. In short, Iriye's centrist position makes him see China as ontologically different. But he does believe that China could achieve a deeper self-confidence if it were to retrieve some universally shared values. Both Japan and the USA should and could accomplish this as well.

In contrast to Iriye's centrist approach, which resolves conflict by recognizing a shared humanity, other scholars stress China's distinct status and insist on conformity with specific principles. The UK-based English School solidarist Hidemi Suganami, for example, does not support the creation of a Japanese or a Chinese school of International Relations. Although he rarely touches on China in his writings, Suganami notes the different international principles that pervade ancient Chinese history.[17] His reflections on a national school of International Relations and his appreciation of these national histories allow him to readily accept China as a distinct nation. His solidarism, however, predisposes him to advocate for China's conformity with globally shared human rights standards.[18] A comparison of Iriye with Suganami shows similarity in their designation of China in accordance to their home (equal with China) and host (in the West) country identities. Nevertheless, their expectations differ. Iriye stresses peace more than the kind of human rights that Suganami cherishes. Furthermore, for Suganami, war is not unthinkable. Iriye prefers micro-level communication, while Suganami focuses on macro-level management. Sinicization would compel Suganami to think seriously about intervention in China's human rights policy. It poses a practical challenge to solidarism and the principles that define him as a solidarist. In comparison, for Iriye, Sinicization means a more urgent need to help China to establish mutual appreciation and cooperation with solidarists like Suganami.

The personal and national context

Although a pacifist, Iriye takes an epistemological stance quite similar to that of the Kyoto School of Philosophy. His father Keishiro Iriye (1903–78), also a student of diplomatic history and China expert who consciously promoted a centrist methodology, belonged to the early Kyoto School's generation.[19] Some members of that school supported the war fought in the name of the Great East Asian Co-prosperity Sphere. According to their philosophy of nothingness, Hegelian contradiction needs no synthesis. To be universal is the ability to be both Oriental and Occidental.

This means that one must exist in a place of nothingness. Retreat to nothingness philosophically brings one back to the origin of civilizations and enables re-entry into a differing cultural context, leading one to appreciate all without changing any. In its time, the Kyoto School inspired important scholars such as Takeuchi Yoshimi, once Japan's most influential literary critic. He suggested that Asia should be conceived of as a method of self-denial to shield us from preoccupation with any specific values or commitment to any specific standpoint.[20] Today, Nobukuni Koyasu, in particular, carries on the legacy of the Kyoto School legacy. He argues that East Asia is a method that reveals itself through an unending process of becoming.[21] Since it is a process, East Asia can never be a piece of territory to be occupied. Hence there exists no conceptual room for a revival of imperialism. The late Yuzo Mizoguchi similarly advocated treating China rather than East Asia as a method, enabling the Japanese to learn to view others without considering Japan's own condition. Thus, Japan can aim to become truly universal.[22] This preoccupation with attaining the universal without resolving obvious contradictions echoes the Kyoto School's view of both Orient and Occident as partial. To follow the logic of nothingness, the rise of China is a development that does not affect Japan, as it occurs in an altogether different context. Although Iriye is not necessarily fully cognizant of their various political varieties, the philosophy of nothingness and the world history standpoint are epistemologically embedded in his centrism, his idea of the importance of inter-cultural relations, and his commitment to an Asian Community. His determined pursuit of peace through regional and global community-building gives this seemingly passive philosophy a fresh meaning and an impulse for political action diametrically opposed to the support of imperialist policies that the Kyoto School represented before World War II.

Iriye's scholarship owes a great deal to his mentor, John K. Fairbank, who helped him throughout his career. World War II presented the question of whether Japan (his home country) or the United States (where he made his life) was to blame for the war. He resolved that difficult question by insisting that the war resulted mostly from colossal misunderstandings on both sides, thus sidestepping the issue of who was right and who was wrong. Even at a time when war between China, Japan, and the United States is highly unlikely, Iriye continues to advocate for peace as if the threat of war were real. It is, of course, real for anyone who bears the burden of war in his or her choice of identity. Without China's participation, Japan can never become the representative of the East, seeking genuine peace with the United States and the West. The rise of China could pose an intellectual threat if China does not support the goal of Asia joining the world, since there would be no East to engage in cultural exchange with the West. That should be sufficient reason for Iriye's attempt to persuade his audience that China is a rising civilization that poses no threat whatsoever. Rather, it offers a historic opportunity. Iriye's favored civilizational relationship preserves all cultures and could not become a reality if China's rise were political. Conceived of as a bridge, Japan facilitates inter-civilizational understandings. It thus might lessen the chances of a future confrontation that would force Japan, and Iriye, to choose sides.

Along with other prewar thinkers who re-appropriate the retreat discourse, each on their own terms, to overcome Japan's war legacy, Iriye distinguishes himself by associating the retreat/centrist discourse with peace activism, a personal cause throughout his scholarly career. He thus develops an earlier anti-China narrative into a brand new, morally infused scholarship that reconnects China, the Pacific, and the world. The cognitive capacity of the prewar Kyoto School to tolerate the incongruence between an older China-oriented Japan and a modern Western-oriented Japan does not yield the same bridging result. Iriye thus clearly differs from the Kyoto philosophers. To favor Orient at one time and Occident at another is not simply a spontaneous act. Consciousness has to be taught and cultivated. Iriye appreciates the merits of both sides of this civilizational divide. His peace is not as bitter as that of the war-accepting Kyoto School. For Iriye, war would betray consciousness, which should validate and secure all sides to all possible conflicts. Furthermore, war would threaten his relationship with his mentor. Iriye is thus very insistent on preaching peace and on teaching his audiences everywhere how to appreciate other civilizations. He tackles directly the mutual animosities in Chinese and Japanese society, urging both sides to adopt an inter-civilizational rather than a national perspective and thus transcending his Japanese identity by making it politically irrelevant or universal. Iriye respects all perspectives, potentially including both the Kyoto School and his own contrarian position that advocates personal diplomacy. The rise of China confirms his view of China as a civilization rather than a state. This helps him to appreciate Japan and China as civilizations that need their inter-civilizational relationships, thus protecting his own centrist position.

Samuel Kim[23]

A diasporic Korean on China

Kim likes to combine all of the analytical perspectives on China into one composite model. He began his career by writing about the Christian missionary Anson Burlingame, who later served as China's ambassador to Europe.[24] If China could be represented in Europe by an American missionary, he posited, it simply could not be all that different from the West. Kim's moral commitment to his subject implied that China could join a world of like-minded countries. This interest led him to the study of peace and war, international organization and world order.[25] His involvement in world order studies fostered the argument that China has to fulfill its duty when conducting its international affairs, and an interest in the study of how China had acquired its sense of membership in international organizations and sought to fulfill its international obligations. In contrast with conventional opinion prevailing in the 1970s, he argued that China was not a troublemaker in the United Nations. To the contrary, it painstakingly chose political gestures that signaled its disagreement with specific policies without disrupting UN procedures.[26] Even in areas in which a legacy of deep conflict remained, China acquiesced and gradually came to adopt UN procedures it had vehemently opposed. At the same time, it tried hard to adhere to the stance of most Third World countries. Kim also notes China's attentiveness to improving its own image. From the perspective of world order studies, there is no great difference between China and other states. Kim edited a book on conflict that incorporates virtually all related theories. His other edited volumes similarly address most of the existing theories about China, covering a broad spectrum of bilateral and multilateral arrangements.[27] Specifically, Kim sees different theories as accounting for different aspects of Chinese foreign policy.

Kim characterizes his scholarship as "synthetic," using the arenas of world order and China to display his collection of theories. To the extent that Kim does not support or oppose specific theories, his work resembles Iriye's. But synthesis differs from centrism. Kim develops his own theoretical perspective, typically well rounded and rarely provoking others. In this, too, he is similar to Iriye. However, in contrast to Iriye, Kim does not hesitate to articulate his own position. Kim's quest in scholarship is to combine and reconcile different intellectual positions and thus to transcend the limitations specific theoretical perspectives inevitably entail. In his writings, Kim does not view China as a country seeking to demonstrate its uniqueness. Instead, he attempts to understand how China adapts to new challenges such as the rules of the World Trade Organization in the era of globalization. Kim's focus on the negotiation process suggests that he views China as just another state.

In comparison to Kim's synthetic approach, US-based David Kang is an ardent defender of a Chinese worldview unfamiliar to Western theories informed by the Westphalian state system. As a Californian, Kang develops an argument that is critical of popular notions of the balance of power. Furthermore, he considers China's neighbors to agree with, indeed embrace, a hierarchical worldview.[28] This agreement generates collectively shared expectations about relationships with which even China, located at the top, must comply. Both US scholars, Kim and Kang are critics of all versions of realism. Instead, Kang argues that the East Asian order has been maintained not by balancing, but by bandwagoning. Located at the center, China has always been a familiar phenomenon to its East Asian neighbors, who began engaging in conflict only during China's periods of weakness. Although far from a synthesis, Kang's criticism of realism is a plea for peace, stability, and prosperity[29] – everything that Washington would cherish. For Kim, the establishment of a world order requires practical work. For Kang, realism is the main danger, threatening conflict and war. For Kim, Sinicization offers opportunities to incorporate previously excluded regimes such as Pyongyang into the world order. For Kang, it consolidates an alternative to realism that promises a world order actually desired by today's major powers.

The personal and national context

Samuel Kim made his career choices on the background of the Cold War, the division of Korea, and containment policy. Shaped by a mixture of cultural and social forces, this context offered numerous opportunities, which Kim seized with alacrity. He learned English on his own so that he could teach Koreans and translate for Americans, scraping together enough funds for a trip to America. Kim supported himself from the beginning as he entered the field of China studies. Later, he became the first American Fulbright professor teaching in China. Throughout his career, he has had no enemies. When he was upset about the Tiananmen uprising, as a scholar he did not act. Kim has always looked for the confluence of diverse factors that would help him to explain complicated events. Concerns over human rights in China simply could not yield one general assessment. Similarly, the rise of China does not push Kim to embrace one simple theory as many other intellectuals do. During the last decade, his attention has shifted away from Chinese to Korean politics. If Communist China failed in shaping China's destiny in the past, China's rise surely would not have a teleological destiny either.

Before settling in the United States, Kim was constantly on the move. Born in what later became North Korea, he learned Japanese as his first and Russian as his second foreign language. But he was determined to live in the United States. To improve his chances of finding a job, he made the shrewd decision to avoid a focus on Korea at the outset of his career. China appeared to be a better choice. Thus, he began to learn Chinese as his fifth foreign language – having studied English and French in college. Later, he shied away in his scholarship from a power politics perspective and instead favored a normative approach. The normative high ground allowed him to avoid making judgments about political developments that had previously pushed his personal life in directions not under his control. Not surprisingly, Kim insists that China is simply too complicated a subject to be encapsulated in a nutshell. A description of China must be nuanced and qualified. This approach mirrors his own career. Kim is very much aware of the puzzle posed by his own identity, and he is cognizant of and sensitive to his seemingly inferior social position. In North Korea, he seems to recognize something of himself when he says that North Korea is no longer a shrimp because the shrimp has learned multiple languages. Kim is a self-professed pacifist. He wants China to become a democracy, but without external pressure. He pays great attention to China's increasing conformity to the norms of international organizations.[30] Unlike realists, and especially offensive realists, he is not alarmed by China's rise. In his writings he shuns extreme positions such as "China threat" or "China collapse." Instead of adhering to a neutral and centrist position like Iriye, Kim draws useful lessons from all sides. Since his scholarship on China is always synthetic, Kim's understanding of China does not point to one clear path. Interestingly, his self-conscious avoidance of teleologies is rooted in the combining of many different teleological arguments. Kim is comfortable with the notion of Sinicization, which for him is an open-ended process. And he readily acknowledges that Korea and Japan were both deeply influenced by China. His attention to and sympathy for North Korea is embedded in his never-alarmist views on China.[31]

John Wong[32]

A diasporic Cantonese on China

John Wong's China is usually placed in a macro-structural context often reflected in the titles of his many publications. Taking a problem-solving approach, he puts himself as much as possible in the shoes of Chinese leaders. Wong addresses China's economic, social, and political problems using a scientific methodology, often relying on statistics as well as models that seek to describe the situation faced by Chinese leaders in objective terms. Occasionally, he is willing to propose policy solutions. He is particularly sensitive to China's relationship with its Southeast Asian neighbors.[33] John Wong publishes more on China's economic development than on any other issue. Although his analysis is always problem-centered, Wong rarely, if ever, shows any interest in the notion of China's collapse. Instead, he is interested in why and how Chinese leaders cope with difficult challenges. And he does not romanticize their ability to resolve any of them.

Wong wants to understand the contemporary challenges Chinese leaders face because this kind of knowledge is put in the service of the Singapore government. His analysis rests on the recognition that China's rise offers Singapore a unique opportunity.[34] In their Chineseness, Singapore and China share common sensibilities. Singapore's relationship with its Southeast Asian neighbors is vulnerable to domestic ethnic quarrels that center on the existence of important Chinese minorities. Wong understands and presents China's policy toward its Southeast Asian neighbors as one of caution. In his depiction of East Asian international relations, there exists no Sinocentric world. For Wong, China is just another country. His analysis is based on national statistics. However, to the extent that China could not simply apply experiences gained elsewhere to resolve the problems it faces, China's experience and capacity are specific and distinctive, illustrated by issues such as leadership succession, socialist reform, and crisis management of issues such as SARS.[35] China's distinctiveness, not its uniqueness, thus makes it possible for Singapore, with easy access to Chinese informants, to contribute to English-language social science scholarship on China.

In comparison to Wong's treatment of China as an object of scientific analysis, China-born, US-trained, and currently Singapore-based Yongnian Zheng takes Chinese scholars very seriously as a vital source of knowledge. Zheng argues that Chinese nationalism has both pragmatic and emotional aspects.[36] Both Wong and Zheng agree that China can be studied objectively. China is not any different from other countries that similarly abide by realist logic (for Wong) or subscribe to nationalism (for Zheng). However, the two scholars differ on the subject of empathy with Chinese feelings as an essential ingredient to the understanding of China. Sympathy with China could mean deep trouble for Wong's Singaporean host. Zheng is less sensitive to the ethnic issues that surround the position of Chinese in Southeast Asia. Both agree, however, that China has its own way of doing things. This explains why both rely on Chinese sources. Neither lives in the West now, and both have lived in Chinese settings – Wong's Hong Kong and Zheng's Zhejiang. For Wong, Sinicization is illustrated by Singapore's greater sensitivity toward and compliance with Chinese practices. For Zheng, it is demonstrated by China's pragmatic nationalism.

The personal and national context

Since 75 percent of Singapore's multi-ethnic population is Chinese, Singapore's relations with China are delicate. Some scholars of Chinese origin, writing in Singapore on Southeast Asian Chinese affairs, dispute the very notion of a Chinese diaspora, insisting that Southeast Asia's Chinese are native. Because of China's potential intervention in local ethnic politics,[37] Singapore's government has traditionally tended to discourage the study of China, in large part due to its anti-Communism and ethnic sensibilities. However, facing the rise of China, this city-state, which so heavily relies on international management and financial flow, simply cannot afford to lag behind in the analysis of developments in China. Such analysis was first disguised as Confucian studies and subsequently carried on under the name of East Asian Studies. In fact, East Asian Studies is primarily about China and secondarily about Taiwan. To desensitize further the study of China, the East Asian Institute (EAI) now virtually monopolizes all of Singapore's resources in the field of China studies. To this end, Singapore's government has decided to rely exclusively on overseas Chinese, temporary appointments, English writing, and social science approaches. In focusing on these four institutional traits, it hopes to prevent Singapore-produced knowledge on China from becoming a political linkage to China. Born in China, raised in anti-Communist Hong Kong, trained in English, and accustomed to annual reunions with his emigrant family in Canada, John Wong offers an ideal fit to assuming a leading position in the field.

Both Wong's Hong Kong background, in which individuals had no say about their political future, and his experience as an immigrant cultivated a self-awareness of having escaped from a Communist takeover, helping to create a feeling of distance from the object of his studies. Recruited from a foreign country, with little intellectual connection to the local community, and without the protection of tenure, Wong could rely on no one but his direct superior, former Deputy Prime Minister Keng Swee Goh and, indirectly, on then Prime Minister Kwang Yew Lee. Wong recruits researchers – increasingly from China – who stay for no longer than five years and receive coaching to write policy papers. His superiors expect a pragmatic approach in the EAI's publications so that the institute's research is of benefit to the government. Anti-China sentiment has never factored into Wong's research, which also includes the study of Southeast Asian Chinese. His interest in and concern for Chinese and China is very evident in his policy analysis. To him, the rise of China is largely a Chinese matter. China's rise has caused Chinese problems and Chinese ways to resolve them.

Wong has shown little nationalist emotion in his writing. He began to recruit Chinese scholars only because Goh insisted on the importance of developing perspectives on China from within China. Goh's belief that anti-Communism would not work has also affected Wong's approach. He has faithfully observed Lee's pragmatism and Goh's strategic thinking. Consequently, EAI's research on China has no connection to Singapore's society. Wong thinks that Southeast Asian Chinese are increasingly becoming less Chinese, while his work brings him increasingly in touch with China. Wong sees it as his main task to present China to Western audiences.[38] Like Lee, his position on China is friendly and neutral. Lee wants the EAI to copy neither Western nor PRC perspectives. Wong is able to achieve this objective because he can justifiably claim that the EAI knows more about China through its Chinese researchers, and that their objectivity results from reliance on social science models and English language. However, the more the EAI's research succeeds in preparing Singapore's participation in China's rise, the less Wong is keeping Singapore away from China. In short, the rise of China is enticing Chinese identity consciousness and eliciting responses from neighboring states.

Chung Tan[39]

A diasporic Chinese and China

Chung Tan's father, Yun-shan, helped Rabindranath Tagore to establish the first China studies institute in India. He has adopted Tagore's conviction that China and India are two civilizations that could not possibly threaten each other. Tagore treated individuals as meeting places of civilizations, and Tan expanded on that theme. Chung Tan began and ends his professional career by criticizing John Fairbank's study of the tribute system, and he is very critical of Samuel Huntington's thesis of the clash of civilizations.[40] Tan believes that both have misread China profoundly, consistently arguing how harmonious and peaceful Chinese political thought and practice have been. He debates some of his Indian colleagues about their concerns over the threat China may pose to India. For Tan, the historical relationship between the two countries centers on two civilizations, each one capable of giving to and learning from the other. It is inconceivable to him that either China or India could pursue imperialist or hegemonic policies and become enemies. At the same time he debates his Chinese and Taiwanese colleagues by insisting that, besides exporting Buddhism, Indian civilization is an important source of Chinese civilization, illustrated by its export to China of the image of the dragon and the idea of equality. He likes to evoke the image of an Indian elephant dancing together with a Chinese dragon.[41]

After his retirement, as a critique of the concepts of geo-politics and geo-economics, Tan developed the concept of "geo-civilization."[42] Although he criticizes geo-politics for its obsession with power competition, he agrees with the geo-economic perspective about the importance of interconnections between China and India. Tan looks to the Himalaya as the origin of four great river systems, two of which laid the foundation for Indian and two for Chinese civilization. He develops the concept of "Chindia" to convey the existence of "great harmony between China and India." In the rise of China, Tan discerns a different model of international behavior that will show the world how it is possible not to challenge anyone. For example, in its long history and despite its superior strength, China has never tried to conquer India. China does not have to treat India or any other state as a rival. Instead, China is a civilization with its own inner logic and spirit. Civilizations highlight rather than threaten one another. Neither India nor America needs to worry that a powerful China would compel them to adopt a specific lifestyle.

In comparison with Tan's strident anti-imperialism, Wang Gungwu – born in China, raised in Malaysia, trained in England, and having taught in Australia, Hong Kong, and Singapore – shows no stridency in his scholarship. Yet he sees China as inhabiting a different world that contrasts with the West. Wang views the Chinese in Southeast Asia as fractured into different kinds.[43] For the sake of convenience, one could categorize his approach to China with a "commonwealth" metaphor, as he recognizes differences in each locality without denying that they share a thin layer of Chinese identity. For Wang, it is a mistake to judge all Chinese by one standard. As a concept, "Chinese" is much broader than the notion of a territorial state and thus not suitable for judgment based on a single standard. Through his scholarship, Wang personifies a perspective that is very tolerant of hybridity, fluidity, and uncertainty. Tan defends strongly China's uniqueness. In contrast, Wang would like to see hybridity as a result of local conditions evolve into difference. Tan argues that the intermixing of civilizations stems from all kinds of interconnections. For Tan, Sinicization bears witness to China's enhanced capacity for learning. For Wang, it could yield a thickening of Chinese identity and a reversal of hybrid identities.

The personal and national context

Tan began his career in Tagore's tradition. The outbreak of the Sino-Indian war in 1962 cost him his job as interpreter for the National Defense Ministry, as his Chinese origin was thought to be incompatible with the loyalty required by his position. Chung Tan has devoted his career to criticizing imperialism and American scholarship on China. He succeeded in convincing his Indian colleagues that it was possible to use Chinese history to establish a perspective outside of the mainstream literature – an orientation that is appreciated in the Indian academic world, where intellectuals are especially sensitive to their indebtedness to the British perspectives that many struggle to resist. Specifically, he demonstrates that the pre-modern tribute paid to the Chinese court was sheer etiquette rather than a system of trade.[44] Chung Tan shows how the imperialist desire for trade had led Fairbank to misunderstand the meaning of tribute for the Chinese. Through his historical scholarship on China, after the 1962 war, Chung Tan reoriented Indian perspectives on China in general toward an anti-imperialist approach to China studies.[45] The historiography of Tan's anti-imperialist epistemology preserved the civilizational sensibility in Tagore's worldview and that of his father, Yun-shan. His politically incorrect ethnic identity was neutralized by his politically correct anti-imperialist standpoint.

Tan has not only tried to improve China's image in India. He also tries to encourage his Chinese colleagues to take India seriously. In their times, Tagore and Yun-shan tried to do the same with little success. Tan follows Tagore's approach by tracing India's contribution to Chinese civilization, drawing serious criticism from Chinese and Taiwanese colleagues but fascinating his audience nonetheless. Tan wants to prove that Chinese civilization is capable of learning and adapting without sacrificing its authenticity. The first argument reconnects China with India; the second assures China's independent position outside the West. Tan wants his Chinese colleagues to be mindful of the rewards that China has reaped by learning from India. His lifelong struggle for better Indo-Chinese relations rests on his insistence that ancient China borrowed from Indian civilization to become today's China. Furthermore, India has much to learn from China in order to make a genuine break from its painful experience with Western imperialism and colonialism. This is a remarkable parallel with Tagore and Yun-shan, who cherished the fact of Buddhism's original export from India to China and promoted the return of Buddhism to India from China in the future.

Over four decades after the 1962 border war, which created enormous pressure on anyone who wanted to prevent further confrontation, the rise of China provides Tan with a new opportunity to reconnect the two civilizations. His writings on geo-civilization have, since his retirement, been hastily published in a number of books that reiterate his long-held views.[46] The Shanghai Academy of Social Science's bi-annual World China Forum, initiated in 2004, has featured Tan as a keynote speaker addressing over one thousand participants. Here, Tan enjoys the opportunity to be part of China's rise amongst Chinese colleagues enjoying improved self-image and self-confidence. His writings have gained attention as he has introduced his civilizational analysis through book and newspaper publications and, most efficiently, through Chinese web pages.[47] While others see China's rise as posing a challenge to India, Tan sees a new opportunity to remind his audiences of the importance of civilizational interconnections.

Sinicization: embedded and multiplying in individual careers

Asian diasporic scholarship typically is written in English. Even though it does not determine its impact, this language prerequisite shapes the audience it will primarily serve. While this common feature is shared by almost all diasporic scholars, those involved in Sinicization differ in at least two ways. First, sensitivity, if not sympathy, toward Chinese history among Asian diasporic scholars gives substance to the process of Sinicization. Second, this sensitivity has repercussions inside and outside of territorial China. Chinese audiences thus appropriate and re-appropriate the interpretations and insights diasporic scholarship provides, with the effect that

China and so-called Chinese concepts encounter all kinds of interventions that can lead to processes of re- as well as de-Sinicization.

Part-time Sinicization in the Anglo world

The Anglo aspects of these scholars' careers make Sinicization a total experience. Each of the four scholars discussed in this chapter has his own intellectual agenda. In addition, each spends a good deal of his professional career as well as leisure time in either his home or his host country. That said, the Anglo-Chinese scholarship of Tan and Wong differs from the Anglo-Asian scholarship of Iriye and Kim. Anglo-Chinese scholarship deals with the English world, the hosting society, and China; Anglo-Asian scholarship with the English world, the home society, and China. Sinicization processes that make the world adapt to Chinese values are only one part of the lives of these four scholars. There are also attempts at influencing those acting on behalf of China by supplying them with certain larger analytical causes, chosen to represent the four scholars' academic independence. Nonetheless, Wong's preoccupation with greater China's economic development, Iriye's insistence on the necessity of a Japanese apology to China for wartime crimes, Tan's celebration of Chinese anti-imperialism, and Kim's support of China's entry into international organizations all share, to different degrees, a profound sensitivity and at times sympathy for China. When they contribute in their writings to the scholarship on China, they take an active part in processes of Sinicization.

The engagement with other, larger causes differs among these four scholars and illustrates processes of recalibration. Wong stresses scientism to justify his core proposition that China's distinctive national conditions call for indigenous treatment; Iriye emphasizes peace and humanist values to support his criticism of the insensitivity of American and Japanese conservatives to different national and cultural perspectives; Kim articulates an idealist world order to justify his refusal to support either China after the suppression of the pro-democracy movement or Western sanctions imposed on China in the aftermath; and Tan supports a geo-civilizational connectivity to justify his optimistic articulation of the hope for a long-term human evolution away from egoistic nationalism. These larger causes, more than their substantive interest in and preoccupation with China, also help define their scholarship. This is not to deny that Wong's preoccupation with the greater China is shared by many who do not trust Western scientism; that widespread Japan-phobia in China might not be assuaged by the kind of apology that Iriye is advocating; that China's participation in international organizations has failed to bring about the world order Kim is advocating; and that anti-imperialism has been used to justify China's confrontation with India, putting into doubt Tan's central claim.

Furthermore, beyond their interests in and preoccupation with China, all four scholars have felt some professional or personal duty toward their respective host or home countries, leading to the waxing and waning of de- and re-Sinicization processes during their careers. Wong must pay heed to Singapore's strategic objective, participation in the Chinese market; Tan has endeavored to establish respect for India in China; Kim wishes to rectify the distorted image of Pyongyang; and Iriye wants to persuade the Japanese people not to change the Peace Constitution. All four feel a profound obligation to help their Asian home or host country. For the two Anglo-Asian scholars, Kim and Iriye, their connections to China are linked intimately to their personal identities. For Kim, China and North Korea are basically in the same camp in world politics. For Iriye, China is a somewhat foreign land to be managed by means of an idealist and personal diplomacy. For the two Anglo-Chinese scholars, Wong and Tan, their self-image is deeply implicated by their relationships with China and their respective Asian host country. For Wong, professional work and emotional loyalty have led him to discover a China that the West does not fully understand. And for Tan, the West embodies an imperialism that should be eliminated in Asia.

Historicized China in four life histories

Our four diasporic scholars have generally avoided direct involvement in the politics of their host societies. Dealing with China has remained for all of them a strictly academic subject. This was less true, however, when they were connected back to their home countries, either while visiting or while greeting visitors from back home. But since all four spent most of their careers abroad, this tended to be the exception. Nonetheless, their frequent travels and their stature as internationally renowned scholars has confronted them with all kinds of practical inquiry, often political in nature, thus illustrating the non-linear feature of Sinicization processes. This was the case, for example, when Iriye began to return to Japan regularly as a university guest lecturer, in the course of his globe-spanning travels, and when he accepted invitations to China where he agreed to interviews. The same has been true for Kim, who is often in South Korea; Tan, who now lives in Chicago while also organizing and attending events in China and India; and Wong, with his frequent professional meetings in China, regular engagements with Chinese scholars in Singapore, annual family reunions in Canada, and Canadian academic position following his retirement from the EAI.

Iriye's guest teaching career in Japan began in 1997. While there, he has consistently expressed strong disagreements with Japanese nationalism, military build-up, and constitutional revision. He once criticized former Premier Abe Shinzo as a second George W. Bush Jr. and expressed his preference for the peace advocate Yasuo Fukuda over nationalist Aso Taro, both former premiers. He also has rejected the impression of the United States' decline and noted the vibrancy of American civil society and the civil society as the future of the world.[48] He specifically welcomed the more recent Premier Yukio Hatoyama's call for an East Asian Community which, Iriye argued, should include the United States. In fact, he hopes that the East Asian Community might eventually evolve into an Asia-Pacific Community. Interestingly, in speaking to a Chinese audience, he argued that a still powerful United States would no longer be a superpower. His Chinese hosts are invariably interested in his criticism of Japanese nationalism. However, when in China, Iriye encourages his audiences to focus on China's civilizational rather than political influence; in that spirit, he describes this as "China's 21st century."[49] In his early scholarship, Iriye had written about what had gone so terribly wrong to cause war in Asia. Later, while traveling especially in China, he encountered the very same forces still at work. Continuing to view China as a victim is no longer an adequate response to the forces transforming world politics. Rather, the most urgent task is to persuade China away from the path of political competition by showing how other states, especially the USA and Japan, are not fearful of China's rise. Promoting the civilizational correlates of a rising China thus substitutes for earlier empathy with China's victimization over the last two centuries.

Kim's increasing contacts with Korea are also reflected in his increasing interest in and concerns over policy issues on the Korean Peninsula. In contrast to Iriye, however, this shift in attention has led him a step away from China, since few Koreans regard China as an actual or potential threat. Kim's analysis of the Korean situation is subtly critical of US policy.[50] On the one hand, this is made easier because China's rise restrains Washington's dominance in the region. On the other hand, US dominance is taken for granted. In contrast with Kim's ambivalence about the USA, Tan's anti-imperialist engagement shows some ambivalence about China's rise. Tan welcomes the rise of China because, he believes, it embodies a non-imperialist way of being a great country; yet he also worries about the negative attitudes toward India that it may engender. Since settling in Chicago, Tan has primarily written articles for Chinese web pages, criticizing the United States and promoting India. Among our four scholars, Wong is the only one who has found complete satisfaction in his increasing contact with China, where he is able to receive respect, meet key policymakers, and make policy suggestions openly without worrying about anxious Southeast Asian neighbors. More recently, he has organized delegations to China, spending weeks there each time.

In the form of rupture or return, the subject of China appears to provoke anxiety in Iriye and Tan, and passion in Kim and Wong as well as Tan. This anxiety centers on a possible confrontation between host and home country – the United States and China for Iriye, and India and China for Tan. Passion reflects the presence of growing opportunities. For Tan, it is the opportunity for China to fulfill its civilizational ideal and for him to continue his father's legacy in China. For Kim, it is the opportunity to give fair treatment to North Korea. And for Wong, it is the opportunity to celebrate his identification with China. Both Iriye and Kim had their host societies, Japan and the United States, in mind in the early stages of their careers as they self-consciously refused to take a specific theoretical and political position. Now they do not question China's rise, demanding that the USA and Japan adapt. Tan and Wong are facing China when they travel from India or Singapore. English plays a smaller role in their China travels than for Iriye and Kim. Iriye operates in English when in China and in Japanese when in Japan, while Kim lectures in English wherever he goes. In form as well as content, Sinicization thus has changed over time for all four.

Finally, our four scholars treat China differently over time. To different degrees in the early stages of their careers, they have viewed China as an object – of imperialism, misperception, Cold War, or ignorance of how to get things done internationally. But with China's rise, their perceptions have shifted, leading them all to recognize a specific form of return: China has again become the subject of its own future. Iriye and Tan are very sensitive to the openness of that future, which for Iriye swings between the poles of civilization and power politics. Although Japan has a clear responsibility to prevent China from choosing the path of power politics, Iriye is telling his Chinese audiences that the choice is theirs alone. Similarly, Tan leaves no doubt that China has taken full ownership over its India policy. Despite his advocacy of a harmonious order of "Chindia," he is keenly aware of a possible future filled with conflict and recrimination. Kim and Wong take China's rise very much for granted. For Kim, what matters is not his support of China but the support the world assumes China gives to Pyongyang; this is what makes his writings about Korea so useful for American audiences. Wong is the only one of the four who feels clear support in China. Both Kim and Wong thus view China as having unquestioned and rightful agency over its own future.

Conclusion: Sinicization as mutual constitution

Sinicization describes processes of civilizational evolution. These processes adapt both internal needs and external contacts with various agents (here, four diasporic scholars) who substantially, though not fully, share worldviews, values, self-understanding, and life practices. Appropriating knowledgeable practices across civilizational boundaries encourages adaptation. Sinicization thus rests on the readiness of its agents to conceptualize and practice new ways of self-understanding.

Encounter and choice are the mechanisms that define agency. Sinicization is premised upon the encounter between Chinese and other civilizations. Encounters push agents to adapt, as they must choose between resistance, teaching, learning, or a combination of all three. Consciously or not, each agent is constantly involved in choosing different strategies of adaptation. If encounters thus can generate fresh possibilities for innovation and recombination, Sinicization is multi-sited. In processes of cross-civilizational encounters, no two agents will adapt their practices in exactly the same way. And although such encounters are occurring all over the world, because of the size of China's population and its peaceful rise, Sinicization is of increasing significance.

Sinicization has grown in vitality and resonance. It has facilitated the spreading of American practices of market capitalism to China's economy, nationalism and rights rhetoric to Chinese politics, balance of power to China's foreign policy, and multiculturalism to China's global diasporic communities. Conceptual and institutional adaptations to Sinicization and the different forms of resistance, re-appropriation, and feedback they engender have made Sinicization more important. All responses push agents to be cognizant of the positions they occupy between different civilizations, and all require knowledge of both Euro-American and Chinese civilizations.

Invariably, agents of Sinicization cannot do without the use of English, with unavoidable ideological, practical, and institutional consequences. Sinicization often implicates not simply China as a nation state, but also the Chinese in Indochina and Taiwan, who mediate between Chinese and their various forms of identity. They act as both producers and consumers of civilization who maneuver among collective, familial, and individual centers of allegiance. Self-knowledge is the foundation of Sinicization. Sinicization consists of multi-sited processes that deconstruct stereotypical notions of China's rise in the twenty-first century. Our four scholars have actively participated in Sinicization disguised as social science (Wong), wished for an improved geo-civilizational Chindia (Tan), managed from an imagined place of mediation to achieve peace (Iriye), and explored as a harbinger for an order in which the world could accommodate North Korea (Kim). Since their strategic choices are shaped by specific historical contexts, these adaptations have varied widely. Positioned at different sites, I conclude, individual agents respond differently to China's rise.

Notes

1 Callahan 2004, 39, 45.
2 Fitzgerald (1996, 94–5) argues that, for the Chinese nationalists to face the world, the assumption must be that there has been an authentic Chinese people beyond doubt.
3 Wang, Gungwu 2000.
4 Goodman and Zang 2008, 1; Ling et al. 2010, 39; He 2009; Suryadinata 1997a, 21–2.
5 For discussions on the politics of China studies in the Anglophone and Sinophone communities, see Shih and Chang 2011; Barmé 2005.
6 Bloom and Bloom 1981, 31–2; Kim-Rivera 2002, 261–81; Chan 2002, 271–85.
7 Chen et al. 2009, 749; Chen 2002, 79.
8 One version of the mix of these larger forces includes realism, idealism, Confucianism, and Islamism (Wang 2008). Another version is Korea between China and Japan, Socialism and Capitalism, and East and West (Kim and Hodges 2006, 513–45).
9 See Katzenstein and Shiraishi 2006. Incidentally, Prasenjit Duara (2009) argues that the rise of China is a replacement of one configuration by the other that is characterized by transnational forces including religion and capitalism.
10 For example, the return of Hong Kong to China marked such a psychological process (Ma and Fung 1999).
11 See Kuo 2008, 112–16.
12 For a vivid example, see Ray Huang's recollection of his position facing the charge of American imperialism (Huang 2001, 284, 521).
13 Ding 2008a; Tsai 2009, 172–5.
14 Unless otherwise specified, the source is an interview with Akira Iriye on 17–18 October 2007 (Iriye 2007).
15 Iriye 1998, 139–41.
16 Iriye 1997, 60.
17 Linklater and Suganami 2006, 192.
18 Ibid., 254; Suganami 1989.
19 Williams 2005, Goto-Jones 2005.
20 Takeuchi and Calichman 2005, 164–5.
21 Koyasu 2004.
22 See Mizoguchi, Yuzo 1989.

23 Unless otherwise specified, the source is from an interview with Samuel Kim on 5, 7, and 12 June 2007 (Kim 2007).
24 Kim 1966.
25 Falk and Kim 1981; Falk, Kim, and Mendlovitz 1991.
26 Kim 1979.
27 In the first of four editions on the state of the art in Chinese foreign policy, two of his authors criticize that those who cannot analyze, write about the state of the art (Babrow and Chan 1984).
28 Kang 2007, 4.
29 Ibid., 201.
30 Kim 2009, 36.
31 For example, Kim's *The Two Koreas and the Great Powers* (2006), in which he formally claims a synthetic approach, and *Korea's Democratization* (2003b).
32 Unless otherwise specified, the source is from an interview with John Wong on 5–9 November 2007 (Wong 2007).
33 Wong 1984; Wong and Lai 2006.
34 Wong, John 2003; 2004, 31–44.
35 Zheng and Wong 2004.
36 For example, see Zheng 2007; 1999.
37 Suryadinata 1997b, 15–22; 1997a, 2–4.
38 Chen and Yang 2009, 158.
39 Tan is the family name. Although Chung Tan always goes by the style of family name first in all his professional activities, this book expediently adopts the standardized form of placing the given name first. Unless otherwise specified, the source is an interview with Chung Tan on 18, 19, and 30 May 2008 (Tan 2008).
40 Huntington 1996.
41 Tan and Uberoi 2009.
42 Tan 2008.
43 Malvezin 2004, 49–57.
44 Tan 1978.
45 Tan and Thakur 1998.
46 Tan and Uberoi 2009, 231.
47 Among them, the two most popular with Chinese readers are probably www.zaobao.com and www.chinareviewnews.com, based in Singapore and Hong Kong respectively.
48 Iriye 2006, 38.
49 Liu, Xuan 2006; Liu and Ma 2006.
50 Kim 2003a.

7
BECOMING "CHINESE" IN SOUTHEAST ASIA[1]

Caroline S. Hau

Over the past three decades, it has become "chic"[2] to be "Chinese" or to showcase one's "Chinese" connections in Southeast Asia. Leaders ranging from President Corazon Cojuangco Aquino of the Philippines to Prime Minister Kukrit Pramoj of Thailand to President Abdurrahman Wahid of Indonesia have proclaimed their Chinese ancestry. Since 2000, Chinese New Year (Imlek) has been officially celebrated in Indonesia, after decades of legal restrictions governing access to economic opportunities and Chinese-language education, use of Chinese names, and public observance of Chinese customs and ceremonies.

Beyond elite and official pronouncements, popular culture has been instrumental in disseminating positive images of "Chinese" and "Chineseness." In Thailand, for example, the highly rated TV drama *Lod Lai Mangkorn* (Through the Dragon Design, 1992), adapted from the novelistic saga of a penurious Chinese immigrant turned multimillionaire and aired on the state-run channel, has claimed the entrepreneurial virtues of "diligence, patience, self-reliance, discipline, determination, parsimony, self-denial, business acumen, friendship, family ties, honesty, shrewdness, [and] modesty" as "Chinese" and worthy of emulation.[3] The critical acclaim and commercial success of another "rags-to-riches" epic from the Philippines, *Mano Po* (I Kiss Your Hand, 2002), spawned six eponymous "sequels."[4] In Indonesia, the biopic *Gie* (2005) sets out to challenge the stereotype of the "Chinese" as "material man," communist, and dictator's crony by focusing on legendary activist Soe Hok Gie. In Malaysia, the award-winning *Sepet* (Slit-eyes, 2005) reflects on the vicissitudes of official multiracialism through the story of a well-to-do Malay girl whose passion for East Asian pop culture leads her to befriend, and fall in love with, a working-class Chinese boy who sells pirated Video Compact Discs.

The term "re-Sinicization" (or "resinification") has been applied to the revival of hitherto devalued, occluded, or repressed "Chineseness," and more generally to the phenomenon of increasing visibility, acceptability, and self-assertiveness of ethnic Chinese in Southeast Asia and elsewhere.[5] The phenomenon of "re-Sinicization" marks a significant departure from an era in which "China" served as a model for the localization of socialism and propagation of socialist revolution in parts of Southeast Asia in the 1950s and 1960s, and Southeast Asian "Chinese" were viewed and treated as economically dominant, culturally different, and politically disloyal Others to be "de-Sinicized" through nation-building discourses and policies. All of these illustrate the non-linear, reversible and reinforcing characteristics of Sinicization.

For want of a better word, the term "re-Sinicization" has served as an expedient signpost for the variegated manifestations and revaluations of such Chineseness. Its use does not simply affirm the conventional understanding of Sinicization as a unilinear, unidirectional, and foreordained process of "becoming Chinese" that radiates (or is expected to increasingly radiate) outward from mainland China.[6] Since the "Sinosphere"[7] was inhabited by different "Chinas" at different times in history, the process of modern "Sinicization" cannot be analyzed in terms of a self-contained, autochthonous "China" or "Chinese" world, let alone "Chinese" identity. These "Chinas" were themselves products of hybridization[8] and acculturation born of their intimate and sometimes contentious cultural, economic, and military contacts with populations across their western continental frontiers, most notably Mongols and Manchus, and with Southern Asia (India and Southeast Asia) across their southern frontiers.[9] This Sinosphere began to break down in the mid-nineteenth century. In their modern articulations, "China," "Chinese," and "Chineseness" are relational terms that, over the past century and a half, point to a history of conceptual disjunctions and historical hybridizations arising from the hegemonic challenges that the maritime powers of the "West" posed to the Sinocentric world. And in that world, social, economic, cultural, and intellectual interactions among many different sites were intense and largely enabled by the regional and global flows and movements of capital, people, goods, technologies, and ideas within and beyond the contexts of British and, later, American hegemony in East and Southeast Asia.

Without discounting China's contribution to modern world-making[10] over the past century and a half, this chapter complicates the idea of "Sinicization" as a mainland state-centered and driven process of remaking the world (and the ethnic Chinese outside its borders) in its own image. Instead, it proposes to understand "Sinicization" as a complex, historically contingent process entailing not just multiple actors and practices, but equally important, multiple sites from which they, over time, have created, reinvented, and transformed received meanings associated with "China," "Chinese," and "Chineseness." Sinicization cannot be studied apart from the related concepts of re-Sinicization and de-Sinicization; taken together, they can best be understood as a congeries of pressures and possibilities, constraints and opportunities for "becoming-Chinese" that are subject to centripetal and centrifugal forces – as Wang Gungwu[11] has noted for the cultural context of territorialization and de/reterritorialization.[12] One crucial implication is that in this process of recalibration no single institution or agent, not even the putative superpower People's Republic of China, has so far been able to definitively claim authority as the final cultural arbiter of what constitutes "Chinese" and "Chineseness" or even, for that matter, "China."

Conceptual disjunctions

From the mid-nineteenth century onwards, Qing China confronted a hegemonic challenge, not from across its continental borders to the west, but from the maritime world to its east. The Opium Wars and more crucially the Taiping rebellion – both manifestations in foreign relations and domestic ramifications of the explosive "clash of empires"[13] – were instrumental in the breakdown of a regional system in the east. That system had hitherto been organized in terms of a China-centered tributary trade system along with what was called, in the late Ming and Qing periods, "mutual markets" (*hushi/goshi*, in which traders could visit Chinese ports without accompanying a tributary mission), with two different dynastic regimes of "China" as its core state.[14] The ensuing century and a half has been characterized by the Chinese as a period of chaos (*luan*), one that has borne witness to large-scale deterritorialization through outmigration from the mainland: a massive outflow of people that would only be reduced, and then only briefly, when Communist China was formally cut off from its non-communist neighbors and the American-led world between the late 1940s and the mid-1970s.

A far-reaching consequence of this period is that the genesis of the modern term *Zhongguo* = China and related signifiers such as *Zhonghua* = "Chinese" and "Chineseness" (a term for which there is no exact Chinese-language equivalent) are characterized by reterritorializing as well as deterritorializing impulses that arise from conceptual disjunctions in the Zhongguo = China equation. Since the late nineteenth and continuing through most of the twentieth century, "China" was incorporated into the international system. Rising nationalist sentiments made "Chinese/ness" an issue of paramount importance for "China" in its multiple discursive, territorial, and regime manifestations, and for the so-called "Chinese" in Southeast Asia (the principal region of immigration from the mainland) and their host states and societies. This created multiple disjunctions between territory, nation, state, culture, and civilization – key concepts in the study of modern politics – in the signifiers "China" and "Chinese/ness."

Not only is it problematical to conflate the concepts of territory, nation, state, culture, and civilization when one talks about "China." The conceptual disjunctions described above are further complicated by China's modern history of translating concepts from other languages (discussed in the next section), embedding thousands of foreign words in the Chinese language. Terms like "feudalism," "imperialism," "colonialism," "naturalism," and "modernity" not only carry with them the history of their usages and circulation in English, Japanese, German,

French, and Russian, among other languages, but the history as well of their localization and (re)signification in the Chinese context. This complex history of global, regional, and local circulation and appropriation makes phrases such as "Han (Chinese) imperialism" and "Han colonization of south and southwestern China" the subject of highly charged debates.

This is not to argue that the concepts of territory, nation, state, culture, and civilization lack any referent; on the contrary, modern Chinese history is an account of the prodigious time and energy expended, not to mention the blood-sweat-tears spilled, on determining, fixing, or challenging and changing the proper cultural, political, territorial, and civilizational referents of "China".[15] The fact that "China" was and continues to be a floating signifier[16] – that is, its referents are variable, sometimes indeterminate and unspecifiable – does not in any way suggest that "China" is purely a discursive construction; it only means that there is an irreducibly discursive dimension to ethnic "Chinese's" relationship with "China." Taxonomic studies of ethnic "Chinese" political loyalty and orientations, and multiple manifestations of "Chineseness," can best be understood as attempts at making sense of the multiplicity of assertions, commitments, persuasions, declarations, and expressions generated by the floating signifier "China." They highlight the productive potential of the signifier "China" to be made to mean and do something, conditioning practices and claims made in the name of "China" and "Chinese."

Between the late nineteenth and the mid-twentieth century, there was a political disjunction as various entities and movements at various times – from late Qing provincial and central authorities, to reformers such as Kang Youwei and Liang Qichao, to revolutionaries such as Sun Yat-sen, and on to warlords, the Kuomintang and the Chinese Communist Party – reached out to the "Chinese" in "China" as well as Nanyang (Southeast Asia) and elsewhere.[17] Motivated by imperatives of mobilizing human, financial, and affective resources, each of these appeals to the "Chinese" accomplished two tasks. It drew on or tapped different wellsprings of attachment to and identification with native place(s), ancestry, and origins; and it articulated competing political visions of community, people, nation, and state. Political disjunction meant that there was no easy or necessary fit between nation and state.[18] Different political movements, whose activities and mobilization sometimes took place outside of the territory of "China," targeted specific "Chinese" localities and communities and competed to capture the state and remake society in the image of their visions of the nation. "China"-driven Sinicization thus represents various attempts on the part of different "Chinese" regimes and actors to propound their notions of Chineseness and mobilize "Chinese" capital, resources, labor, and specific talents/skills for economic, political, and cultural objectives inside and outside the territorial boundaries of "China."

Such attempts to reterritorialize the "Chinese" in Southeast Asia were in some ways successful. They helped to create a new political, and more importantly, mobilizable entity called the *huaqiao*, a term that came into general use at the end of the nineteenth century but acquired its territorializing connotations only at the beginning of the twentieth.[19] But these efforts often came up short against competing deterritorializations and reterritorializations of "Chinese" and "Chineseness" that had taken place for at least three centuries in the colonial states of Southeast Asia – especially the Spanish Philippines, Dutch East Indies, British Malaya, and French Indochina. Illustrating the non-linear, multi-sited, reversible, and reinforcing characteristics of Sinicization, their regimes promoted, cemented, and reinvented specific forms of "Chinese" identification and identities while curtailing or repressing others.[20]

In the early years of colonial rule, for example, hoping for the eventual disappearance of the *sangley* community, the Spanish in the Philippines relied on the category of *mestizo* (mixed blood) to administratively distinguish the Philippine-born offspring of *sangley* ("Chinese")-native unions from their (China-born and Christian converted) *sangley* fathers. Their access to their fathers' capital and their socialization in their mothers' native cultures made the *mestizos* among the most socially mobile and hybrid strata of the colonial population. Acquiring economic clout by taking over the hitherto *sangley*-dominated trade during the prohibition of *sangley* immigration between 1766 to 1850, these *mestizos* were instrumental in appropriating the term "Filipino" (a term originally denoting Spanish creoles) and giving it a national(ist) signification. But while this resignification promoted hybridity as a nationalist ideal, it effectively occluded these *mestizos'* "Chinese" ancestry and connections and codified the "Chinese" as Filipino nationalism's Other. This double move helped to promote identification with "white" Europe and America.

Thailand exemplifies a different historical trajectory: at the turn of the twentieth century, cultural notions of Chineseness had been far less important in the eyes of the Chakri kings than the political fealty and economic utility of these "subjects" to the monarchical state. That preeminent symbol of Chineseness, the pigtail, as Kasian Tejapira[21] has cogently argued, at first signified identification with the Qing empire. Later transformed into a marker of cultural nativism among the *jeks*, it was mainly viewed by the Thai state as a signifier for a specific administrative category, a specific tax value, and opium addiction. Only later, when Chinese republicanism came to be seen as a political threat to the state, did the Thai monarch Vajiravudh (Rama VI) actively propound a racial conception of Thai-ness that was opposed to Chineseness.[22]

In Indonesia and Malaysia, intermarriages between Chinese and natives had produced a stable "third culture" of *peranakan* and *baba*, whom Dutch and British colonial policies classified as "Chinese" and whom the colonial systems of social hierarchy, privileges, and incentives discouraged from assimilating into native society. Fresh waves of migration from China in the late nineteenth century created pressures to Sinicize on the part of the *baba*. As their political awakening preceded that of the successful anti-Manchu revolution in China, the *peranakan* worked through their modern identification as "Chinese" by means of active participation in Indies politics.[23]

The most salient feature of the colonial Southeast Asian state's treatment of the "Chinese" is the association of "Chinese" with commerce and capital, an identification that originated in the context of maritime trade and colonial economic enterprise but glosses over the existence of sizeable communities of Chinese laborers, especially in Malaysia. Such identification effectively conditioned the socialization of "Chinese" migrants as "material men" who played an indispensable role in the colonial economies. Reproduced and perpetuated through social relations of production that were characteristic of "Chinese" enterprise in the region,[24] this socialization enabled the "Chinese" to take advantage of the opportunities that were available in the colonial states and economies. But it also rendered them vulnerable to nationalist opprobrium that stigmatized "alien Chinese" as economically dominant and politically unreliable. This made them ready targets of nationalist policies aimed at disentangling the link between ethnicity and class through domestication of "cultural" differences (via assimilation and integration) and redistribution of wealth. Even though a combination of generational change and global/regional economic development has in recent decades produced sizeable urban professional middle classes that include not only "Chinese" but also non-Chinese Southeast Asians, economic regionalization has further cemented this identification of "Chinese" with capital. The crucial difference is that in the throes of economic and social transformation, postcolonial states and societies have generally revalued the identification of Chinese with capital in positive terms. This continuing identification of Chinese with capital is the source of "Chinese" assertive self-empowerment but also of continuing vulnerability to popular-nationalist ressentiment in contemporary Southeast Asia. Oscillating between these two poles, popular media portray Chinese as "heroes" of regional economic development and "villains" in times of economic crisis (and easy targets of violence, as in the case of Chinese Indonesians during the Asian crisis of 1997–98).

Deterritorialization through migration did not simply transplant "Chinese" and "Chineseness" to places outside China. These sites of immigration provided their own settings and cultural matrices for the invention, reinvention, and transformation of "Chineseness," testing even the most expansive notion of Chinese "civilization" that defined Chineseness not in racial terms, but through written language and subscription to "Chinese" core values. Indeed, there were communities in Southeast Asia who called themselves or were treated by their states as "Chinese," but who neither spoke, read, nor wrote "Chinese," practiced "Chinese" customs or rituals, or looked "Chinese." The East Indies *peranakan* were classified by the Dutch as "Chinese," even though their culture exhibited pronounced hybridization of Javanese and other cultural elements that made them appear "un-Chinese" in the eyes of visiting Qing officials.[25] Until the early 1980s, to take another example, Indonesia's Kalimantan province had a community of stateless "Chinese" whom Indonesian government officials call *hitacis* (pronounced "hitachis," a word play on the Japanese appliance maker) or *hitam tapi cina* (black but Chinese). Indonesian officials confessed to being unable to distinguish these individuals from native Indonesians,[26] and they do not readily fit the accepted racial, linguistic, civilizational, and cultural criteria for Chineseness. This illustrates how "Chinese" and "Chineseness," in the hands and eyes of the Dutch East Indies colonial state and Indonesian postcolonial state, are rendered arbitrary by the exigencies and whims of the state and government officials.

The *hitacis* are not an exceptional case. What constitutes "Chinese" culture in the modernist sense of the term is continually enriched by the development of hybrid "Chinese" cultures that owe a great deal to the local histories of settlement and cultural contacts in social spaces outside the purview of the mainland state. The politicized *huaqiao* nationalism among "Chinese" immigrants and their descendants was a "peripheral" sort that was dependent and conditional on developments and contestations on the mainland. Physical and psychological distance from China gave it leeway to define its various "Chinese" cultures according to the pressures operating and opportunities open in the countries of residence.[27] At the same time, *huaqiao* activities had an impact on the mainland. Overseas Chinese support for the nationalist movement led Sun Yat-sen to call the *huaqiao* the "mother of revolution" (*geming zhi mu*). Southeast Asian Chinese provided substantial financial support for "national salvation" activities against the Japanese in the 1930s and 1940s. Moreover, in the decades since the reopening of China, in deeply interactive processes, investment by ethnic Chinese from Hong Kong, Taiwan, Southeast Asia, America, and elsewhere has been crucial to the economic modernization of the mainland.[28]

To complicate the issue, during the first half of the twentieth century the mainland "Chinese" state was not unitary, weakened as it had been during the late Qing and the Republican years. Its reach and capacities were undermined by defeat at the hands of the British. In the twentieth century, the threat of dismemberment and secession loomed large as China was subject to decentralized rule by competing warlords, occupation by imperial Japan, and a civil war between the KMT and CCP. The enduring myth of historical continuity that rests on the ideal of a unitary state[29] belies the reality of fragmentation of power and authority, with the state(s) serving as object(s) of intense competition among different forces.

Another disjunction arises from the modern state's fraught and contested inheritance of the territorial boundaries established by the Qing (with precedents in boundaries set by the Mongols and claimed by the Ming). While huge tracts of Mongolia were able to gain independence after the breakdown of the Qing empire, territories such as Tibet and Xinjiang, which did not join the Chinese Republic, have been occupied and placed under the control of the mainland party state. They are now viewed as indispensable parts of China, a view that does not square with the opinions of Tibetan and Uyghur separatists. Attempts at promoting an inclusive nationalist discourse in the mainland coexist alongside a Han-Sinocentrism that defines "Chineseness" in exclusivist terms.[30]

"China's" internal division was not the only significant disjunction. Equally important was the physical fragmentation around the edges of the Qing empire, particularly the loss of Hong Kong to the British and Taiwan to the Japanese. These geopolitical "splits" were to have crucial consequences during the Cold War era, when the mainland was "closed" to the American-dominated "Free Asia," and Taiwan and Hong Kong emerged as interlinked (but not necessarily overlapping) purveyors, respectively, of state-authorized and market-driven "Chinese" culture and "Chineseness" through the circulation of media and popular culture. In the post-Cold War era, the status of Taiwan remains a flashpoint as mainland China's integration into (and increasing importance in) the "East Asian" trade system has proceeded alongside its continuing exclusion from the hub-and-spokes security framework.

On the international front, Taiwan and mainland China competed, with varying degrees of success, for the attention and support (if not loyalty) of overseas Chinese during the Cold War era.[31] For all of Taipei's attempts to establish itself as a "cultural substitute" for the mainland[32] and success in creating multiple linkages between Taiwan, Hong Kong, and the overseas Chinese during that period, ethnic Chinese familial memories of, and ties to, the ancestral land in mainland China were neither easily nor completely replaceable[33] by a transfer of loyalty to Taipei. Nor could interest in developments in mainland China and pride in "China's" achievements be fully rechanneled to Taiwan, given the disconnection between the KMT-controlled Taiwan state and the mainland territory of "China" to which the ethnic Chinese in Southeast Asia and elsewhere traced their ancestry/origin. At the same time, the geopolitical identification of the mainland with socialism by non-communist states in the region curtailed any means of direct contact between ethnic Chinese in "Free Asia" and "China." Furthermore, for more than twenty years after World War II, emotional attachment to the place of ancestral origin did not necessarily translate into political (let alone economic) identification with the Communist state.[34] Wang Gungwu[35] rightly notes the centripetal and centrifugal forces that have led to the creation of multiple cultural centers of Chineseness, and the inability of the current regime on the mainland to claim cultural authority as the sole legitimate representative of China and arbiter of Chineseness.

This does not mean, however, that these geopolitical sites of Chinese representations and contestations were totally discrete and mutually exclusive. Despite the "closing" of mainland China to Free Asia in the Cold War years, there existed some channels of communication among the authorities in the mainland, Taiwan and Hong Kong, and parts of the mainland. During the Cold War, for example, the Fujian and Guangdong Provinces continued to be linked, through small-scale migration and material inflows, to Hong Kong, Taiwan, Southeast Asia, Japan, and the United States. The opening of China after 1978 has seen further deterritorialization through large-scale migration from China as well as re-migration of ethnic Chinese from Northeast and Southeast Asia to mainly English-speaking countries of America and the Commonwealth of Nations. Simultaneously, reterritorializations have occurred as the crisis of faith engendered by the retreat of socialism and socialist thought created a vacuum filled by versions of nationalist and Confucianist discourses propounded by diverse states, markets, communities, and individuals inside and outside China.[36] Various actors sought to fill the void through literature, mass media such as newspapers, films, and television shows, and cybermedia, as well as regime sponsorships of Confucianism, Taiwanese cultural nationalism, and other undertakings.

"Sino-Japanese-English" hybridization in the age of collective imperialism

Conceptual disjunction is not the only characteristic feature of the modern term "China" and its attendant signifiers. A specific sort of hybridization has also been crucial to the emergence of modern "China" and its culture and politics. It has long been accepted that cultural inflows traditionally entered imperial China mainly through continental (particularly Inner) Asia and through the overland routes that brought Buddhism from India. Several times in its history, "China" was ruled by non-Han: the Mongols, who incorporated China into the first world-empire in history; and the Manchus, who presided over a multi-ethnic empire and cemented their legitimacy among the Han Chinese by selectively Sinicizing themselves (without, however, completely erasing their ethnic identification as Manchus) and acting as principal sponsors of state-propagated Confucianism.[37]

Rather than its lack of interest in exporting its institutions, social practices, and values,[38] limits to the reach and might of the mainland state were instrumental in delineating its relations with neighbors to the east.[39] Its relations with Korea and Vietnam, with whom it shared borders, were historically organized in terms of a China-centered tributary system, periodically backed by military power, allowing for a flexible range of appropriations of – and acculturation to – things Chinese by neighboring states.[40] Even as Vietnam closely modeled its institutions and practices after China, it actively engaged in a form of appropriation that drew on "civilizational" notions shared among different polities in the East Asian region while abstracting the term for China from its geographical reference to the mainland.[41] This abstraction enabled the Vietnamese court and scholar-officials to enthusiastically adopt Confucian institutions and norms while simultaneously resisting political domination by the mainland state.[42] Farther removed from China's reach, some polities in the region, such as Malaka and Butuan, sent tributary missions to China to secure economic benefits and accrue social prestige, without adopting wholesale Chinese institutions and social practices.

The hybridization that arose during the maritime period from the collision between China and the "West" entailed a different cultural politics. The flows of people and modes of transmission of new political and cultural ideas – as well as the new conceptions of community that entered and circulated in China from the West – ran through pathways and networks created in the East. Consequently, the making of "China" in the modern period is crucially mediated by two non-Chinese communicative spheres, Japanese and English (both British and American), which were created by the regional system in the East in which Britain, Japan, and the USA competed for dominance. Between the late nineteenth century and the 1930s, the formation of an East-based system of collective imperialism linked the territories and economies of China, Japan, and Southeast Asia, providing the bridges and avenues through which peoples, commodities, languages, and ideas moved into China.

This pattern of flows to, through, and from China is nested in a specific regional structure of power and wealth. Although western powers dominated the international order that provided the institutional framework for "forced free trade" in the region, the economic impact of the West on China was confined mainly to the littoral regions.[43] It was intra-Asian trade, mediated by western collective imperialism, that penetrated China's hinterlands and connected China to the world market. In this sense, the impact of the West was principally mediated through intra-Asian regional links and connections among China, Japan, and the various colonies in Southeast Asia. Chinese merchants and the development of colonial economies, underpinned in part by Chinese labor, played a crucial role in this connecting process.[44] This regional system, rather than the "West" per se, played a central part in China- and world-making. In its cultural matrix, Japanese was an important linguistic mode of transmission of western concepts, while English served as the de facto regional and commercial lingua franca.

The relationship between China and the so-called "West" was crucially mediated by the reconfigured relationship between China and Japan. Japan's victory over Qing China in the Sino-Japanese War of 1894–95 was a spectacular reversal of traditional China-to-Japan unidirectional cultural flows. From the final years of the nineteenth century to the first half of the twentieth, the number of Chinese students who received their education in Japan surpassed the combined numbers of their compatriots in Europe and America.[45] These Chinese *ryūgakusei/liuxuesheng* were key agents in the "translingual practices" (to use Lydia Liu's term) that decisively shaped the very terms by which, for intellectual and political purposes, the "West" was discursively constructed and deployed in a China–West binary.[46] Through these practices, basic vocabulary such as politics (*zhengzhi*), economy (*jingji*), and culture (*wenhua*) entered the Chinese lexicon and circulated in China through "Sino-Japanese-English" translations in which not only Japan-educated Chinese and Japanese, but also western missionaries, played important roles.[47] More than half of the loan words in the Chinese language are from Japanese;[48] one Chinese scholar has gone so far as to argue that 70 percent of the modern terms regularly used in the social sciences and humanities are imported from Japanese.[49] Some of these Japanese terms were neologisms first coined by western missionaries and subsequently re-imported to China via Japanese texts. Others were either neologisms rendered in *kanji* (Chinese character) form by the Japanese, or old classical kanji/Chinese terms that were assigned new and modern meanings by the Japanese, and then re-imported into China.

An early political form taken by these translingual practices was Asianism, for which Tokyo/Yokohama served as the main hub, with smaller hubs in San Francisco, Singapore, Siam, and Hong Kong. Here, a kind of Sino-Japanese kanji/hanyu communicative sphere helped create a network that linked, at different times, personalities such as Kim Okgyun of Korea, Inukai Tsuyoshi and Miyazaki

Tōten of Japan, Sun Yat-sen of China, and Phan Boi Chau of Vietnam.[50] But it is also instructive to note that English became the second lingua franca of this Asianist network, connecting Suehiro Tetchō to Jose Rizal, and Sun Yat-sen and An Kyong-su to Mariano Ponce. Sun Yat-sen communicated with his Japanese friends and allies through Chinese (often in brush conversations or *bitan/hitsudan*) as well as English. He switched completely to English when communicating with Filipino nationalist Mariano Ponce, as did Japanese activists like Suehiro Tetchō and Miyazaki Tōten.

In fact, along with his connections with Japan and Korea through the medium of written Chinese, Sun also exemplifies a specific kind of "modern Chinese" that first emerged in port cities such as Shanghai, Tientsin, Canton, and Amoy, as well as sites of Chinese immigration in Southeast Asia and America. The "Anglo-Chinese" (to use a term coined by Takashi Shiraishi[51]) were part of the British formal and commercial empire in the region in the nineteenth century.[52] In Hong Kong and Southeast Asia, Anglo-Chinese – who, along with a smaller number of their Japanese counterparts, were often educated by Christian missionaries – staffed the bureaucracy and constituted the nascent middle classes of professionals (such as doctors) and scions of Chinese merchants. Educated in both Chinese and English and sometimes only in English, and interpellated as "Chinese" by the colonial policies of their respective domiciles, these Anglo-Chinese were proficient in local and colonial languages such as Cantonese, Hokkien, Malay, Javanese, Tagalog, Dutch, Portuguese, and French. Their multilingualism (and especially their proficiency in the commercial regional lingua franca) gave them the cultural resources to move across social and linguistic hierarchies in their polyglot colonial societies and beyond.[53]

These multicultural/hybrid Chinese include the Penang (Malaysia)-born Lim Boon Keng (Lin Wenqing, 1869–1957), a doctor by profession who was educated in Edinburgh. He was an associate of Sun Yat-sen and later president of Xiamen (Amoy) University, and a key figure in the propagation of Confucianism in Singapore, Malaya, and the Dutch East Indies. Spurred by his exposure to English texts on China and Chinese classics, and the colonial dispensation that labeled him "Chinese," his attempt at creating a "modern Chinese identity" entailed the elevation of Confucianism to a national as well as a universal philosophy and religion comparable to, and on a par with, Christianity.[54] His idea of an emergent Chineseness was not rooted in outward or physical signs of Chineseness (for example, costume or hairstyle), but rather in a personal code or morality that prepared the Chinese for progress. At the same time, as Wang Gungwu has pointed out, Lim's advocacy of Confucian education was complemented by his support for a modern curriculum that included the teaching of science. Famously delivered in English at his presidential address at Xiamen University[55] on 3 October 1926, his vision of revivified Confucian teachings for the present time offered a distinctive platform for modernization in China. Despite differing sharply from the anti-tradition Chinese modernity envisioned by the Sino-Japanese hybrid Lu Xun, it was in all respects as modern as Lu's.[56]

Two other exemplary Anglo-Chinese from opposite ends of the political spectrum are conservative Ku Hung-ming (Gu Hongming, 1857–1928) and May 4th activist Lee Teng Hwee (Li Denghui, 1872–1947). Like Lim Boon Keng, Ku Hung-ming was born in Penang and educated in Edinburgh, but he also studied in Leipzig and Paris. Fluent in English, Chinese, French, and German, among other languages, he translated Confucian and other classic texts into English, worked for the Qing government, and advocated a form of orthodox Confucianism that, counterposed to European civilization, proved to be unpopular even among Chinese.[57] Lee was born near Batavia (now Jakarta, Indonesia) and educated at the Anglo-Chinese School in Singapore and Yale University in the USA. He founded the Yale Institute and taught at the Tiong Hwa Hwee Koan in Batavia, and later became the first president of Fudan University in Shanghai.[58]

The impact of political Asianism was limited and eventually curtailed by Japanese imperialism. It spurred the development of Chinese nationalism by providing Chinese nationalists with an identifiable enemy against which the Chinese people could be mobilized. Sino-Japanese-English translingual practices arguably had a far more widespread influence especially on Chinese culture, politics, and military organization.[59] Such translingual practices transformed Chinese institutions and practices, bearing out the discursive and dispositional aspects of Sinicization. Their political impact is readily apparent in the crucial role they played in the introduction of socialist thought into China, via translation from Japanese. Ishikawa Yoshihiko's[60] study reveals that, between 1919 and 1921, 13 out of 18 Chinese translations of texts by Marx and Engels, as well as other Marxist figures – including *The Communist Manifesto* – were based on Japanese translations. Writings by Japanese anarchists and Marxists such as Kōtoku Shūsui, Ōsugi Sakae, and Kawakami Hajime also were read in China, Korea, and Vietnam, and influenced the development of socialism in these countries.[61] Where political surveillance of and crackdowns against Bolshevism restricted its transmission from Japan to China, Bolshevist thought, including its visual imagery, entered China via translations from English (many of them published in America) through the treaty port of Shanghai. The port city of Shanghai itself is a spatial representation of this Sino-Japanese-English hybridization: the British provided the policing and administration; the Japanese constituted the largest foreign contingent; and the gray zones created by the administratively segmented International Settlements enabled nationalists and communists from Asia and beyond to flourish, allowing figures such as Tan Malaka, Nguyen Ai Quoc (Ho Chi Minh), Hilaire Noulens, and Agnes Smedley (who communicated with each other in English, a lingua franca of the Comintern) to meet, mingle, and organize their respective political projects in the name of the nation and international solidarity.

Beyond mainland China, the Sino-Japanese-English cultural nexus was an enabling ground not only for the revolutionary movement in the Philippines, but also for the political awakening of the Indies Chinese, whose activities would provide models and inspiration for Indonesian nationalist activism. Tiong Hwa Hwee Koan, the first social and educational association established in 1900, recruited staff from Chinese *ryūgakusei* in Japan to teach not only Chinese but also English.[62] Its textbooks, which were published in Japan and later in Shanghai, had originally been designed for use by Chinese students in a Yokohama school run by a Yokohama Chinese; that school's opening had been graced by Sun Yat-sen and Inukai Tsuyoshi.[63] The Indonesian writer Pramoedya Ananta Toer would memorialize the Chinese influence on Indonesian nationalism through the revolutionary Khouw Ah Soe – a graduate of an English-language high school in Shanghai. Although Soe does not publicly acknowledge this, he had in fact lived for some years in Japan before being sent to do political organizing among the Indies Chinese. In *Anak Semua Bangsa* (Child of All Nations, 1980),[64] the protagonist Minke learns from Soe about anticolonial struggles in the Philippines and China. In a little over one generation, this political awakening and educational trend would produce Anglo-Chinese Indonesians such as Njoo Cheong Seng (1902–62), whose popular Gagaklodra series of martial-arts fiction features the eponymous half-Chinese, half-Javanese protagonist. Njoo typified a new generation of Indonesian Chinese who were comfortable not only with Indonesian (and Dutch), but in particular with English. In imagining an Indonesian nationalism that was not incompatible with Chinese patriotism, he drew inspiration from both British and American literary traditions and popular cultures (especially American comics and Hollywood films).[65]

Thailand offers another interesting case study, of a different path of transmission of radical nationalism through the regional circulation of people and transmission of ideas. Communism came to Thailand not from the West, but via the East through Chinese and Vietnamese immigrants. Considered part of the Communist Party of Malaya, Thailand's Communist Party would in turn make Siam a strategic base and hub for the establishment of communist cells in Laos and Cambodia by Ho Chi Minh.[66] Although gifted Sino-Thais were able to obtain their education in England and, less frequently, in France, English education at the time was limited to Thai aristocrats, bureaucrats, and the nascent middle class. Sino-Thais received their education in China or in nearby Straits Chinese schools. The bilingual Thai-born *lukjin*, who were instrumental in translating socialist texts into Thai, bonded with their Thai counterparts in prison. During the American-led Cold War period, they achieved proficiency in English, enabling them to work on translation along with Thai radicals. This pattern of increasing proficiency in the language of British and later American regional domination would be of great consequence in the post-Cold War period.

The rise of the Anglo-Chinese under American hegemony

Japan's primacy as a translingual hub was undermined by Japanese imperialism and its failed attempt to establish hegemony in the region. After its defeat, Japan was incorporated into the American-led "Free Asia" through a hub-and-spokes regional security system (anchored in the US–Japan alliance and bilateral treaties between the USA and its Southeast Asian allies) and a triangular trade system involving the

USA, Japan, and the rest of "Free Asia" that officially excluded (in the name of "containment") Communist China.[67]

Of equal import was the fact that for the first quarter century of this new regional arrangement, ethnic Chinese migrants faced a great deal of pressure from postcolonial nation-states in Southeast Asia to de-Sinicize. This pressure reached its apotheosis in the anti-Chinese discrimination practiced in Indonesia, which actively sought to erase all visible (and auditory) signs of Chineseness. Along with the postcolonial states in Malaysia and the Philippines, Indonesia aimed to regulate if not restrict the economic activities of ethnic Chinese through economic nationalism and affirmative-action programs favoring *bumiputera* ("sons of the soil"). While these de-Sinicizing policies and the absence of direct contact with mainland China succeeded in nationalizing the Chinese minority, erasing Chineseness by granting the Chinese Indonesian a form of second-class citizenship ironically reinforced and perpetuated the treatment of the ethnic Chinese as "alien" nationals.[68] The situation of the Chinese in the Philippines, however, shows how changing diplomatic and economic imperatives led to shifts in state policies, as the re-establishment of diplomatic relations between the Philippines and China in 1975 paved the way for the mass granting of Filipino citizenship to large numbers of Chinese. The hitherto alien Chinese, through college education, were drawn into closer and more frequent social contact with Filipinos and came to identify themselves as "Filipino," thus facilitating their incorporation into both the national imaginary and the body politic.

State-driven attempts at de-Sinicizing the Chinese and more recent market-driven re-Sinicization of the Chinese occurred with novel forms of hybridization. Anglophone education in the region and abroad and the acquisition of linguistic proficiency in English (or more accurately, Englishes) became a widespread phenomenon that reached beyond the elites and professionals and scions of rich merchants of the earlier period to encompass the growing middle classes and urban populations. This hybridization also involves nationalization that incorporates elements and languages of Southeast Asia's indigenous cultures. The product and agent of this process is the "Anglo-Chinese" (and, in the case of the Southeast Asian Chinese, "Anglo-Chinese-Indonesian," and so on). The term "Anglo-Chinese" was originally applied to schools (sometimes western missionary-run) where sons (and later daughters) of ethnic Chinese businessmen received the kind of education that prepared them for business and/or professional careers. A version of the Confucian classics was taught in Chinese (*Guoyu*), alongside English and practical subjects such as accounting. Such "hybrid" schools were established in the Nanyang territories (mainly in the British colonies of Singapore and Malaya, but also in Indonesia and the Philippines), and in the port cities of Hong Kong, Tientsin, Canton, Amoy, and Shanghai; some of their graduates went on to pursue higher education either in China or, more commonly, in England and America.

A term that originated in the maritime-Asian world under British hegemony can thus be fruitfully applied to the contemporary regional context of the East

Asian hybridization of Chinese under American hegemony. The crucial linguistic continuity from British to American English marked the transition from British to American hegemony and promoted the use of English as a regional and commercial lingua franca. What followed was the widespread dissemination of Hollywood films and, eventually, the Americanization of bureaucratic elites and professional middle classes and their worldviews. Like their forefathers in this region, the Anglo-Chinese tend to have the following characteristics: they are at least bilingual (with English as one of their major languages); they received a western-style education (which normally includes secondary or tertiary or graduate education in America or Britain);[69] they have some grounding in the school systems in their respective countries and intend to educate their children in the same way; they are well versed in "international" (mainly Anglo-American) business norms and values; and they have relied on their hybrid skills (whether linguistic or cultural) and connections to enter business and work as professionals. One can also speak of comparable processes of Anglo-Japanization of Japanese, Anglo-Koreanization of Koreans, Anglo-Sinicization of Taiwanese, and comparable phenomena among segments of Southeast Asian middle and upper classes. In Chapter 6, Chih-yu Shih provides the biographical details of China specialists whose careers illustrate these various processes.

Far removed from the context of anti-imperialist nationalism that was the engine of "China"-driven Sinicization in the first half of the twentieth century, "re-Sinicization" is today more a component of, rather than an alternative to, ethnic Chinese Anglo-Sinicization. Now primarily market-driven, it is propelled as much by economic incentives for learning Mandarin Chinese and seeking jobs in a rapidly growing China and East Asian region as by the desire to learn "Chinese" culture in a more hospitable political environment. Wang Gungwu[70] calls this the new *huaqiao syndrome*, in which the mainland Chinese nation-state is an increasingly important, but by no means the only, source of economic opportunities and cultural identification and validation. Contemporary Sinicization is recalibrating established routines. This process may entail a form of Sinicization that involves the Mandarinization of erstwhile provincialized/localized *huaqiao* identities, as the pressures and incentives among Anglo-Chinese to learn *putonghua* (as well as the simplified Chinese script) increase with China's economic rise. But it is not likely to happen at the expense of ongoing Anglo-hybridization, and may very well complement it. Moreover, the process of selective Anglo-hybridization involves not only ethnic Chinese, but also non-Chinese Southeast Asian elites and middle classes. It prepares the ground for the creation of an encompassing and inclusive cultural frame of reference and communicative meeting ground for interaction among the Southeast Asian middle and upper classes, and between these classes and their counterparts in other areas of the world. Along with fellow Anglo-hybrid elites in their respective countries, Anglo-Chinese parlay their proficiency in the global lingua franca and their familiarity with Anglo-American norms and codes into cultural, social, and material capital.

Ethnic Chinese were erstwhile subject to pressures to declare loyalty to their respective country of residence. During the Cold War, their lack of direct access to mainland China meant that the elder generation, who considered themselves sojourners, could no longer dream of returning to China. The younger generation grew up with the firm notion that their home was in the Philippines, Thailand, or other parts of Southeast Asia. "China" remained for them a geographical and symbolic marker whose image was now mediated by Taiwan and Hong Kong in the form of films, television programs, newspapers, and news reports. In the age of collective imperialism, and especially in conjunction with anti-Japanese nationalism, this condition of extended absence from the mainland had already created the phenomenon of "abstract" or "taught" nationalism among the so-called *huaqiao*.[71] In the 1930s and 1940s, this type of nationalism inspired some of them to return to China during the Sino-Japanese war. In postcolonial Southeast Asia across the Taiwan Strait, a bitter rivalry between two governments claiming to speak in the name of a legitimate "China" played out in Chinatowns across Southeast Asia, America, and elsewhere. This, despite the fact that younger generations, increasingly rooted in their countries of birth, looked to Southeast Asia for their identities. Some chose assimilation; others, still identifying themselves as Chinese, practiced a form of abstract nationalism that enabled identification with (an often imaginary) "China" without necessarily supporting either the mainland or the Taiwanese state.[72]

Moreover, Taiwan and especially Hong Kong emerged as hubs for the popular cultural dissemination of images of and knowledge about China, in the form of newspapers, books, movies, television shows, and pop music. This development was conditioned in large part by the potentials and restrictions inherent in the regional system created in America's "Free Asia." The example of Hong Kong cinema in the postwar period is instructive of how conceptual disjunction and historical hybridization influenced the development of the film industry. In the early postwar era, the production of Hong Kong films relied heavily on financing by overseas Chinese and pre-selling to distributors in Southeast Asia. Replacing prewar Shanghai as the "Hollywood of the East," Hong Kong had a preeminently regional cinema. Starting in the 1950s, during the Cold War, Taiwan emerged as the Hong Kong film industry's main market and a leading source of non–Hong Kong financing. Hong Kong's ability to capture the regional market of American-led "Free Asia" was made possible in part by Taiwan's ruling Kuomintang Party. By classifying Hong Kong films as part of its "national cinema," it promoted exchanges between Hong Kong and Taiwan (as well as "Free Asia" overseas Chinese communities). This made Hong Kong films eligible for consideration by Taiwan's film-awarding organizations, and offered incentives for import and production of Mandarin-language films through subsidies and preferential taxation.[73] The intensification of indigenous nationalism in Southeast Asia in the late 1960s and 1970s had an adverse impact by restricting the circulation of Hong Kong films as well as Southeast Asian Chinese investment in the Hong Kong film industry. This led to a shift in focus from serving émigré-community markets to developing domestic along with national markets in the region and beyond. Hong Kong's regional émigré and overseas market in turn defined Hong Kong's film tradition, genres, and conventions. Mandarin and other Sinophone films of the 1950s drew from the folk opera tradition and prewar Shanghai film conventions of featuring songs, historical themes and settings, and love and martial arts genres[74] – conventions on which even mainland Chinese filmmakers had to draw during the past decade when, in collaboration with their Hong Kong and Taiwanese counterparts, they began producing films for the international market.

Through the "Free Asia" regional system, Japan also became connected to Hong Kong and Taiwan. In line with the Sino-Japanese-English hybridization of modern China, Shanghai's film studios in the 1920s and 1930s were modeled not only after Hollywood, but also after Japan.[75] The postwar period witnessed an increase in popular culture flows from Japan (through film, music, *manga*, and anime) into Taiwan and Hong Kong. *Jidai-geki* (pre-Meiji historical drama) films from Japan, for example, inspired Hong Kong filmmakers to create their own swordplay movies. Taiwanese popular music has historical roots in Japanese *enka*, with superstars such as Teresa Teng (Teng Li-chün, who has a huge fan base in China) cementing their domestic and international reputations by making it big in Japan, and going on to record songs not just in Mandarin, Cantonese, Japanese, and English, but also in Korean, Vietnamese, and Indonesian. Film technicians were trained in Japan, and Japanese talent were hired in Hong Kong. In the early 1950s, Japanese filmmakers initiated the establishment of the Southeast Asian Motion Picture Producers' Association and the Southeast Asian Film Festival. This move would eventually lead to the expansion of a regional film network under the designations of "Asia" and "Asia-Pacific."[76] Hong Kong films were shot on location in Japan, Singapore, Malaysia, South Korea, Taiwan, and the Philippines; co-productions and talent inflows were initiated with Japan, South Korea, the Philippines, and Thailand;[77] and from the 1970s onward, Hong Kong's domestic as well as other national markets (rather than just émigré-community markets) in Asia, America, and other areas became an important source of Hong Kong film revenues.

The reopening of China in the late 1970s marked the beginning of China's economic reintegration with the regional system. Hong Kong, Taiwan, and ethnic Chinese entrepreneurs, professionals, and companies in Southeast Asia, America, and other regions played an important role in this process. In sharp contrast, on questions of security, China remains outside the US-led hub-and-spokes system. A look at the cooperative and collaborative connections and networks in and around Hong Kong cinema reveals how the patterns and densities of regional exchanges have changed over time.[78] Although China had opened and embarked on reform, in the late 1970s and early 1980s it was still in the process of being integrated into the regional system. The integration of "Free Asia" was already very much in place, as illustrated by the prominent presence of Taiwanese and the importance of Southeast Asian financing and distribution networks in Hong Kong films. Japanese inflows of money and talent peaked at the height of Japan's bubble years in the

1980s, when the country led the flying-geese pattern of regional development. As China became more integrated into the regional system and emerged as the locomotive of regional development after the Asian financial crisis of 1997–98, mainland Chinese financing and talent inflows gained importance in Hong Kong films. Taiwanese actors/actresses have always formed an important contingent in Hong Kong films; in the 1990s, mainland actors came to constitute an equally important group that overtook their Taiwanese counterparts by the early 2000s.

Large-scale flows and exchanges between Hong Kong and China have resulted in a form of re-Sinicization, defined by Eric Ma as "the recollection, reinvention and rediscovery of historical and cultural ties between Hong Kong and China."[79] Despite the rise of cultural nationalism that has sought to articulate a uniquely Taiwanese national identity (entailing a reassessment of Japan's role in Taiwan's modernization), post-Cold War contacts and deepening economic ties with the mainland engendered a "Mainland Fever" in Taiwan that was fed by books, films, and music from and about mainland China.[80] In the meantime, the "porous" nature of the regional system has enabled people and capital to go transnational.[81] This trend has become clearer in recent years through an increase in the "unclassifiability" of East Asians such as the actor Takeshi Kaneshiro. He holds a Japanese passport, and his father is Japanese and mother Taiwanese. Conversant in Mandarin, Hokkien, Japanese, English, and Cantonese, he debuted as a singer under the Japanese name "Aniki" and gained fame first in Taiwan before appearing in Hong Kong and Japanese films.

The cultural impact of ongoing regionalization is far less understood and remarked upon. Japanization, which reached its peak in the 1980s and 1990s as Japan-led economic growth planted the seeds for regional economic integration, has now been subsumed under a broader process of East Asian regionalism and regionalization that has created variegated sources of cultural flows going well beyond Japan and Greater China. It is subject to interesting and novel recombinations, as when increasing numbers of mainland Chinese students opt to study in Japan rather than in America, Taiwanese *manga* artists begin publishing their works in Japan, mainland Chinese produce films using East Asian pop culture formats, Singaporeans follow Hong Kong and Taiwanese fashion trends, Filipinos fall in love with Taiwan's pop-idol band *F4* and Japanese with Korean teledramas, and Koreans learn English in the Philippines rather than in America or Britain. "Re-Sinicization" and Japanization are but two streams of this multi-sited, uneven process of hybridization.[82]

Some implications of multi-sited "Chineseness"

The conceptual disjunctions and historical hybridizations that make "China" a floating signifier create multiple meanings of and identifications with "China," "Chineseness," and "Chinese culture/civilization." In *practice*, no single political entity/regime embodies or exercises ultimate authority on "China," "Chinese," and "Chineseness." Although its importance has greatly increased in economic and geopolitical terms, the mainland has so far not emerged as the preeminent cultural arbiter of Chineseness. Indeed, China is distinguished by a relative lack of soft power.[83] Nor has the economic rise of China and the market-driven Mandarinization of "Chineseness" substantively reduced or simplified the multi-sited claims and belongings exercised by the ethnic "Chinese" in Southeast Asia.

What we see, instead, are multiple instances of cultural entrepreneurship that do not necessarily affirm the primacy of mainland China as the cultural center and arbiter of (Mandarin) Chineseness. An example is the Dragon Descendants Museum, located northwest of Bangkok in Suphan Buri Province. A brainchild of former Thai prime minister (and himself Sino-Thai) Banharn Silpa-archa, the museum was conceived for the commemoration of the twentieth anniversary of the establishment of diplomatic relations between Thailand and China. Launched in late 2008, its celebration of "5,000 years" of Chinese history illustrates just how much ideas of China and Chineseness owe to the incorporation of a standardized version of Chinese history, taught in Thai Chinese schools, into the narrative of "Chinese" contribution to the development of Thailand. More telling is its subscription to a version of Chinese history that is mediated by Taiwan's and Hong Kong's culture industries. One striking example of this Hong Kong/Taiwan pop-cultural mediation of Chineseness is the prominence accorded to the historical figure of Judge Pao (Bao Zheng), whom Thais came to know through the Taiwanese TV mini-series that was a huge hit not only in Taiwan, but also in Hong Kong and mainland China.[84] It was in fact the enormous popularity of the Judge Pao series among Thai viewers that made Chineseness "chic" in the 1990s.[85]

Cultural entrepreneurs like Malaysia's Lillian Too (born in Penang) and Thailand's Chitra Konuntakiet (born in Bangkok) have turned Chineseness into a profitable business venture. Lillian Too has built her career on a curriculum vitae that emphasizes her MBA from the Harvard Business School; her position as the first woman CEO from Malaysia to head a publicly listed company, the Hong Kong Dao Heng Bank; and her self-reinvention as founder of the World of Feng Shui. Her website sells her English-language geomancy (*fengshui*) books, which target the "30 million English-speaking non-Chinese Asians" worldwide.[86] Educated in an elite school in Thailand before obtaining her Master's degree in the United States, Thailand's Chitra Konuntakiet overcame her experience of anti-Chinese racism in school by becoming a successful columnist, radio personality, and novelist. Her books on Chinese culture (as filtered through her Teo-chiu upbringing) – *Chinese Knowledge from the Old Man, Chinese Children, Nine Philosophy Stories,* and most recently the novel *A-Pa* – have sold more than 600,000 copies to date.[87] Both Lillian Too and Chitra Konuntakiet propound notions of Chineseness that fall beyond the purview of state-sanctioned and mainland-originating discourses: in the case of Lillian Too, through access to a belief system that is not accorded official recognition in mainland China but is part of folk beliefs and practices in Taiwan, Hong Kong, Chinatowns elsewhere, and mainland China; and in the case of Chitra Konuntakiet, through access to familial memories and ideas of

Chinese customs and practices that were rooted primarily in her father's immigrant experience in Thailand rather than in received notions of Chineseness promoted by the mainland and Taiwan's China scholarship.[88]

Enforced for much of the twentieth century by the political turmoil on the mainland, "Chinese" migrants and their descendants' existential experiences of extended physical absence from their putative places of "origin" have meant that political contestation over the meanings of "China" did extend across the mainland and into Nanyang and Hong Kong. Yet there were important limits to the deterritorialization of these struggles, as illustrated by "the China factor" in the Hong Kong riots of 1967.[89] Even when political and cultural movements succeeded in capturing the state, their ability to use the state to propound their vision of the "Chinese" nation remains constrained by the limited reach of the "Chinese" state. Through competing strategies of territorialization, deterritorialization, and reterritorialization, authorities and institutions impose constraints on ethnic Chinese, within both Chinese and non-Chinese territories. The spatial, political, cultural, and economic disjunctions that inform the different processes of Sinicization have lent an irreducibly "imaginative" dimension to "Chinese" identification without predetermining the practical consequences and outcomes of these identifications and projects.

Moreover, mainland China has not remained immune to the appeal of these different sources and centers of "Chineseness."[90] An important example of spirited debate on China's identity in the post-Maoist era is the one sparked by the controversial six-part TV documentary series *Heshang* (River Elegy, 1988), which relied on the spatial metaphors of land-versus-sea to contrast the isolationism of so-called "traditional" "Chinese" culture, symbolized by the Great Wall, with the openness of the maritime-world "blue" ocean into which the Yellow River flows.[91] Some enterprising companies have embarked on making films, set in China, that showcase China's regional connections and participation in shared urban regional lifestyles. One example is the successful mainland Chinese production of the East Asian romantic comedy genre *Lian Ai Qian Gui Ze* (My Airline Hostess Roommate, 2009) which deals with a Beijing-based flight attendant who falls in love with her roommate, a Taiwanese visual artist who creates a cute cat character modeled after Japanese anime. Another example is the persistence and continuing popularity of the traditional Chinese script, despite government attempts to impose and propagate a simplified system; traditional script continues to proliferate in China via the Internet, overseas news media, movies, books, and even shop signs (despite government prohibition). Thus it retains its usefulness as a means by which mainland Chinese can communicate with Taiwan and overseas Chinese communities.[92] The Chinese government is even promoting the production of cartoon animation, drawing in part on the visual language and conventions of Japanese anime that were popularized through Taiwan and Hong Kong. One example of a successful venture is *Xi Yang Yang yu Hui Tai Lang* (Pleasant Goat and Big Big Wolf), a television cartoon series produced by the Guangdong-based Creative Power Entertaining, whose 2009 movie version broke box office records for the Chinese animated film.⁹³ The cartoon series is now aired in 13 Asian countries and regions.⁹⁴

By erasing their revolutionary past and in its place highlighting local and regional identities that carry traces of "traditional" or "folk" elements, and with the rise of regional/local identities, China's provinces in the hinterlands have sought to transform themselves into revenue-generating tourist attractions, thus challenging the "ultrastable spatial identity of Chineseness."⁹⁵ Nor have coastal provinces been remiss in self-promotion. Tourist-service companies in Xiamen, for example, have turned hybridity into a cultural asset as a way of attracting tourists from Taiwan, Hong Kong, and Southeast Asia, with which Xiamen has close historical connections. For example, a tourist brochure put out by the Xiamen Min'nan Tourism and Culture Industry Co. invokes international as well as local contexts to package Xiamen's attractions. Published in Chinese, English, and Japanese, the brochure features a series of stage shows that celebrate, through song and dance, the heritage of "Magic Min'nan" (Southern Min).⁹⁶ Min'nan is presented as a hybrid culture, a product of the historical position of Fujian as the "starting point" of the Maritime Silk Road, a "hotbed of reform" that played an important role in the reopening of post-Maoist China, and a "pioneer in the Western littoral of the Taiwan Straits." Alongside its ancient South China (*Guyue*) heritage, this brochure plays up Xiamen's shared cultural links with Taiwan and Inner Asia and its free-port access to the "West" and the world, thus laying simultaneous claim to western-oriented modernity and classical Chinese civilization.

Moreover, the highlighting of a hybrid South China culture with multiple traditions and connections rewrites the narrative of Chinese civilization, stressing its heterogeneity and, in particular, the openness and hybridity of the "south" as opposed to the "north."⁹⁷ It affirms an idea first propounded by Fu Ssu-nien (Fu Sinian) and Ku Chieh-kang (Gu Jiegang) in the 1920s and 1930s⁹⁸ and revitalized during the past three decades by new archeological findings that prove the existence of a number of regional cultures (other than the one along the Yellow River in the Central Plains). These regional contacts formed a "core" which, by 3000 BCE, linked a geographic area consisting of Shaanxi–Shanxi–Henan, Shandong, Hubei, lower Yangtze, the southern region from Poyang to the Pearl River delta, and the northern region by the Great Wall that would subsequently be called "China."⁹⁹ This idea of multiple sources and origins of Chinese civilization decenters the traditional claim of the Yellow River as the cradle of Chinese civilization without relinquishing altogether the idea of a civilizational "core."

The centripetal and centrifugal forces of territorializing and de/reterritorializing China and Chineseness thus define ethnic Chinese attitudes and responses toward claims to cultural authenticity by mainland Chinese. The outcry in Hong Kong and Guangzhou against a proposal by the Chinese People's Political Consultative Conference Guangzhou Committee to increase the ratio of Mandarin-language to Cantonese content in Guangzhou Television's programming – an attempt to proscribe Cantonese-language coverage of the 2010 Asian Games – indicates that there are limits to how much restriction mainland authorities can impose on the use of local "dialects."[100] Sometimes derided as "culturally inferior" to their fellow "Chinese" on the mainland, some Southeast Asian Chinese have responded by claiming access, via their own local "Chinese" culture, to an authentic "ancient" China that survives through centuries-long, transplanted Chinese customs and rituals no longer practiced – or, for a time, proscribed by the government – in their places of ancestral origins in mainland China.[101] Negotiating between their self-identifications as "overseas Chinese" (*huaqiao*) and "ethnic Chinese" (*huaren*) has on occasion enabled Southeast Asian Chinese to lay claim to speaking, not in the name of China and Chinese unification, but as the voice of China itself. This happened, for example, in the coverage of Hong Kong's turnover and the Taiwan Question by the Malaysian Chinese newspaper *Kwong-Wah Yit Poh*.[102] In other cases, the response may take the form of a compensatory gesture of defensive ethnocentrism. An Internet document circulated by and addressed to the "49 million Hokkien-speakers" all over the world, for example, valorizes the Minnan "dialect" as "the imperial language" of the Tang Dynasty and "the language of your ancestors."[103] Advocating a Han-Sinocentric approach while denying the equation of Chineseness with the state-promoted national language, Mandarin, the anonymous author appeals to "all Mandarin-speaking friends out there – do not look down on your other Chinese friends who do not speak Mandarin – whom you guys fondly refer to as 'Bananas.' In fact, they are speaking a language which is much more ancient & linguistically complicated than Mandarin." Mandarin is characterized as an alien tongue spoken by a non-Han minority, "a northern Chinese dialect heavily influenced by non-Han Chinese." In attesting to its ancient Chinese lineage, this argument is grounded in a comparison of vocabulary and pronunciation, not with other local Chinese "dialects" but with foreign languages such as Japanese and Korean that were part of the "Golden Age" of the Tang China-centered Sinosphere. Such an argument conveniently overlooks the complex ways in which ethnic identity and differences were constructed during the Tang dynasty, and the fact that the ancestry, cultural practices, and geographic focus of the Tang elites were in large part already oriented toward Inner Asia and "barbarized" northern China.[104] The above example is revealing of "pressures" brought to bear on Southeast Asian Chinese to learn and speak *putonghua*/Mandarin, when their "dialects" had long been the basis of their claim to a Chinese ethnic identity. This "Mandarinization" of Hokkien-, Teochiu-, or Cantonese-based "Chinese" identities, however, also constitutes proof of an internal contestation over what "Chinese" means, who can claim Chineseness, who counts as Chinese, and who can "represent" it.

Multiple cultural sites and centers of Chineseness produce different, at times competing, visions of Chineseness. Two opposing views are laid out in Shanghai-born and Hong Kong-based director Wong Kar-wai's *2046* (2004) and mainland China-based Zhang Yimou's *Hero* (2002). Set in 1960s Hong Kong, *2046* tells the story of a young author of erotic newspaper serials. Among the women with whom this writer falls in love is his landlord's daughter, whom he eventually helps to reunite with her Japanese lover. In this movie, Wong not only imagines the possibility of a Japanese–Chinese rapprochement, couched in the language of romantic love and family reconciliation – a vision that stands in stark contrast to the worsening of China–Japan relations owing to Prime Minister Koizumi's 2001 and 2002 visits to the Yasukuni Shrine. More important, Wong lets his characters speak to each other in the language with which they are most comfortable, even though Cantonese, Mandarin, and Japanese are in reality mutually unintelligible. The lingua franca is not found in the movie, but rather *on* the movie, in the form of subtitles, the language of which varies from one market or set of audiences to another. In this way, the film evades the politically charged hierarchy of languages based on the assumed standard set by Mandarin or *putonghua* that is audibly rendered in such films as Ang Lee's *Crouching Tiger, Hidden Dragon* (2003) and, more problematically, Zhang Yimou's *Hero*. Writes critic and scholar Gina Marchetti,[105]

> In *Hero*, mainland Chinese director Zhang Yimou also takes a chance, through his proxy Nameless (Jet Li), that the world is ready for the return of the wandering hero. Nameless/Jet Li travels from the PRC to Hong Kong, to Hollywood and back again to China. *Hero* also repatriates Hong Kong's Tony Leung (as Broken Sword) and Maggie Cheung (as Flying Snow) as well as Chinese-American Donnie Yen (as Sky) who sacrifice themselves to maintain the Chinese nation-state. The diasporic Chinese from the far edges of the world symbolically capitulate to the central authority of the Emperor Qin (Chen Daoming)/Beijing/the PRC/Chinese cinema.[106]

Conclusion

Scholars who look at China from a broader, international perspective have generally been wary of subscribing to culturalist arguments. Wang Gungwu,[107] for example, offers an important refutation of cultural essentialist arguments about "Chinese" economic success. Such scholars have highlighted instead the importance of the specific situatedness and locations of the "Chinese" in China, Southeast Asia, and beyond. Questions of "roots" and "routes"[108] are of paramount concern and have real consequences – including life-and-death ones – for the "Chinese" in Southeast Asia. In making sense of the historical construction of "China," "Chinese," and "Chineseness," in their modern articulations, their concern has been to emphasize the importance of both structure and agency.

Wei-ming Tu's[109] notion of symbolic universes that make up "cultural China," and Jamie Davidson's[110] attempt to explain the restructuring of Southeast Asian countries by economic globalization as a form of "Chinese-ization" or becoming "structurally Chinese" of urban, middle-class, capitalist Southeast Asian societies, are useful reminders that asserting the heterogeneity and historical variability of "becoming-Chinese" is the starting point, not the concluding statement, of any inquiry into questions and issues of "China," "Chinese," and "Chineseness." The propensity in overseas Chinese studies for taxonomic essays that classify ethnic

Chinese according to their political orientations and loyalty is both an instructive symptom of the uneasy fit among the core concepts of territory, people, nation, culture, state, and civilization, and a valiant attempt to catalogue the various manifestations of their critical disjunctions. "Transnational" approaches that purport to move beyond the strictures of nation- and state-centered analysis to stress the "different ways of being Chinese"[111] or "deconstruct modern Chineseness"[112] offer nuanced case studies. Because they invoke "China" as a self-explanatory straw figure against which transnational or diasporic difference is *then* asserted, however, they overlook the broader implications of critical disjunctions and historical hybridization. William Callahan's sophisticated study of "Greater China" is rightly critical of binary thinking in China/West and center/periphery studies, advocating "an understanding of China and civilization in terms of popular sovereignty, heterotopia, and an open relation to Otherness."[113] Yet Callahan's analysis is marked by aporia with regard to Japan's mediating role in "Chinese" modernity, be it historical or contemporary. This is apparent in his exclusion of Japan on methodological grounds. Although for Callahan it "is very important to regional economics and is crucial to a geopolitical understanding of East Asia, it is not included here, since Japan is peripheral to the transnational relations and theoretical challenges of Greater China."[114]

The "problem of clarifying what 'China' is"[115] is hardly novel. This chapter suggests that looking into the pressures and opportunities for "becoming Chinese" by colonial, "China"-driven, postcolonial (national), and market-driven processes of Sinicization in the region that we now call "East Asia" enables us to specify not just individual differences across time and space, but just as importantly, identify *patterns of differences* – or *differance*[116] – that are historically identified and lived as "Chinese" in China, Southeast Asia, and beyond. Among the most important of these patterns of differences is the identification of "Chinese" with commerce and capital in Southeast Asia; a comparable process happened also in Hong Kong and to the *benshengren* in Taiwan. Another pattern of difference is the regional circulation of socialist ideas and creation of revolutionary networks in Southeast Asia. The historical incarnation of economic capital by "Chinese" bodies is a personification by which capital, and the "pragmatic" values, habits, and practices associated with it, are actively/passively/forcibly incorporated by living beings as "second nature." This process cannot be understood apart from the cultural matrices that embed two historical processes: Sino-Japanese-English hybridization after the middle of the nineteenth century; and the Anglo-Sinicization, regionalization, and globalization of the ethnic "Chinese" in China and Southeast Asia, especially in the second half of the twentieth century.

Patterns of differences also account for the complexity and diversity of "Chinese" responses to, and perceptions of, power and authority in China and elsewhere, which range from enthusiastic accommodation with the mainland state on the part of so-called "Red Capitalist" taipans of Hong Kong, to militant challenges against the colonial state posed by the communist guerrillas of Malaya, to hedging by Chinese-Filipino businesspeople who contribute to the campaign coffers of all presidential candidates. "Chinese" identification with capital has meant a greater awareness of and sensitivity to the arbitrary exactions of the state and the vicissitudes of business. Anglo-Chinese who are safely nationalized and whose citizenships are not under question are under less pressure to be "apolitical" compared to earlier generations of "overseas Chinese."[117] Long distance nationalism, however, continues to shape overseas Chinese responses to mainland China.

The existence of multiple actors, acts, and sites of Chineseness foregrounds the importance of lived experiences in complicating commonsensical notions of "Chinese" identity. Civilizational notions of "Chineseness" continue to be haunted by race, nation, and territory. Cultural, political, and circumstantial ideas of "Chineseness" are often articulated as Han-Chinese ethnic identity; and Han-Chineseness as ethnic identity is, in turn, inflected by modern ideas of race.[118] Yet these ideas actually encompass older notions of patrilineal kinship that are concerned less with racial purity than with often mythical origins. The genealogy they construct is flexible and capable of transcending place, disregarding physical appearances, encompassing intermarriage and adoption, and incorporating diverse cultural practices, including "non-Chinese" ones.[119] Patrilineal kinship may be linked to the ideology of "Confucian culturalism" and its (ethnocentric) claims to absorb "outsiders" and Sinicize them. But as lived experience – and despite the pressures exerted by colonial, "China"-driven, postcolonial, and market-driven Sinicization – becoming-Chinese is neither preordained nor unidirectional or assimilational.

Rather, Sinicization entails an interactive and dialogical process capable not just of blurring the lines between "Self" and "Other," but of transforming them across territorial boundaries and civilizational divides. Viewed in these terms, the phenomenon of "re-Sinicization" might be better understood not as recovery or revival (implied by the prefix "re-") of long-occluded Chineseness, but as *a* process of "becoming-Chinese" whose origins are traceable neither to the "core" nor to the "periphery" of so-called "Cultural China," but to the vicissitudes of the broader phenomena of multi-sited state-, colony- and nation-, region-, and world-making.

Contrary to the idea that mainland China is currently remaking the region and the world in its image, parts of mainland China – particularly its urban, middle-, and upper-class populations in the coastal areas – are actually undergoing a form of Anglo-Sinicization that makes specific groups and communities more like the modern hybrid "Anglo-Chinese" that emerged, in the course of 150 years, out of the region we now call "East Asia" (which includes Northeast and Southeast Asia). These mainland Anglo-Chinese have more in common – in terms of lifestyle, upbringing, education, mores, and values – with urban, educated, middle-class "East Asians" than with the rural and impoverished peoples who remain rooted within China, East and especially Southeast Asia, and beyond. This does not discount the possibility that mainland China's political and economic dynamics over the next few decades – especially if a Sinocentric order were actually to emerge and a power shift occur in China's favor, changing the rules and norms of doing business and politics, for example – might create pressures and incentives toward Sinicization that will be substantively different from the current phenomenon of Anglo-Sinicization. Compared to the processes discussed in this chapter, the evidence for this mainland-driven form of becoming-Chinese – such as the proliferation of simplified Chinese newspapers among overseas Chinese communities, the popularity of mainland Chinese popular culture (particularly historical dramas) among non-mainland Chinese migrant communities, de-Anglicization in Hong Kong[120] – exists to some extent; but its capacity to supplant other forms of becoming-Chinese remains debatable.[121]

This chapter's main concern is to identify the broader historical patterns of hybridization and analyze how these patterns, arising from multiple sites and sources of creating "differences" that are lived as "Chinese," complicate the notion of Sinicization. The signifier "China" is the enabling as well as the delimiting condition of a politics of *identification*, which is not necessarily a politics of *identity* rooted in, as Rey Chow[122] has argued, the dominant myths of consanguinity and claims to ethnic oneness about "China." The challenge, then, is not simply one of retelling the various discourses *about* "China" and attempts by different agents to fix the meaning of Chineseness. Nor is it a simple issue of repudiating or resisting all claims to "Chineseness" in terms of origins or ancestry. Instead, the challenge is to understand how processes of territorializing and de/reterritorializing "China" and "Chineseness" regulate the complex interplay of proximity and distance in the geographical, political, economic, and cultural identifications among the "Chinese." This interplay allows migrants and their descendants – at certain times, in certain places, and under specific circumstances – to claim, and base their actions on, commonalities and/or differences with Southeast Asians, *other* "Chinese," and others. What is at stake in the rise of China and processes of "Sinicization" is nothing less than how "Chineseness" is constituted out of forces both of its making and beyond its control, and what kinds of capacities, effects, possibilities, and limits structure these processes and the "Chinese's" "in/human condition."[123]

Notes

1 I would like to thank Andrew Abalahin, Chitra Konuntakiet, Chris Baker, Daniel A. Bell, Allen Carlson, Pheng Cheah, Kasian Tejapira, Peter Katzenstein, Khoo Boo Teik, David Leheny, Francis Loh Kok Wah, Gregory Noble, Pasuk Phongpaichit, Shih Chih-yu, Tan Pek Leng, Wang Gungwu, and the participants of the Beijing workshop for their insights and comments, and Sarah Tarrow for her editorial support. I especially thank Takashi Shiraishi for his support and encouragement. Research for this chapter was in part funded by the Japan Society for the Promotion of Science research grant (21401011) on "The Rise of China and the Political and Social Transformation of Southeast Asia: International, Transnational and National Perspectives."
2 Phongpaichit and Baker 1996, 135.
3 Tejapira 1997, 76.
4 Hau 2005.

5 See the definition, among many such works, provided by Tjon Sie Fat 2009, 360.
6 See, for example, the critique of Chan and Tong 2001, 9, and Crossley, Siu, and Sutton 2006, 6–7; on resinification as an ideological activity of inventing unity through the production of "Chineseness," see Dirlik 1997, 308.
7 Fogel 2009, 4, drawing on Matisoff 2003, 6.
8 The use of the word "hybridization" (and related terms like "hybrid") in this chapter is not meant to imply that there is a pre-existing purity that is then subject to cultural mixture.
9 Shaffer 1994, 8–12. For a succinct discussion of the history of China's southward expansion and the impact of differing dynastic policies toward the southern frontier on Southeast Asia, see Sun 2010.
10 Liu 2004.
11 Wang 2004, 224.
12 Territorialization, deterritorialization, and reterritorialization are routinely employed alongside "coding," "recoding," and "decoding" across a range of single- and co-authored texts written by Deleuze and Guattari (1983, 1987) to refer to particular instances of configuration, deconfiguration, and reconfiguration of "territory" understood in its spatial/physical, representational, social, psychoanalytic, economic, and political senses. I use these terms insofar as their emphasis on both fluidity and fixity of cultural flows and identities encourages critical thinking about, as well as beyond, the concepts of territory, nation, and sovereignty that inform studies of the "Chinese" in Southeast Asia.
13 Liu 2004.
14 The so-called "tributary trade system," organized around tributary missions to "China" that were also accompanied by traders (and, in some states, established through military intervention), reached its zenith in the fifteenth century under the first Ming emperors. Qing emperors focused their energies on the north and northwestern frontier, adopting a policy of disengagement while encouraging maritime trade (see Sun 2010). Some states such as Siam and Burma continued to send tributary missions until the mid-nineteenth century. Tokugawa Japan and Qing China did not establish state-to-state relations, but Chinese traders could visit Nagasaki for trade.
15 Duara 1997, 40.
16 Levi-Strauss 1987 (1950), 63.
17 Duara 1997; Godley 1981.
18 Guo 2004.
19 Wang 1992a, 6–7.
20 According to Anthony Reid, terms such as *Chijs*, *Cina*, and *sangley* were already in use in Southeast Asia during the sixteenth century to refer to traders and artisans from Guangdong and Fujian, regardless of the regional or linguistic variations among them (Reid 2010, 53–4). It is instructive to note that a term like *sangley*, which was used in the Philippines and South Sulawesi, does not necessarily denote place-name or ethnicity; its ambiguous etymology – the term is said to have been derived from *shanglu* (a classical Chinese term for merchant traveler), *sengdi* (Hokkien for "commerce"), or *sionglai* (Hokkien for *changlai*, "frequently coming") – distinguishes this group of (mainly Fujian) "frequent comers" by their occupation and mobility.
21 Tejapira 2001b.
22 Tejapira 1997.
23 Coppel 1976, 31.
24 Chun 1989.
25 Duara 1997.
26 I owe this information to Nobuhiro Aizawa.
27 Wang 1981, 156–7.
28 Suryadinata 1995, 195, 208, 209–15.
29 Fitzgerald 1995.
30 Guo 2004.

31 Oyen 2010.
32 Chun 1995.
33 Wickberg 2006, 25.
34 Following the Bandung Afro-Asian Solidarity Conference in 1955, mainland China renounced its Dual Nationality claims in an effort to improve relations with its Southeast Asian neighbors. However, Taiwan under Chiang Kai-shek was reluctant to give up its claims on the diasporic Chinese, leading to a divergence in policy between the Republic of China and US policies on the overseas Chinese (Oyen 2010, 90–1). Taiwan's relations with overseas Chinese have been reconfigured in recent decades as attention has shifted to "overseas Taiwanese" rather than "overseas Chinese" among Taiwan policymakers, particularly the Democratic Progressive Party, in the Overseas Chinese Affairs Commission. Interest in and calls for "Taiwanization" do not normally include the "overseas Chinese." I thank Gregory Noble for the information on recent developments in Taiwan.
35 Wang 2004, 224.
36 See, for example, Bell 2008 for a discussion of the Confucian revival in China.
37 Huang 2011.
38 Kang 2010a, 91.
39 The salience of maritime geography can be seen in the fact that, over a period of 11 years from 743 to 754 CE, the Chinese Buddhist monk Jianzhen (Ganjin) attempted five times to cross the East China Sea into Japan before succeeding on the sixth try. It was the Mongols' success in developing the capability to move large numbers of troops by ships that enabled them to reach Japan and Java, but even then, they were beaten back. Although maritime technology had developed sufficiently to enable, for instance, the movement of large numbers of troops at the time of Hideoyoshi's attempt to conquer Korea toward the end of the sixteenth century, insurmountable logistical problems made it practically impossible to sustain long-term military campaign and pacification. Only in the nineteenth century did advances in steamship technology make the large-scale movement of people a fact of life.
40 Reid and Zheng 2009; see also Giersch 2006 on Qing expansion into Yunnan, whose Tai elites also had relations with Burma and Siam.
41 Wang Gungwu (2011) offers a caveat on the use of the word "civilization": "although 'civilization' is a word introduced into China quite recently, there was an ancient consciousness derived from ideas that were eventually codified in the *Yijing*, *Laozi*, *Yinyang* writings, Confucian stress on ancestors and individual cultivation, down to the later Daoists, Buddhists and Neo-Confucians that together distinguished the peoples of East Asia. The ideas were drawn from the many kinds of ethnic and social groups who were within reach of the lands of eastern Asia, and who interacted and intermingled with one another over the millennia. For this, using the modern word civilization may be misleading. The process involved was more important than the total content." See Kelley's (2005, 31–5) discussion of Sino-Vietnamese relations in terms of Vietnamese self-conceptions of their country as a "domain of manifest civility." The strong cultural identification with and acknowledgment of Vietnam's political subservience to China expressed in Vietnamese envoy poetry raise interesting questions about audience, intention, and reception that complicate (rather than simply affirm) commonsensical notions of "Sinicization." On the dynamism of acculturation and hybridization and their impact on Qing institutions and borderland societies along the Sino-Southeast Asian "frontiers," see Giersch 2006 and Shepherd 1993.
42 Woodside 1971, 18–19, 21.
43 Sugihara 2005a, 2, 8–9.
44 Sugihara 2005c.
45 Lu 2004, 25, 39.
46 Liu 1995, xviii, 17–19, 31–42.

47 Ibid., especially the lists in appendices B, C, D, and E.
48 Wong 1979, 5.
49 Wang, Binbin 2000, 164–5.
50 Shiraishi and Hau 2009; Hau and Shiraishi 2009.
51 Shiraishi 2010b. The term "Anglo-China" has been used to refer to the nineteenth-century "realm of economic, political and cultural exchange" with British Hong Kong as a capital (Munn 2009 [2001], 2). The use of "Anglo-Chinese" in this chapter highlights the importance not only of the territories under British and American colonial rule or commercial influence, but of a specific pattern of hybridization that produced a certain type of "Chinese." "Anglo" refers primarily to linguistic proficiency acquired through Anglophone (which includes British, American, and other Englishes) education in the region as well as in Britain, the USA, and Canada.
52 The reach and might of the British commercial empire could be felt even in non-British territories such as Siam, Spanish Philippines, the Dutch Indies, and French Indochina in the nineteenth and early twentieth centuries. The extent of Spanish Philippines' dependence on trade with Great Britain (as well as the United States), mediated by British, American, and Chinese country traders, provoked Spanish complaints that "From the commercial point of view the Philippines is an Anglo-Chinese colony with a Spanish Flag" (Recur 1879, 110, quoted in Wickberg 1965, 280). As a consequence, English became the de facto regional lingua franca, although colonial states also imposed their own languages on the elites in their territories. The scale, however, was far smaller compared to the spread of English under American hegemony in the postwar and post-Cold War periods.
53 Lim and Ku were exceptionally gifted men of letters and published books in English. Not all Anglo-Chinese at the turn of the twentieth century could write in English (a notable example of a bilingual who also wrote in English is Zhang Ailing/Eileen Chang [1920–95], the celebrated Shanghai-born writer), but they nevertheless had reading and to a lesser extent speaking abilities in that language. It is instructive to note that China's foremost translator of the time, the Fujian-born Lin Shu (1852–1924), had no foreign languages himself, but instead relied on bilingual collaborators to translate Anglo-American (and to a lesser extent French) writings into literary Chinese.
54 Yamamoto 1995, 37–45; Li 1991, chapters 2 and 3.
55 Wang 2003, 166.
56 Ibid., 176.
57 Wang Gungwu 2011.
58 I thank Wang Gungwu for his great help in identifying Ku and Lee as exemplary Anglo-Chinese.
59 Lee 1999, 315–21; Shih 2001, 4; Lu 2004.
60 Ishikawa 2001, 459–84.
61 Dirlik 2008, 156.
62 Williams 1960, 72.
63 Ibid., 74.
64 Toer 1980.
65 Chandra 2011.
66 Tejapira 2001a.
67 Shiraishi 1997, 175–9.
68 The situation in Suharto's Indonesia differs from the Sukarno era, when China's cultural diplomacy and the circulation of Chinese literary principles informed Indonesia's cultural politics, especially the discursive construction of a "national allegory" (Liu Hong 2006).
69 In some instances, owing to the vicissitudes of language policies, some Anglo-Chinese may be functional in English and their mother tongue (Malay, Tagalog, Hokkien, Cantonese) but not necessarily in Mandarin. The situation has changed as economic opportunities created by the rise of China have given Anglo-Chinese more incentives to learn Mandarin. Efforts to promote Mandarin in Singapore since the late 1970s, for

example, have been successful, but at the expense of marginalizing non-Mandarin Chinese "dialects" such as Hokkien.
70 Wang 2004, 166.
71 Wang 1981, 157.
72 Teo 1997, 111.
73 Law and Bren (with Ho) 2004, 291, 295.
74 Bordwell 2000, 66.
75 For an account of Japanese involvement in the wartime Chinese film industry, see Fu 2003.
76 Yau 2009, 169.
77 Law and Bren (with Ho) 2004, 203–10, 221.
78 Hau and Shiraishi forthcoming.
79 Ma 1999, 45.
80 Hsiau 2000, 109.
81 Katzenstein 2005, 18.
82 Katzenstein 2006a, 4–14; Chua Beng Huat 2003; Qiu 2010.
83 Li 2008b.
84 I thank Kasian Tejapira for his insights into the Dragon Descendants Museum's "strange" cultural politics of Chineseness (Interview with Kasian Tejapira, Bangkok, 17 October 2009).
85 Phongpaichit and Baker 1996, 139–40.
86 Lim 2006.
87 Interview with Chitra Konuntakiet, Bangkok, 19 October 2009; see also Pungkanon 2008.
88 A more recent example is Yale University professor Amy Chua, whose article "Why Chinese Mothers are Superior" (Chua 2011) provoked fierce debates on the Internet over the merits (and demerits) of her self-proclaimed "Chinese" style of strict parenting. The Anglo-Chinese Chua invoked her own upbringing by her parents, who were Chinese Filipino migrants to the USA, as an inspiration.
89 Bickers and Yep 2009, 11–12.
90 Wang 2004, 210–26.
91 Su and Wang 1991.
92 Guo 2004, 109.
93 I thank Allen Carlson for first alerting me to this anime series. In November 2009, the Chinese government established the China Animation Comic Group to promote animation production, technology, and marketing. Plans include the building of a national hub, China Animation Game City, in Beijing. The government also provides subsidies to Chinese animation companies (Hosaka 2010).
94 "Chinese Cartoon to Land in International Market" 2009.
95 Oakes 2000, 668. See Friedman 1994 and Gladney 1994 on the reinvention of national identity in the post-Mao era.
96 Xiamen Min'nan Tourism and Culture Industry Co. 2010.
97 Friedman 1994, 83–7.
98 Wang, Fan-sen 2000, 98–123.
99 Chang 1999, 58–9.
100 Tellingly, among the songs sung at the protests which took place in Guangzhou and Hong Kong were a Cantonese song by the Hong Kong boy band *Beyond*, and a Cantonese adaptation of the theme song from the Japanese anime, *Dr. Slump* (Zhu 2010). A recent example of hybridization at work in *putonghua* itself is *geili* (literally, "to give force or power"; awesome, cool, exciting), whose antonym *bugeili* (boring, dull) was first popularized over the Internet by a Chinese-language dubbing of a Japanese anime based on the Chinese classic, *Xi You Ji* (Journey to the West), and quickly transmuted into the English "gelivable" and "ungelivable" and the French "guélile" ("Geili" 2010).

101 I thank Francis Loh Kok Wah for providing information on the Penang Hokkien Chinese's "re-exporting" of rituals and ceremonies associated with ancestor worship back to their lineage/family associations in Fujian, China. See the valuable research by Liu Zhaohui (2005, especially 143–4).
102 Lee 2009, 57. I thank Shih Chih-yu for directing me to Lee's insightful analysis.
103 "Ancient Imperial Language of China – 2,000 Years Ago" 2009.
104 Abramson 2008, xxi.
105 Marchetti 2007, 7.
106 Marchetti's (2007) critique cites Hong Kong-born and New York-based filmmaker Evans Chan's (2004) scathing analysis of *Hero*'s political subtext of legitimizing the authoritarian mainland Chinese state through the subordination of Greater China.
107 Wang 1992b.
108 Clifford 1997.
109 Tu 1994a.
110 Davidson 2008, 222.
111 Nonini and Ong 1997, 26.
112 Ong and Nonini 1997a, 326.
113 Callahan 2004, 96.
114 Ibid., xxix.
115 Young 1999, 63; Chow 2009, x.
116 Derrida 1982.
117 I thank Wang Gungwu for prodding me to think about the relationship between power and capital.
118 Dikötter 1992.
119 Ebrey 2003, 165–76.
120 The leading Chinese-language dailies in Southeast Asia continue to use traditional Chinese script, although there are now newspapers that use simplified script. Mainland Chinese TV dramas are widely available on cable and are watched by overseas Chinese, but do not as yet command a wide following among non-Chinese Southeast Asians as Korean, Japanese, and Taiwanese dramas do.
121 Increased enrollment in Chinese-language programs of study in mainland China and the establishment of Confucius Institutes around the world are often taken as evidence of "Sinicization." It should be noted, however, that just as incentives to learn Mandarin have increased among Anglo-Chinese as well as non-Chinese, learning English – now mandatory from Elementary Grade 3 onwards in China – has become a big business in China, with well-to-do mainland Chinese sending their children abroad for English-language education (Thorniley 2010). Moreover, no power shift has (yet) happened in favor of China. In the absence of a significant social formation in which acquisition of Chinese language involves internalization of "Chinese" norms, regulations, and values on a scale that is comparable to what happened to Anglo-Chinese with English in the regional historical context of British and American hegemony, it is difficult to ascertain the degree to which "Sinicization" is actually taking place among people who are learning *putonghua* (except on a limited, individual basis), and preparing the ground for the emergence of a Sinocentric order. It is instructive to note, for example, that Liang's (2010) call for making Mandarin the primary medium of instruction in publicly funded schools in Hong Kong remains rooted in the assumption of a multilingual Hong Kong in which Cantonese and English continue to be spoken. A proof of mainland-driven Sinicization would be if large numbers of people, whether ethnic Chinese or not, want to change their passports for a PRC passport, or *putonghua* becomes the regional lingua franca that is spoken even among non-Chinese, or Chinese norms (whether in business or politics) are accepted as legitimate in the region. So far the evidence seems to point in the opposite direction, with (Anglo-)Chinese professionals from the mainland as well as international movie stars such as Jet Li and Gong Li taking Singaporean citizenship and Zhang Ziyi taking Hong Kong citizenship, mainly for the purpose of

protecting their assets and properties. A notable contrary trend, however, is the fact that Hong Kong lawmakers have been under increasing pressure from the mainland government (which does not recognize Dual Citizenship, following its experience in Southeast Asia) to give up their foreign passports/nationalities.
122 Chow 1993, 24–6.
123 Cheah 2006, 7, 10.

PART IV

8

SINICIZATION IN COMPARATIVE PERSPECTIVE[1]

Peter J. Katzenstein

The opening stanza of Rudyard Kipling's *Ballad of East and West* reads:

Oh East is East and West is West and never the twain shall meet
Till earth and sky stand presently at God's great Judgment seat.[2]

Yet, contra Kipling, there exists no sharp division separating East from West.[3] Although all civilizations and civilizational processes are distinct, grounded as they are in different local settings, they are embedded in a common global context. Like America, Islam, Japan, Europe, and India, China is an exemplar of a distinctive, richly pluralist civilization that draws on both East and West.

Sinicization is complex. Except within the borders of the Chinese empire, in the past it did not mean "becoming Chinese." Rather, resulting from sustained interaction, Sinicization created shared understandings overlaying a mosaic of local diversity. Sinicization, writes Charles Holcombe, was "an open-ended dialogue between local customs and international East Asian norms and not some simple duplication of everything Chinese."[4] In Chinese terminology, Sinicization can create a harmonious environment. Harmony in this context does not refer to dull uniformity but to interesting diversity (*he er bu tong*).[5] In European social theory, Gramsci's concept of hegemony is a reasonable analogue to the Chinese concept of harmony. Power wielded through hegemony or harmony tends to be invisible, as the existence of that power is taken for granted.

Rather than trying to explain large civilizational processes such as Sinicization with invariant models of power mobilization, transition, or diffusion, following Charles Tilly's advice it seems wiser to focus on the subprocesses of Sinicization illustrated by the six case studies in this book, with particular emphasis on specific elements of practice and policy.[6] Practices and policies underline that civilizations are marked by vigorous disagreements in both action and speech.[7] Together, they generate different outcomes. One such outcome, cultural imperialism, describes the unilateral imposition of the norms and practices of one civilization upon another that it seeks to absorb, displace, or destroy. A second outcome describes the wholesale adoption by local actors of the form or content of imported policies and practices. Finally, a third outcome – the one that is most typical in the relations among major civilizations and most readily observed in the book's six case studies – describes hybridization of local norms and practices through selective appropriation in the give-and-take that defines civilizational processes: the exchange of cultural material in the form of information, ideas, values, norms, and identities. Hybridization highlights the shifting balances of policy and practice among civilizations. In brief, Sinicization is reflected in processes of transcivilizational engagements, intercivilizational encounters, and occasional civilizational clashes.

Sinicization is comparable to processes of Europeanization, Americanization, Japanization, Indianization, and Islamicization. Such civilizational processes occur at all times; they gain special public attention as the power of states, polities, or empires rises; and they linger while power slips away. Sinicization is creating an international milieu that China and the Chinese find welcoming. These processes are relational. They do not only affect others by radiating outward from China. Instead, by exposing China to more intensive relations with other civilizations, they also help remake China. Importantly, they can affect China's organization of power. This book inquires into Sinicization as a set of processes that are reflected in a variety of practices and policies, which can be traced empirically in the domains of security, political economy, and culture.

Sinicization is a concept that incites the imagination of many Chinese. They feel perfectly comfortable with a conceptual vocabulary that corresponds closely to their shared beliefs in the unity of the Chinese people and to a shared sense of inevitability of the rise of China after a long period of unjust and unjustified humiliation.[8] Not so in America. Among historians and social scientists in particular, the concept of Sinicization receives a bad press. It connotes flatness in a world full of nooks and crannies. It appears to entail an intellectually unacceptable and historically invalid teleology implying that in the end, everyone will become Chinese. This book argues that on empirical and analytical grounds, both views are inaccurate and unwarranted. In contrast to the applause and criticism that greet the concept of Sinicization in some quarters, this book seeks to develop an approach that makes it analytically and empirically tractable. Rather than talking about Sinic civilization in the singular and Sinicization as a simple, uniform, and unidirectional process, I conceive of Sinic civilization as constituted by multiple and often conflicting traditions and Sinicization as a complex set of processes.[9]

In pointing to the internal pluralism of civilizations in a world of plural civilization, I begin this chapter with a discussion of how to avoid the illusion of singularity in civilizational analysis. I then provide a theoretical and empirical analysis of civilizational processes, mechanisms, policies, and practices that draws on the chapters in this book before discussing Indianization and India, and Japanization and Japan, as two Asian examples that provide a comparative context for this book's focus on Sinicization and China. A brief conclusion sums up the main themes of this chapter.

Civilizational analysis: a conceptual overview

Civilizations provide us with the broadest social context and worldviews in both space and time; they equal "culture writ large."[10] Civilizations do not act; political entities act within civilizations. More specifically, as Lydia Liu writes, "civilizations do not clash; empires do."[11] In a similar vein Ian Morris insists that culture "is less a voice in our heads telling us what to do than a town hall meeting where we argue about our options."[12] It thus helps to shape everyday practice and policy through the exercise of power in institutions. As Gary Hamilton argues, "world images have decisive effects on how such spheres of activity are actually interpreted and organized as going concerns."[13] Actors in all civilizations engage in the illusion that they are singular and thus blind themselves to the existence of other ways of imagining and living life. It is, however, undeniable that we live in a world of plural and pluralist civilizations. The illusion of singularity is often fostered by intellectual and political entrepreneurs who seek to serve particular interests through discursive moves and political strategies. Under the cold light of evidence, past claims to singularity do not hold up.[14] Civilizations are distinctive and differentiated, not unique or unified. As for the future, it is conceivable that we will witness a clash between Civilization, capitalized and in the singular, and Nature. To survive that clash a new kind of singularity may evolve – lodged in what Jeremy Rifkin calls an empathic civilization – that would transcend East and West. A successor to the contested traditions and modernities of plural and pluralist civilizations, such empathic civilization may be humankind's best hope for avoiding global nightfall.[15] For now, however, it exists only in embryonic form.[16]

Civilizations are indelibly bound up with political power – in both its visible–behavioral as well as its invisible–symbolic dimensions.[17] Materialist accounts of civilizations are inclined to stress the former, ideational ones the latter. In reality, both play their parts. Civilizational politics is partly driven by the interests of elites. Seeking to expand their power and prestige across geographic and symbolic spaces, these elites rely on civilizational imageries in an instrumental fashion. More characteristic and less straightforward is a second civilizational dynamic in which elite interests are defined by civilizational discourses and practices that impose their own logic over material structures, incentives, and the interests derived from them. Power in civilizations is primarily social, revealed in identities and interests and in the processes, policies, and practices that flow from them. In short, the broad social context that civilizations provide shapes how political actors, not civilizations, mobilize power.

Language and religion

The two most important and distinctive characteristics of a civilization are its religious and literary traditions. Separately and together, they provide ample raw material from which to fashion the multiple traditions that constitute civilizational life. Language is a central element of civilization. In Japan, Korea, and Vietnam for millennia Chinese was used for writing, even though these countries retained their indigenous languages and in some cases their own scripts.[18] In the eighteenth century, French language and court manners were epitomes of civilization emulated in polite society throughout Europe. Frederick the Great spoke German – but only to his dogs.

In India, language is also a central marker of civilization.[19] The very choice between "Hindu" or "Indian" civilizations poses a central question. "Hindu civilization" suggests religion as the one overarching cultural component that overrides all others. "Indian civilization" makes space for numerous cultural components and for healthy contestation among them. Susanne Hoeber Rudolph chooses the composite over the coherence view. The Indian subcontinent encompasses states that are divided in terms of religion but share linguistic, literary, and other cultural characteristics, thus giving credence to the concept of Indian civilization. Furthermore, Rudolph argues, India invalidates the distinction between civilized and uncivilized based on the existence of a written language. With Brahmins trained in an oral tradition of reciting the Vedas, Sanskrit survived for hundreds of years under the social convention of oral transmission; writing would have violated the sacred. Yet, the emphasis on language and elite culture, Rudolph also points out, overlooks the importance of language as a vehicle of xenophobic nationalism and, in the case of India, of imperialism and colonialism.

Bruce Lawrence argues similarly that Islamic civilization arose in the context of nomadism with strong oral traditions.[20] The absence of a written language at the origin, as in Islam, or over prolonged periods, as in India, shows that in the evolution of civilizations, language plays important though varying roles. Indian scholars continue to debate the question of what is the language of Indian civilization. As a practical matter, Indian elites rely widely on English. However, while this permits India's service sector to leap-frog over other developing economies, nobody thinks of it as India's language. Here, as in other linguistically fluid situations such as the Philippines, English is accepted as a lingua franca but not as a mother tongue.[21] What, then, is the precise status of English as the latest in a long history of world languages? Nicholas Ostler argues that the world is moving not to a monolingual but to a multilingual future, without a successor to English as a lingua franca.[22] For now, at least, that primacy is beyond doubt as English presents the lion's share of all published translations.[23] Still, Ostler's detailed analysis of the use of mother tongue and of English as a lingua franca suggests a world of linguistic diversity.[24] Indeed, as a lingua franca English is experiencing a limited process of differentiation into distinguishable varieties.[25] English will not displace the diversity of mother tongues in a multicivilizational world marked by linguistic regionalism.[26] And it may itself be undermined or displaced by the evolution of language technologies that is now beginning to revolutionize processes of translation.

Religion is a second marker of civilization. Samuel Huntington, for example, refers to "Western religion" rather than "Western Christendom" as the successor to "Latin Christendom," the term of choice before the Enlightenment.[27] Western Christendom was in fact a deeply divided religious tradition. In the sixteenth and seventeenth centuries, that division was revealed in Protestant and Catholic mass slaughters during the Thirty Years War. As late as the turn of the twentieth century, Protestants viewed Catholics with much suspicion as a subversive transnational religion, just as many Catholics and Protestants today regard Muslims. James Kurth builds and elaborates on Huntington's argument about the importance of Reform Protestantism for the origin and evolution of Western and American civilization.[28] Especially provocative is Kurth's argument that the Protestant core of the American Creed has come to include the civil religion of a secularized Protestantism – what he calls the heretical, neo-pagan religion of America's secular elite. Religious diversity rather than universal religion marks the resurgence of religious vitality in many contemporary civilizations. Multiple traditions of secularisms, in the plural, point to the intensification or persistence of religious consciousness and politics with which these secularisms must engage. While Christianity and Islam have expanded in the twentieth century, so have various forms of nonreligious and atheistic belief systems. Varieties of religious and secular belief systems thus continue to exist side by side. Russian civilization illustrates clearly this pluralist theme.

Russia

Throughout its history, Russia has remained open to very different external influences, occupying a peripheral position, especially in relation to Western Europe. This illustrates the point that civilizations do not emerge as self-contained entities with crystallized values which they subsequently diffuse. Rather, they emerge in the interstices and at the crossroads of other civilizational complexes.[29] Yet, in sharp contrast to Africa, Russia is readily recognized as a distinct civilization.[30] The reason inheres less in Russia itself and more in Europe's intellectual reimagination of East and West during the Enlightenment. For centuries, Europe had been organized intellectually along a north–south gradient. But during the Enlightenment West European elites invented Eastern Europe as a foil to highlight their own civility and progress against the supposed backwardness and barbarity of the East. The idea of Eastern Europe was thus deeply entangled with Europe's Orientalist tradition. "The new idea of civilization," writes Larry Wolff, "was the crucial and indispensible point of reference that made possible the consolidation and articulation of the inchoate idea of Eastern Europe," not as an antipode to civilization but rather as an intermediary point on a civilizational gradient that declined from West to East.[31]

Even though Russia's borders have been wide open, Russian scholars have embraced the notion of constituting a distinctive civilization. Language, literature, and religion are vital parts of Russia's self-consciousness.[32] Greek missionaries and the pervasive influence of Byzantium provided deeply intertwined legacies that made Russia both integral and marginal to European civilization. Russian Orthodoxy evolved under the influence of these open-ended, transcivilizational processes.[33] By the early twentieth century, Russian religion had taken on firm ideological functions, with Marxism becoming Russia's official, civil religion.

The collapse of the Soviet Union reopened Russian debates about its contested identity.[34] Russian intellectuals and policymakers rejected as ethnocentric Francis Fukuyama's liberal, international and Samuel Huntington's realist, cultural ideas.[35] Although these theorists hold mutually exclusive views, Russian intellectuals widely considered both to be inadequate. Liberal internationalism overemphasizes the global sources of civilizational identity, while cultural realism overstates the local. For Russian intellectual sensibilities, both arguments are too linear and overlook the dialectical relationship between the global and the local. Furthermore, Russian civilizational discourse revealed the existence of different political camps and schools of thought marked by vigorous disagreements: Liberal, Social Democrat, Statist, and National Communist. Each of these traditions holds to distinct views on the sources, strengths, and contents of Russia's cosmopolitan and local traditions. And all are marked by the capacity for dialectical thought strikingly absent from Fukuyama's and Huntington's writings.[36]

In this view of Russian civilization, the separatist tendencies that are of growing importance in contemporary Russia mirror ethnocentric and exclusive American views. The reassertion of the trinity of Orthodoxy, autocracy, and nationality signals a return to nineteenth-century Tsarism and a decline of liberal and Social Democratic traditions.[37] Russia's new Conservatism points with great pride to traditional values, as conservatism does everywhere. Yet, like all forms of conservatism, it has no compelling answer to the criticism that traditional values come in various types: traditions of serfdom and traditions of peasant uprisings, for example, or traditions of Tsarist authoritarianism, Stalinist totalitarianism, and Russian liberalism. Contemporary Russia is a civilizational state that continues to debate the relevance of its multiple traditions for its role in the modern world. And that debate reveals a broad continuum of contemporary civilizational practices and discourses that stretches from liberal Eurocentrism to post-Soviet Eurasianism.[38] In brief, this sketch of Russian civilizational politics illustrates the pitfalls of styles of analysis that make us think about Russia, the East, or any civilization in unique or unified terms.

Pluralist civilizations in one civilization of modernity or unitary civilizations in the international state system?

Civilizational analysis should avoid being trapped by the illusion of singularity.[39] There are two basic views on civilization. This book takes a pluralist view that sees civilizations as embedded in a more encompassing context. It thus extends further the perspective of pre-modern civilizations as a Eurasian or Afro-Eurasian ecumene.[40] Civilizations are grounded in and encompass the material infrastructure of world affairs – cities, commerce, travel, trade, alliances, and warfare. Scouring the scattered testaments of long-forgotten collectors of Indian and Egyptian artifacts in the eighteenth and nineteenth centuries, Maya Jasanoff is able to track "how much the process of cultural encounter involved crossing and mixing."[41] Ian Morris has argued similarly that over the long course of human history, all large groupings of peoples have been endowed with similar inherent capacities; understood in geographic terms, West and East have enjoyed variable ecological advantages leading to shifting advantages of one over the other; the recent lead of Western over Eastern civilizations will either reverse during the coming century or, more likely, be rendered irrelevant by transformative changes that will eliminate the significance of territory in the universal explosion of knowledge.[42] Today's civilization of modernity stands for the known world and the manifold connections between different civilizational complexes. Although it retains for now territorial roots, it is defined also by non-territorial processes that express a forever changing historical consciousness. And it constitutes a universal system of knowledgeable practices that are characteristic of contested, multiple modernities. The history of civilizations is one of mutual borrowing that does not endanger a civilization's character.[43] The movement of peoples between hills and valleys and across continents and oceans, as well as the tensions within and between religious and literary traditions, account for the plurality and pluralism of civilizations.

An alternative view of civilizations holds that they are unitary cultural programs, organized hierarchically around uncontested core values that yield unambiguous criteria for judging good conduct.[44] This view was a European invention of the eighteenth century. In the nineteenth century, it was enshrined in the concept of one standard of civilization. That standard was grounded in race, ethnic affiliation, religion, and a firm belief in the superiority of European civilization over all others. The distinction between civilized and uncivilized peoples, however, is not specific to the European past. It enjoys broad support today among many conservative supporters of Huntington's thesis of the clash of civilizations – a book that was translated into 39 languages.[45] Paradoxically, it is also held by many liberals who are committed to improving the rule of law and global standards of good governance. Furthermore, the unitary argument is widely used by non-Europeans in their analysis of civilizational politics. Everywhere and at all times, so-called barbarians have knocked on the doors of civilizations.[46]

Where civilizations appear to cohere around uncontested core values, we are witnessing political and intellectual innovations created for particular purposes rather than inherent cultural traits of unchanging collective identities and practices. Samuel Huntington's *Clash of Civilizations* restates the old, unitary thesis for our times. For Huntington, civilizations are coherent, consensual, invariant, and equipped with a state-like capacity to act. Huntington succeeded brilliantly in his objective of providing a new paradigm for looking at world politics after the end of the Cold War. His correct anticipation of 9/11 gave the book a claim to validity that helps account for its continued relevance. Less noticed in public than in academic discourse is the fact that Huntington greatly overstates his case. Numerous analyses have established beyond any reasonable doubt that clashes occur primarily within rather than between civilizations.[47] Furthermore, the book's appeal has not been undermined by the failure of the second of its two main claims. Since the end of the Cold War, the relations between Sinic and American civilizations are summarized best by terms such as encounter or engagement rather than clash.

A very similar, anti-Western counter-discourse, also steeped in Western reasoning, has long existed in Asia. Lee Kuan Yew and his advisor Tommy Koh are outspoken supporters of the Asian values view.[48] Another well-known public intellectual in Singapore, Kishore Mahbubani, is a champion of Asia. His recent book details a seismic shift in power from "West" to "East."[49] And then there is the dialogue between Mohammad Mahathir and Shintarō Ishihara, which develops the same point more stridently.[50] The voices proclaiming the dawn of Asia's civilizational primacy may shift from yesterday's Japan, to today's China and tomorrow's India. But these voices are growing louder. Like "Orientalism," "Occidentalism" characterizes East and West in the singular.[51]

Primordialism as political construction

The widespread use of East and West in the singular creates a discursive category that is endowed with actor-like dispositions. It is then deployed under specific political conditions and for specific political purposes.[52] It is not the category, but the act of reification or construction that is politically consequential and that requires political analysis. In convincing ourselves and others of a specific mental map, and aligning our identities and interests with that map, we rely on rhetorical constructions to impute meaning that otherwise eludes us.

Primordialism is a simplifying crystallization of social consciousness. It can focus on civilization as it does on gender, kinship, territory, language, or race. The specific collective identity invoked is defined either in terms of "civility" (drawing boundaries between "us" and "them" with a specific focus on rules of conduct and social routines) or in terms of sacredness (drawing boundaries between "us" and "them" with specific reference to the transcendental, defined as God or Reason).[53] We need to understand both: how civilizations become, and what they are. Indeed, in primordial constructions of Self and Other, action and speech are deeply entangled with one another rather than existing side by side. Our analysis thus needs to encompass both to capture the broad and deep consensus about the very term "civilization."[54]

Samuel Huntington's unitary conception of civilization illustrates this point. For Huntington, civilizations are competing in an international system rather than constituting a global civilization of modernity. Hence, Huntington articulates as a policy maxim "the commonalities rule," pointing as an urgent need to something that exists already in abundance: the search for values, institutions, and practices that are shared across civilizations.[55] In his view, civilizations balance power rather than reflecting open-ended processes and a broad range of human practices. Neglecting all the evidence of a restless, pluralist, and at times seething West, Huntington's analysis sees the West as a civilizationally reactive status quo power that reluctantly engages the upsurge of revisionist non-Western civilizations.

Rather than focusing on actors such as states, polities, or empires that are embedded in civilizational complexes, in Huntington's analysis civilizations themselves become actors. And, implausibly, he measures civilizational power solely by material capabilities such as population, GNP, and military expenditures. His clash of civilizations thus looks remarkably similar to a clash of large states or empires. In my view, instead, civilizations are the broadest cultural context for world politics.

Civilization of modernity and a balance of practice

The civilization of modernity as an encompassing context for all civilizations enhances the pluralism that inheres in a world of civilizations. That context is not the international system or global markets, frequently deployed concepts that suffer from excessive sparseness and abstraction. Recognition of the importance of this context is central to the trenchant self-critique that William McNeill wrote of his brilliant *The Rise of the West*, more than a quarter of a century after he had completed it and six years before the publication of Huntington's book.[56] For McNeill, civilizations are internally variegated, loosely coupled, elite-centered social systems that are integrated in a commonly shared global context. He argues that his earlier path-breaking book was wrongheaded, based on the faulty assumption of the existence of civilizations conceived as separate groupings whose interaction was the main engine of world history. Instead, McNeill now insists that an adequate account must give proper consideration to the broader context in which all civilizations are embedded. Since civilizations are internally differentiated, they transplant selectively. And since they are loosely integrated, they generate debates and contestations that tend to make them salient to others. What historically was true for South Asia and the Islamic world, under the impact of modern communications technologies is even more true for all contemporary civilizations. All of today's civilizations are embedded in one all-encompassing civilization of modernity.

Civilizational politics is therefore syncretic in blending global and international processes with religious, secular, and national ones.[57] For Fernand Braudel, at first sight "every civilization looks rather like a railway goods yard, constantly receiving and dispatching miscellaneous deliveries."[58] Deeply meaningful to many members of the cultural elite, as self-conscious and lived identities, civilizations do not rank at the top for most people and typically do not manifest themselves in an everyday sense of strong belonging. Making civilizations primordial is arguably a political project aimed at creating a taken-for-granted sense of reality that helps in distinguishing between Self and Other, and between right and wrong. It requires elimination of the awareness that civilizations exist in plural forms and are constituted by multiple traditions creating diverse processes, policies, and practices.

In sum, the conceptualization I offer here is attuned to both the emergence of new political forces that reflect the richness of the political repertoires made available by various civilizations, and the political backlash that novelty and change will frequently create. Closely tied to political power, shifting balances of policies and practices are thus producing and reproducing behavioral and symbolic boundaries within and between civilizations.

Civilizational processes and practices

We lack the conceptual framework for the analysis of civilizational processes in international politics that Norbert Elias developed for domestic affairs.[59] We do know, however, that civilizational processes in global affairs occur in a setting that lacks a monopoly over the means of violence. This structural condition points to non-linear, multi-sited, multidirectional, reinforcing, and reversible processes of Sinicization.

Civilizational processes

Sinicization invites a distinctive style of analysis that in recent decades has become increasingly common in the social sciences. This is illustrated by the growing interest in processes and mechanisms that has complemented a more traditional, variable-based language indebted to the logic of covering-law explanations and the correlational logic of statistical explanations. Mechanisms are lower-level process links that are embedded within, but potentially independent from, a higher-level causal story.[60] Conversely, a causal model, theory, or narrative often relies on configurations of multiple processes to explain how some set of initial conditions in one or more contexts generates some set of outcomes or variations. Civilizational analysis that focuses on processes, policies, and practices fits into this research tradition.

Beyond this general understanding, there exists little agreement on what constitutes process or mechanism.[61] For starters, civilizational processes cannot be analyzed only with a materialist definition, as is common in the natural sciences and engineering.[62] Instead, as in other fields of social science analysis, they contain some irreducibly unobservable aspects of social reality, such as the conceptual and semiotic systems that can affect processes and objects without the intervention of observable, concrete mechanisms.[63] Furthermore, civilizational processes exist at a level of generality that goes beyond specific spatial or temporal contexts. They are abstract representations that specify the logic of a process that is unfolding in different contexts.[64]

Scholars have identified numerous mechanisms in various studies. In his historical work, for example, Charles Tilly has focused on strategic exchange and bargaining, diffusion with threshold effects, and tipping points in network structures.[65] Iain Johnston's analysis of China and international institutions has highlighted the importance of social influence, mimicking, and persuasion.[66] Referencing the work of Tanja Börzel and Thomas Risse, Kevin Featherstone has distinguished among asymmetrical patterns of absorption, accommodation, and transformation.[67] And in his analysis of multiple modernities, Jürgen Kocka has focused on imposition, imitation, adaptation, and negotiation.[68] These different mechanisms, and others we could add to the list, potentially help us to specify the causal relationships among situation, actor, discourse, action, and emergent structural properties of different contexts. Thus we can generate a preliminary inventory of mechanisms connecting civilizational processes to policies and practices.

For example, Allen Carlson focuses in Chapter 2 on the mechanism of conceptualization. The rising importance of non-traditional security concerns gives renewed importance to China's policies toward its northern frontier. Embryonic changes are beginning to affect China's conceptual maps. Carlson tracks these carefully so as to understand better the directions of future policy changes. In Chapter 3, Xu Xin develops an explanation of China's Taiwan policy as a process of adaptation. Various constraints and opportunities of China's past and present political conditions are shaping the path it seeks to chart in its unification policy, reining in Taiwan's secessionist impulses while drawing on what Xu Xin calls a tradition of "loose reign." Brokerage and competition are the two mechanisms that are central to Tianbiao Zhu's analysis of China's compressed development in Chapter 4. They are of critical importance for the policy flexibility that he identifies as a central aspect of "vertical" Sinicization in the past and "horizontal" border-spanning Sinicization in the present. In Chapter 5, Takashi Shiraishi's analysis of the regional impact of China's economic rise highlights two mechanisms: diffusion of Chinese business practices to neighbors that are not well integrated into the global economy, and bargaining with neighbors that are. Chih-yu Shih focuses in Chapter 6 on the mechanism of appropriation and reappropriation of Chinese products and symbols by four scholars who coped with very different life trajectories. Finally, Caroline Hau highlights in Chapter 7 the invention and reinvention of what it means to be Chinese in various Southeast Asian locales and time periods. In sum, conceptualization, adaptation, brokerage and competition, diffusion and bargaining, appropriation and invention are mechanisms that play a role in non-linear, multi-sited, multidirectional, reinforcing, and reversible processes of Sinicization.

This inventory is no more than a first small step. Eventually, process and mechanism analysis may offer plausible hypotheses at the individual level for aggregating disparate individual practices, and at the collective level for identifying some observable uniformities.[69] Operating at both levels, civilizational analysis highlights the causal complexity of processes, policies, and practices.[70]

What should we expect from this analysis? Minimalists insist that civilizational processes are so complex, impenetrable, and contingent as to defy systematic analysis altogether. We can perhaps describe, interpret, and assess the meaning of processes, but we cannot aim at explaining them.[71] Maximalists argue that causal mechanisms are "structures and entities that have the capacity to generate observed associations between macrophenomena."[72] They tell us that something occurs with regularity, as well as why and how it occurs. An adequate account of how the world works combines credible causal mechanisms that produce a given phenomenon or event.

This book establishes its claim between these two positions. Its motivation disagrees with the minimalist position. But since the field of civilizational analysis is in its infancy and since this analysis draws on only a few case studies, the maximalist position is unrealistically ambitious. The task at hand is to illustrate the existence of important connections within and between the processes, policies, and practices that constitute Sinicization. The analysis of specific episodes in the fields of security, political economy, and culture may help to offer some plausible claims about the existence of possibly robust components and connections.[73] Eventually, but not here, process- and mechanism-based accounts may thus lead us to the search for recurrent configurations.

This middle position is close to that of Peter Hedström and Martha Finnemore. Hedström differentiates among law-like explanations, statistical explanations, and mechanism explanations.[74] Each differs in its motivating explanatory principle – subsumption under a causal law, identification of a statistical relationship, specification of a social mechanism. And each emphasizes different key explanatory factors – law-like relation to the event to be explained, statistical relevance, identification of action-relevant entities and activities and their various linkages. "The core idea behind the mechanism approach is that we explain not by evoking universal laws, or by identifying statistically relevant factors, but by specifying mechanisms that show how phenomena are brought about."[75] Martha Finnemore, rather than examining a process, such as Sinicization, and asking what it is, looks instead at the activities of actors and asks how they describe and interpret their activities in different contexts.[76] Her methodology is a "narrative explanatory protocol." These protocols are, first, descriptive in laying out a chronological sequence and, second, configurative in articulating a coherent structure in arranging them in a particular way. Following Charles Pierce and John Ruggie, Finnemore bridges induction and deduction with the method of "abduction," a dialectical combination of both.

Civilizational practices

International relations theory has in recent years rediscovered the categories of pragmatism and practice. Influenced among others by Pierre Bourdieu and Jürgen Habermas, both concepts help clarify some of the most vexing questions in the field.[77] Practices express what Vincent Pouliot calls "the logic of practicality" – a close cousin of Bourdieu's "logic of practice" – which operates alongside and complementary to the logic of consequence, appropriateness, and argumentation.[78] Practices vary in their degree of competence and in the balance between discursive and material elements. They can exist in parallel without significant mutual interference; they can evolve symbiotically, forming coherent wholes in which different ensembles create mutually reinforcing relationships; they can form hybrid interactions with one another to create new practices; and they can exist in relations of mutual subordination.[79] Practices can be unselfconscious, based on unspoken "background" or "common" knowledge that express differently structured life worlds; and they can be conscious. Practice, in the singular, refers to the contingent and often creative part of human existence that plays itself out case by case.

Practices, in the plural, refer to the habitual and routinized actions shared by a group of people.[80]

In the case of civilizations, the logic of practicality includes representational models of action that are fictional, not rationalist. In contrast to literary fiction, imagined future states of the world often remain undisclosed, are seen as separate from the real world, and are perceived as naturalized representations of the future.[81] Without reducing uncertainty, fictions thus can provide parameters for choices in an uncertain world. They can help in the emergence of new practices. And they are non-verifiable. Practice informed by fiction complements unselfconscious civilizational processes.

Language is a specific social practice. It has a generative capacity that allows for novelty and creativity rather than mere repetition. Practices can generate conventions and symbols that stabilize meanings and make it possible to adhere to the protocols of instrumental decision making. Some human practices can reveal civilizational and other identities by activating myths and metaphors. The same is true of international diplomacy and law. They, too, are ongoing conversations and negotiations in search of workable translations and thus contribute to establishing contingent and evolving collective systems of shared reference. Political practice is the only way of telling whether, and to which extent, translation of civilizational and other differences has actually succeeded. In general, transcivilizational engagement creates more successful translations than intercivilizational encounters. Civilizational clash signifies a fundamental rupture of peaceful systems of reference while creating a shared world of violence.

Vincent Pouliot takes this observation, if not my terminology, as the starting point for his analysis of the relations between West and East, exemplified by NATO and Russia after the Cold War and the disintegration of the Soviet Union.[82] The Cold War clash between NATO and the Soviet Union was not transformed through political practices into peaceful engagements, but ended up as a series of symbolic power struggles. For many reasons, these encounters have not spilled over into overt conflict. But neither have they led to deep engagement in a security community marked by the emergence of dependable expectations of peaceful change. "NATO–Russia power politics seems to have uneasily migrated from the realm of war, however cold, to that of normalized diplomacy."[83] Pouliot's conclusion is supported by other scholars. Russia is currently coming into its own because its civilizational encounter with the West makes it into a semi-periphery that exists in relative isolation.[84] In separate analyses, Ted Hopf and Iver Neumann have also concluded that Russia remains Western Europe's "Eastern Other" and Western Europe remains Russia's "External Other."[85]

Processes and practices

Chapters 2–7 illustrate a broad range of processes and practices in different empirical domains. Allen Carlson focuses in Chapter 2 on the discursive politics that accompanies the reimagining of China's interior frontier. On the issue of China's borders, the rhetorical space was wide open in the distant past, was narrowly constrained after 1949, and is cautiously and gradually opening up in recent years. In the past, the relation between China and the frontier lacked firm contours. There were no rigid preconceptions about the extension of the domain of China's rightful rule. Borders were thought of as contested zones. This conceptual flexibility created space for a broad array of practices that allowed for Sinicization processes across China's northern frontier. Starting in the middle of the nineteenth century, Chinese intellectuals took up with alacrity European concepts of sovereignty and territoriality that eliminated China as the symbolic center of the world. Old and new notions of China coexisted for about a century, with the new gaining at the expense of the old. After the founding of the PRC in 1949, discursive rigidity and silence replaced dialogue and debate, an unmistakable sign that Western concepts of territorial sovereignty had been fully accepted by China and its new Communist government. A univocal discourse of territorial sovereignty *über alles* replaced vibrant disagreements and debates. Whatever the status of the Great Wall in history, after 1949 China was walled off from the outside world. The Communist government also developed a system of classification of different nationalities and autonomous regions.

After 1979, a new pragmatism in Chinese politics and policy led to modifications in the treatment of minorities as well as some changes in official discourse. The collapse of the Soviet Union improved dramatically the security environment of the PRC along its northern border. As a matter of policy and political practice, China's active participation in setting up the Shanghai Five in 1996, and its successor the Shanghai Cooperation Organization in 2001, pointed to growing flexibility and trust in multilateral approaches to Central Asian affairs. Increased cross-border interactions and the encouragement of ethnic tourism followed in due course.[86] In parallel with these changes, a discursive space that had been closed off for half a century reopened gradually. In recent years, elite discourse is cautiously reengaging issues associated with China's northwestern border. In doing so, all proponents reach back to past discourses and seek hidden answers or meanings that may be relevant for China's contemporary predicaments. In addition, they are unavoidably affected by concepts and modes of thinking developed outside of China. The contemporary debate emphasizes frontier studies (linked to traditional concerns with space), frontier security (linked to new conceptions of societal security), and points at least embryonically to a rethinking away from established concepts and practices of regional autonomy and nationality classifications. In Carlson's analysis, Sinicization contains an irreducible, discursive dimension that implicates deeply how Chinese actors conceive of the relationships between Self and Other. He demonstrates that these relationships vary widely across time and political regimes. As open-ended spatial, temporal, and discursive processes, Sinicization is highly changeable. It remains to be seen whether the limited conceptual innovations of recent years will broaden the dialogue further or whether domestic repression will once again narrow the scope of debate. As in the past, political practices and policies are sure to accompany these changes in political discourse.

With specific reference to Taiwan, Xu Xin's analysis in Chapter 3 focuses on China's maritime border to the south, with more attention to policy and practice than to discourse. The Taiwan issue highlights the primacy of national reunification. Sinic civilization and Sinicization are put to good use in serving the goal of defending, maintaining, and regaining national unity. Conflicting pressures and processes converge on the issue of Taiwan – a perennial problem for regime legitimacy, national identity, state security, and Chinese foreign relations. The Chinese approach of "one country, two systems" bears the imprint of two complementary conceptions of international relations: the modern Westphalian one of territorial sovereignty ("one country") and an older Sinic one of a hierarchical world that gives the center some latitude in dealing with an autonomy-craving periphery ("two systems"). Exclusive jurisdictional claims exist side by side with flexible practices and policies, and pragmatic governance arrangements. While Carlson in Chapter 2 and Shih in Chapter 6 track primarily the ups and down of discourse, Xu Xin, like Zhu's analysis of compressed development in Chapter 4, focuses primarily on policies and practices that exemplify Sinicization.

Xu Xin's analysis demonstrates that the policies, practices, and discourses around the issue of national unification are adopted, acted out, and deployed in changing clusters of meanings of what China was, is, will, and should be, rather than being expressed monolithically and linearly. Resonating with the analysis provided by Shih (Chapter 6) and Hau (Chapter 7), both Western and Sinic conceptions and practices are regularly brought into play, often in different and novel combinations. Specifically, contemporary Chinese diplomacy reflects aspects of traditional concepts and practices, thus helping the Chinese government to bridge the gap between the aspiration for one united China and the existence of a political reality that falls far short of it.

The history of China's changing relations with Taiwan reflects many crosscurrents of re- and de-Sinicization that reflect and shape processes of identity constructions on both sides of the Taiwan Strait. The mainland experienced the rise of Chinese nationalism during the Republican period and socialist revolution under Mao's rule; and it rediscovered Sinic traditions with Deng's reforms. Taiwan meanwhile underwent de-Sinicization and forced Japanization under Japanese colonial rule, re-Sinicization under Chiang Kai-shek's authoritarian regime, and de-Sinicization and Taiwanization under Lee Teng-hui's and Chen Shui-bian's indigenous and democratic governments. These processes, furthermore, unfolded in the dramatically changing geopolitical contexts of Japanese military aggression, World War II, the Cold War, and American hegemony. The dialectics of Sinicization illustrate the contested nature of China's nation building in the twentieth century.

Wrapped in the language of one sovereign China, the government's tolerance for calls for independence by previous Taiwanese administrations resembles traditional practices of "loose reign." Mao's concept of "peaceful" liberation and Deng's of "peaceful" reunification both speak to the patience that very different Chinese regimes have displayed in dealing with autonomous political entities in the periphery. Just as peace means self-restraint and forbearance, sovereignty often means symbolic central authority. Throughout much of Chinese history, cultural and political frontiers have not coincided. The Taiwan problem thus is not a unique episode as much as the recurrence of a deeply painful experience with which the Chinese government copes by drawing on its cultural capital. The claim for universal preeminence thus coexists with pragmatic and differentiated governance concepts. The behavioral compellingness of this social myth of universalism may be low; but its implications for regime legitimacy and sense of self are nonetheless significant. It is not clear whether China's sense of cultural unity is larger than Western-style nationalism as John Fairbank has argued.[87] But the pragmatism that Xu Xin analyzes may well be grounded in a deeply rooted and secure sense of self. Confronted with the challenge of Taiwanization on the road to reunification, some intellectuals who enjoy good access to top politicians are unafraid of looking to the mutual constitution of Taiwan and China for a further enhancement of one future China. This is a Chinese version of the European pooling of sovereignty in an ongoing, sincere search for making the one China everyone professes to want a reality. In dealing with the Taiwan problem, defining China in more encompassing, civilizational terms thus has proven politically advantageous.

In Chapter 4, Tianbiao Zhu's analysis of China's compressed development and multiple traditions focuses on a number of economic processes that help constitute Sinicization and encourage flexible policies and practices. They are distinctively Chinese and differ substantially from policies and practices that typify liberal market and developmental statist economies. Characteristic of compressed development is simultaneity rather than sequencing. What once comprised discrete stages of development now flows together into tightly linked and often contradictory processes of industrialization and de-industrialization. Policies and practices no longer focus on one overriding national goal; instead, they speak to the different logics of action brought about by the new condition of simultaneity.

Compressed development thus intensifies both political brokerage and market competition. Reflected in and responding to contradictory developments, China's property rights regime is multilayered. China's flexible policy repertoire defies the summary labels offered by regulatory or developmental models of policy making.[88] China differs, therefore, from both South Korea's vertical integration of national champions and Taiwan's horizontal, networked economy. Reminiscent of the pragmatic diplomatic practice of "loose reign" and the primacy of correct practice over correct belief discussed in Chapter 3, Zhu's discussion of "policy stretch" encompasses practices that are distinctively Chinese. The Chinese system generates experimentation and improvisation as normal rather than deviant outcomes. Illustrated by the central government in the early 1990s and the financial sector beginning in the late 1990s, bending the rules and searching for practical ways of adaptation are more important than following standard operating procedures.

Brokerage and competition apply also to the approach that China's government takes to the private sector and inter-governmental relations. The government approaches different private actors by following a system of "graduated control," ranking these actors by their ability to pose political challenges as well as the value of the public goods they provide. It thus limits the ability of social and economic organizations to disrupt China's economic and political life. Far from being dysfunctional, fragmented rather than coherent policy implementation is a systematic outcome. The relations between the central, provincial, and local governments thus share dynamics similar to policy stretch and graduated control. Problem solving drives the government's agenda setting and bargaining tactics. If there is one policy dictum, it is "no one size fits all."

Along a north–south gradient, China's government influence diminishes as the importance of the private sector increases in the middle of the country and foreign investors, many of them overseas Chinese, dominate the economy in the south. The government's acquiescence to provincial and local governments as well as foreign investors speaks volumes about its pragmatic and adaptable approach to economic issues. China's economy and especially its foreign and private sectors are built on the backs of migrant workers, typically disenfranchised and discriminated against by local governments. "Informalism" is a crucially important mechanism for the success of China's manufacturing sector, especially during the last 15 years. From 15,000 workers in 1978, the informal sector of the economy grew by 2006 to 168 million workers or just under 60 percent of the urban workforce.[89] Informalism also required cheap land which local governments have made readily available to foreign investors, with often dismal environmental consequences. Tolerated or encouraged by the central government, informality provides a decisively important connection between local governments, foreign investors, migrant workers, and peasants.

Takashi Shiraishi traces in Chapter 5 the variability of processes, policies, and practices that accompany China's outward economic expansion into Southeast Asia. Without denying that China's rise has been a very important fact throughout East and Southeast Asia, Shiraishi's analysis stresses not the uniformity of China's outward expansion but the variability of how Sinicization processes are incorporated into different countries. All of the conventional concepts that scholars of international relations deploy – soft-balancing, limited alignment, hedging, accommodation, or bandwagoning – are too blunt to capture the interplay of processes, policies, and practices. Thailand, Indonesia, Vietnam, and Myanmar, for example, react very differently to Sinicization processes. The more fully integrated into regional and global economic networks, the more open and unthreatened the response to China's economic rise, as is true of Thailand. Although it welcomes the economic opportunities that China's economic rise creates, domestic ethnic divisions make Indonesia more cautious in fully engaging China. Vietnam, too, seizes on the economic opportunities of China's rise. However, as it confronts a more powerful and assertive China over disputed territorial issues, Vietnam also balances against China for reasons of national security, directly with Japan and indirectly with the United States. Finally, threatened by economic sanctions and politically isolated, Myanmar depends heavily on China for both economic capital and political support. Shiraishi's analysis points to three interrelated factors that condition the response to Sinicization: position in the US-centered security system, extent of embeddedness in the regional and global economy, and domestic politics for regime maintenance and national unity.

Shiraishi pushes the analysis one step further as he focuses on the transnational dimension of China's rise, particularly official and private economic and trade cooperation, military assistance, and resource diplomacy. Rather than involving only state-owned banks and corporations, as in the 1980s and 1990s, the changing structure of China's economy now creates what Shiraishi calls "transnational politico-business alliances," which involve trade, finance, investment, official assistance, and state guarantees in a fusion so deep that state, political party, and business can no longer be disentangled. Only projects of great strategic importance continue to involve the top leadership on official state visits. In the case of Myanmar's power industry, for example, Shiraishi details how transnational business alliances are backstopped by financial guarantees provided by the state. These deals reflect, in his terminology, "partial" Sinicization processes. Shiraishi finds the same pattern in Chinese investments in the Laotian mining sector. More generally, he argues, this is most likely to happen in countries that are poorly integrated into the regional or global economy, in situations in which Chinese corporations face few local or transnational non-Chinese competitors, and in contexts in which they can deal with military officials or party cadres. Partial Sinicization is akin to Hirschman's influence effect in that it creates a community of interests across national borders that permits the influence of social power.[90] Collusion and corruptions are less important than the transferring of a model of business–government relations from China to neighboring countries. These alliances have built into them one particular feature that could create a very different dynamic in a very short time. Should large private investments fail, loans would be converted into stocks, and economic cooperation would change into direct foreign investment. In that eventuality, Chinese state corporations would end up owning substantial parts of a country's economic infrastructure. In short, in times of economic crisis, opaque business deals and partial Sinicization might turn into overtly political processes of Sinicization.

Sinicization works differently when countries are fully integrated into the regional and global economy and are not dominated by military or party cadres, as is true of Indonesia and Thailand. In Indonesia a large project of thermal power plant construction made Chinese firms move aggressively to drive out foreign competitors, eventually insisting on the renegotiation of those contracts and imposing more onerous conditions, thus eliminating the price advantage that had made Chinese firms highly competitive in the early bidding stages. The outcome, unhappy for Indonesia in terms of economic cost, was not a political disaster. The story was different in the Philippines. In a similar episode of transnational business deals, a factionalized Filipino political class exposed vulnerable business practices of Chinese firms and drew these firms into contentious and politically volatile domestic quarrels. In this and all the other cases, Sinicization is a differentiated set of processes, encompassing a variety of practices and policies that have a family resemblance but play themselves out very differently in different national contexts.

Everywhere, we see the seizing of economic advantages and political hedging; both phenomena are affected by China's economic rise, especially in countries not well integrated into Asia's regional or the global economy. In their specifics, however, the practices and policies that attend Sinicization are modulated and country-specific; they defy description under any general label.

In Chapter 6, Chih-yu Shih examines the work of four world-class diasporic scholars (Akira Iriye, Samuel Kim, Chung Tan, and John Wong) writing outside of China and, for the most part, for English-speaking audiences. Their cultural and linguistic skills and varied life stories speak to their multiple, cultural–geographical selves. Their work illustrates both a liminal position between East and West as well as China and Asia, and meaningful choices that are shaped, though not determined, by different contexts. In Shih's analysis, Sinicization is a set of multidirectional, multi-sited, discursive processes. Sinicization presupposes agents who appropriate and reappropriate Chinese symbols and practices for their own use and that of interested groups. Their transnational lives and work put into question an exclusive focus on territorially bounded nation states as the only unit of analysis in China's rise. Shih inquires into how these four scholars have coped with their specific situations, and how their lives were adapted to different circumstances. The interaction between an imagined China and Asian diaspora extends well beyond China and its surrounding territories. Crucial for processes of Sinicization are scholars acting as cultural brokers who mediate between China and the world. Sinicization captures processes of self-discovery and self-interpretation that reconstruct China in various imaginations and languages to a broader world.

At an individual level, rethinking and adaptation prompted by the encountering of ever changing life conditions are the cultural mechanisms that contribute to civilizational evolution. Shih examines these processes in the lives of his four scholars, whose professional lives centered on thinking deeply about China, in English as well as in their native languages, and for professional communities outside of China as well as Chinese audiences. Expressed in their writings and speeches, scholarly acts of imagination and conceptualization thus are components of Sinicization. It helps the effort to identify with China and to build bridges between different academic and national communities. In Shih's analysis, China is a temporal rather than a spatial concept. The meaning of engaging China depends on the time and site of these four scholars' lives and work rather than on what a tangible China is or does. A meaningful China lives in the scholarly imagination more than in its material manifestations. And there exists no central force or agency that in the name of China can harness or determine how these scholars represent China.

Caroline Hau's analysis of processes of hybridized Sinicization in Chapter 7 locates them in a specific regional, global, and geopolitical context during the past 150 years. Because it is a complex and historically contingent process, for Hau Sinicization involves numerous actors, practices, and sites, and is closely related to re- and de-Sinicization. The result of these processes is to create, reinvent, and transform the meaning of "China" and "Chineseness" in various Southeast Asian locales and also in China itself. In these processes Japan, Southeast Asia, Britain, and the USA are crucial to the making of "modern" Chineseness and China. Hybridized processes of Sinicization have regional and global scope and reach. Hau's analysis thus goes well beyond conceptualizations that take the "China" of "Cultural China" or "Greater China" as a given. Even when proponents of Cultural and Greater China emphasize the multi-sitedness of "Chineseness," somehow they do not factor in the causal power of regional and global contexts which enable different forms and variable strengths of identification with China and of Chineseness. It is thus important that China is located within, rather than abstracted from, a broader regional and global terrain. Throughout, Hau's analysis focuses on "becoming" rather than "being" Chinese.

Hau's approach does not take the colonial and the nation state as units of analysis. The state is useful only insofar as it helps account for different incentives shaping the variable trajectories of becoming Chinese. Colonial policies helped to segment populations in Southeast Asia and imposed new language regimes on colonial elites. Her analysis does not privilege the point of departure, as is done frequently in studies of transnationalism; it does not assign hybridity to the very act and consequences of the physical "travel" by individuals; it does not leave the category of "China" unexamined by holding to the unconscious assumption that China is monolithic; and it does not share in the all-too-common belief of the unity of the Chinese people, as if "China" were itself not made plural and hybridized by the very same historical experiences that shaped, for example, the emergence of the Anglo-Chinese in Southeast Asia.

Language plays a crucial role in hybridized Sinicization processes. "Translingual practices," specifically English, Japanese, and (during the Communist years) Russian, made concepts enter, circulate, and localize in modern Chinese. Linguistic continuity across the British and American empires is crucial to the rise of the Anglo-Chinese. Translations are always uneven and contingent processes. Furthermore, translations are always sites of political, intellectual, and cultural contestations. Acts of coding, decoding, and recoding thus are always involved in cultural flows, for example over the meaning of "Han imperialism/colonialism," or the ways in which the concepts of "great unity" (*da yitong*) or "All-under-heaven" (*tianxia*) are resignified or appropriated in different geopolitical eras.

According to the modern Chinese philosopher Hu Shih, "civilization is not created in a vague and general fashion, it is created bit by bit, and drop by drop."[91] As Chapters 2–7 amply illustrate, civilization is not a condition but a set of processes created by human practices. These practices sum, in the aggregate, to civilizational processes such as Sinicization and thus produce and reproduce behavioral and symbolic boundaries.

Civilizational processes and identities: Indianization and India, Japanization and Japan

Although they deserve much more sustained attention than I can offer here, civilizational processes involving Japan and India provide a comparative context in which to view Sinicization and China. India's diaspora shares important similarities with China's and differs from the relative inwardness of Japan.[92] At the same time, Japan has arguably had more exposure to and influence on Sinicization and China, at least in recent decades, than has India.

Japanization and Japan[93]

In his analysis of Japan, Shmuel Eisenstadt identifies two key characteristics: continuous internal institutional change, and a great receptivity to outside influences coupled with an astonishing capacity to internalize these influences.[94] Japan is often called a country of imitators. At the same time, Japan has displayed an unrelenting insistence on reinforcing its basic political conceptions of social order. One clear example is the colonization of Hokkaidō and the "catastrophic de-culturation, dispossession and subjugation of the island's indigenous population, the Ainu," carried out in a manner reminiscent of, though more brutal than, the occupation of Okinawa, Korea, and Taiwan.[95] External changes have rarely displaced Japan's governing premises. Although Buddhism and Confucianism had a large influence on Japan, they were greatly transformed in the process of incorporation. In contrast to other civilizations, Japan has never seen itself as part of a broader civilization with which it might share some basic principles or identities.

If a macro-historical perspective stresses Japanization as a form of adaptation to external change, more recent analyses have been impressed by Japan's prowess as an industrial behemoth in world markets. Japanization is intimately linked to the global spread of an American consumption culture. Since America has become the land of excessive and conspicuous consumption, especially in recent decades, that culture is met in Japan with considerable ambivalence since it values thrift and investment too little and growing inequalities too much.[96] Still, by the late 1960s, the Japanese had come to accept American products of mass consumption – TV, washing machines, refrigerators – as Japanese and proceeded to produce and export them, and subsequent generations of consumer goods, to America, the rest of Asia, and the world.

Japanization as a process has been studied carefully in the global automobile and popular culture industries.[97] In automobiles, electronics, and other export industries, Japanese producers succeeded in creating large gains in productivity, flexibility, and quality that assured them of a preeminent position in regional and global markets. Japanese firms behaved differently in different markets. In Britain, for example, Japanese automobile producers were eager to create a new system of industrial relations. In the USA they rushed to open production facilities in a market threatened by high tariff walls. Detailed studies support the conclusion that Japanization does not offer any fixed benchmarks by which to measure its spread. It involves, rather, relatively open-ended processes of diffusion, emulation, and the adoption of distinctive patterns of production and consumption. It offers no clear templates that can simply be replicated in different national or local settings. Instead, Japanization appears to involve variable combinations of deliberate organizational designs, shared cognitive schemas and normative orders, and conflicting political interests.

Japan's popular culture industries offer a second illustration.[98] Japanese modernity exists alongside others. Its civilizational self-understanding is grounded in the notion that Japan can translate Western standards of modernity for the rest of Asia without sacrificing its own distinct identity. During Japan's reckless militarist expansion in the first half of the twentieth century, as well as its relentless mercantilist growth in the second half, Japanese widely believed in the country's civilizational myth or mission. Culturally, Japan's distinctive hybridity of multiple modernities "domesticates anxieties about foreign influence," as Japanization intermingles with the incorporated modernities of its neighbors.[99] Artistically creative and economically dynamic, Japan's popular culture industries have flowered, especially in Asian markets. Japan has specialized in cultural imports, from baseball to Christmas. Japanese producers thus acquired the cultural know-how of American and European producers and are reselling that know-how in the form of indigenous production to their avid customers in Japan, East Asia and beyond. As Japanese products have no trouble being "understood,"[100] Japan's culture industries have had astounding success in creating cultural similarity with other countries, especially in East Asia. The elimination of distinctive Japanese characteristics is of paramount importance in the energetic pursuit of glocalization.[101] Having adapted many of the products of American popular culture, Japanese producers regard themselves as particularly well positioned to translate Western leisure products for Asian sensibilities. In both importing and exporting, they are creating a sameness in consumption styles that is distinctly different from those of America and Europe. In popular music, TV dramas, and *manga*, among others, the electronic revolution so readily embraced in East Asia diffuses Japanese images and values, while at the same time opening the Japanese market to cultural influences from South Korea, Taiwan, Hong Kong, China, and Southeast Asia.

Like China, Japan has its own multiple, contested traditions. In his broad overview of Japanese civilization as the only distinctly non-Axial age civilization, Eisenstadt has stressed Japan's continuous, autonomous, and turbulent history up to and including modern times.[102] Japan lacked what the other Axial age civilizations had – the urge to implement in the mundane world of the here and now the precepts of a higher ethical or metaphysical order. Non-Axial age civilizations, such as the Mongols, quickly succumbed to Axial-age civilizations. Not Japan, which articulated and retained a strong sense of self in its encounters with Buddhism, Confucianism, and other civilizations.

It is not surprising therefore that Japan's national polity (*kokutai*) has timeless, almost mystical connotations.[103] The conservative politics of a prescriptive, cultural familism roots the contemporary Japanese state deeply in the unbroken history of a family headed by the emperor. This focus has given state officials and the conservative camp in Japanese politics a culturally grounded vision that helped motivate and legitimate the twentieth-century military attempt to make all of East Asia children of the Japanese emperor, and subsequently to provide an astonishingly successful economic model for all of East Asia to imitate. Before 1945, Shintoism was a cultural and political program seeking to assist Japan's imperialist venture. After 1945, official discourse invoked Japan as a family nation, and familial metaphors crop up frequently in the corporate world. Indeed, the family as a corporate and pre-political unit is in the conservative reading of Japan the most important bedrock of Japan's civilizational polity. The family that is being invoked, however, varies. On the one hand, it refers to the multigenerational household (*ie*), which some scholars at the time of Japan's rise in the 1980s viewed as the central source of Japanese success.[104] But it refers also to the nuclear family as it has emerged in the modernizing Japan after World War II. Much of the failure of official rhetoric and public policy has to do with the discrepancy between the image of Japan's "family way" in the singular, and the lived experience and commonsense understanding of the plurality and diversities in the literal and unscripted familial units that constitute Japan now as they have throughout the ages. Against conservative wishes, today it is students, slackers, singles, seniors, and strangers that are transforming Japan's family, state, and nation.[105]

What realists regard as Japan's unique civilization is thus marked by multiple traditions. Two stand out and have engaged in an unending tug of war in recent decades. A primordial construction of a unique Japanese essence competes with a self-understanding of Japan as an ensemble of infinitely flexible and adaptive discourses and practices. At enormous costs to itself, Japan has resisted strong pressures, especially from its Asian neighbors, to take full responsibility for the unspeakable suffering that its imperialist venture and war of aggression brought in the 1930s and 1940s. At the same time, dependent on the United States as its most important ally and trade partner, Japan has shown an almost infinite flexibility in adjusting to the demands of a typically protectionist US Congress. Over a period of decades, Japanese officials have permitted a gradual opening of domestic markets. At the same time, however, Japan's techno-nationalist proclivities have remained so strong as to put Japanese business at a competitive disadvantage in an era of outsourcing and transnational technological collaborations. And with decreasing success, more than other civilizational states Japan has tried to maintain an ethnically homogenous population. Since the 1980s, Japan's growing internationalization has been closely linked to a deepening of its nationalism. Opening up to the world and digging deeper into Japanese traditions and culture are twin processes.

Indianization and India[106]

Admittedly, "Indianization" is an awkward though accurate neologism. It points to the fact that India's civilizational engagements with the world is largely sidelining India's 150 million Muslims. Historically, these processes were structured around the Indian Ocean, which put India at the center of trade routes connecting Southeast and East Asia, the Middle East, the Mediterranean, and Africa.[107] This location at the central switchpoint of the Afro-Eurasian world was important both before and after the arrival of the European powers. The contacts between India and the Islamic world, specifically Iran, deserve explicit mention.[108] "Greater India" stretched from Southeast Asia to Iraq. Tagore's travels explored that realm and went beyond it.[109] In modern times, India staffed and provided many of the shock troops of the British empire: merchants, workers, policemen, and soldiers. As Britain's "jewel in the crown," India and the networks spanning the Indian Ocean were indispensable for helping to finance and defend Britain's global empire. That empire was not only a hub-and-spoke arrangement centering on London but also a web of horizontal filaments, with India a subimperial center of great importance.[110] It remains an open question whether for a century India was parasitic on Britain's global empire, or whether Britain was parasitic on the set of civilizational, commercial, cultural, and political networks that had grown around the Indian Ocean, with India at its center. The Great Depression, World War II, and Indian independence ended this symbiotic relationship. For Britain, the loss of India in 1948 meant the loss of its empire. For India it meant becoming the world's largest democracy.

Contemporary India is marked by multiple processes of Indianization. An illustrious group of Indian writers such as Salman Rushdie, a Muslim, Vikram Seth, and Arundhati Roy are contributing an enormous amount of artistic talent to world literature, with an avid readership all over the English-speaking world.[111] Indeed, Anglo-Indian literature, in the opinion of some, constitutes India's most important contribution to the world of books.[112] In the area of film, with an annual production of about 1,000 movies, Bollywood dwarfs Hollywood in sheer numbers if not in profitability. Bollywood's rise was helped by the Cold War. Because of its shortage of Western currencies, during the Cold War the most important market for Indian movies was in the Socialist world. Produced in 1951, *Awaara* was probably the most widely watched movie of its era, and Raj Kapoor the most admired film star of the 1950s and 1960s. Even today, the former member states of the Soviet Union continue to be important outlets for an industry which, compared to Hollywood, enjoys little if any political support.[113] Indian movies and the artistic and social sensibilities they express continue to be hugely popular also in Greece, Egypt, Iran, and Pakistan.[114] More recently their appeal, both commercial and artistic, has also been strong in the Commonwealth countries, the United States, and wherever there exists a large Indian diaspora.[115] Moreover, as India's second largest media company, Rupert Murdoch's STAR-TV provides India's movie and TV industry with ready-made, direct access to an Asian market of about 300 million.

Other examples of Indianization readily come to mind. At the Bandung Conference in 1955, Nehru's India was in the forefront of defining for Third World countries a zone of diplomatic autonomy outside of Cold War structures imposed by the two superpowers.[116] In the form of Hindutva, India has in recent decades been exporting religion to the United States, Britain, and to wherever a substantial Indian diaspora can be found.[117] That diaspora's vibrancy challenges the notion of increasing cultural homogeneity in the era of globalization.[118] Indian cuisine has spread around the globe, both as *haute cuisine* and as cheap restaurant or street food.[119] In the globalization of sports, cricket's most recent TV-friendly reorganization will give India a preeminent, and South Asia an overwhelming, market share.[120] And at the elite level, a group of expatriate Indian economists, working primarily in Britain and the United States, is unrivaled in the academic world. These scholars are producing cutting-edge research while retaining a much broader intellectual outlook and harboring much bigger intellectual ambitions than their more narrowly and professionally focused British or American colleagues.[121]

India has also been on the receiving end of processes of engagement, most notably in the financial crisis of 1991. The adoption of economic liberalization has transformed important aspects of the Indian economy. Liberalization has brought affluence and a consumer society in which social trust and engagement have become more precarious, self-centered behavior more prevalent, and the ecological barriers to long-term growth much greater. In this new consumer society, old problems such as public health are recast as a component of an individualized political economy of pleasure.[122] Though still relatively recent, the effects of liberalization have already proven to be profound, illustrating how processes of civilizational encounters and engagements are always multi-sited and multidirectional.

For Jawaharlal Nehru, India was a place to be discovered, a singularity in a defined time and space.[123] Nehru viewed the Taj Mahal and the reign of the Mughal emperors as the fountainhead and crystallization of Indian civilization. By linking India's Muslim past with its most spectacular architectural symbol, Nehru hoped, perhaps, to affirm a secular image of the Indian nation state and challenge the Vedic origins of the India that many Indians believe in. Similarly, Sunil Khilnani chose to talk of the idea of India – in the singular.[124] So did Louis Dumont in his characterization of India as a typical traditional society. Dumont's analysis stressed social inequality and conflated structural principles with Brahmin conceptions, which he regarded as a stand-in for all of Indian society.[125]

Such conceptualizations seem oddly out of touch with contemporary scholarship. India is not to be discovered, either as a place or as an idea. Instead, India is continually reinvented, and it is deeply divided. Several centuries of Muslim conquest, settlement, and rule have not succeeded in making 150 million Muslims an integral part of India. Instead, Indian history remains a focal point of contestation – most recently, since the 1980s, with the rise of Hindutva. Prasenjit Duara calls Hindutva a syndicated, political, and monolithic form of Hindu nationalism favored by the Bharatiya Janata Party (BJP – Indian People's Party) and Shiv Sena.[126] Indeed, the rise of Hindu nationalism has been the central event in the crisis of Indian secularism.[127] Side by side with Nehru's secular and incorporating form of Hinduism, there exists now a religious and exclusive form, articulated by Golwalkar as early as 1948. It seeks to elevate Hinduism above all other religions and regards Islam as a foreign element in the Indian body politic. As is true of Europeans and Americans, Indians are thus continuously asking themselves, "who are we?"[128] And as is true elsewhere, they are drawing on multiple traditions to give their contested and tentative answers. For, as Amartya Sen points out, Indians are an argumentative lot, and not only in Bengal.[129] Their arguments are recurrent attempts to rearticulate, recombine, renegotiate, and relive India's various traditions. Even though it is designated as a single state, India does not exist in the singular. Instead, it exists as an ongoing set of conversations, political quarrels, and at times bloody fights, as over the Mughal Babri Mosque in Ayodhya.

This is one of Mahatma Gandhi's many legacies.[130] Like Tagore, Gandhi favored the political plurality of Indian civilization that preceded the introduction and imposition of Western concepts of state and nation under British rule. From this vantage point, India appears as a heterogeneous civilizational polity rather than a homogeneous nation state.[131] Indian plurality emerged as the successor of a vast transnational ecumene in which Sanskrit texts, which had monopolized world literary production, had circulated for a millennium.[132] It is still unknown why, between 1000 and 1500, the people in South Asia chose to produce texts in languages that did not travel as far as Sanskrit while at the same time joining an extended Persephone ecumene. Whatever the reason, this history created a degree of diversity that was not regretfully accepted, as in medieval Europe, but openly celebrated. Gandhi embraced the social and cultural pluralism that claimed his life at the very moment that India gained independent statehood.

Gandhi's folk-based, critical traditionalism differed from Tagore's classical universalism and from the modern, secular concept of the nation state which, Gandhi thought, would dehumanize life and diminish or eliminate India's distinctiveness.[133] Informed by this view, Gandhi sought to articulate an Indian identity that he regarded as a distinctive contribution to the world. His own biography made Indian identity a diasporic intellectual construct, forged in the marginalized position Gandhi had occupied in England and in the position of leadership that he subsequently held among Indian expatriates in Africa. For Gandhi, there actually existed a homeland that needed to be liberated, with methods that were well suited to his and India's characteristics – allowing him and Nehru, despite all their differences, to become comrades-in-arms in the most unusual struggle for national liberation the world has seen. Gandhi drew on a variety of indigenous sources to articulate an Indian identity. He knew those sources much better than did Karl Marx, who wrote, "Indian society has no history at all, at least no known history. What we call its history, is but the history of the successive intruders who founded their empires on the passive basis of that unresisting and unchanging society."[134] Marx's and Gandhi's views shared some similarity with nineteenth-century European Orientalist discourse that characterized India as rural, poor, religious, ascetic, and deeply spiritual. But we should not forget the profound impact that India's pre-modern technology had on Europe's material culture – specifically the manufacture of cotton clothing and steel, the two leading edges of Britain's Industrial Revolution; this undermines decisively the myth of India's merely philosophical and other-worldly character.[135]

To search for the essence of India is a losing proposition. To engage the argumentative tradition about India's multiple traditions is not. Today the Hindutva movement interprets the Hindu past as a form of cultural nationalism stretching back to Vedic times, a nationalism that is deeply entangled with Indian civilization. In sharp contrast, secular anti-colonial nationalism, Hindutva activists argue, can offer no more than a critique of oppressive colonialism and lacks a positive message resonating with India's Hindu majority. This view overlooks the contribution of British rule to the strengthening of religious boundaries in India. Since no natural categories such as Hindu or Muslim existed before Britain's arrival, it was British rule that made the emergence of a self-contained notion of Hinduism a possibility in the first place.[136] Neo-Gandhians, among others, are thus resisting the attempt to render a single version of the Indian past, stressing instead the ideal of multiplicity and the combinatorial richness it entails for the evolution of India as a civilizational complex. The contest over balancing the uniformity of individual rights in India's civil code with the diversity of personal laws protected by minority rights thus is a historically grounded, open-ended story – an important example of India's civilizational politics writ large.[137]

Conclusion

Our world of civilizations is plural and pluralist. It readily accommodates China as a distinctive rather than exceptional case. To insist on uniqueness is quite normal, not only in China but also in Japan and India. Indeed, in this, all three are quite comparable to Islam and the West.

All of these civilizations are nested in one encompassing global civilization containing multiple modernities. Civilizational processes express continually reconstructed multiple traditions, supported by different political coalitions and embodied in different institutions. Civilizational traditions and processes express specific antinomies: transcendental and mundane, universalistic and particularistic, totalistic and pluralistic, orthodox and heterodox. In civilizational politics, as in other kinds of politics, actors reveal to others and discover for themselves who they are; who they are drives what they do; and what they do shapes who they are.[138] Chinese, Japanese, and Indian civilizational identities and processes thus constitute an important context for political action.

Civilizational analysis often connotes a hierarchical view of the world that distinguishes "advanced" from "backward" peoples and polities, as Mao himself argued.[139] Supporters of Sinicization are less conscious of this fact than was Norbert Elias. As a twentieth-century German, he was acutely aware that civilizational processes can be easily reversed as yesterday's civilizers become today's uncivilized. Elias's theory of civilizing process is a historicization of Freud's superego, tracking the path from spontaneous, instinctual expressions to social and then internal control in the form of self-restraint.[140] The monopolization of force by the state, which disarmed a warring aristocracy and helped create a society of courtiers in domestic politics, is not an option in the society of states. What may instead be working weakly at the global level are two universal sentiments in particular: human rights grounded in the rights revolution of the last half-century, and human well-being grounded in the increasing importance of science and technology in the last three centuries. Both have become so broadly accepted that all but a handful of states and political actors adhere to the script they provide – without necessarily adhering to their implementation.[141]

Civilizations are not actors. They cannot clash. Instead they provide a context in which actors encounter and engage one another, as illustrated by the record of the last two decades in the relations between Sinic and American civilizations. This is not to deny the possibility of clash. But to date, at least, Samuel Huntington has been wrong in his prediction about a clash between Western and Sinic civilization. Furthermore, his theory is arguably culpable of helping those who promote such a clash and who would welcome its occurrence. Sinic civilizational consciousness dates back many centuries and reflects the fact that many different ethnic and social groups constituting the peoples of East Asia intermingled with one another over centuries and millennia.[142] The conceptual language of civilizational analysis, however, has become part of the Chinese vocabulary only in recent times. It needs to be honed to match the depth of consciousness.

Dynamic processes and practices that constitute encounters of, engagements with, and clashes between civilizations exist in the realm of becoming rather than being. Will they express in the future processes of hyphenated civilizational convergence, as Emanuel Adler and his colleagues argue?[143] Or will perhaps one civilization of empathy emerge, in which a new biosphere consciousness replaces older forms of civilizational consciousness inhering in multiple modernities, as Jeremy Rifkin suggests?[144] For now, these remain open questions that only the future can answer. The past, however, gives us some sense of the possibilities and limitations of a hyphenated or reinvented civilizational world.[145] Anglo-Indians are Indian citizens whose paternal line leads to Europe. They were the creation of eighteenth- and nineteenth-century British imperialism. Having lived only in India, Anglo-Indians were for the most part Christian, with English as their first and often only language. At the time of independence they formed a half-caste of about half a million people, which has dwindled since to no more than one third that size today. Their distinctive culture was and is neither Indian nor British. While that generation will not reproduce Anglo-Indian culture, their children have a relatively easy time finding good jobs in the Anglo-American world. Multinational corporations in search of profits, NGOs pursuing justice, and governments and international organizations bargaining and negotiating – they all look for intermediaries with bicultural backgrounds and an excellent command of English. Anglo-Indians join the veneer of cultural intermediaries who, like British expats and American businesspeople, live between worlds. The emergence of such a veneer is providing some cross-civilizational bridging in the Sinic world, in specific geographical areas such as Hong Kong and in particular social pockets such as the bi- or trilingual urban and professional elites in maritime Asia.[146]

The fact remains that civilizations are most similar not in their cultural coherence, isolation, or tendency toward clash, but in their pluralist differences, in their plurality, and in their encounters and engagements. We should resist the temptation of excessive simplification and the fallacy of misplaced polarities entailed in binary distinctions between East and West. Instead, we should embrace the intellectual and political opportunities of what Kwame Anthony Appiah has called the "contaminated cosmopolitanism" of our multi-civilizational world.[147] The opening stanza of Kipling's famous *Ballad of East and West*, I have argued here, is wrong: East and West are connected through manifold civilizational processes, policies, and practices. Dividing his life between India, a house in South Africa, a ranch in North America, Egypt, Britain, and many other places, Kipling certainly would have concurred.[148] For in his poem's second stanza he writes, with due allowance for the politically incorrect usage of gender and some imperfections in cadence:

> But there is neither East nor West, border nor breed nor birth
> When two strong men stand face to face, tho they come from the ends of the earth.[149]

Notes

1 For their criticisms, comments, and suggestions I would like to thank Martin Bernal, Jian Chen, Nicola di Cosimo, Gregory Noble, Miles Kahler, David Leheny, Wendy Leutert, Rudra Sil, Sidney Tarrow, Wang Gungwu, Tingyang Zhao, the participants in workshops held at Peking University in January 2010 and March 2011, my co-authors in this book, and the anonymous reviewers of the book manuscript. Mary Katzenstein read the penultimate draft and insisted on clarifications and corrections that helped me make this a much better chapter. For their invaluable research assistance I am indebted to Emma Clarke, Elisa Charbonnel, and Jill Lyon. Finally, I would like to acknowledge with enormous gratitude the generous financial support that I received in 2009–10 from the Louise and John Steffens Founders' Circle Membership at the Institute of Advanced Studies in Princeton.
2 Beecroft 1956, 425.
3 See Katzenstein 2012a for an analysis of Western civilization with a specific focus on Anglo-America. For a general overview of civilizational politics, see Katzenstein 2010a and Arnason 2010a, 2010b.
4 Holcombe 2001, 224, 219–23.
5 I thank Qingguo Jia for pointing this out to me in private correspondence (9 November 2009).
6 Tilly 2001, 37.
7 Laitin 1988.
8 Callahan 2010.
9 Katzenstein 2010b; Holcombe 2001, 221.
10 Lawrence 2010, 157; Huntington 1996, 41; Müller, 1999, 31–4.
11 Liu 2004, 1.
12 Morris 2010, 568.
13 Hamilton 2010, 37.
14 Morris 2010.
15 Kurzweil 2005; Rifkin 2009.
16 Katzenstein 2012b.
17 Barnett and Duvall 2006. Knöbl (2007) stresses the importance of political power in civilizational analysis.
18 Kang 2010a.
19 Rudolph 2010; Sen 2006, 46–9.
20 Lawrence 2010.

21 Ostler 2010, 20.
22 Ibid.
23 Ibid., 10.
24 Ostler's analysis is at odds with the three circle view that distinguishes among native English, official English, and English as a first foreign language, as developed by Braj Kachru (1985).
25 Ostler 2010, 47–55.
26 Ibid., 225–41.
27 Huntington 1996.
28 Kurth 2010.
29 I would like to thank Sinja Graf, who sharpened my thinking on this point.
30 Huntington 1996, 45.
31 Wolff 1994, 12, 14.
32 Worth 1998.
33 Rzhevsky 1998, 2, 4.
34 Tsygankov 2003, 56–8; 2008, 767–8.
35 Fukuyama 1989; Huntington 1996.
36 Tsygankov 2008, 763.
37 Coalson 2008.
38 Tsygankov 2008, 768–72.
39 I restate here some of the main arguments and themes first published in Katzenstein 2010a and 2010b.
40 Hodgson 1974 and 1993; McNeill 1990. See also Lawrence 2010, 157.
41 Jasanoff 2005, 7.
42 Morris 2010.
43 Braudel 1993, 8.
44 Bowden 2009.
45 Huntington's publisher signed 57 foreign contracts. Information provided by Valerie Borchardt, 1 December 2009, personal communication. Huntington amplified and extended a similar thesis first advanced by Bernard Lewis (1990).
46 Callahan 2010; Pocock 2005; Brody 2001.
47 Fox 2001; Ben-Yehuda 2003; Chiozza 2002; Henderson and Tucker 2001; Russett, Oneal, and Cox 2000; Neumayer and Plümper 2009; Schimmelfennig 2003, 150; Ferguson 2011, 312–14.
48 Zakaria 1994; Koh, Yeo, and Latif 2000.
49 Mahbubani 2008.
50 Mahathir and Ishihara 1995.
51 Chen 1992; Buruma and Margalit 2004.
52 See also Katzenstein 2010a, 11–13.
53 Eisenstadt and Schluchter 1998, 14–15.
54 Ferguson 2007, 191, 195.
55 Huntington 1996, 320; Brooks 2011.
56 McNeill 1990, 1963.
57 Haas 2000.
58 Braudel 1993, 29.
59 Elias 1978, 2000.
60 Stinchcombe 1991, 380–2; Mayntz 2004, 243–5.
61 Mahoney 2001, 579–80; Hedström 2005, 24–5.
62 Bunge 2004, 191.
63 Hedström and Swedberg 1998, 13; George and Bennett 2005, 143; McAdam, Tarrow, and Tilly 2008.
64 Elster 1998, 45; Hernes 1998, 74–8. For dissenting views, see Wight 2004, 290; Flyvbjerg 2001, 43.
65 Tilly 1997, 47.

66 Johnston 2008.
67 Featherstone 2003, 19–20.
68 Kocka 2001.
69 Schelling 1998, 32–3; Kuran 1998; Petersen 1999; George and Bennett 2005, 137, 141–2; Tilly 2001, 24–5.
70 Bunge 2004, 193; Tilly 2001, 25; Sil and Katzenstein 2010a, 2010b, 419–21.
71 Tilly 2001, 22–4.
72 Waldner 2007, 153.
73 Tilly 2001, 24–6; Hedström 2005, 11, 25–6, 33.
74 Ibid., 11.
75 Ibid., 24.
76 Finnemore 2003, 10–11, 13–15.
77 Adler and Pouliot 2011a; Guzzini 2010; Sil and Katzenstein 2010a and 2010b; Sabel and Zeitlin 2010; Pouliot 2010; Brunnee and Toope 2010; Hopf 2010; Adler 2005.
78 Pouliot 2010, 13–14.
79 Adler and Pouliot 2011b, 6–8, 19–21.
80 Guzzini 2010, 307. Pouliot's (2010, 29) systematic presentation of practical knowledge (*knowing how*) differentiates it sharply from representational knowledge (*knowing that*) through a set of ideal-typical distinctions highlighting its cognitive status (tacit, inarticulate, automatic vs. conscious, verbalizable, intentional), mode of learning (experiential unspoken practice vs. formal reflexive schemes), relation to practice (knowledge lies in the practice vs. knowledge precedes practice), nature of inference (implicit vs. explicit), direction of fit (world-to-mind doing vs. mind-to-world observing), type of reasoning (unthinking vs. instrumental or normative), and popular categories (commonsense, experience, intuition, knack, skill vs. scheme, model, theory, calculation, reasoning). These binary distinctions are helpful for alerting us to the possible existence of different micro-logics that motivate civilizational practices.
81 Beckert 2011, 2.
82 Pouliot 2010.
83 Ibid., 2.
84 Hopf 2011.
85 Hopf 2002; Neumann 1999.
86 Extending the traditional approach of Mao's China, however, the government has remained unwavering in clamping down hard on ethnic mobilization and dissent.
87 Fairbank 1983, 461.
88 Mertha 2009b.
89 Huang 2009, 406; 2011.
90 Hirschman 1980/1945.
91 Quoted in Wang 1984, 1.
92 The contrast between outward looking and diasporic India and inward looking and nationalist Japan provides an interesting starting point for a comparative analysis that might replicate the different configurations between inward, northern and outward, southern China.
93 I would like to thank Victor Koschmann for his freely shared insights. David Leheny's (2010) analysis stresses an enduring discourse of Japanese distinctiveness as a liminal bridging of tradition and modernity, East and West, and all other binaries. Eisenstadt's (1996) analysis inquires into Japan's distinctive practices. Both styles of analysis enrich our understanding, and I thus refrain from making an a priori choice between them.
94 Eisenstadt 1996, 14–16.
95 Blaxell 2009.
96 Garon and Maclachlan 2006.
97 Katzenstein 2006b, 4–7; 2005, 162–7, 202–4.
98 Otmazgin 2008, 2007; Iwabuchi 2002.
99 Zuberi 2005, 112.

100 Faiola 2003.
101 Shimemura 2002.
102 Eisenstadt 1996; Knöbl 2007, 92–110; Elvin 1996, 261–301. It should be noted that Eisenstadt's reception of Jasper's Greece-centered argument is debatable, as Martin Bernal has reminded me. Hindu religion and culture were socially deeply embedded before Buddha. Confucius thought of himself as extending ancient traditions dating back to the Shang dynasty. Many scholars of Iran now date Zoroaster in the second millennium rather than the sixth century. And Axial age theories tend to exclude Mesopotamia and Egypt dating back to 3000 BCE. This is another illustration that the dating of an unambiguous point of origin of any civilization is a hopeless enterprise in a world of interaction and exchange.
103 Gluck 1985, 144–6.
104 Murakami 1984; Rohlen 1985, 1989.
105 Pyle 2007, 3, 18; Kelly and White 2006.
106 I would like to thank Durba Ghosh, Mary Katzenstein, Susanne Rudolph, and Robert Travers for their critical comments on and helpful suggestions for my discussion of India.
107 Bose 2006; Bayly 2007; Chaudhuri 1990.
108 Cole 2002a, 2002b.
109 Bharucha 2006.
110 Metcalf 2007, 7.
111 Rajan and Sharma 2006b.
112 Pollock 1998, 70.
113 Ashreena 2007.
114 Bokhari 2007; Eleftheriotis 2006; Iordanova et al. 2006.
115 Rajan and Sharma 2006a.
116 Acharya 2009.
117 Bhatt and Mukta 2000.
118 Shukla 2003.
119 Collingham 2006.
120 Appadurai 1996, 89–113.
121 The group includes, among others, Amartya Sen, Abhijit Banerjee (MIT), Pranab Bardhan (Berkeley), Kaushik Basu (Cornell), Partha Dasgupta (Cambridge, UK), Dilip Mookherjee (Boston University), and Sendil Mullainathan (Harvard).
122 Mazzarella 2003, 59–98.
123 Nehru 1990.
124 Khilnani 1997.
125 Dumont 1980; Arnason 2003, 231.
126 Duara 1991. See also Ludden 1996; Varshney 1993; Dalrymple 2005.
127 Needham and Sunder Rajan 2007.
128 Huntington 2004a, 2004b.
129 Sen 2005.
130 Gandhi 1997.
131 Kumar 1989; 1997, 407.
132 Pollock 1998, 2006.
133 Nandy 1983, 47–63, 100–6.
134 Marx 1973, 320. I would like to thank Leonard Seabrooke for this reference.
135 Bernal 2005.
136 Rudolph and Rudolph 1997, 224–5; Kinvall 2007, 100.
137 Ibid., 236.
138 Pouliot 2010, 39.
139 Mao 1978.
140 Collins 2010, 440.
141 Katzenstein 2012b.
142 Wang Gungwu, personal communication, 9 January 2011.

143 Adler 2005; Adler et al. 2006.
144 Rifkin 2009.
145 Ridge 2010.
146 I would like to thank Takashi Shiraishi for clarifying this point for me. For a discussion of the limits and possibilities of Anglo-China in nineteenth-century Hong Kong, see Munn 2001.
147 Appiah 2006, 101.
148 Braudel 1993, 507.
149 Beecroft 1956, 425.

REFERENCES

Abdelal, Rawi and Kirshner, Jonathan (1999/2000) "Strategy, Economic Relations, and the Definition of the National Interest," *Security Studies* 9(1): 123–62.
Abramson, Marc S. (2008) *Ethnic Identity in Tang China*, Philadelphia: University of Pennsylvania Press.
Acharya, Amitav (2009) *Whose Ideas Matter? Agency and Power in Asian Regionalism*, Ithaca, NY: Cornell University Press.
Adler, Emanuel (2005) *Communitarian International Relations: The Epistemic Foundations of International Relations*, New York: Routledge.
Adler, Emanuel, Bicchi, Federica, Crawford, Beverly, and Del Sarto, Raffaella A. (eds) (2006) *The Convergence of Civilizations: Constructing a Mediterranean Region*, Toronto: University of Toronto Press.
Adler, Emanuel and Pouliot, Vincent (eds) (2011a) *International Practices*, Cambridge: Cambridge University Press.
—— (eds) (2011b) "International Practices: Introduction and Framework," in Emanuel Adler and Vincent Pouliot (eds), *International Practices*, Cambridge: Cambridge University Press, pp. 3–35.
Ajia Keizai Kenkyusho (2007) "Ajia Doko Nenpo 2007" [Yearbook of Asian Affairs, 2007], Tokyo: Ajia Keizai Kenkyusho (Institute of Developing Economies – Japan External Trade Organization).
Alam, M. Shahid (2003) "Articulating Group Differences: A Variety of Autocentrisms," *Science & Society* 67(2): 205–17.
Amako, Satoshi (2010) "Chugoku no Taito to Taigai Senryaku" [The Rise of China and Its External Strategy], in Satoshi Amako and Emi Mifune, *Bocho-suru Chugoku no Taigai Kankei: Pakkus Sinika to Shuhen-koku* [External Relations of the Expanding China: Pax Sinica and States in its Vicinities], Tokyo: Keiso Shobo, pp. 3–54.
Amako, Satoshi and Mifune, Emi (2010) *Bocho-suru Chugoku no Taigai Kankei: Pakkus Sinika to Shuhen-koku* [External Relations of the Expanding China: Pax Sinica and States in its Vicinities], Tokyo: Keiso Shobo.
"Ancient Imperial Language of China – 2,000 Years Ago" (2009) Online. Available at: http://iangohs.wordpress.com/2009/01/02/ancient-imperial-language-of-china – 2000-years-ago/ (accessed 25 October 2010).

Appadurai, Arjun (1996) *Modernity at Large: Cultural Dimensions of Globalization*, Minneapolis: University of Minnesota Press.

Appiah, Kwame Anthony (2006) *Cosmopolitanism: Ethics in a World of Strangers*, New York: W.W. Norton.

Arnason, Johann P. (2003) "East and West: From Invidious Dichotomy to Incomplete Deconstruction," in Gerard Delanty and Engin F. Isin (eds), *Handbook of Historical Sociology*, Thousand Oaks, CA: Sage, pp. 220–34.

—— (2010a) "Introduction: Domains and Perspectives of Civilizational Analysis," *European Journal of Social Theory* 13(1): 5–13.

—— (2010b) "The Cultural Turn and the Civilizational Approach," *European Journal of Social Theory* 13(1): 67–82.

Arrighi, Giovanni (2007) *Adam Smith in Beijing: Lineages of the Twenty-First Century*, London and New York: Verso.

—— (2008) "Historical Perspectives on States, Markets and Capitalism, East and West." Online. Available at: http://japanfocus.org/products/details2630 (accessed 14 January 2008).

—— (2009) "China's Market Economy in the Long Run," in Ho-Fung Hung (ed.), *China and the Transformation of Global Capitalism*, Baltimore, MD: Johns Hopkins University Press, Chapter 2.

Arrighi, Giovanni, Hamashita, Takeshi, and Selden, Mark (eds) (2003) *The Resurgence of East Asia: 500, 150 and 50 Year Perspectives*, London and New York: Routledge.

Arrighi, Giovanni, Hui, Po-Keung, Hung, Ho-fung, and Selden, Mark (2003) "Historical Capitalism, East and West," in Giovanni Arrighi, Takeshi Hamashita, and Mark Selden (eds), *The Resurgence of East Asia: 500, 150 and 50 Year Perspectives*, London and New York: Routledge, Chapter 7.

ASEAN–Japan Centre (2011) "Nippon, ASEAN, Chugoku no taigai boeki" [External Trade of Japan, ASEAN and China]. Online. Available at: http://www.asean.or.jp/ja/asean/know/statistics/3.html (accessed 13 February 2011).

Ashreena, Tanya (2007) "Promoting Bollywood Abroad Will Help to Promote India," *Chilli Breeze* (Oct.). Available at: http://www.chillibreeze.com/articles/Indian-films.asp (accessed October 2007).

Asian Development Bank (ADB) (2010a) "Key Indicators for Asia and the Pacific." Online. Available at: http://www.adb.org/Documents/Books/Key_Indicators/2010/default.asp (accessed 13 February 2011).

—— (2010b) "Myanmar," Key Indicators for Asia and the Pacific. Online. Available at: www.adb.org/Statistics (accessed 13 February 2011).

Babrow, Davis B. and Chan, Steven (1984) "On a Slow Boat to Where? Analyzing Chinese Foreign Policy," in Samuel Kim (ed.), *China and the World: Chinese Foreign Policy in the Post-Mao Era*, Boulder, CO: Westview, pp. 32–56.

Bakar, Osman and Cheng, Gek Nai (1997) *Islam and Confucianism: A Civilizational Dialogue*, Kuala Lumpur: University of Malaya Press.

Barma, Naazneen, Chiozza, Giacomo, Ratner, Ely, and Weber, Steven (2009) "A World without the West? Empirical Patterns and Theoretical Implications," *Chinese Journal of International Politics* 2(4) (Winter): 525–44.

Barmé, Geremie (2005) "On New Sinology," Online. Available at: http://rspas.anu.edu.au/pah/chinaheritageproject/newsinology/newsinology.php (accessed 20 April 2010).

Barnett, Michael and Duvall, Raymond (eds) (2006) *Power in Global Governance*, Cambridge: Cambridge University Press.

Barth, Boris and Osterhammel, Jürgen (eds) (2005) *Zivilisierungsmissionen; Imperiale Weltverbesserung seit dem 18. Jahrhundert*, Konstanz: UVK Verlagsgesellschaft.

Bartlett, Beatrice S. (1991) *Monarchs and Ministers: The Grand Council in Mid-Ch'ing China, 1723–1820*, Berkeley: University of California Press.

Bayly, Susan (2007) *Asian Voices in a Postcolonial Age: Vietnam, India and Beyond*, Cambridge: Cambridge University Press.

Beckert, Jens (2011) "Imagined Futures: Fictionality in Economic Action," *MPfG Discussion Paper* 11/8, Cologne: Max Planck Institute for the Study of Societies.

Beecroft, John (1956) *Kipling: A Selection of His Stories and Poems*, Garden City, NY: Doubleday.

Beeson, Mark (2009) "Hegemonic Transition in East Asia? The Dynamics of Chinese and American Power," *Review of International Studies* 35: 95–112.

Bell, Daniel A. (2008) *China's New Confucianism: Politics and Everyday Life in a Changing Society*, Princeton, NJ: Princeton University Press.

—— (2009) "War, Peace, and China's Soft Power: A Confucian Approach," *Diogenes* 56(1): 26–40.

Bell, Daniel A. and Hahm, Chaibong (eds) (2003) *Confucianism for the Modern World*, Cambridge: Cambridge University Press.

Bennett, D. Scott and Stam, Allan (2003) *The Behavioral Origins of War*, Ann Arbor: University of Michigan Press.

Ben-Yehuda, Hemda (2003) "The 'Clash of Civilizations' Thesis: Findings from International Crises, 1918–94," *Comparative Civilizations Review* 49: 28–42.

Berenson, Alex (2009) "Plotting Thrillers in the Fog of China," *New York Times*, Week in Review (29 Nov.): 4.

Bernal, Martin (1987) *Black Athena: The Afroasiatic Roots of Classical Civilization*, New Brunswick, NJ: Rutgers University Press.

—— (2005) "India in the Making of Europe," *Journal of the Asiatic Society* (Calcutta) 46(4): 37–66.

Bernstein, Richard J. and Munro, Ross (1997) "China I: The Coming Conflict with America," *Foreign Affairs* 76(2): 18–32.

Bert, Wayne (2003) *The United States, China and Southeast Asian Security: A Changing of the Guard?* New York: Palgrave Macmillan.

Bezlova, Antoaneta (2006) "China's New Cultural Revolution," *Asia Times* (29 July).

Bharucha, Rustom (2006) *Another Asia: Rabindranath Tagore and Okakura Tenshin*, New Delhi: Oxford University Press.

Bhatt, Chetan and Mukta, Parita (2000) "Hindutva in the West: Mapping the Antinomies of Diaspora Nationalism," *Ethnic and Racial Studies* 23(3) (May): 407–41.

Bianjiang, Yanjiu Zhongxin (2004) Bianjiang de Dingyi [The Definition of Frontier]." Online. Available at http://chinaborderland.cass.cn/show_News.asp?id=%272053%27.

Bickers, Robert and Yep, Ray (2009) *May Days in Hong Kong: Riot and Emergency in 1967*, Hong Kong: Hong Kong University Press.

Blanchard, Jean-Marc F. (2011) "Chinese MNCs as China's New Long March: A Review and Critique of the Western Literature," *Journal of Chinese Political Science* 16: 91–108.

Blaxell, Vivian (2009) "Designs of Power: The 'Japanization' of Urban and Rural Space in Colonial Hokkaidō," *JapanFocus*. Online. Available at: http://japanfocus.org/articles/print_article/3211 (accessed 5 September 2009).

Bloom, A.H. and Bloom, Alfred H. (1981) *The Linguistic Shaping of Thought: A Study in the Impact of Language on Thinking in China and the West*, Hillsdale, NJ: Lawrence Erlbaum.

Boeisho/Jieitai (Ministry of Defense, Japan) (2010) *Heisei 23 nendo iko ni kakawaru Boei Keikaku no Taiko ni tsuite* [Principles of the Defense Plan from 2011 onward]. Online. Available at: http://www.mod.go.jp/j/approach/agenda/guideline/index.html.

Bokhari, Farhan (2007) "Engaging Indians: Bollywood Breaches Borders," *Financial Times* (11 Apr.). Online. Available at: http://search.ft.com/ftArticle?queryText=farhan+bokhari+bollywood&y=4&aje=true&x=16&id=070412000737&ct=0> (accessed 30 March 2007).

Bordwell, David (2000) *Planet Hong Kong: Popular Cinema and the Art of Entertainment*, Cambridge, MA: Harvard University Press.

Bose, Sugata (2006) *A Hundred Horizons: The Indian Ocean in the Age of Global Empire*, Cambridge, MA: Harvard University Press.

Bowden, Brett (2009) *The Empire of Civilization: The Evolution of an Imperial Idea*, Chicago, IL: University of Chicago Press.

Bowden, Brett and Seabrooke, Leonard (eds) (2006) *Global Standards of Market Civilization*, New York: Routledge.

Brandt, Loren, Rawski, Thomas G., and Zhu, Xiaodong (2007) "International Dimensions of China's Long Boom," in William Walton Keller and Thomas G. Rawski (eds), *China's Rise and the Balance of Influence in Asia*, Pittsburgh, PA: University of Pittsburgh Press, pp. 14–46.

Braudel, Fernand (1993) *A History of Civilizations*, New York: Penguin.

Breslin, Shaun (2000) "Decentralisation, Globalisation and China's Partial Re-engagement with the Global Economy," *New Political Economy* 5(2): 205–26.

Brody, Hugh (2001) *The Other Side of Eden: Hunters, Farmers, and the Shaping of the World*, New York: North Point Press.

Brooks, David (2011) "Huntington's Clash Revisited," *New York Times* (3 March). Online. Available at: http://www.nytimes.com/2011/03/04opinion/04brooks.html?_r=2&pagewanted=print (accessed 25 May 2011).

Broomfield, Emma V. (2003) "Perceptions of Danger: The China Threat Theory," *Journal of Contemporary China* 12: 265–84.

Brown, Frederick Z. (2010) "Rapprochement between Vietnam and the United States," *Contemporary Southeast Asia* 32(3): 317–42.

Brown, Michael E., Coté, Owen R. Jr., Lynn-Jones, Sean M., and Miller, Steven E. (eds) (2000) *The Rise of China: An International Security Reader*, Cambridge, MA: MIT Press.

Brunnee, Jutta and Toope, Stephen (2010) *Legitimacy and Legality in International Law*, Cambridge: Cambridge University Press.

Bunge, Mario (2004) "How Does It Work? The Search for Explanatory Mechanisms," *Philosophy of the Social Sciences* 34(2): 182–210.

Burns, John P. (2003) "'Downsizing' the Chinese State: Government Retrenchment in the 1990s," *China Quarterly* 175: 775–802.

Buruma, Ian and Avishai, Margalit (2004) *Occidentalism: The West in the Eyes of Its Enemies*, New York: Penguin.

Buzan, Barry (2010) "China in International Society: Is 'Peaceful Rise' Possible?" *Chinese Journal of International Politics* 3(1): 5–36.

Cai, Hongbin and Treisman, Daniel (2006) "Did Government Decentralization Cause China's Economic Miracle?" *World Politics* 58(4): 505–35.

Callahan, William A. (2003) "Beyond Cosmopolitanism and Nationalism: Diasporic Chinese and Neo-Nationalism in China and Thailand," *International Organization* 57(3): 481–517.

—— (2004) *Contingent States: Greater China and Transnational Relations*, Minneapolis and London: University of Minnesota Press.

—— (2007) "How To Understand China: The Dangers and Opportunities of Being a Rising Power," *Review of International Studies* 31: 701–14.

Callahan, William A. (2008) "Chinese Visions of World Order: Post-hegemonic or a New Hegemony," *International Studies Review* 10: 749–61.
—— (2010) *China: The Pessoptimist Nation*, New York: Oxford University Press.
Carlson, Allen (2005) *Unifying China, Integrating with the World*, Stanford, CA: Stanford University Press.
—— (2010) "An Unconventional Tack: Nontraditional Security Concerns and China's 'Rise,'" *Asia Policy* (July): 49–64.
—— (2011) "Moving Beyond Sovereignty? A Brief Consideration of Recent Changes in China's Approach to International Order and the Emergence of the *Tianxia* Concept," *Journal of Contemporary China* (Jan.): 89–102.
Caulfield, Janice L. (2006) "Local Government Reform in China: A Rational Actor Perspective," *International Review of Administrative Sciences* 72: 253–67.
CCP Taiwan Work Office and State Council Taiwan Affairs Office (1998) *Zhongguo Taiwan Wenti [China's Taiwan Issue]*, Beijing: Jiuzhou Tushu Chubanshe.
Central Documentaries Office (1998) *Deng Xiaoping Sixiang Nianpu, 1975–1997 [Chronology of Deng Xiaoping Thought, 1975–1997]*, Beijing: Central Documentaries Press.
Cha, Seong Hwan (2003) "Modern Chinese Confucianism: The Contemporary Neo-Confucian Movement and Its Cultural Significance," *Social Compass* 50(4): 481–91.
Cha, Victor (1998) "Defining Security in East Asia: History, Hotspots, and Horizon-gazing," in Eunmee Kim (ed.), *The Four Asian Tigers: Economic Development and the Global Political Economy*, San Diego, CA: Academic Press, pp. 33–58.
Chan, Elaine (2002) "Beyond Pedagogy: Language and Identity in Post-colonial Hong Kong," *British Journal of Sociology of Education* 23(2): 271–85.
Chan, Evans (2004) "Zhang Yimou's Hero – The Temptations of Fascism," *Film International* no. 8. Online. Available at: http://www.filmint.nu/netonly/eng/heroevanschan.htm/ (accessed 15 December 2007).
Chan, Kwok Bun and Tong, Chee Kiong (2001) "Positionality and Alternation: Identity of the Chinese of Contemporary Thailand," in Chee Kiong Tong and Kwok Bun Chan (eds), *Alternate Identities: The Chinese of Contemporary Thailand*, Singapore: Times Academic Press, pp. 1–8.
Chandra, Elizabeth (2011) "Fantasizing Chinese/Indonesian Hero: Njoo Cheong Seng and the Gagaklodra Series," *Archipel* 82: 83–112.
Chang, Kwang-chi (1999) "China on the Eve of the Historical Period," in Michael Loewe and Edward L. Shaughnessy (eds), *The Cambridge History of Ancient China: From the Origins of Civilization to 221 B.C.*, Cambridge: Cambridge University Press, pp. 33–73.
Chaudhuri, Kirti N. (1990) *Asia before Europe: Economy and Civilisation of the Indian Ocean from the Rise of Islam to 1750*, New York: Cambridge University Press.
Cheah, Pheng (2006) *Inhuman Conditions: On Cosmopolitanism and Human Rights*, Cambridge, MA: Harvard University Press.
Chen, Boyu, Hwang, Ching-Chane, and Ling, L.H.M. (2009) "Lust/Caution in IR: Democratising World Politics with Culture as a Method," *Millennium* 37(3): 743–66.
Chen, Chang-hung and Yang, Yuan-ning (2009) "Two Diasporic Approaches to China among Chinese Overseas" [Huayi liqun renshi zhongguo de liangzhong keneng tujing]. *Southeast Asian Journal* [Dongnanya xuekan] 6(2): 135–76.
Chen, Jian (2001) *Mao's China and the Cold War*, Chapel Hill: University of North Carolina Press.
Chen, Kuan-Hsing (2002) "Why Is 'Great Reconciliation' Impossible? De-Cold War/Decolonization, Or Modernity and Its Tears (Parts I–II)," *Inter-Asia Cultural Studies* 3(1): 77–100.

Chen, Xiaomei (1992) "Occidentalism as Counterdiscourse: 'He Shang' in Post-Maoist China," *Critical Inquiry* 18(4): 686–712.
Cheng, Yung-nien (2010) "The Chinese Model of Development: An International Perspective," *Social Sciences in China* 31(2): 44–59.
Cheow, Eric Teo Chu (2004) "China's Rising Soft Power in Southeast Asia," *Pacific Forum CSIS* (3 May): 1–2.
Cheung, Jennifer (2006) "China's Rise: The Forgotten Chapter on Its Soft Power," Cornell University, unpublished paper.
Chicago Council on Global Affairs (in Partnership with East Asia Institute, EAI) (2008) *Soft Power in Asia: Results of a 2008 Multinational Survey of Public Opinion*, Chicago, IL: Chicago Council on Global Affairs.
"Chinese Cartoon to Land in International Market" (2009) ChinaA2Z.com News (3 July). Online. Available at: http://news.chinaa2z.com/news/html/2009/20090703/20090703082238338604/20090703082556451481.html (accessed 8 May 2010).
Chiozza, Giacomo (2002) "Is There a Clash of Civilizations? Evidence from Patterns of International Conflict Involvement, 1946–97," *Journal of Peace Research* 39(6): 711–34.
Chow, Rey (1993) *Writing Diaspora: Tactics of Intervention in Contemporary Cultural Studies*, Bloomington and Indianapolis: Indiana University Press.
—— (2009) "Foreword," in Elaine Yee Lin Ho and Julia Kuehn (eds), *China Abroad: Travel, Spaces, Subjects*, Hong Kong: Hong Kong University Press.
Christensen, Thomas J. (2006) "Fostering Stability or Creating a Monster? The Rise of China and U.S. Policy toward East Asia," *International Security* 31(1): 81–126.
—— (2009) "Shaping the Choices of a Rising China: Recent Lessons for the Obama Administration," *Washington Quarterly* 32(3): 89–104.
Chua, Amy (2011) "Why Chinese Mothers are Superior," *Wall Street Journal* (8 Jan.). Online. Available at: http://online.wsj.com/article/SB10001424052748704111504576059713528698754.html (accessed 5 March 2011), pp. ix–xii.
Chua, Beng Huat (2003) *Life is Not Complete without Shopping: Consumption Culture in Singapore*, Singapore: Singapore University Press, National University of Singapore.
Chun, Allen (1989) "Pariah Capitalism and the Overseas Chinese of Southeast Asia: Problems in the Definition of the Problem," *Ethnic and Racial Studies* 12(2): 233–56.
—— (1995) "An Oriental Orientalism: The Paradox of Tradition and Modernity in Nationalist Taiwan," *History and Anthropology* 9(1): 27–56.
Clifford, James (1997) *Routes: Travel and Translation in the Late Twentieth Century*, Cambridge, MA: Harvard University Press.
Clough, Ralph N. (1978) *Island China*, Cambridge, MA: Harvard University Press.
Coalson, Robert (2008) "Russian Conservatives Challenge Notion of 'Universal Values.'" Online. Available at: http://www.rferl.org/Content/Russian_Conservatives_Challenge_Notion_Of_Universal_Values/1358106.html (accessed 23 December 2008).
Cohen, Paul A. (1996) *Discovering History in China: American Historical Writing on the Recent Chinese Past*, 2nd edn, New York: Columbia University Press.
Cole, Juan Ricard I. (2002a) "Iranian Culture and South Asia, 1500–1900," in Nikki R. Keddie and Rudi Matthee (eds), *Iran and the Surrounding World: Interactions in Culture and Cultural Politics*, Seattle: University of Washington Press, pp. 15–35.
—— (2002b) *Sacred Space and Holy War: The Politics, Culture and History of Shi'ite Islam*, London: I.B. Tauris.
Collingham, Lizzie (2006) *Curry: A Tale of Cooks and Conquerors*, New York: Oxford University Press.
Collins, Randall (1998) *The Sociology of Philosophies: A Global Theory of Intellectual Change*, Cambridge, MA: Harvard University Press.

Collins, Randall (2004) "Civilizations as Zones of Prestige and Social Contact," in Saïd Amir Arjomand and Edward A. Tiryakian (eds), *Rethinking Civilizational Analysis*, Thousand Oaks, CA: Sage, pp. 132–47.
—— (2010) "A Dead End for a Trend Theory," *European Journal of Sociology* 50(3): 431–41.
Coppel, Charles A. (1976) "Patterns of Chinese Political Activity in Indonesia," in J.A.C. Mackie (ed.), *The Chinese in Indonesia*, Honolulu: University Press of Hawai'i, Honolulu and Australian Institute of International Affairs, pp. 19–76, 215–26.
Crossley, Pamela Kyle, Siu, Helen F., and Sutton, Donald S. (2006) *Empire at the Margins: Culture, Ethnicity and Frontier in Early Modern China*, Berkeley: University of California Press.
Dædalus (1991) *The Living Tree: The Changing Meanings of Being Chinese Today* (Spring).
Dalrymple, William (2005) "India: The War over History," *New York Review of Books* 52(6): 62–5.
Davidson, Jamie S. (2008) "The Study of Political Ethnicity in Southeast Asia," in Erik Martinez Kuhonta, Dan Slater, and Tuong Vu (eds), *Southeast Asia in Political Science: Theory, Region, and Quantitative Analysis*, Stanford, CA: Stanford University Press, pp. 199–226, 352–4.
Deleuze, Gilles and Guattari, Félix (1983 [1972]) *Anti-Oedipus: Capitalism and Schizophrenia*, trans. Robert Hurley, Mark Seem and Helen R. Lane, Minneapolis: University of Minnesota Press.
—— (1987 [1980]) *A Thousand Plateaus: Capitalism and Schizophrenia*, trans. Brian Massumi, Minneapolis: University of Minnesota Press.
Deng, Xiaoping (1984) "Speech at the Third Plenary Session of the Central Advisory Commission of the Communist Party of China," 22 October, *Collected Works of Deng Xiaoping*, Vol. III. Online. Available at http://web.peopledaily.com.cn/english/dengxp/vol3/text/c1280.html.
—— (1987) "Speech at a Meeting with the Members of the Committee for Drafting the Basic Law of the Hong Kong Special Administrative Region," 16 April, *Collected Works of Deng Xiaoping*, Vol. III. Online. Available at http://web.peopledaily.com.cn/english/dengxp/vol3/text/c1710.html.
Deng, Yong and Wang, Fei-Ling (2005) *China Rising: Power and Motivation in Chinese Foreign Policy*, Lanham, MD: Rowman & Littlefield.
Derrida, Jacques (1982) "Difference," in *Margins of Philosophy*, trans. Alan Bass, Chicago, IL: University of Chicago Press, pp. 3–27.
Deutsch, Karl W. (1966) *Nationalism and Social Communication: An Inquiry into the Foundations of Nationality*, 2nd edn, Cambridge, MA: MIT Press.
Dikötter, Frank (1992) *The Discourse of Race in Modern China*, Stanford, CA: Stanford University Press.
Ding, Sheng (2008a) "Digital Diaspora and National Image Building: A New Perspective on Chinese Diaspora Study in the Age of China's Rise," *Pacific Affairs* 80(4): 627–48.
—— (2008b) *The Dragon's Hidden Wing: How China Rises with Its Soft Power*, Lanham, MD: Lexington Books.
Dirlik, Arif (1997) "Critical Reflections on 'Chinese Capitalism' as Paradigm," *Identities* 3(3): 303–30.
—— (2008) "Socialism in China: A Historical Overview," in Kam Louie (ed.), *The Cambridge Companion to Modern Chinese Culture*, Cambridge: Cambridge University Press, pp. 155–72.
Duan, Hong (2007) "Tu Weiming and New Confucianism on Mainland China," Cornell University, unpublished paper (April).

Duan, Jinsheng (2009) Shilun Zhongguo Bianzhengxue de Yanjiu Neirong jiqi Xueke Jianshe [A Discussion of Constructing the Substance and Research Contents of China's Frontier Governance Studies], Chuxiong Shifan Daxue Xuebao 5: 49–56.

Duara, Prasenjit (1991) "The New Politics of Hinduism," *Wilson Quarterly* 15(3) (Summer): 42–50.

—— (1995) *Rescuing History from the Nation: Questioning Narratives of Modern China*, Chicago, IL: University of Chicago Press.

—— (1997) "Nationalists among Transnationals: Overseas Chinese and the Idea of China, 1900–1911," in Aihwa Ong and Donald Nonini (eds), *Ungrounded Empires: The Cultural Politics of Modern Chinese Transnationalism*, New York and London: Routledge, pp. 39–60.

—— (2009) "Periodizing the Cold War: The Imperialism of Nation States," a lecture at the Institute of Modern History, Academia Sinica, Taipei, 22 June.

Duchesne, Ricardo (2001/02) "Between Sinocentrism and Eurocentrism: Debating Andre Gunder Frank's *ReOrient: Global Economy in the Asian Age*," *Science & Society* 65(4): 428–63.

—— (2003) "The Post-Malthusian World Began in Western Europe in the Eighteenth Century: A Reply to Goldstone and Wong," *Science & Society* 67(2): 195–205.

Duckett, Jane and Hussain, Athar (2008) "Tackling Unemployment in China: State Capacity and Governance Issues," *International Organization* 62(2): 211–29.

Dumont, Louis (1980) *Homo Hierarchicus: The Caste System and Its Implications*, Chicago, IL: University of Chicago Press.

Ebrey, Patricia Buckley (2003) "Surnames and Chinese Han Identity," in Patricia Buckley Ebrey, *Women and the Family in Chinese History*, London and New York: Routledge, pp. 165–76, 247–9.

The Economist (2008) "Economic Focus: An Aberrant Abacus" (3 May): 85.

—— (2009) "Enter the Dragon" (11 July): 84–5.

—— (2010a) "The Beijing Consensus is to Keep Quiet" (8 May): 41–2.

—— (2010b) "East or Famine: The Balance of Economic Power" (27 Feb.): 79–80.

—— (2010c) "Not Just Another Fake" (16 Jan.): 67–9.

Economy, Elizabeth and Oksenberg, Michel (eds) (1999) *China Joins the World: Progress and Prospects*, New York: Council on Foreign Relations Press.

Eisenstadt, S.N. (1986) "The Axial Age Breakthrough in China and India," in S.N. Eisenstadt (ed.), *The Origins and Diversity of Axial Age Civilizations*, New York: State University of New York Press, pp. 325–59.

—— (1996) *Japanese Civilization: A Comparative View*, Chicago, IL: University of Chicago Press.

Eisenstadt, S.N. and Schluchter, Wolfgang (1998) "Introduction: Paths to Early Modernities – A Comparative View," *Dædalus* 127(3): 1–18.

Eleftheriotis, Dimitris (2006) "A Cultural Colony of India: Indian Films in Greece in the 1950s and 1960s," *South Asian Popular Culture* 4(2): 101–12. Available at: http://wfsearch.webfeat.org.proxy.library.cornell.edu (accessed 30 October 2007).

Elias, Norbert (1978) *The History of Manners*, Oxford: Blackwell.

—— (1982) *The Civilizing Process*, Vol. 2. *Power and Civility*, trans. Edmund Jephcott, New York: Pantheon.

—— (2000) *The Civilizing Process: Sociogenetic and Psychogenetic Investigations*, revised edition, Oxford: Blackwell.

Ellerman, David (2010) "Pragmatism versus Economics Ideology in the Post-Socialist Transition: China versus Russia," *Real-world Economics Review* 52: 2–27.

Elliott, Mark C. (2001) *The Manchu Way: The Eight Banners and Ethnic Identity in Late Imperial China*, Stanford, CA: Stanford University Press.

Elster, Jon (1998) "A Plea for Mechanisms," in Peter Hedström and Richard Swedberg (eds), *Social Mechanisms: An Analytical Approach to Social Theory*, New York: Cambridge University Press, pp. 45–73.
Elvin, Mark (1973) *The Pattern of the Chinese Past*, Stanford, CA: Stanford University Press.
—— (1996) *Another History: Essays on China from a European Perspective*, Canberra: Wild Peony.
Engardio, Pete (ed.) (2007) *Chinindia: How China and India are Revolutionizing Global Business*, New York: McGraw.
Executive Yuan Mainland Affairs Council (2011) "Comparative and Selective Statistics about Cross-Strait Exchanges, December 2010." Online. Available at http://www.mac.gov.tw/lp.asp?ctNode=5713&CtUnit=3971&BaseDSD=7&mp=1 (accessed 1 February 2011).
Faiola, Anthony (2003) "Japan's Empire of Cool: Country's Culture Becomes Its Biggest Export," *Washington Post Foreign Service* (23 Dec.): A01.
Fairbank, John K. (1964) *Trade and Diplomacy on the China Coast: The Opening of the Treaty Ports*, Cambridge, MA: Harvard University Press.
—— (ed.) (1968) *The Chinese World Order*, Cambridge, MA: Harvard University Press.
—— (1974) "Varieties of Chinese Military Experience," in Frank Kierman Jr. and John K. Fairbank (eds), *Chinese Ways in Warfare*, Cambridge, MA: Harvard University Press, pp. 1–26.
—— (1983) *The United States and China*, 4th edn, enlarged, Cambridge, MA: Harvard University Press.
Falk, Richard and Kim, Samuel (1981) *The War System: An Interdisciplinary Approach*, Boulder, CO: Westview.
Falk, Richard, Kim, Samuel, and Mendlovitz, Saul (eds) (1991) *The United Nations*, New Brunswick, NJ: Transaction Publishers.
Featherstone, Kevin (2003) "Introduction: In the Name of 'Europe,'" in Kevin Featherstone and Claudio M. Radaelli (eds), *The Politics of Europeanization*, New York: Oxford University Press, pp. 3–26.
Feltenstein, Andrew and Iwata, Shigeru (2005) "Decentralization and Macroeconomic Performance in China: Regional Autonomy Has Its Costs," *Journal of Development Economics* 76: 481–501.
Feng, Huiyun (2009) "Is China a Revisionist Power?" *Chinese Journal of International Politics* 2(3): 313–34.
Feng, Yi (2006) "Sources of Political Capacity: A Case Study of China," *International Studies Review* 8(4): 597–606.
Feng, Youlan (1985) *Zhongguo Zhexue Jianshi [A Short History of Chinese Philosophy]*, Beijing: Peking University Press.
Ferguson, Niall (2011) *Civilization: The West and the Rest*, London: Allen Lane.
Ferguson, Niall and Schularick, Moritz (2009) "The End of Chimerica," Harvard Business School, Working Paper 10–037.
Ferguson, Yale H. (2007) "Pathways to Civilization," in Martin Hall and Patrick Thaddeus Jackson (eds), *Civilizational Identity: The Production and Reproduction of "Civilizations" in International Relations*, New York: Palgrave, pp. 191–7.
Finnemore, Martha (2003) *The Purpose of Intervention: Changing Beliefs about the Use of Force*, Ithaca, NY: Cornell University Press.
Fishman, Ted C. (2005) *China Inc.: How the Rise of the Next Superpower Challenges America and the World*, New York: Scribner.
Fitzgerald, John (1995) "The Nationless State: The Search for a Nation in Modern Chinese Nationalism," *Australian Journal of Chinese Affairs* 33 (Jan.): 75–104.

—— (1996) *Awakening China: Politics, Culture and Class in the Nationalist Revolution*, Stanford, CA: Stanford University Press.
Flyvbjerg, Bent (2001) *Making Social Science Matter*, New York: Cambridge University Press.
Fogel, Joshua A. (2009) *Articulating the Sinosphere: Sino-Japanese Relations in Space and Time*, Cambridge, MA: Harvard University Press.
Foot, Rosemary and Walter, Andrew (2011) *China, the United States, and Global Order*, Cambridge: Cambridge University Press.
Fox, Jonathan (2001) "Clash of Civilizations or Clash of Religions: Which Is a More Important Determinant of Ethnic Conflict?" *Ethnicities* 1: 295–320.
Frank, Andre Gunder (1998) *ReOrient: Global Economy in the Asian Age*, Berkeley: University of California Press.
Fravel, M. Taylor (2008) *Strong Borders, Secure Nation: Cooperation and Conflict in China's Territorial Disputes*, Princeton, NJ: Princeton University Press.
French, Howard W. (2006) "Another Chinese Export Is All the Rage: China's Language," *New York Times* (11 Jan.): A3.
Friedberg, Aaron (1988) *The Weary Titan: Britain and the Experience of Relative Decline, 1895–1905*, Princeton, NJ: Princeton University Press.
—— (2000) "The Struggle for Mastery in Asia," *Commentary* 110(4): 17–26.
Friedman, Edward (1994) "Reconstructing China's National Identity: A Southern Alternative to Mao-Era Anti-Imperialist Nationalism," *Journal of Asian Studies* 53(1): 67–91.
Frost, Ellen L. (2007) "China's Commercial Diplomacy in Asia: Promise or Threat?" in William Walton Keller and Thomas G. Rawski (eds), *China's Rise and the Balance of Influence in Asia*, Pittsburgh, PA: University of Pittsburgh Press, pp. 95–117.
Fu, Poshek (2003) *Between Shanghai and Hong Kong: The Politics of Chinese Cinemas*, Stanford, CA: Stanford University Press.
Fujita, Koichi (2008) "*Myanmar no 'Hinkon' Mondai: Shokuryo Seisaku to no kanren wo chushin ni*" [Myanmar's 'Poverty' Problem: with special reference to Food Policy] in Kudo Toshihiro (ed.), *Myanmar Keizai no Jitsu-zo* [Real Pictures of Myanmar's Economy], Tokyo: Ajia Keizai Kenkyusho.
Fukuyama, Francis (1989) "The End of History?" *National Interest* 16 (Summer): 3–16.
—— (1995) *Trust: The Social Virtues and the Creation of Prosperity*, New York: Free Press.
Gandhi, Mahatma (1997) *Hind Swaraj and Other Writings*, edited by Anthony J. Parel, Cambridge: Cambridge University Press.
Garon, Sheldon and Maclachlan, Patricia L. (eds) (2006) *The Ambivalent Consumer: Questioning Consumption in East Asia and the West*, Ithaca, NY: Cornell University Press.
Gates, Hill (1996) *China's Motor: A Thousand Years of Petty Capitalism*, Ithaca, NY: Cornell University Press.
George, Alexander and Bennett, Andrew (2005) *Case Studies and Theory Development in the Social Sciences*, Cambridge, MA: MIT Press.
"Geili" (2010) *The New York Times*, "Schott's Vocab: A Miscellany of Modern Words and Phrases*" (18 Nov.). Online. Available at: http://schott.blogs.nytimes.com/2010/11/18/geili/ (accessed 5 March 2011).
Gerschenkron, Alexander (1962) *Economic Backwardness in Historical Perspective: A Book of Essays*, Cambridge, MA: Harvard University Press.
Giersch, C. Patterson (2006) *Asian Borderlands: The Transformation of Qing China's Yunnan Frontier*, Cambridge, MA: Harvard University Press.
Gill, Bates and Huang, Yanzhong (2006) "Sources and Limits of Chinese 'Soft Power,'" *Survival* 48(2): 17–36.
Gladney, Dru C. (1994) "Representing Nationality in China: Refiguring Majority/Minority Identities," *Journal of Asian Studies* 53(1): 92–123.

Gladney, Dru C. (1996) *Muslim Chinese: Ethnic Nationalism in the People's Republic*, 2nd edn, Cambridge, MA: Harvard University Asia Center.
Glaser, Bonnie S. and Medeiros, Evan S. (2007) "The Changing Ecology of Foreign Policy-Making in China: The Ascension and Demise of the Theory of 'Peaceful Rise,'" *China Quarterly*. Doi: 10.1017/S0305741007001208.
Gluck, Carol (1985) *Japan's Modern Myths: Ideology in the Late Meiji Period*, Princeton, NJ: Princeton University Press.
Godley, Michael R. (1981) *The Mandarin-Capitalists from Nanyang: Overseas Chinese Enterprise in the Modernization of China 1893–1911*, Cambridge: Cambridge University Press.
Goldstein, Avery (1997/98) "Great Expectations: Interpreting China's Arrival," *International Security* 22(3): 36–73.
—— (2005) *Rising to the Challenge: China's Grand Strategy and International Security*, Stanford, CA: Stanford University Press.
Goldstone, Jack A. (2003) "Europe vs. Asia: Missing Data and Misconceptions," *Science & Society* 67(2): 184–95.
Gomez, Edmund Terence and Benton, Gregor (2004) "Introduction: De-essentializing Capitalism: Chinese Enterprise, Transnationalism, and Identity," in Edmund Terence Gomez and Hsin-Huang Michael Hsiao (eds), *Chinese Enterprise, Transnationalism and Identity*, London and New York: RoutledgeCurzon, pp. 1–19.
Gomez, Edmund Terence and Hsiao, Hsin-Huang Michael (2001a) "Introduction: Chinese Business Research in Southeast Asia," in Edmund Terence Gomez and Hsin-Huang Michael Hsiao (eds), *Chinese Business in Southeast Asia: Contesting Cultural Explanations, Researching Entrepreneurship*, Richmond, Surrey, UK: Curzon, pp. 1–37.
—— (eds) (2001b) *Chinese Business in Southeast Asia: Contesting Cultural Explanations, Researching Entrepreneurship*, Richmond, Surrey, UK: Curzon.
—— (eds) (2004) *Chinese Enterprise, Transnationalism and Identity*, London and New York: RoutledgeCurzon.
Gong, Gerrit W. (1984) *The Standard of "Civilization" in International Society*, Oxford: Clarendon Press.
—— (1985) "China's Entry into International Society," in Hedley Bull and Adam Watson (eds), *The Expansion of International Society*, New York: Oxford University Press, pp. 185–99.
Goodman, David and Zang, Xiaowei (2008) "The New Rich in China: The Dimension of Social Changes," in David S.G. Goodman (ed.), *The New Rich in China: Future Rulers, Present Lives*, London: Routledge.
Goto-Jones, Christopher (2005) *Political Philosophy in Japan: Nishida, the Kyoto School, and Co-Prosperity*, Leiden: Routledge Leiden Series in Modern East Asia.
Gries, Peter Hays (2005) "Social Psychology and the Identity–Conflict Debate: Is a 'China Threat' Inevitable?" *European Journal of International Relations* 11(2): 235–65.
Guo, Yingjie (2004) *Cultural Nationalism in Contemporary China: The Search for National Identity under Reform*, London and New York: Routledge.
Guzzini, Stefano (2010) "Imposing Coherence: The Central Role of Practice in Friedrich Kratochwil's Theorising of Politics, International Relations and Science," *Journal of International Relations and Development* 13: 301–22.
Haan, Arjan de (2010) "Will China Change International Development as We Know It?" *Journal of International Development* (28 July).
Haas, Ernst B. (2000) *Nationalism, Liberalism, and Progress, Volume 2. The Dismal Fate of New Nations*, Ithaca, NY: Cornell University Press.
Hamashita, Takeshi (1997) "The Intra-regional System in East Asia in Modern Times," in Peter J. Katzenstein and Takashi Shiraishi (eds), *Network Power: Japan and Asia*, Ithaca, NY: Cornell University Press, pp. 113–35.

—— (Linda Grove and Mark Selden, eds) (2008) *China, East Asia and the Global Economy*, London: Routledge.
Hamilton, Gary G. (1996) "Overseas Chinese Capitalism," in Weiming Tu (ed.), *Confucian Traditions in East Asian Modernity: Moral Education and Economic Culture in Japan and the Four Dragons*, Cambridge, MA: Harvard University Press, pp. 328–42.
—— (2006a) *Chinese Capitalism? The Organization of Chinese Economics*, New York: Routledge.
—— (2006b) *Commerce and Capitalism in Chinese Societies*, London and New York: Routledge.
—— (2010) "World Images, Authority, and Institutions: A Comparison of China and the West," *European Journal of Social Theory* 13(1): 31–48.
Han, Nianlong (ed.) (1987) *Dangdai Zhongguo Waijiao* [Contemporary China's Diplomacy], Beijing: Chinese Social Sciences Press.
Hansen, Valerie (2000) *The Open Empire: A History of China to 1600*, New York: Norton.
Hara, Yonosuke, Souknilanh, Keola, and Yamada, Norihiko (2011) "Chugoku to no Kankei wo Mosaku suru Laos" [Laos groping for its relations with China]. Online. Available at: http://www.rieti.go.jp/jp/publications/summary/11010016.html.
Harrell, Stevan (1995) "Introduction: Civilizing Projects and the Reaction to Them," in Stevan Harrell (ed.), *Cultural Encounters on China's Ethnic Frontiers*, Seattle: University of Washington Press, pp. 3–36.
Hatch, Walter (2010) *Asia's Flying Geese: How Regionalization Shapes Japan*, Ithaca, NY: Cornell University Press.
Hau, Caroline S. (2005) "Conditions of Visibility: Resignifying the 'Chinese'/'Filipino' in *Mano Po* and *Crying Ladies*," *Philippine Studies* 53(4): 491–531.
Hau, Caroline S. and Shiraishi, Takashi (2009) "Daydreaming about Rizal and Tetcho: On Asianism as Network and Fantasy," *Philippine Studies* 57(3): 329–88.
—— (forthcoming) "Regional Contexts of Cooperation and Collaboration in Hong Kong Cinema," in Nissim Otzmagin and Eyal Ben-Ari (eds), *Cultural Collaboration in East Asian Popular Culture*, Kyoto and Singapore: Kyoto University Press and NUS Press.
He, Qinglian (2009) "Why Have China's Peasants Become the Major Force in Social Resistance?" China Rights Forum online. Available at: http://hrichina.org/public/contents/article?revision%5fid=169453&item%5fid=169452 (accessed 1 April 2010).
Hedström, Peter (2005) *Dissecting the Social: On the Principles of Analytical Sociology*, Cambridge: Cambridge University Press.
Hedström, Peter and Swedberg, Richard (1998) "Social Mechanisms: An Introductory Essay," in Peter Hedström and Richard Swedberg (eds), *Social Mechanisms: An Analytical Approach to Social Theory*, New York: Cambridge University Press, pp. 1–31.
Henderson, Errol A. and Tucker, Richard (2001) "Clear and Present Strangers: The Clash of Civilizations and International Conflict," *International Studies Quarterly* 45: 317–38.
Hernes, Gudmund (1998) "Real Virtuality," in Peter Hedström and Richard Swedberg (eds), *Social Mechanisms: An Analytical Approach to Social Theory*, New York: Cambridge University Press, pp. 74–101.
Hirschman, Albert O. (1980/1945) *National Power and the Structure of Foreign Trade*, Berkeley: University of California Press.
Ho, Ping-Ti (1998) "In Defense of Sinicization: A Rebuttal of Evelyn Rawski's 'Reenvisioning the Quing,'" *Journal of Asian Studies* 57(1): 123–55.
Hobson, John M. (2004) *The Eastern Origins of Western Civilisation*, New York: Cambridge University Press.
Hodgson, Marshall G.S. (1974) *The Venture of Islam: Conscience and History in a World Civilization*, 3 vols, Chicago, IL: University of Chicago Press.

Hodgson, Marshall G.S. (1993) *Rethinking World History: Essays on Europe, Islam and World History* (edited with introduction and conclusion by Edmund Burke IV), Cambridge: Cambridge University Press.

Holcombe, Charles (2001) *The Genesis of East Asia 221 B.C.–A.D. 907*, Honolulu: University of Hawai'i Press.

Hopf, Ted (2002) *Social Construction of International Politics: Identities and Foreign Policies, Moscow, 1955 and 1999*, Ithaca, NY: Cornell University Press.

—— (2010) "The Logic of Habit in International Relations," *European Journal of International Relations* 16(4): 539–61.

—— (2011) "Russia Is Becoming Russia: A Semi-Periphery in Splendid Isolation," unpublished manuscript (May).

Hosaka, Tomoko A. (2010) "Chinese Version of Animé Catches the Eye," *International Herald Tribune* (30 Mar.): 15.

Howell, Jude (2006) "Reflections on the Chinese State," *Development and Change* 37(2): 273–97.

Hsiau, A-chin (2000) *Contemporary Taiwanese Cultural Nationalism*, London and New York: Routledge.

Huang, Philip C.C. (2008) "Centralized Minimalism: Semiformal Governance by Quasi Officials and Dispute Resolution in China," *Modern China* 34: 9–35.

—— (2009) "China's Neglected Informal Economy: Reality and Theory," *Modern China* 35: 405–38.

—— (2010) "Beyond the Right–Left Divide: Searching for Reform from the History of Practice," *Modern China* 36: 115–33.

—— (2011) "The Theoretical and Practical Implications of China's Development Experience: The Role of Informal Economic Practices," *Modern China* 37: 3–43.

Huang, Ray (2001) *Huanghe qingshan* [Yellow River and Blue Mountains], Taipei: Lien Ching.

Huang, Xiaoming (2002) "What is 'Chinese' about Chinese Civilization? Culture, Institutions, and Globalization," in Mehdi Mozaffari (ed.), *Globalization and Civilizations*, New York: Routledge, pp. 218–41.

Huang, Yanzhong and Ding, Sheng (2006) "Dragon's Underbelly: An Analysis of China's Soft Power," *East Asia* 23(4): 22–44.

Huang, Ying-che (2007) *"Qu Ribenhua" "Zai Zhongguohua": Zhanhou Taiwan Wenhua Chongjian, 1945–1947* [Uprooting Japan; Implanting China: Cultural Reconstruction in Postwar Taiwan, 1945–1947], Taipei: Rye Field Publications.

Hughes, Christopher (1997) *Taiwan and Chinese Nationalism: National Identity and Status in International Society*, London: Routledge.

Hui, Victoria Tin-bor (2005) *War and State Formation in Ancient China and Early Modern Europe*, New York: Cambridge University Press.

—— (2006) "Toward a Multicultural Approach to the Liberal Peace: A Comparison of Historical China and Historical Europe," Paper prepared for presentation at the 102nd Annual Meeting of the American Political Science Association, Philadelphia, 31 Aug.–3 Sept.

Hung, Ho-fung (ed.) (2009) *China and the Transformation of Global Capitalism*, Baltimore, MD: Johns Hopkins University Press.

Hunt, Michael H. (1996) *The Genesis of Chinese Communist Foreign Policy*, New York: Columbia University Press.

Hunter, Alan (2009) "Soft Power: China on the Global Stage," *Chinese Journal of International Politics* 2(3): 373–98.

—— (n.d.) "China: Soft Power and Cultural Influence," unpublished paper, Centre for Peace and Reconciliation Studies, Coventry University, Coventry, UK.

Huntington, Samuel P. (1996) *The Clash of Civilizations and the Remaking of World Order*, New York: Simon & Schuster.

—— (2004a) "The Hispanic Challenge," *Foreign Policy* (Mar.–Apr.): 31–45.

—— (2004b) *Who Are We? The Challenges to America's National Identity*, New York: Simon & Schuster.

Ida, Koji (2007) "Chugoku no tai-Myanmar Enjo Toshi no Jittai" [The Reality of Chinese Assistance and Investment in Myanmar], in Japan External Trade Organization, Overseas Research Division (ed.), *Higasi Ajia Keizai Renkei Foram 2007* [East Asia Economic Partnership Forum], Tokyo: JETRO.

Ikenberry, G. John (2008a) "The Rise of China and the Future of the West," *Foreign Affairs* 87(1): 23–37.

—— (2008b) "The Rise of China: Power, Institutions, and the Western Order," in Robert H. Ross and Zhu Feng (eds), *China's Ascent: Power, Security, and the Future of International Politics*, Ithaca, NY: Cornell University Press, pp. 89–114.

—— (2011a) *Liberal Leviathan: The Origins, Crisis, and Transformation of the American World Order*, Princeton, NJ: Princeton University Press.

—— (2011b) "The Future of the Liberal World Order: Internationalism after America," *Foreign Affairs* 90(3): 1–14.

Institute of International Strategic and Development Studies (2009) *The Rise of China's Power and International Role*, Tsinghua University, School of Public Policy and Management (June).

Iordanova, Dina et al. (2006) "Indian Cinema's Global Reach," *Journal of South Asian Popular Culture* 4(2): 113–40. Webfeat. Available at: http://wfsearch.webfeat.org.proxy.library.cornell.edu (accessed 30 October 2007).

Iriye, Akira (1997) "Stepping Out: Japan Can Help Shape the Emerging Asia Pacific: Is It Ready?" *Harvard Asia Pacific Review* 1(1): 56–60.

—— (1998) "East Asia and the Emergence of Japan, 1900–1945," in Michael Howard and Wm. Roger Louis (eds), *The Oxford History of the Twentieth Century*, New York: Oxford University Press, pp. 205–15.

—— (2006) "The Role of Philanthropy and Civil Society in U.S. Foreign Relations," in Yamamoto Tadashi, Akira Iriye, and Iokibe Makoto (eds), *Philanthropy and Reconciliations: Rebuilding Postwar U.S.–Japan Relations*, Tokyo: Japanese Center for International Exchange, pp. 37–60.

—— (2007) "Oral History Interview," 17–18 Oct. Research and Educational Center for China Studies and Cross-Strait Relations of the Department of Political Science, National Taiwan University. Online. Available at: http://140.112.150.151/RAEC/act/interviewJ+Iriye+1–2.doc (accessed 31 March 2010).

Ishikawa, Yoshihiro (2001) *Chūgoku Kyōsantō Seiritsu-shi*, Tokyo: Iwanami Shoten.

Ito, Takeshi (2007) "Enjo Kyoyo-koku to shite no Chugoku" [China as Assistance-providing State], in Overseas Research Division, Japan External Trade Organization (ed.), *Higasi Ajia Keizai Renkei Foram 2007* [East Asia Economic Partnership Forum 2007], Tokyo: JETRO.

Iwabuchi, Koichi (2002) *Recentering Globalization: Popular Culture and Japanese Transnationalism*. Durham, NC: Duke University Press.

Jacobs, Andrew (2011) "Confucius Stood Here, But Not for Very Long," *New York Times* (23 Apr.): A4.

Jacques, Martin (2009) *When China Rules the World: The End of the Western World and the Birth of a New Global Order*, New York: Penguin.

Jain, Purnendra and Groot, Gerry (2006) "Greater China," *Asia Times* (17 May).

Jasanoff, Maya (2005) *Edge of Empire: Lives, Culture, and Conquest in the East, 1750–1850*, New York: Alfred A. Knopf.

JETRO (Japan External Trade Organization) (2010a) "China: Kiso teki keizai shihyo" [China: Basic Economic Indicators], most recently updated on 22 Nov. Online. Available at: http://www.jetro.go.jp/world/asia/cn/stat_01/ (accessed 13 February 2011).
—— (2010b) "Vietnam: Kiso teki keizai shihyo" [Vietnam: Basic Economic Indicators], most recently updated on 22 Nov. Online. Available at: http://www.jetro.go.jp/world/asia/vn/stat_01/ (accessed 13 February 2011).
Jia, Haitao and Shi, Cangjin (2007) *Haiwai Yinduren yu Haiwai Huaren Guoji Yingxiangli Bijiao Fenxi* [A Comparative Study on the International Influence of the Indian Diaspora and Chinese Diaspora], Jinan: Shangdong People's Publisher.
Jia, Qingguo (2009) "Unipolarity: Implications for China, the US and the World," in Quansheng Zhao and Guoli Liu (eds), *Managing the China Challenge: Global Perspectives*, New York: Routledge, pp. 217–29.
Jin, Guantao and Liu, Qingfeng (2009) *Guannian Shi Yanjiu: Zhongguo Xiandai Zhongyao Zhengzhi Shuyu de Xingcheng* [The Study of Ideas History: The Formation of Modern Chinese Political Concepts], Beijing: Law Press.
Jin, Raoru (1998) *Zhonggong Xianggang Zhengce Miwen Shilu* [Inside Story of the CCP's Hong Kong Policy], Taipei: Greenfield Bookstore.
Johnston, Alastair Iain (1995) *Cultural Realism: Strategic Culture and Grand Strategy in Chinese History*, Princeton, NJ: Princeton University Press.
—— (1996) "Cultural Realism and Strategy in Maoist China," in Peter J. Katzenstein (ed.), *The Culture of National Security: Norms and Identity in World Politics*, New York: Columbia University Press, pp. 216–68.
—— (2004) "Beijing's Security Behavior in the Asia-Pacific: Is China a Dissatisfied Power?" in J.J. Suh, Peter J. Katzenstein, and Allen Carlson (eds), *Rethinking Security in East Asia: Identity, Power, and Efficiency*, Stanford, CA: Stanford University Press, pp. 34–96.
—— (2008) *Social States: China in International Institutions, 1980–2000*, Princeton, NJ: Princeton University Press.
Johnston, Alastair Iain and Ross, Robert S. (eds) (1999) *Engaging China: The Management of an Emerging Power*, London: Routledge.
Kachru, Braj (1985) "Standards, Codifications, and Sociolinguistic Realism: The English Language in the Outer Circle," in R. Quirk and H. Widdowson (eds), *English in the World*, Cambridge: Cambridge University Press, pp. 11–30.
Kang, David C. (2003) "Getting Asia Wrong: The Need for New Analytic Frameworks," *International Security* 27(4) (Summer): 57–85.
—— (2003/04) "Hierarchy, Balancing, and Empirical Puzzles in Asian International Relations," *International Security* 28(3): 165–80.
—— (2004) "The Theoretical Roots of Hierarchy in International Relations," *Australian Journal of International Affairs* 58(3): 337–52.
—— (2005) "Hierarchy in Asian International Relations: 1300–1900," *Asian Security* 1(1): 53–79.
—— (2007) *China Rising: Peace, Power, and Order in East Asia*, New York: Columbia University Press.
—— (2010a) "Civilization and State Formation in the Shadow of China," in Peter J. Katzenstein (ed.), *Civilizations in World Politics: Plural and Pluralist Perspectives*, London and New York: Routledge, pp. 91–113.
—— (2010b) *East Asia before the West: Five Centuries of Trade and Tribute*, New York: Columbia University Press.
Kang, Xiaoguang and Han, Heng (2008) "Graduated Controls: The State–Society Relationship in Contemporary China," *Modern China* 34(1): 36–55.

Kastner, Scott L. (2008) "The Global Implications of China's Rise," *International Studies Review* 10: 786–94.

Katzenstein, Peter J. (2000a) "Regionalism and Asia," *New Political Economy* 5(3): 353–68.

—— (2000b) "Varieties of Asian Regionalisms," in Peter J. Katzenstein, Natasha Hamilton-Hart, Kozo Kato, and Ming Yue, *Asian Regionalism*, Ithaca, NY: Cornell University East Asia Series, vol. 107, pp. 1–34.

—— (2005) *A World of Regions: Asia and Europe in the American Imperium*, Ithaca, NY: Cornell University Press.

—— (2006a) "East Asia – Beyond Japan," in Peter J. Katzenstein and Takashi Shiraishi (eds), *Beyond Japan: The Dynamics of East Asian Regionalism*, Ithaca, NY: Cornell University Press, pp. 1–33.

—— (2006b) "Multiple Modernities as Limits to Secular Europeanization?" in Timothy A. Byrnes and Peter J. Katzenstein (eds), *Religion in an Expanding Europe*, Cambridge: Cambridge University Press, pp. 1–33.

—— (2008) "China's Rise: East Asia and Beyond," *EAI Working Paper Series 12* (Apr.), Seoul, East Asia Institute. Online. Available at: http://www.eai.or.kr/type_k/panelView.asp?bytag=p&catcode=&code=kor_report&idx=8156&page=5 (accessed 30 June 2011).

—— (ed.) (2010a) *Civilizations in World Politics: Plural and Pluralist Perspectives*, London and New York: Routledge.

—— (2010b) "A World of Plural and Pluralist Civilizations: Multiple Actors, Traditions and Practices," in Peter J. Katzenstein (ed.), *Civilizations in World Politics: Plural and Pluralist Perspectives*, New York: Routledge, pp. 1–40.

—— (ed.) (2012a) *Anglo-America and Its Discontents: Civilizational Identities beyond West and East*, New York: Routledge.

—— (2012b) "Many Wests and Polymorphic Globalism," in Peter J. Katzenstein (ed.), *Anglo-America and Its Discontents: Civilizational Identities beyond West and East*, New York: Routledge, pp. 207–247.

Katzenstein, Peter J. and Shiraishi, Takashi (eds) (1997) *Network Power: Japan and Asia*, Ithaca, NY: Cornell University Press.

—— (eds) (2006) *Beyond Japan: The Dynamics of East Asian Regionalism*, Ithaca, NY: Cornell University Press.

Kaufman, Stuart J. (1997) "The Fragmentation and Consolidation of International Systems," *International Organization* 51(2): 173–208.

Kaufman, Stuart J., Little, Richard, and Wohlforth, William (eds) (2007) *The Balance of Power in World History*, New York: Palgrave.

Keidel, Albert (2007) "The Limits of a Smaller, Poorer China," *Financial Times* (14 Nov). Online. Available at: http://www.carnegieendowment.org/publications.index.cfm?fa=view…(accessed 11 December 2007).

Keller, William Walton and Rawski, Thomas G. (2007) *China's Rise and the Balance of Influence in Asia*, Pittsburgh, PA: University of Pittsburgh Press.

Kelley, Liam C. (2005) *Beyond the Bronze Pillars: Envoy Poetry and the Sino-Vietnamese Relationship*, Hawai'i: University of Hawai'i Press.

Kelly, William W. and White, Merry I. (2006) "Students, Slackers, Singles, Seniors, and Strangers: Transforming a Family-Nation," in Peter J. Katzenstein and Takashi Shiraishi (eds), *Beyond Japan: The Dynamics of East Asian Regionalism*, Ithaca, NY: Cornell University Press, pp. 63–82.

Kennedy, Scott (2005) *The Business of Lobbying in China*, Cambridge, MA and London: Harvard University Press.

Kerr, David (2007) "Has China Abandoned Self-reliance?" *Review of International Political Economy* 14(1): 77–104.

Khilnani, Sunil (1997) *The Idea of India*, New York: Farrar Straus and Giroux.
Kim, Myonsob and Hodges, Horace Jeffery (2006) "Korea as a Clashpoint of Civilizations," *Korea Observer* 37(3): 513–45.
Kim, Samuel (1966) *Anson Burlingame: A Study in Personal Diplomacy*, PhD dissertation, Columbia University.
—— (1979) *China, the United Nations, and World Order*, Princeton, NJ: Princeton University Press.
—— (ed.) (1998) *China and the World: Chinese Foreign Policy in the Post-Mao Era*, Boulder, CO: Westview.
—— (2003a) "China–North Korean Relations at a Crossroads," *International Journal of Korean Studies* 7(1): 39–55.
—— (2003b) *Korea's Democratization*, Cambridge: Cambridge University Press.
—— (2006) *The Two Koreas and the Great Powers*, Cambridge: Cambridge University Press.
—— (2007) "Oral History Interview," 5, 7, 12 June. Research and Educational Center for China Studies and Cross-Strait Relations of the Department of Political Science, National Taiwan University. Online. Available at: http://140.112.150.151/RAEC/act/Sam20%Kim20%Interviews.doc (accessed 30 April 2010).
—— (2009) "China and Globalization: Confronting Myriad Challenges and Opportunities," *Asian Perspective* 33(3): 41–80.
Kim-Rivera, E.G. (2002) "English Language Education in Korea under Japanese Colonial Rule," *Language Policy* 3(1): 261–81.
Kinvall, Catarina (2007) "Civilizations, Neo-Ghandianism and the Hindu Self," in Martin Hall and Patrick Thaddeus Jackson (eds), *Civilizational Identity: The Production and Reproduction of "Civilizations" in International Relations*, New York: Palgrave, pp. 95–107.
Kirshner, Jonathan (2008) "The Consequence of China's Economic Rise for U.S.–Sino Relations: Rivalry, Political Conflict, and (Not) War," in Robert Ross and Zhu Feng (eds), *Rising China: Theoretical and Policy Perspectives*, Ithaca, NY: Cornell University Press, pp. 238–59.
—— (2010) "The Tragedy of Offensive Realism: Classical Realism and the Rise of China," *European Journal of International Relations*: 1–23 (17 Aug.). doi:10.1177/1354066110373949. Available at: http://ejt.sagepub.com/content/early/2010/08/16/1354066110373949.abstract.
Kissinger, Henry (2011) *On China*, New York: Penguin.
Knöbl, Wolfgang (2007) *Die Kontingenz der Moderne: Wege in Europa, Asien und Amerika*, Frankfurt/New York: Campus.
Kocka, Jürgen (2001) "Multiple Modernities and Negotiated Universals," Paper prepared for the conference on Multiple Modernities, Social Science Research Center (WZB), Berlin, 5–7 May.
Koh, Tommy, Yeo, Lay Hwee, and Latif, Asad (2000) *Asia and Europe: Essays and Speeches*, Singapore and River Edge, NJ: World Scientific Pub. and Asia-Europe Foundation.
Kokubun, Ryosei and Wang, Jisi (eds) (2004) *The Rise of China and Changing East Asian Order*, Tokyo: JCIE.
Komiya, Masataka (2009) "Beichu-kankei no naka no Nihon to Tonan Ajia: Indonesia no Shiten" [Japan and Southeast Asia in the Sino-US relationship], unpublished manuscript.
Koyasu, Nobukuni (2004) *On East Asia: Japanese Modern Thoughts in Critical Perspectives* [dongya lun: riben xiandai sixiang pipan]. In Jinghua Zhao (trans.). Changchun: Jilin People's Press.
Krasner, Stephen D. (1999) *Sovereignty: Organized Hypocrisy*, Princeton, NJ: Princeton University Press.

Kubota, Izumi (2011) "Reisen-go Chugoku no 'Gunji Gaiko' " [China's Military Diplomacy in the Post-Cold War Era], unpublished manuscript.

Kuhn, Philip A. (1990) *Soulstealers: The Chinese Sorcery Scare of 1768*, Cambridge, MA: Harvard University Press.

Kumagai, Satoru (2007) "Comparing the Networks of Ethnic Japanese and Ethnic Chinese in International Trade," Tokyo, Institute of Developing Economies, Discussion Paper No. 113.

Kumar, Ravinder (1989) *The Making of a Nation: Essays in Indian History and Politics*, New Delhi: Manohar.

—— (1997) "State Formation in India: Retrospect and Prospect," in Martin Doornbos and Sudipta Kaviraj (eds), *Dynamics of State Formation: India and Europe Compared*, London: Sage, pp. 395–410.

Kuo, Chia-chia (2008) *Lisanzhe de zhongguo minzuzhuyi: huayi xuezhe Zhao Suisheng yu Zheng Yongnian miandui zhongguo de shenfen celue* [Chinese Diaspora's Nationalism: The Identity Strategies of Chinese Overseas Scholars Zhao Suisheng and Zheng Yongnian in Facing China], Taipei: Research and Educational Center for China Studies and Cross-Taiwan Strait Relations, Department of Political Science, National Taiwan University.

Kuran, Timur (1998) "Social Mechanisms of Dissonance Reduction," in Peter Hedström and Richard Swedberg (eds), *Social Mechanisms: An Analytical Approach to Social Theory*, New York: Cambridge University Press, pp. 147–71.

Kurlantzick, Joshua (2006) "China's Charm: Implications of Chinese Soft Power," *Carnegie Endowment Policy Brief* 47 (June).

Kurth, James (2010) "The United States as a Civilizational Leader," in Peter J. Katzenstein (ed.), *Civilizations in World Politics: Plural and Pluralist Perspectives*, London and New York: Routledge, pp. 41–66.

Kurzweil, Ray (2005) *The Singularity Is Near: When Humans Transcend Biology*, New York: Vintage.

Kuwamori, Hiroshi and Okamoto, Nobuhiro (2007) "Industrial Networks between China and the Countries of the Asia-Pacific Region," Tokyo, Institute for Developing Economies, Discussion Paper No. 110.

Kynge, James (2006) *China Shakes the World: A Titan's Rise and Troubled Future – and the Challenge for America*, Boston, MA: Houghton Mifflin.

LaFraniere, Sharon (2010) "China's Zeal for 'Avatar' Crowds out 'Confucius,'" *New York Times* (30 Jan.): B1–B2.

Laitin, David (1988) "Political Culture and Political Preferences," *American Political Science Review* 82(2): 589–93.

Lake, David A. (1988) "The State and American Trade Strategy in the Pre-Hegemonic Era," *International Organization* 42(1): 33–58.

—— (2009) *Hierarchy in International Relations*, Ithaca, NY: Cornell University Press.

Lam, Peng Er, Ganesan, Narayanan, and Durkop, Colin (2010) *East Asia's Relations with a Rising China*, Seoul: Konrad Adenauer Stiftung.

Lantis, Jeffrey S. (2002) "Strategic Culture and National Security Policy," *International Studies Review* 4(3): 87–113.

Latham, A.J.H. and Kawakatsu, Heita (eds) (2006) *Japanese Industrialization and the Asian Economy*, London: Routledge.

Law, Kar and Bren, Frank (with the collaboration of Sam Ho) (2004) *Hong Kong Cinema: A Cross-Cultural View*, Lanham, MD, Toronto, and Oxford: Scarecrow Press.

Lawrence, Bruce B. (2010) "Islam in Afro-Eurasia: A Bridge Civilization," in Peter J. Katzenstein (ed.), *Civilizations in World Politics: Plural and Pluralist Perspectives*, London and New York: Routledge, pp. 157–75.

Lee, Chin Chen (Li Zheng Xian/Steve Lee) (2009) *Malaixiya Guanghua Ribao de Zhongguo Renshi – Zai Huaqiao yu Huaren Liang Zhong Shenfen Zhijian* [Malaysia-based *Kwong-Wah Yit Poh*'s Understanding of China: Between *Huaqiao* and *Huaren* Identities], Taipei: Research and Educational Center for China Studies and Cross-Taiwan Strait Relations, Department of Political Science, National Taiwan University.

Lee, Jennifer (2008a) *The Fortune Cookie Chronicles*, New York: Twelve.

—— (2008b) "Solving a Riddle Wrapped in a Mystery inside a Cookie," *New York Times* (16 Jan.).

Lee, Leo Ou-fan (1999) *Shanghai Modern: The Flowering of a New Urban Culture in China, 1930–1945*, Cambridge, MA and London: Harvard University Press.

Lee, Teng-hui (1999) *Taiwan de Zhuzhang* [Taiwan's Claim], Taipei: Yuan-Liou Publishing.

Legro, Jeffrey W. (2007) "What China Will Want: The Future Intentions of a Rising Power," *Perspectives on Politics* 5(3): 515–34.

Leheny, David (2010) "The Samurai Ride to Huntington's Rescue: Japan Ponders Its Global and Regional Roles," in Peter J. Katzenstein (ed.), *Civilizations in World Politics: Plural and Pluralist Perspectives*, London and New York: Routledge, pp. 114–36.

Leibold, James (2007) *Reconfiguring Chinese Nationalism: How the Qing Frontier and its Indigenes Became Chinese*, New York: Palgrave Macmillan.

Leightner, Jonathan E. (2010) "Alternative Property Systems for China," *China: An International Journal* 8(2): 346–59.

Leonard, Mark (2008) *What Does China Think?* New York: Public Affairs.

Levi-Strauss, Claude (1987 [1950]) *Introduction to the Work of Marcel Mauss*, trans. Felicity Baker, London: Routledge.

Lewis, Bernard (1990) "The Roots of Muslim Rage," *Atlantic Monthly* (Sept.): 47–60.

Li, Dongyan (2007) "China's Approach to Non-Traditional Security," Paper presented at the "Non-Traditional Security Challenges in Asia Conference," Berkeley, 8 March. Online. Available at: http://ieas.berkeley.edu/events/pdf/2007.03.08_Li_Dongyan.pdf.

Li, Hongbin and Zhou, Li-An (2005) "Political Turnover and Economic Performance: The Incentive Role of Personnel Control in China," *Journal of Public Economics* 89 (Sept.): 1743–62.

Li, Mingjang (2008a) "China Debates Soft Power," *Chinese Journal of International Politics* 2(2): 287–308.

—— (2008b) "Soft Power in Chinese Discourse: Popularity, Prospect and Parameter," *Chinese Journal of International Politics*: 1–22.

Li, Rex (2009) *A Rising China and Security in East Asia: Identity Construction and Security Discourse*, New York: Routledge.

Li, Yizhou (2009) "Guanyu dui Tai Juece Zhanlue Tiaozheng" [On Strategic Adjustment of Policy-making toward Taiwan], ChinaTaiwan Website. Available at http://www.chinataiwan.org/plzhx/zhjzhl/zhjlw/200912/t20091223_1198804.htm (accessed 23 December 2009).

Li, Yuanjin (Lee Guan Kin) (1991) *Lin Wenqing de sixiang–Zhongxi wenhua de huiliu yu maodun* [The Thought of Lim Boon Keng: Convergency and Contradiction between Chinese and Western Culture], Singapore: Singapore Society of Asian Studies.

Li, Zehou (1987) *Zhongguo Xiandai Sixiang Shilun* [Historical Comments on Modern Chinese Thought], Beijing: Dongfang Chubanshe.

Liang, Hongfu (James Leung) (2010) "Mandarin Proficiency Will Aid Hong Kong," *China Daily* (3 June). Online. Available at: http://www.chinadaily.com.cn/opinion/2010-06/03/content_9925813.htm (accessed 22 March 2011).

Lieberthal, Kenneth (1992) *Bureaucracy, Politics, and Decision Making in Post-Mao China*, Berkeley: University of California Press, Chapter 1.

Lieberthal, Kenneth and Oksenberg, Michel (1988) *Policy Making in China: Leaders, Structures, and Processes*, Princeton, NJ: Princeton University Press.

Lim, Carolyn (2006) "How Lillian Too Creates the Right Space at the Right Time," *Wall Street Journal* (2 Oct.), reprinted on Lillian Too's Official Website, http://www.lillian-too.com/news_wsjoct06.php (accessed 12 April 2010).

Ling, L.H.M., Hwang, Ching-Chane, and Chen, Boyu (2010) "Subaltern Straits: 'Exit,' 'Voice,' and 'Loyalty' in the United States–China–Taiwan Relations," *International Relations of the Asia-Pacific* 10: 33–59.

Linklater, Andrew (2011) *The Problem of Harm in World Politics: Theoretical Investigations*, New York: Cambridge University Press.

Linklater, Andrew and Suganami, Hidemi (2006) *The English School of International Relations: A Contemporary Reassessment*, Cambridge: Cambridge University Press.

Liu, Bo and Ma, Juan (2006) "Wenming de jiaorong: rang women gengjia xianghu yilai" [The Fusion of Civilizations: Let Us Depend More on Each Other]. *21 Shijie jingji baodao* [The 21st Century Economy Report], 11 Nov. Online. Available at: http://view.news.qq.com/a/20061212000023_1.htm (accessed 20 January 2009).

Liu, Hong (2006) "The Transnational Construction of 'National Allegory': China and the Cultural Politics of Postcolonial Indonesia," *Critical Asian Studies* (London) 38(3): 179–210.

Liu, Lydia H. (1995) *Translingual Practice: Literature, National Culture, and Translated Modernity – China, 1900–1937*, Stanford, CA: Stanford University Press.

—— (2004) *The Clash of Empires: The Invention of China in Modern World Making*, Cambridge, MA: Harvard University Press.

Liu, Wei-qiang (2008) "Zhongguo Feichuantong Anquan mianlin de Tiaozhan ji Ying dui Celue," [The Challenges and the Corresponding Strategy on Nontraditional Security in China], *Tianshui Xingzheng Xueyuan Xuebao*, #1.

Liu, Xuan (2006) "Guoji wenhuazhuyizhe Ru Jianzhao huyu chaoyue guojia de wenming jiaoliu" [International Culturalist Iriye Akira: Calling for Civilizational Exchanges to Transcend Nation-states]. PKU News (6 Nov.). Online. Available at: http://pkunews.pku.edu.cn/xwzh/2006-11/06/content_110280.htm (accessed 6 January 2011).

Liu, Yia-Ling (1992) "Reform from Below: The Private Economy and Local Politics in the Rural Industrialisation of Wenzhou," *China Quarterly* 130.

Liu, Zhaohui (2005) *Chaoyue xiangtu shehui: yi ge qiao xiang cun luo de lishi wenhua yu shehui jiegou* [Beyond Peasant Society: History, Culture and Social Structure in a Qiao Xiang Village], Beijing: Minzhu Chubanshe.

Lohr, Steve (2011) "Maybe Japan Was Just a Warm-Up," *New York Times*, Business Section (23 Jan.): 1, 6.

Long, Denggao, Zhao, Liang and Ding, Qian (2008) "Haiwai Huaren Touzi Zhongguo Dalu: Jieduanxing Tezheng yu Fazhan Qushi" [Investment of Overseas Chinese in Mainland China: Features and Trends], *Huaqiao Huaren Lishi Yanjiu* [Overseas Chinese History Studies] 2 June.

Lu, Jinyong (2010) "Zhongguo Duiwai Touzi Fazhan Qushi yu Zhanwang" [Development and Prospect of China's Outward Foreign Investment], *Cai Jing Jie* [Money China] 23: 5–8.

Lu, Yan (2004) *Re-Understanding Japan: Chinese Perspectives, 1895–1945*, Honolulu: Association for Asian Studies and University of Hawai'i Press.

Ludden, David (ed.) (1996) *Making India Hindu: Religion, Community, and the Politics of Democracy in India*, Bombay: Oxford University Press.

Lynch, Daniel (2009) "Chinese Thinking on the Future of International Relations: Realism as the *Ti*, Rationalism as the *Yong*?" *China Quarterly* 197: 87–107.

Ma, Dazheng (2003) "Guanyu Gouzhu Zhongguo bianjiangxue de Duan Xiang" [Concerning the Ongoing Development of China's Frontier Studies], Zhongguo Bianjiang Shidi Yanjiu #3: 10–13.
—— (2007) "Shenhua Bianjiang Lilun Yanjiu yu Tuidong Zhongguo Bianjiangxue de Gouzhu" [Deepening the Theoretical Research in Frontier Studies and Promoting the Construction of China's Frontier Studies], Zhongguo Bianjiang Shidi Yanjiu #1: 1–5.
—— (2008) Bianjiang YanjiuYinggai you yige da Fazhan [There Should Be a Major Development in Frontier Studies], Dongbei Shidi #4: 2–7.
Ma, Eric K.W. (1999) *Culture, Politics and Television in Hong Kong*, London and New York: Routledge.
Ma, Eric K.W. and Fung, Anthony Y.H. (1999) "Re-sinicization, Nationalism and the Hong Kong Identity," in Clement So and Joseph Chan (eds), *Press and Politics in Hong Kong: Case Studies from 1967 to 1997*, Hong Kong: Hong Kong Institute for Asia-Pacific Studies.
Ma, Licheng (2005) *Da Tupo: Xin Zhongguo Siying Jingji Fengyunlu* [The Big Breakthrough: Review of Private Economy in New China], Beijing: Zhonghua Gongshang Lianhe Publisher.
Ma, Rong (2004) "Lijie Minzu Guanxi de Xin Silu" [A New Perspective to Studying Ethnic Relations], Beijing Daxue Xuebao #6: 122–33.
—— (2007) "A New Perspective in Guiding Ethnic Relations in the Twenty-first Century: 'De-politicization' of Ethnicity in China," *Asian Ethnicity* 3: 199–217.
—— (2009) "The Key to Understanding and Interpreting Ethnic Relations in Contemporary China," ISS (International Institute of Social Studies of Erasmus University Rotterdam). Online. Available at: http://www.iss.nl/DevISSues/Articles/The-key-to-understanding-and-interpreting-ethnic-relations-in-contemporary-China.
McAdam, Doug, Tarrow, Sidney and Tilly, Charles (2008) "Methods for Measuring Mechanisms of Contention," *Qualitative Sociology* 31: 307–31.
McGregor, James (2006) *One Billion Customers: Lessons from the Front Lines of Doing Business in China*, New York: Free Press.
McNeill, William H. (1963) *The Rise of the West: A History of the Human Community*, Chicago, IL: University of Chicago Press.
—— (1990) "*The Rise of the West* after Twenty-Five Years," *Journal of World History* 1: 1–21.
Maddison, Angus (2006) *The World Economy: A Millennial Perspective*, Paris: Development Centre of the Organisation for Economic Co-operation and Development.
Maddison, Angus and Wu, Harry X. (2008) "Measuring China's Economic Performance," *World Economics* 9(2): 13–44.
Mahathir bin Mohamad and Ishihara, Shintar (1995) *The Voice of Asia: Two Leaders Discuss the Coming Century*, New York: Kodansha International.
Mahbubani, Kishore (2008) *The New Asian Hemisphere: The Irresistible Shift of Global Power to the East*, New York: Public Affairs.
Mahoney, James (2001) "Beyond Correlational Analysis: Recent Innovations in Theory and Method," *Sociological Forum* 16(3): 575–93.
Maier, Charles S. (1978) "The Politics of Productivity: Foundations of American International Economic Policy after World War II," in Peter J. Katzenstein (ed.), *Between Power and Plenty: Foreign Economic Policies of Advanced Industrial States*, Madison: University of Wisconsin Press, pp. 23–50.
Makeham, John (ed.) (2003) *A New Confucianism: A Critical Examination*, New York: Palgrave Macmillan.
Maliniak, Daniel, Oakes, Amy, Peterson, Susan, and Tierny, Michael J. (2007) "Inside the Ivory Tower," Foreign Policy (Mar./Apr.). Online. Available at: http://www.foreignpolicy.com/story/cms.php?story_id=3718&print=1 (accessed 26 February 2007).

Malvezin, Laurent (2004) "The Problems with (Chinese) Diaspora: An Interview with Wang Gungwu," in Gregor Benton and Hong Liu (eds), *Diasporic Chinese Ventures, The Life and Work of Wang Gungwu*, London: RoutledgeCurzon.

Mancall, Mark (1984) *China at the Center: 300 Years of Foreign Policy*, New York: Free Press.

Mao, Zedong (1978) *Collected Works, 1917–1949.* Vols. 1–9. Compiled, edited, and published by the US Government's Joint Publications Research Service (JPRS).

Marchetti, Gina (2007) *Andrew Lau and Alan Mak's* Infernal Affairs – The Trilogy, Hong Kong: University of Hong Kong Press.

Maruya, Toyojiro (2010) "Saikin no Chugoku-Keizai to Nicchu-Keizai-Kankei: Genjo to Tenbo" [Recent Chinese Economy and Sino-Japanese Economic Relations: The Current Situation and Prospects], unpublished manuscript.

Marx, Karl (1973) "The Future Results of British Rule in India," in David Fernbach (ed.), *Surveys from Exile, Political Writings*, New York: Vintage Books, pp. 307–16.

Matisoff, James A. (2003) *Handbook of Proto-Tibeto-Burman*, Berkeley: University of California Press.

Mayntz, Renate (2004) "Mechanisms in the Analysis of Macro-Social Phenomena," *Philosophy of the Social Sciences* 34(2): 237–59.

Mazzarella, William (2003) *Shoveling Smoke: Advertising and Globalization in Contemporary India*, Durham, NC: Duke University Press.

MCC (Ministry of Commerce, China) (ed.) (2010) *Zhongguo Duiwai Touzi Hezuo Fazhan Baogao* [Report on Development of China's Outward Investment and Economic Cooperation], Shanghai: Jiaotong University Press.

Mearsheimer, John J. (2001) *The Tragedy of Great Power Politics*, New York: Norton.

—— (2006) "China's Unpeaceful Rise," *Current History* (Apr.): 160–2. Online. Available at: http://mearsheimer.uchicago.edu/pdfs/A0051.pdf (accessed 7 February 2011).

Mertha, Andrew (2009a) "'Fragmented Authoritarianism 2.0': Political Pluralization in the Chinese Policy Process," *China Quarterly* 200: 995–1012.

—— (2009b) "From 'Rustless Screws' to 'Nail Houses': The Evolution of Property Rights in China," *Orbis* 53(2): 233–49.

Metcalf, Thomas R. (2007) *Imperial Connections: India in the Indian Ocean Area 1860–1920*, Berkeley: University of California Press.

Mintz, Sidney W. (2009) "Asia's Contributions to World Cuisine," *Asia-Pacific Journal*, 18-2-09 (1 May). Online. Available at: http://japanfocus.org/articles/print_article3135 (accessed 4 May 2009).

Miyamoto, Yuji (2010) *Korekara Chugoku to do tsukiau ka* [How to Engage China from now on], Tokyo: Nihon Keizai Sinbunsha.

Miyata, Toshiyuki (2011) "Chugoku Shijo toTai Kaori-mai Jasumin Rice: Naze Sekai Saidai no Kome Seisankoku Chugoku ga Tai-mai wo Yunyu suru no ka?" [Thai Fragrant Jasmine Rice for the Chinese Market: Why does China, the largest rice producing country, import Thai rice?]. Online. Available at: http://www.rieti.go.jp/jp/publications/dp/11j005.pdf.

Mizoguchi, Yuzo (1989) *China as Method* [Hōhō toshite no Chūgoku], Tokyo: Tokyo Daigaku Shuppankai.

Montinola, Gabriella, Qian, Yingyi and Weingast, Barry R. (1996) "Federalism, Chinese Style: The Political Basis for Economic Success," *World Politics* 48(1): 50–81.

Moore, Thomas G. (1996) "China as a Latecomer: Toward a Global Logic of the Open Policy," *Journal of Contemporary China* 5(12): 187–208.

—— (2002) *China in the World Market: Chinese Industry and International Sources of Reform in the Post-Mao Era*, Cambridge: Cambridge University Press.

Morris, Ian (2010) *Why the West Rules – For Now: The Patterns of History, and What They Reveal about the Future*, New York: Farrar, Straus and Giroux.

Müller, Harald (1999) *Das Zusammenleben der Kulturen: Ein Gegenentwurf zu Huntington*, Frankfurt am Main: Fischer.

Munn, Christopher (2001) *Anglo-China: Chinese People and British Rule in Hong Kong 1841–1880*, Richmond, Surrey, UK: Curzon.

—— (2009 [2001]) *Anglo-China: Chinese People and British Rule in Hong Kong, 1841–1880*, Hong Kong: Hong Kong University Press.

Murakami, Yasusuke (1984) "Ie Society as a Pattern of Civilization," *Journal of Japanese Studies* 10(2): 281–363.

Murphy, Ann Marie (2010) "US Rapprochement with Indonesia: From Problem State to Partner," *Contemporary Southeast Asia* 32(3): 362–87.

Nandy, Ashis (1983) *The Intimate Enemy: Loss and Recovery of Self under Colonialism*, Delhi: Oxford University Press.

Naughton, Barry (1996) *Growing Out of the Plan: Chinese Economic Reform, 1978–1993*, Cambridge: Cambridge University Press.

—— (ed.) (1997) *The China Circle: Economics and Technology in the PRC, Taiwan, and Hong Kong*, Washington, DC: Brookings Institution Press.

—— (2007a) "Reframing China Policy: The Carnegie Debates," *Journal of Chinese Economic and Business Studies* 5(3): 193–202.

—— (2007b) *The Chinese Economy: Transitions and Growth*, Cambridge, MA: MIT Press.

Needham, Anuradha Dingwaney and Sunder Rajan, Rajeswari (eds) (2007) *The Crisis of Secularism in India*, Durham, NC: Duke University Press.

Nehru, Jawaharlal (1990) *The Discovery of India*, New York: Oxford University Press.

Neumann, Iver (1999) *Uses of the Other: "The East" in European Identity Formation*, Minneapolis: University of Minnesota Press.

Neumayer, Eric and Plümper, Thomas (2009) "International Terrorism and the Clash of Civilizations," *British Journal of Political Science* 39: 711–34.

Nguyen, Vu Tung (2010) "Vietnam: Kokka Anzen Hosho he no Aratana Aprochi to Kokubo-Gaiko Seisaku he no Eikyo" [Vietnam: a new approach for national security and influence on defense and foreign policy], in Boeisho Boei Kenkyusho [Defense Research Institute, Ministry of Defense] (ed.), *Ajia Taiheiyo Shokoku no Anzen Hosho jo no Kadai to Kokubo Bumon he no Eikyo* [Security Tasks in Asia-Pacific States and their Influence on Defense Sectors], Tokyo: Boeisho Boei Kenkyusho, pp. 117–34.

Nonini, Donald M. and Ong, Aihwa (1997) "Chinese Transnationalism as an Alternative Modernity," in Aihwa Ong and Donald Nonini (eds), *The Cultural Politics of Modern Chinese Transnationalism*, New York and London: Routledge, pp. 3–33.

Nye, Joseph S. Jr. (1990) *Bound to Lead: The Changing Nature of American Power*, New York: Basic Books.

—— (2004) *Soft Power: The Means to Success in World Politics*, New York: Public Affairs.

—— (2005) "The Rise of China's Soft Power," *Wall Street Journal Asia* (29 Dec.).

Oakes, Tim (2000) "China's Provincial Identities: Reviving Regionalism and Reinventing 'Chineseness,'" *Journal of Asian Studies* 59(3): 667–92.

Oi, Jean C. and Walder, Andrew G. (eds) (1999) *Property Rights and Economic Reform in China*, Stanford, CA: Stanford University Press.

Oksenberg, Michel (2001) "The Issue of Sovereignty in the Asian Historical Context," in Stephen D. Krasner (ed.), *Problematic Sovereignty: Contested Rules and Political Possibilities*, New York: Columbia University Press, pp. 83–104.

Ong, Aihwa and Nonini, Donald M. (1997a) "Toward a Cultural Politics of Diaspora and Transnationalism," in Aihwa Ong and Donald Nonini (eds), *The Cultural Politics of Modern Chinese Transnationalism*, New York and London: Routledge, pp. 323–32.

—— (eds) (1997b) *Ungrounded Empires: The Cultural Politics of Modern Chinese Transnationalism*, New York: Routledge.

Ono, Gary (2007a) "Japanese American Fortune Cookie: A Taste of Fame and Fortune, Part I." Online. Available at: http://www.discovernikkei.org/forum/en/node/1934 (accessed 3 February 2009).

—— (2007b) "Japanese American Fortune Cookie: A Taste of Fame and Fortune, Part II." Online. Available at: http://www.discovernikkei.org/forum/en/node/1935 (accessed 3 February 2009).

Osiander, Andreas (2008) *Before the State: Systemic Political Change in the West from the Greeks to the French Revolution*, Oxford: Oxford University Press.

Osterhammel, Jürgen (2005) "'The Great Work of Uplifting Mankind': Zivilisierungsmission und Moderne," in Boris Barth and Jürgen Osterhammel (eds), *Zivilisierungsmissionen*, Konstanz: UVK Verlagsgesellschaft, pp. 363–425.

Ostler, Nicholas (2010) *The Last Lingua Franca: English until the Return of Babel*, New York: Walker.

Otmazgin, Nissim Kadosh (2007) "Regionalizing Culture: The Political Economy of Japanese Culture in East and Southeast Asia, 1988–2005," PhD dissertation, Graduate School of Asian and African Area Studies, Kyoto University (March).

—— (2008) "Contesting Soft Power: Japanese Popular Culture in East and Southeast Asia," *International Relations of the Asia-Pacific* 8: 73–101.

Overholt, William H. (1993) *The Rise of China: How Economic Reform Is Creating a New Superpower*, New York: W.W. Norton.

Oyen, Meredith (2010) "Communism, Containment and the Chinese Overseas," in Zheng Yangwen, Hong Liu, and Michael Szonyi (eds), *The Cold War in Asia: The Battle for Hearts and Minds*, Leiden and Boston: Brill, pp. 59–93.

Page, Benjamin I. and Xie, Tao (2010) *Living with the Dragon: How the American Public Views the Rise of China*, New York: Columbia University Press.

Pan, Wei (2010a) "Western System versus Chinese System," *EAI Background Brief* No. 530 (20 May).

—— (2010b) "Contemporary Chinese System," Public presentation, roundtable "Explaining the Rise of China: A Challenge to Social Science Theories?" Yenching Institute, Harvard University, Cambridge, MA (5 Apr.).

Paradise, James F. (2009) "China and International Harmony? The Role of Confucius Institutes in Bolstering Beijing's Soft Power," *Asian Survey* 49: 647–69.

Pearson, Margaret M. (1997) *China's New Business Elite: The Political Consequences of Economic Reform*, Berkeley: University of California Press.

—— (2005) "The Business of Governing Business in China: Institutions and Norms of the Emerging Regulatory State," *World Politics* 57(2): 296–322.

Pempel, T.J. (2010) "More Pax, Less Americana in Asia," *International Relations of the Asia-Pacific* 10: 465–90.

Perlez, Jane (2004) "Chinese Move to Eclipse U.S. Appeal in South Asia," *New York Times* (18 Nov.): A2.

Petersen, Roger (1999) "Mechanisms and Structures in Comparison," in John R. Bowen and Roger Petersen (eds), *Critical Comparisons in Politics and Culture*, New York: Cambridge University Press, pp. 61–77.

Pew Research Center for the People & the Press (2009) *America's Place in the World 2009: An Investigation of Public Leadership Opinion about International Affairs*. Pew Research

Center for the People & the Press in association with the Council of Foreign Relations (Dec.).
Phongpaichit, Pasuk and Baker, Chris (1996) *Thailand's Boom!* Bangkok: Silkworm Books.
Pijl, Kees van der (2007) *Nomads, Empires, States*. Vol. 1. *Modes of Foreign Relations and Political Economy*, London: Pluto Press.
—— (2010) *The Foreign Encounter in Myth and Religion*. Vol. 2. *Modes of Foreign Relations and Political Economy*, London: Pluto Press.
Pocock, J.G.A. (2005) *Barbarism and Religion*, New York: Cambridge University Press.
Pollock, Sheldon I. (1998) "India in the Vernacular Millennium: Literary Culture and Polity, 1000–1500," *Dædalus* 127(3): 41–74.
—— (2006) *The Language of the Gods in the World of Men: Sanskrit, Culture, and Power in Premodern India*, Berkeley: University of California Press.
Pomeranz, Kenneth (2000) *The Great Divergence: China, Europe, and the Making of the Modern World Economy*, Princeton, NJ: Princeton University Press.
Pouliot, Vincent (2010) *International Security in Practice: The Politics of NATO–Russia Diplomacy*, New York: Cambridge University Press.
PRC Foreign Ministry and Central Documentaries Office (1990) *Zhou Enlai Waijiao Wenxuan* [Selected Diplomatic Works of Zhou Enlai], Beijing: Central Documentaries Press.
PRC Foreign Ministry Diplomatic History Research Office (1993) *Zhou Enlai Waijiao Huodong Dashiji, 1949–1975* [Chronology of Zhou Enlai's Diplomatic Activities, 1949–1975], Beijing: World Affairs Press.
Pungkanon, Kupluthai (2008) "Tales of the Father," *Daily Xpress* (29 Dec.). Online. Available at: http://www.dailyxpress.net/2008/12/29/lifestyle/lifestyle_5242.php (accessed 26 April 2010).
Purdue, Peter (2005) *China Marches West*, Cambridge, MA: Harvard University Press.
Pye, Lucian W. (1988) *The Mandarin and the Cadre: China's Political Cultures*, Ann Arbor: Center for Chinese Studies, University of Michigan.
—— (1990) "China: Erratic State, Frustrated Society," *Foreign Affairs* 69(4): 56–74.
—— (1992) *The Spirit of Chinese Politics*, Cambridge, MA: Harvard University Press.
Pyle, Kenneth B. (2007) *Japan Rising: The Resurgence of Japanese Power and Purpose*, New York: Public Affairs.
Qi, Mingtian and Chen, Lixu (2001) *Wenhua yu Zhejiang Quyu Jingji Fazhan* [Culture and Economic Development in Zhejiang Area], Hangzhou: Zhejiang People's Publisher.
Qiang, Shigong (2010) *Zhongguo Xianggang: Zhengzhi yu Wenhua Shiye* [Hong Kong, China: Political and Cultural Vision], Beijing: SDX Joint Publishing Company.
Qin, Yaqing (2010) "International Society as Process: Institutions, Identities, and China's Peaceful Rise," *Chinese Journal of International Politics* 3(2): 129–53.
Qiu, Shu Ting [Kinnia Yau Shuk-ting] (2010) *Zhong-Ri-Han Dianying: Lishi, Shehui, Wenhua* [Chinese–Japanese–Korean Films; History, Society, Culture], Hong Kong: Hong Kong University Press.
Qu, Wanwen (2009) "Ganchao Gongshi Jiandu Xia de Zhongguo Chanye Zhengce Moshi: Yi Qiche Chanye Weili" [The Chinese Model of Industrial Policy under Catch-up Consensus Supervision: The Case of the Automobile Industry], *Jingjixue* [*China Economic Quarterly*] 8(2): 501–32.
Rachman, Gideon (2007) "The Hard Evidence that China's Soft Power Policy is Working," *Financial Times* (20 Feb.): 13.
Rajan, Gita and Sharma, Shailja (2006a) *New Cosmopolitanisms: South Asians in the US*, Stanford, CA: Stanford University Press.

—— (2006b) "Theorizing Recognition: South Asian Authors in a Global Milieu," in Gita Rajan and Shailja Sharma (eds), *New Cosmopolitanisms: South Asians in the US*, Stanford: Stanford University Press, pp. 150–69.
Ramo, Joshua Cooper (2004) "The 'Beijing Consensus,'" Unpublished paper, Foreign Policy Centre, London.
—— (2007) "Brand China," Unpublished paper, Foreign Policy Centre, London (Feb.).
Rauch, James E. and Trindade, Vitor (2002) "Ethnic Chinese Networks in International Trade," *Review of Economics and Statistics* 84(1): 116–30.
Ravenhill, John (2006) "Is China an Economic Threat to Southeast Asia?" *Asian Survey* 46(5): 653–74.
Rawski, Evelyn S. (1996) "Presidential Address: Reenvisioning the Qing: The Significance of the Qing Period in Chinese History," *Journal of Asian Studies* 55(4): 829–50.
Recur, Carlos (1879) *Filipinas. Estudios administrativos y comerciales* [The Philippines: Administrative and commercial studies], Madrid: Imprenta de Ramón Moreno y Ricardo Rojas.
Reid, Anthony (2010) *Imperial Alchemy: Nationalism and Political Identity in Southeast Asia*, Cambridge: Cambridge University Press.
Reid, Anthony and Zheng, Yangwen (2009) *Negotiating Asymmetry: China's Place in Asia*, Singapore: National University of Singapore Press.
Ren, Xiao (2008) "Toward a Chinese School of International Relations?" in Wang Gungwu and Yongnian Zheng (eds), *China and the New International Order*, New York: Routledge, pp. 293–309.
Ridge, Mian (2010) "Fadeout for a Culture that's neither Indian nor British," *New York Times* (15 Aug.): 6.
Rifkin, Jeremy (2009) *The Empathetic Civilization: The Race to Global Consciousness in a World Crisis*, New York: Jeremy P. Tarcher/Penguin.
Rigger, Shelley (1999) *Politics in Taiwan: Voting for Democracy*, London: Routledge.
Riles, Annelise (2011) *Collateral Knowledge: Legal Reasoning in the Global Financials Markets* [sic], Chicago, IL: University of Chicago Press.
Rizal, Sukma (2009) "Chugoku no Taito he no Indonesia no taio" [Indonesia's Response to the Rise of China], in Jun Tsunekawa (ed.), *Chugoku no Taito: Tonan Ajia to Nihon no Taio* [The Rise of China: Southeast Asian and Japanese Responses], Tokyo: Boei Kenkyusho, Boeisho, pp. 137–54.
Roberts, J.A.G. (2002) *China to Chinatown: Chinese Food in the West*, London: Reaktion Books.
Rohlen, Thomas P. (1985) "When Evolution Isn't Progressive," *Journal of Japanese Studies* 11(1): 65–9.
—— (1989) "Order in Japanese Society: Attachment, Authority, and Routine," *Journal of Japanese Studies* 15(1): 5–40.
Rosecrance, Richard and Guoliang Gu (eds) (2009) *Power and Restraint: A Shared Vision for the U.S.–China Relationship*, New York: Public Affairs/Perseus.
Ross, Robert S. (1995) *Negotiating Cooperation: The United States and China, 1969–1989*, Stanford, CA: Stanford University Press.
Ross, Robert S. and Zhu, Feng (eds) (2008) *China's Ascent: Power, Security, and the Future of International Politics*, Ithaca, NY: Cornell University Press.
Roy, Denny (1994) "Hegemon on the Horizon? China's Threat to East Asian Security," *International Security* 19(1): 149–68.
—— (1996) "The 'China Threat' Issue: Major Arguments," *Asian Survey* 36(8): 758–71.
Rudolph, Lloyd I. and Rudolph, Susanne Hoeber (1997) "Occidentalism and Orientalism: Perspectives on Legal Pluralism," in Sally C. Humphreys (ed.), *Cultures of Scholarship*, Ann Arbor: University of Michigan, pp. 219–52.

Rudolph, Susanne Hoeber (2010) "Four Variants of Indian Civilization," in Peter J. Katzenstein (ed.), *Civilizations in World Politics: Plural and Pluralist Perspectives*, New York: Routledge, pp. 137–56.
Ruggie, John Gerard (1993) "Territoriality and Beyond: Problematizing Modernity in International Relations," *International Organization*, 47(1): 139–74.
Russett, Bruce M., Oneal, John R., and Cox, Michaelene (2000) "Clash of Civilizations, or Realism and Liberalism Déjà Vu? Some Evidence," *Journal of Peace Research* 37(5): 583–608.
Rzhevsky, Nicholas (1998) "Russian Cultural History: Introduction," in Nicholas Rzhevsky (ed.), *Modern Russian Culture*, Cambridge: Cambridge University Press, pp. 1–16.
Sabel, Charles F. and Zeitlin, Jonathan (eds) (2010) *Experimentalist Governance in the European Union: Towards a New Architecture*, New York: Oxford University Press.
Saw, Swee-Hock, Sheng, Lijun, and Chin, Kin Wah (2005) *ASEAN–China Relations: Realities and Prospects*, Singapore: ISEAS.
Schelling, Thomas (1998) "Social Mechanisms and Social Dynamics," in Peter Hedström and Richard Swedberg (eds), *Social Mechanisms: An Analytical Approach to Social Theory*, New York: Cambridge University Press, pp. 32–44.
Schimmelfennig, Frank (2003) *The EU, NATO and the Integration of Europe: Rules and Rhetoric*, New York: Cambridge University Press.
Schwartz, Benjamin I. (1975) "The Age of Transcendence," *Dædalus* 104(2): 1–7.
—— (1968) "The Chinese Perception of the World Order: Past and Present," in John K. Fairbank (ed.), *The Chinese World Order: Traditional China's Foreign Relations*, Cambridge, MA: Harvard University Press, pp. 276–88.
Segal, Adam and Thun, Eric (2001) "Thinking Globally, Acting Locally: Local Governments, Industrial Sectors, and Development in China," *Politics & Society* 29(4).
Sekai Keizai no Neta Cho (2010) "[Material Notebook of World Economy]" Online. Available at: http://ecodb.net/country/CN/imf_gdp.html (accessed 13 February 2011).
Selden, Mark (1997) "China, Japan and the Regional Political Economy of East Asia, 1945–95," in Peter Katzenstein and Takashi Shiraishi (eds), *Network Power: Japan and Asia*, Ithaca, NY: Cornell University Press, pp. 306–40.
—— (2011) "China and India: Marching to the Head of the Queue?" Public lecture, Cornell University (4 Feb.).
Selden, Mark and Grove, Linda (2008) "Editors Introduction: New Perspectives on China, East Asia and the World Economy," in Takeshi Hamashita, *China, East Asia and the Global Economy*, London: Routledge, pp. 1–11.
Selden, Mark and Wu, Jieh-min (2011) "The Chinese State, Incomplete Proletarianization and Structures of Inequality in Two Epochs," *Asia-Pacific Journal* 9(5). Available at: http://japanfocus.org/articles/view/3480 (accessed 21 November 2011).
Sen, Amartya (2005) *The Argumentative Indian: Writings on Indian History, Culture, and Identity*, New York: Farrar, Straus and Giroux.
—— (2006) *Identity and Violence: The Illusion of Destiny*, New York: W.W. Norton.
Shaffer, Lynda (1994) "Southernization," *Journal of World History* (Spring): 1–21.
Shambaugh, David (1996) "Containment or Engagement of China? Calculating Beijing's Responses," *International Security* 21(2): 180–209.
—— (2005a) "Introduction: The Rise of China and Asia's New Dynamics," in David Shambaugh (ed.), *Power Shift: China and Asia's New Dynamics*, Berkeley: University of California Press, pp. 1–20.
—— (2005b) *Power Shift: China and Asia's New Dynamics*, Berkeley: University of California Press.

Sharma, Yojana (2011) "China: Ambitious Plans to Attract Foreign Students," *University World News* (13 Mar.).
Shen, Zhihua (2007) *Mao Zedong, Sidalin ju Chaoxian Zhanzheng* [Mao Zedong, Stalin and the Korean War], Guangzhou: Guangdong People's Press.
Sheng, Ding (2010) "Analyzing Rising Power from the Perspective of Soft Power: A New Look at China's Rise to the Status Quo Power," *Journal of Contemporary China* 19 (Mar.): 255–72.
Shenkar, Oded (2006) *The Chinese Century: The Rising Chinese Economy and Its Impact on the Global Economy, the Balance of Power, and Your Job*, Philadelphia, PA: Wharton School Publishing.
Shepherd, John Robert (1993) *Statecraft and Political Economy on the Taiwan Frontier, 1600–1800*, Stanford, CA: Stanford University Press.
Shevchenko, Alexei (2004) "Bringing the Party Back In: The CCP and the Trajectory of Market Transition in China," *Communist and Post-Communist Studies* 37: 161–85.
Shi, Zhengfeng (2002) "Taiwan Minzhuhua de Tiaozhan" [Challenges of Taiwan's Democratization], Tamkang University Website. Available at: http://mail.tku.edu.tw/cfshih/seminar/20021116.htm#_ftn1 (accessed 16 January 2011).
Shibata, Satoru (2011) *China Impact*, Tokyo: Chuo Koron Shinsha.
Shih, Chih-yu (1994) "The Decline of a Moral Regime: China's Great Leap Forward in Retrospect," *Comparative Political Studies* 27(2): 272–301.
Shih, Chih-yu and Chang, T.C. (2011) "China Studies That Defend Chineseness: The Im/possibility of China-centrism in the Divided Sino-phone World," in Herbert Yee (ed.), *China's Rise: Threat or Opportunity*, London: Routledge, pp. 280–96.
Shih, Shu-mei (2001) *The Lure of the Modern: Writing Modernism in Semicolonial China, 1917–1937*, Berkeley: University of California Press.
Shimemura, Yoichi (2002) "Globalization vs. Americanization: Is the World Being Americanized by the Dominance of American Culture?" *Comparative Civilizations Review* 47: 80–91.
Shiraishi, Takashi (1997) "Japan and Southeast Asia," in Peter J. Katzenstein and Takashi Shiraishi (eds), *Network Power: Japan and Asia*, Ithaca, NY: Cornell University Press, pp. 169–94.
—— (2006) "The Third Wave: Southeast Asia and Middle-Class Formation in the Making of a Region," in Peter J. Katzenstein and Takashi Shiraishi (eds), *Beyond Japan: The Dynamics of East Asian Regionalism*, Ithaca, NY: Cornell University Press, pp. 237–71.
—— (2010a) "Indonesia ni oite Keizai-seicho no Seiji ha ikani shite fukkatsu shitaka" [How has the politics of economic growth come back in Indonesia?], in Otsuka Keijiro and Takashi Shiraishi (eds), *Kokka to Keizai Hatten* [State and Economic Development], Tokyo: Toyo Keizai Sinpo-sha.
—— (2010b) "Shinshun Zadankai: Ajia to Ikiru Nihon" [New Year Dialogue: Japan Living with Asia], *Kokusai Kaihatsu Journal* (1 Jan.): 14–21.
Shiraishi, Takashi and Hau, Caroline S. (2009) "'Ajia-shugi' no jubaku wo koete—Higashi-Ajia kyōdotai saikō" [Overcoming the curse of "Asianism": Revisiting the East Asia Community], *Chūokōron* (Feb.): 168–79.
—— (2010) "Only Yesterday: China, Japan and the Transformation of East Asia," in Yangwen Zheng, Hong Liu, and Michael Szonyi (eds), *The Cold War in Asia: The Battle for Hearts and Minds*, Leiden: Brill, pp. 25–38.
Shirk, Susan (1993) *The Political Logic of Economic Reform in China*, Berkeley: University of California Press.
Shue, Vivienne (1988) *The Reach of the State: Sketches of the Chinese Body Politic*, Stanford, CA: Stanford University Press.

Shukla, Sandhya Rajendra (2003) *India Abroad: Diasporic Cultures of Postwar America and England*, Princeton, NJ: Princeton University Press.

Sil, Rudra and Katzenstein, Peter J. (2010a) *Beyond Paradigms: Analytic Eclecticism in the Study of World Politics*, New York: Palgrave.

—— (2010b) "Analytic Eclecticism in the Study of World Politics: Reconfiguring Problems and Mechanisms across Research Traditions," *Perspectives on Politics* 8(2): 411–31.

Smith, Warren (2008) *China's Tibet: Autonomy or Assimilation*, Lanham, MD: Rowman & Littlefield.

So, Alvin Y. (2009) "Rethinking the Chinese Development Miracle," in Ho-Fung Hung (ed.), *China and the Transformation of Global Capitalism*, Baltimore, MD: Johns Hopkins University Press, Chapter 3.

Song, Xinning (2001) "Building International Relations Theory with Chinese Characteristics," *Journal of Contemporary China* 10: 61–74.

Spence, Jonathan D. (1998) *The Chan's Great Continent: China in Western Minds*, New York: W.W. Norton.

State Statistical Bureau (2011). "China Statistical Yearbook 2009". Online. Available at: http://www.stats.gov.cn/tjsj/ndsj/2009/indexch.htm (accessed 15 February 2011).

Steinfeld, Edward S. (2004) "China's Shallow Integration: Networked Production and the New Challenges for Late Industrialization," *World Development* 32(11): 1971–87.

Stinchcombe, Arthur L. (1991) "The Conditions of Fruitfulness of Theorizing about Mechanisms in Social Science," *Philosophy of the Social Sciences* 21: 367–88.

Stokes, Gale (2001) "Why the West? The Unsettled Question of Europe's Ascendancy," *Lingua Franca* 11(8). Online. Available at: http://www.linguafranca.com/print/0111/cover.html (accessed 20 November 2010).

Su, Xiaokang and Wang, Luxiang (1991) *Deathsong of the River: A Reader's Guide to the Chinese TV Series Heshang*, Ithaca, NY: East Asia Program, Cornell University.

Suettinger, Robert L. (2004) "The Rise and Descent of 'Peaceful Rise.'" *China Leadership Monitor* 12: 1–10. Online. Available at: http://www.hoover.org/publications/china-leadership-monitor/article/7739 (accessed 15 February 2011).

Suganami, Hidemi (1989) *The Domestic Analogy and World Order Proposals*, Cambridge: Cambridge University Press.

Sugihara, Kaoru (2005a) "An Introduction," in Kaoru Sugihara (ed.), *Japan, China, and the Growth of the Asian International Economy, 1850–1949*, Oxford: Oxford University Press, pp. 1–19.

—— (ed.) (2005b) *Japan, China, and the Growth of the Asian International Economy, 1850–1949*, Japan Studies in Economic and Social History, vol. 1, Oxford: Oxford University Press.

—— (2005c) "Patterns of Chinese Emigration to Southeast Asia, 1869–1939," in Kaoru Sugihara (ed.), *Japan, China, and the Growth of the Asian International Economy, 1850–1949*, Oxford: Oxford University Press, pp. 244–74.

Sugiyama, Shinya and Grove, Linda (eds) (2001) *Commercial Networks in Modern Asia*, Richmond, Surrey, UK: Curzon Press.

Sun, Laichen (2010) "Assessing the Ming Role in China's Southern Expansion," in Geoff Wade and Sun Laichen (eds), *Southeast Asia in the Fifteenth Century: The China Factor*, Singapore and Hong Kong: NUS Press and Hong Kong University Press, pp. 44–79.

Suryadinata, Leo (1995) "China's Economic Modernization and the Ethnic Chinese in ASEAN: A Preliminary Study," in Leo Suryadinata (ed.), *Southeast Asian Chinese and China: The Politico-Economic Dimension*, Singapore: Times Academic Press, pp. 193–215.

—— (1997a) *Chinese and Nation-building in Southeast Asia*, Singapore: Singapore Society of Asian Studies.

—— (1997b) *Ethnic Chinese as Southeast Asians*, Singapore: ISEAS.
Sutter, Robert G. (2005) *China's Rise in Asia: Promises and Perils*, Lanham, MD: Rowman & Littlefield.
Swedberg, Richard (2010) "A Note on Civilizations and Economics," *European Journal of Social Theory* 13(1): 15–30.
Tai, Hung-chao (1989) "The Oriental Alternative: An Hypothesis on Culture and Economy," in Hung-chao Tai (ed.), *Confucianism and Economic Development: An Oriental Alternative?* Washington, DC: Washington Institute for Values in Public Policy, pp. 6–37.
Takahara, Akio (2009) "Chugoku no Taito to sono Kinrin Gaiko: Nihon Gaiko he no Shisa" [The Rising China and its diplomacy to neighboring states: Implications for Japan's Diplomacy]. Online. Available at: http://www.rieti.go.jp/jp/publications/summary/09060002.html.
Takeuchi, Yoshimi (2005) "Extreme Slavishness," in Richard F. Calichman (ed. and trans.), *What Is Modernity? Writings of Takeuchi Yoshimi*, New York: Columbia University Press.
Takeuchi, Yoshimi and Calichman, Richard (ed. and trans.) (2005) *What Is Modernity? Writings of Takeuchi Yoshimi*, New York: Columbia University Press.
Tammen, Ronald L. and Kugler, Jacek (2006) "Power Transition and China–US Conflicts," *Chinese Journal of International Politics* 1(1): 35–55.
Tan, Chung (1978) *China and the Brave New World*, Durham, NC: Carolina Academic Press.
—— (2008) "Caiyong 'diyuan wenming' fanshi cujin zhong yin guanxi fazhan" [Promoting Sino-Indian Relations by a Model of "Geo-Civilization"], *South Asian Studies Quarterly* [*nanya yanjiu jikan*] 2: 1–9.
Tan, Chung and Thakur, Ravni (1998) *Across the Himalayan Gap: An Indian Quest for Understanding China*, New Delhi: Indira Gandhi National Centre for the Arts.
Tan, Chung and Uberoi, Patricia (eds) (2009) *Rise of the Asian Giants: The Dragon Elephant Tango*, New Delhi: Anthem Press.
Tao, Xie and Page, Benjamin I. (2010) "Americans and the Rise of China as a World Power," *Journal of Contemporary China* 19: 479–501.
Tejapira, Kasian (1997) "Imagined Uncommunity: The Lookjin Middle Class and Thai Official Nationalism," in Daniel Chirot and Anthony Reid (eds), *Essential Outsiders: Chinese and Jews in the Modern Transformation of Southeast Asia and Central Europe*, Seattle and London: University of Washington Press, pp. 75–98.
—— (2001a) *Commodifying Marxism: The Formation of Modern Thai Radical Culture, 1927–1958*, Kyoto: Kyoto University Press and Trans Pacific Press.
—— (2001b [1992]) "Pigtail: A PreHistory of Chineseness in Siam," in Chee Kiong Tong and Kwok Bun Chan (eds), *Alternate Identities: The Chinese of Contemporary Thailand*, Singapore: Times Academic Press, pp. 41–66.
Teo, Stephen (1997) *Hong Kong Cinema: The Extra Dimension*, London: BFI (British Film Institute) Publishing.
Thayer, Carlyle A. (2010) *Southeast Asia: Patterns of Security Cooperation*, Canberra: Australian Strategic Policy Institute.
Thorniley, Tessa (2010) "Battle Intensifies for $2Bn English-Teaching Business in China," *Guardian Weekly* (13 July). Online. Available at: http://www.guardian.co.uk/education/2010/jul/13/china-english-schools (accessed 5 March 2011).
Thun, Eric (2006) *Changing Lanes in China: Foreign Direct Investment, Local Governments, and Auto Sector Development*, Cambridge: Cambridge University Press.
Thurow, Lester (2007) "A Chinese Century? Maybe It's the Next One," *New York Times*, Business Section (19 Aug.): 4.

Tian, Mingming (2011) "Zhongguo Duiwai Zhijie Touzi de Xianzhuang Fenxi" [Analysis of the Current State of China's Outward Direct Investment], *Jingying Guanlizhe* [Manager Journal] 6.

Tilly, Charles (ed.) (1975) *The Formation of National States in Western Europe*, Princeton, NJ: Princeton University Press.

—— (ed.) (1985) "War Making and State Making as Organized Crime," in Peter B. Evans, Dietrich Rueschemeyer and Theda Skocpol (eds), *Bringing the State Back In*, New York: Cambridge University Press, pp. 169–191.

—— (ed.) (1992) *Coercion, Capital, and European States, AD 990–1992*, Cambridge, MA, and Oxford: Blackwell.

—— (1997) "Means and Ends of Comparison in Macrosociology," *Comparative Social Research* 16: 43–53.

—— (2001) "Mechanisms in Political Processes," *Annual Review of Political Science* 4: 21–41.

Tin, Maung Maung Than (2010) "Myanmar: kokka oyobi Kokugun no Anzen Hosho jo no Kadai" [Myanmar: Security Tasks of the State and the National Army], in Boeisho Boei Kenkyusho [Defense Research Institute, Ministry of Defense] ed., *Ajia Taiheiyo Shokoku no Anzen Hosho jo no Kadai to Kokubo Bumon he no Eikyo* [Security Tasks in Asia-Pacific States and their Influence on Defense Sectors], Tokyo: Boeisho Boei Kenkyusho, pp. 135–53.

Tjon Sie Fat, Paul (2009) *Chinese New Migrants in Suriname: The Inevitability of Ethnic Performing*, Amsterdam: Amsterdam University Press.

Toer, Pramoedya Ananta (1980) *Anak Semua Bangsa: Sebuah Roman* [Child of All Nations: A Novel], Jakarta: Hasta Mitra.

Tong, Shijun (2006) "Chinese Thought and Dialogical Universalism," in Gerard Delanty (ed.), *Europe and Asia beyond East and West*, New York: Routledge, pp. 305–15.

Totten, Sanden (2011) "China Invests in Filmmaking, for Image and Profit." Online. Available at:http://www.npr.org/2011/06/19/137253607/china-invests-in-filmmaking-for-image-and-profit?ft=1&f=1001 (accessed 27 June 2011).

Tsai, Kellee S. (2007) *Capitalism without Democracy: The Private Sector in Contemporary China*, Ithaca, NY: Cornell University Press.

Tsai, Ming-chin (2009) *Revisiting the Cultural Revolution: Taking a Position between Transcendence and Re-presentation* [Huiyi wen ge: zai chaoyue yu zaixian jian de xuanze shiye], Taipei: Research and Educational Center for China Studies and Cross-Taiwan Strait Relations, Department of Political Science, National Taiwan University.

Tsugami, Toshiya (2003) *Chugoku Taito: Nihon wa Nani wo Nasu beki ka* [The Rise of China: What Should Japan Do?], Tokyo: Nihon Keizai Sinbunsha.

Tsui, Kai-yuen and Wang, Youqiang (2004) "Between Separate Stoves and a Single Menu: Fiscal Decentralization in China," *China Quarterly* 177: 71–90.

Tsunekawa, Jun (2009a) *Chugoku no Taito: Tonan Ajia to Nihon no Taio* [The Rise of China: Southeast Asian and Japanese Responses], Tokyo: Boeisho Boei Kenkyusho.

—— (ed.) (2009b) *The Rise of China: Responses from Southeast Asia and Japan*, NIDS Joint Research Series No. 4, Tokyo: National Institute for Defense Studies.

Tsygankov, Andrei P. (2003) "The Irony of Western Ideas in a Multicultural World: Russians' Intellectual Engagement with the 'End of History' and 'Clash of Civilizations,'" *International Studies Review* 5: 53–76.

—— (2008) "Self and Other in International Relations Theory: Learning from Russian Civilizational Debates," *International Studies Review* 10: 762–75.

Tu, Weiming (1991) "Implications of the Rise of 'Confucian' Asia: A Confucian Perspective on the Rise of Industrial East Asia," in Silke Krieger and Rolf Trauzettedl (eds), *Confucianism and the Modernization of China*, Mainz: v. Hase & Koehler, pp. 29–41.

—— (1994a) "Cultural China: The Periphery as Center," in Weiming Tu (ed.), *The Living Tree: The Changing Meaning of Being Chinese Today*, Stanford, CA: Stanford University Press, pp. 1–34.

—— (ed.) (1994b) *The Living Tree: The Changing Meaning of Being Chinese Today*, Stanford, CA: Stanford University Press.

—— (2000) "Multiple Modernities: A Preliminary Inquiry into the Implications of East Asian Modernity," in Lawrence E. Harrison and Samuel P. Huntington (eds), *Culture Matters: How Values Shape Human Progress*, New York: Basic Books, pp. 256–66.

—— (2002) "Multiple Modernities: Implications of the Rise of 'Confucian' East Asia," in Karl-Heinz Pohl and Anselm Müller (eds), *Chinese Ethics in a Global Context: Moral Bases of Contemporary Societies*, Leiden: Brill (Sinica Leidensia, Vol. 56), pp. 55–77.

Uchimura, Hiroko and Jutting, Johannes P. (2009) "Fiscal Decentralization, Chinese Style: Good for Health Outcomes?" *World Development* 37(12): 1926–34.

Uy, Veronica (2007) "Chinese Embassy, Filipino-Chinese Group Slam Santiago 'Slur,'" *Philippine Daily Inquirer* (27 Sept.). Online. Available at: http://globalnation.inquirer.net/news/breakingnews/view_article.php?article_id=91094 (accessed 8 April 2008).

Varshney, Ashutosh (1993) "Contested Meanings: India's National Identity, Hindu Nationalism, and the Politics of Anxiety," *Dædalus* 122(3): 227–61.

Vu, Tuong (2010) "Studying the State through State Formation," *World Politics* 62(1): 148–75.

Vyas, Utpal (2011) *Soft Power in Japan–China Relations: State, Substate and Non-state Relations*, London and New York: Routledge.

Wachman, Alan M. (1994) *Taiwan: National Identity and Democracy*, Armonk, NY: M.E. Sharpe.

—— (2007) *Why Taiwan? Geostrategic Rationales for China's Territorial Integrity*, Stanford, CA: Stanford University Press.

Waldner, David (2007) "Lessons from the Study of Mass Extinctions," in Richard Ned Lebow and Mark Lichbach (eds), *Theory and Evidence in Comparative Politics and International Relations*, New York: Palgrave Macmillan, pp. 145–75.

Waldron, Arthur (1990) *The Great Wall of China*, Cambridge: Cambridge University Press.

Waltz, Kenneth N. (1979) *Theory of International Politics*, Reading, MA: Addison-Wesley.

Wang, Binbin (2000) "Gezai Zhongxi zhi jian de Riben: Xiandai Hanyu zhong de Riyu 'wailaiyu' wenti" [Japan between China and the West: The Question of Japanese-imported Terms in the Chinese Language], in He Xiongfei (ed.), *Shouwang Linghun: Shanghai Wenxue Suibi Jingpin* [Vigilant Spirit: Essays from Shanghai Literature], Shanghai: Zhonghua Gongshang Lianhe Chubanshe.

Wang, Fan-sen (2000) *Fu Ssu-nien: A Life in Chinese History and Politics*, Cambridge: Cambridge University Press.

Wang, Gungwu (1968) "Early Ming Relations with Southeast Asia: A Background Essay," in John K. Fairbank (ed.), *The Chinese World Order: Traditional China's Foreign Relations*, Cambridge, MA: Harvard University Press, pp. 34–62.

—— (1981) "The Limits of Nanyang Nationalism, 1912–37," in Wang Gungwu, *Community and Nation: Essays on Southeast Asia and the Chinese*, Singapore: Heinemann, pp. 142–58.

—— (1984) "The Chinese Urge to Civilize: Reflections on Change," *Journal of Asian History* 18: 1–34.

—— (1992a) "The Origins of Hua-Ch'iao," in Wang Gungwu, *Community and Nation: China, Southeast Asia and Australia*, New South Wales: Association of Asian Studies in Australia and Allen and Unwin, pp. 1–10.

Wang, Gungwu (1992b) "Trade and Cultural Values: Australia and the Four Dragons," in Wang Gungwu, *Community and Nation: China, Southeast Asia and Australia*, New South Wales: Association of Asian Studies in Australia and Allen and Unwin, pp. 301–13.

—— (2000) *The Chinese Overseas: From Earthbound China to the Quest for Autonomy*, Cambridge, MA: Harvard University Press.

—— (2003 [1991]) "Lu Xun, Lim Boon Keng, and Confucianism," in Wang Gungwu, *China and the Chinese Overseas*, Singapore: Eastern University Press, pp. 163–84.

—— (2004) "Cultural Centres for the Chinese Overseas," in Gregor Benton and Hong Liu (eds), *Diasporic Chinese Ventures: The Life and Work of Wang Gungwu*, London and New York: RoutledgeCurzon, pp. 210–26.

—— (2011) E-mail to author, 10 January.

Wang, Hongying (2003) "National Image Building and Chinese Foreign Policy," *China: An International Journal* 1(1): 46–72.

Wang, Jenn-hwan (2006) "China's Dualist Model on Technological Catching Up: A Comparative Perspective," *Pacific Review* 19(3): 385–403.

Wang, Jisi (2005) "China's Search for Stability with America," *Foreign Affairs* 84(5): 39–48.

Wang, Q. Edward (2010) "'Rise of the Great Powers' = Rise of China? Challenges of the Advancement of Global History in the People's Republic of China," *Journal of Contemporary China* 19: 273–89.

Wang, Shaoguang (2003) "China's Changing of Guard: The Problem of State Weakness," *Journal of Democracy* 14(1).

Wang, Wen (2007) "Dong(nan)ya Diqu Huaren Ziben Zai Hua Waishang Zhijie Touzi Xianzhuang ji Qushi Fenxi" [Analysis on the Current Situation and Trend of FDI in China from Chinese Capital in (South) East Asia], *Jingji Jingwei* [Economic Survey] 6.

Wang, Ying and Lie, Ma (2008) "Bid to Attract Foreign Students Gears Up," *China Daily* (24 Apr.): 2.

Wang, Yiwei (2002) "Between Science and Art: Questionable International Relations Theories," *Japanese Journal of Political Science* 8(2): 191–208.

Wang, Yizhou (n.d.) "Definitions of Non-traditional Security and Its Implications for China," translation available at: http://www.irchina.org/en/pdf/wyz07a.pdf.

Wang, Yuan-kang (2001) "Power Politics of Confucian China," PhD Dissertation, University of Chicago.

—— (2002) "Culture and Foreign Policy: What Imperial China Tells Us," Paper prepared for delivery at the Annual Meeting of the Political Science Association, Boston, 29 Aug.–1 Sept.

—— (2011) *Harmony and War: Confucian Culture and Chinese Power Politics*, New York: Columbia University Press.

Wang, Yu-ching (2008) *Tongshi, buguo fenkai: xifang pubianzhuyi lunshu xia de rujia yu yisilan* [Contemporaneous and Yet Separate: Confucianism and Islam in Western Universalist Narratives], Taipei: Research and Educational Center for China Studies and Cross-Taiwan Strait Relations, Department of Political Science, National Taiwan University.

Wang, Zhengyi (1997) "Dongya Guoji Tixi Keyi Chengwei Keneng?" [Is an East Asian International Order Possible?], *World Economics and Politics* 2: 17–20.

Watson, James L. (1993) "Rites or Beliefs? The Construction of a Unified Culture in Late Imperial China," in Lowell Dittmer and Samuel S. Kim (eds), *China's Quest for National Identity*, Ithaca, NY: Cornell University, pp. 80–103.

Wei, Zhongyou (2006) "In the Shadow of Hegemony: Strategic Choices," *Chinese Journal of International Politics* 1(2): 195–229.

Weidenbaum, Murray and Hughes, Samuel (1996) *The Bamboo Network: How Expatriate Chinese Entrepreneurs Are Creating a New Economic Superpower in Asia*, New York: Free Press, Martin Kessler Books.
Whittaker, Hugh D., Zhu, Tianbiao, Sturgeon, Timothy, Tsai, Mon Han, and Okita, Toshie (2010) "Compressed Development," *Studies in Comparative International Development* 45: 439–67.
Wickberg, Edgar (1965) *The Chinese in Philippine Life, 1850–1898*, New Haven, CT: Yale University Press.
—— (2006) "Hokkien–Philippines Familial Transnationalism, 1949–75," in Maria N. Ng and Philip Holden (eds), *Reading Chinese Transnationalisms: Society, Literature, Film*, Hong Kong: Hong Kong University Press, pp. 17–36, 190–2.
Wight, Colin (2004) "Theorizing the Mechanisms of Conceptual and Semiotic Space," *Philosophy of the Social Sciences* 34(2): 283–99.
Williams, David (2005) *Defending Japan's Pacific War: The Kyoto School Philosophers and Post-White Power*, London: RoutledgeCurzon.
Williams, Lea (1960) *Overseas Chinese Nationalism: The Genesis of the Pan-Chinese Movement in Indonesia, 1900–1916*, Glencoe, IL: Free Press.
Wittfogel, Karl (1957) *Oriental Despotism*, New Haven, CT: Yale University Press.
Wolfe, Martin (2011a) "East and West Converge on a Problem," *Financial Times* (12 Jan.): 9.
—— (2011b) "In the Grip of a Great Convergence," *Financial Times* (5 Jan.): 9.
Wolfers, Arnold (1962) *Discord and Collaboration: Essays on International Politics*, Baltimore, MD: Johns Hopkins University Press.
Wolff, Larry (1994) *Inventing Eastern Europe: The Map of Civilization on the Mind of the Enlightenment*, Stanford, CA: Stanford University Press.
Womack, Brantly (ed.) (2010a) *China's Rise in Historical Perspective*, Lanham, MD: Rowman & Littlefield.
—— (2010b) *China among Unequals: Asymmetric Foreign Relationships in Asia*, Singapore: World Scientific Publishing.
Wong, Christine (2009) "Rebuilding Government for the 21st Century: Can China Incrementally Reform the Public Sectors?" *China Quarterly* 200: 929–52.
Wong, John (1984) *The Political Economy of China's Changing Relations with Southeast Asia*, London/New York: Macmillan Press.
—— (2003) "The Rise of China: Bane or Boon to Southeast Asia," *Harvard Asia Quarterly* 7(2): 23–30.
—— (2007) "Oral History Interview," 5–9 November, Research and Educational Center for China Studies and Cross-Strait Relations of the Department of Political Science, National Taiwan University. Online. Available at: http://140.112.150.151/RAEC/act/Singapore-1.doc (accessed 30 April 2010).
Wong, John and Lai, Hongyi (2006) "Changing Academic Challenges of the Southeast Asian Studies Field in China," in Saw Swee Hock and John Wong (eds), *Southeast Asian Studies in China*, Singapore: Institute of Southeast Asian Studies, pp. 8–29.
Wong, R. Bin (1997) *China Transformed: Historical Change and the Limits of European Experience*, Ithaca, NY: Cornell University Press.
—— (2003) "Beyond Sinocentrism and Eurocentrism," *Science & Society* 67(2) (Summer): 173–84.
Wong, Siu-lun (1979) *Sociology and Socialism in Contemporary China*, London: Routledge and Kegan Paul.
Woodside, Alexander (1971) *Vietnam and the Chinese Model: A Comparative Study of Nguyen and Ch'ing Civil Government in the First Half of the Nineteenth Century*, Cambridge, MA: Harvard University Press.

Woodside, Alexander (2006) *Lost Modernities: China, Vietnam, Korea, and the Hazards of World History*, Cambridge, MA: Harvard University Press.
—— (2007) "The Centre and the Borderlands in Chinese Political Theory," in Diana Lary (ed.), *The Chinese State at the Borders*, Vancouver: UBC Press.
World Bank (1993) *The East Asian Miracle: Economic Growth and Public Policy*, New York: Oxford University Press.
Worth, Dean S. (1998) "Language," in Nicholas Rzhevsky (ed.), *Modern Russian Culture*, Cambridge: Cambridge University Press, pp. 1–16.
Wright, Tim (2007) "State Capacity in Contemporary China: 'Closing the Pits and Reducing Coal Production,'" *Journal of Contemporary China* 16(51): 173–94.
Wuthnow, Joel (2008) "The Concept of Soft Power in China's Strategic Discourse," *Issues and Studies* 44(2): 1–28.
Xiamen Min'nan Tourism and Culture Industry Co. (2010) *Magic Min'nan*, Xiamen: Xiamen Min'nan Tourism and Culture Industry Co., Ltd.
Xing, Yuqing (2010) "Facts about and Impacts of FDI on China and the World Economy," *China: An International Journal* 8(2): 309–27.
Xu, Lili and Yu, Xiaofeng (2009a) "Biananxue Chuyi" [An Opinion on the Development of "Frontier Security Studies"], *Zhejiang Daxue Xuebao* #5: 5–18.
—— (2009b) "Lun bianjiang Minzu Diqu Feichuantong Anquan Wenti ji Ying Dui" [Coping with Non-traditional Security Issues in Frontier Nationality Regions], *Minzu Yanjiu* #5: 34–43.
Xu Xin (1993) "Wan Qing Zhongguo Waijiao: Lishi Chongtu zhong de Shiluo yu Gengxin" [Late Qing's Diplomacy: Failure and Renewal in Historical Conflict], in Yuan Ming (ed.), *Kua Shiji de Tiaozhan* [Challenges at the Turn of the Centuries], Chongqin: Chongqin Publishing House.
—— (2008) "The Chinese Concept of 'Twenty Years' Strategic Opportunities' and Its Implications for Asian Security Order," Paper prepared for delivery at the Asian Security Conference, New Delhi.
—— (2009) "The Power of Identity: China and East Asian Security Politics after the Cold War," Cornell University, Government Department, unpublished book manuscript.
Yabuki, Shin (2010) *Zusetsu Chūgoku-ryoku* [China's Power: Diagrams], Tokyo: Soso-sha.
Yamamoto, Nobuto (1995) "Lim Boon Keng ni okeru 'Kindai teki Chūgokujin' no sōzō – 'Shinpo' no jidai ni okeru shoki Nanyō kajin nationalism kenkyū shiron" [Lim Boon Keng and the Creation of the "Modern Chinese": A Preliminary Study of Early Nanyang Chinese Nationalism in the Age of "Progress"], *Hōgaku Kenkyū* 68(5): 27–66.
Yan, Anlin (2008) "Cong 86 Zi Dui-Tai Fangzhen Kan Wang Daohan Huizhang de Weida Renge" [The 86-Character Maxim and Wang Daohan's Great Personality], People's Daily Website. Available at: http://tw.people.com.cn/BIG5/26741/139936/139937/8504213.html.
Yan, Xuetong (2001) "The Rise of China in Chinese Eyes," *Journal of Contemporary China* 10: 33–9.
—— (2006) "The Rise of China and Its Power Status," *Chinese Journal of International Politics* 1(1): 5–33.
—— (2008) "Xun Zi's Thoughts on International Politics and Their Implications," *Chinese Journal of International Politics* 2(1): 135–65.
—— (2010) "Introduction," in Sun Xuefeng, Matt Ferchen, and M. Taylor Fravel (eds), *Rethinking China's Rise: A Chinese Journal of International Politics Reader*, Oxford: Oxford University Press, pp. 1–7.

—— (2011) *Ancient Chinese Thought, Modern Chinese Power*, Princeton, NJ: Princeton University Press.
Yang, Dali L. (2003) "China's Changing of Guard: State Capacity on the Rebound," *Journal of Democracy* 14(1).
—— (2004) *Remaking the Chinese Leviathan: Market Transition and the Politics of Governance in China*, Stanford, CA: Stanford University Press.
Yang, Jiemian (2007) "China's Perspective on International System: Soft Power and Public Goods," *International Review/Global Review* (trial issue): 94–112.
Yang, Kuisong (2010) *Zhongjian Didai de Geming* [Revolution in the Intermediate Zone], Taiyuan: Shanxi People's Press.
Yang, Lien-sheng (1968) "Historical Notes on the Chinese World Order," in John K. Fairbank (ed.), *The Chinese World Order: Traditional China's Foreign Relations*, Cambridge, MA: Harvard University Press, pp. 20–33.
Yang, Yao (2010) "The End of the Beijing Consensus," *Foreign Affairs*. Online. Available at: http://www.foreignaffairs.com/articles/65947/the-end-of-the-beijing-consensus?page=2 (accessed 15 February 2011).
Yang, Ying (2007) "China's Soft Power and Its National Image," Paper presented at the Annual Meeting of the International Studies Association 48th Annual Convention, Chicago, 28 Feb.–3 Mar.
Yao, Zhizhong, and Li, Zhongmin (2011) "Zhongguo Duiwai Zhijie Touzi de Fazhan Qushi yu Zhengce Zhanwang" [China's Outbound FDI: Trends and Policy Outlook], *Guoji Jingji Pinglun* [Review of International Economics] 2: 127–40.
Yau, Shuk-Ting Kinnia (2009) "The Early Development of East Asian Cinema in a Regional Context," *Asian Studies Review* 33: 161–73.
Yeo, Yukyung (2009) "Remaking the Chinese State and the Nature of Economic Governance? The Early Appraisal of the 2008 'Super-Ministry' Reform," *Journal of Contemporary China* 18(62): 729–43.
Yep, Ray (2008) "Enhancing the Redistributive Capacity of the Chinese State? Impact of Fiscal Reforms on County Finance," *Pacific Review* 21(2): 231–55.
Yong, Maj Goh Kong (1999) "Is China Predisposed to Using Force? Confucian–Mencian and Sunzi Paradigms in Chinese Strategic Culture," *Journal of the Singapore Armed Forces* 25(4). Online. Available at: http://www.mindef.gov.sg/safti/pointer/back/journals/1999/Vol25_4/16.htm (accessed 16 March 2008).
Young, Ken (1999) "Consumption, Social Differentiation and Self-Definition of the New Rich in Industrialising Southeast Asia," in Michael Pinches (ed.), *Culture and Privilege in Capitalist Asia*, London and New York: Routledge, pp. 56–85.
Yu, Xintian (2007) "The Role of Soft Power in China's External Strategy," *International Review/Global Review* (trial issue):113–27.
Yu, Ying-shih (1990) "Changing Conceptions of National History in Twentieth-Century China," *Conceptions of National History: Proceedings of Nobel Symposium 78*, pp. 155–74.
Yuan, Yuan, Tao, Sisi, and Zhao, Huan (2010) "Gongzhu Bianjiang Anquan zhi Ji" [Establishing the Foundation of Frontier Security], *Outlook Weekly*. Online. Available at: http://blog.sina.com.cn/s/blog_631636840100hps7.html (accessed 27 July 2011).
Zakaria, Fareed (1994) "Culture is Destiny: A Conversation with Lee Kuan Yew," *Foreign Affairs* 73(2): 109–24.
—— (2006) "The U.S. Can Out-Charm China," *Newsweek* (12 Dec.): 45.
Zeitlin, Jonathan (2000) "Introduction: Americanization and Its Limits: Reworking US Technology and Management in Postwar Europe and Japan," in Jonathan Zeitlin and Gary

Herrigel (eds), *Americanization and Its Limits: Reworking US Technology and Management in Postwar Europe and Japan*, Oxford: Oxford University Press, pp. 1–50.

Zhan, Jing Vivian (2009) "Decentralizing China: Analysis of Central Strategies in China's Fiscal Reforms," *Journal of Contemporary China* 18(60): 445–62.

Zhang, Biwu (2005) "Chinese Perceptions of American Power, 1991–2004," *Asian Survey* 45(5): 667–86.

Zhang, Feng (2009) "Rethinking the 'Tribute System': Broadening the Conceptual Horizon of Historical East Asian Politics," *Chinese Journal of International Politics* 2(4): 545–74.

—— (2010a) "How Hierarchic Was the Historical East Asia System? East Asian International Relations during the Ming–Qing period, 1368–1800," Paper prepared for the roundtable on the nature of political and spiritual relations among Asian leaders and polities from the fourteenth to the eighteenth centuries, Institute of Asian Research, University of British Columbia (19–21 Apr.).

—— (2010b) "The Tianxia System: World Order in A Chinese Utopia," *Global Asia* 4(4): 108–12.

—— (2011) "The Rise of Chinese Exceptionalism in International Relations," Unpublished paper, Murdoch University (January).

Zhang, Kaiyuan (ed.) (2002) *Zhongguo Jingji Shi* [Economic History of China], Beijing: Higher Education Publisher.

Zhang, Nianchi (1998) "Gongtong Dizao Tongyi Fanrong Fuqiang Minzhu Wenming de Xin Zhongguo" [Mutual Constitution of Unified, Prosperous, Strong, Democratic, and Civilized New China], *China Review* 2 (Feb.): 22–8.

Zhang, Ruizhuang (2008) "The Rise of China and Its Implications for the United States," Unpublished paper, Nankai University.

Zhang, Yazhong (2009) "Zhuiyi Wang Daohan Xiangsheng de Gongtong Dizao Lun" [Retrospection of Mr. Wang Daohan's Thesis of "Mutual Constitution"], *ChinaReviewNews.com*. Online. Available at: http://gb.chinareviewnews.com/crn-webapp/mag/docDetail.jsp?coluid=61&docid=101181344 (accessed 16 January 2011).

Zhang, Yongjin (2003) "Reconsidering the Economic Internationalization of China: Implications of the WTO Membership," *Journal of Contemporary China* 12(37): 699–714.

Zhao, Tingyang (2006) "Rethinking Empire from a Chinese Concept 'All-under-Heaven,'" *Social Identities* 12(1): 29–41.

—— (2009a) "A Political World Philosophy in Terms of All-under-heaven (Tian-xia)," *Diogenes* 221: 5–18.

—— (2009b) *Huai Shijie Yanjiu: Zuowei Diyi Zhexue de Zhengzhi Zhexue* [Study of the Bad World: Political Philosophy as the First Philosophy], Renmin University of China Press.

Zheng, Bijian (2005a) *China's Peaceful Rise: Speeches of Zheng Bijian*, Washington, DC: Brookings Institution.

—— (2005b) "China's 'Peaceful Rise' to Great Power Status," *Foreign Affairs* 84(5) (Sept./Oct.): 17–20.

—— (2005c) *Peaceful Rise: China's New Road to Development*, Beijing: Central Party School Press.

Zheng, Yongnian (1999) *Discovering Chinese Nationalism in China: Modernization and International Relations*, New York: Cambridge University Press.

—— (2004) *Globalization and State Transformation in China*, Cambridge: Cambridge University Press.

—— (2006) "Explaining the Sources of de facto Federalism in Reform China: Intergovernmental Decentralization, Globalization, and Central–Local Relations," *Japanese Journal of Political Science* 7(2): 101–26.

—— (2007) "China's Pragmatic Nationalism: Is It Manageable?" *Washington Quarterly*, 29(1): 131–44.
Zheng, Yongnian and Wong, John (eds) (2004) *The SARS Epidemic: Challenges to China's Crisis Management*, Singapore and London: World Scientific.
Zhou, Hong (2010) "The World Implications of the 'Chinese Road' in the Context of Globalization," *Social Sciences in China* 31(2): 5–20.
Zhou, Liqun and Xie, Siquan (eds) (2008) *Zhongguo Jingji Gaige 30 Nian: Minying Jingji Juan* [30 Years of Chinese Economic Reform: Volume on Private Economy], Chongqing: Chongqing University Press.
Zhou, Ping (2008) Woguo de Bianjiang yu Bianjiang Zhili [China's Frontiers and Frontier Governance], Zhengzhixue Yanjiu #2: 68–72.
Zhu, Danting (2010) "Yue chang yue you ai – he ku bao dong gua" [Singing in Cantonese for love of Cantonese: Why bother to speak Mandarin], Nan Fang Du Shi Bao [Southern Metropolitan Daily] (12 Jul.). Nandu Daily. Online. Available at: http://gcontent.oeeee.com/9/ad/9adeb82fffb5444e/Blog/89a/b53716.html (accessed 5 March 2011).
Zhu, Tianbiao (2007) "Rethinking Import-Substituting Industrialization," in Ha-Joon Chang (ed.), *Institutional Change and Economic Development*, New York: United Nations University Press.
Zuberi, Nabeel (2005) "Blessings: Globalization and Culture as Hybrid Discourses," *Global Media and Communication* 1(1): 105–20.
Zweig, David (2002) *Internationalizing China: Domestic Interests and Global Linkages*, Ithaca, NY: Cornell University Press.
Zweig, David and Han, Donglin (2010) "Can a Developing Country Have Too Many Educated Returnees: Are Chinese 'Sea Turtles' Becoming 'Seaweed'?" in Christiane Kuptsch (ed.), *The Internationalization of Labor Markets: The Social Dimension of Globalization*, Geneva: International Labour Organization (ILO), pp. 89–104.

INDEX

Abe Shinzo 126, 170
accommodation: 218; of China 129, 139, 198; as Chinese strategy 26, 37n130, 43, 81, 129, 139
accountability 104
acculturation 13, 176, 183, 202n41
adaptation 29, 104–6, 156, 162, 168–73, 218–19, 224–31
Adler, Emanuel 236
Africa 14, 16, 30–1, 137, 213, 231, 234; Forum on China-Africa Cooperation 31
agriculture 102–3; commodities 112, 184; as foundation 111, 113; private household farming 112; in Thailand 131
aid, foreign 135–8; concessional loans 131, 137, 141–5
All-under-heaven *see under* unity
Americanization 9, 99, 189, 210
Amoy 185, 188
anarchy 36n126, 69
Anglo-Chinese 12, 70–3, 153–4, 185–9, 198–200, 203nn51,52,53, 69, 204n88, 205n121, 228; scholarship 169–70; and US hegemony 187–92
anime 191,194, 204nn93,100
An Kyong-su 185
anti-Chinese 16, 93, 161, 165, 188
APEC 85, 91
Appiah, Kwame Anthony 237
Aquino, Corazon 175
aristocracy 8, 27, 187, 235

ASEAN 30, 120–1, 125–34, 136, 139, 147, 148n32; ADMM-Plus 128, 148n32; ASEAN Plus Three: 23, 125–8; ASEAN Plus Six: 126, 128; ASEAN Regional Forum 25, 30, 125, 127–8, 135
Asian Development Bank 85, 131
Asianism 184–6
Aso Taro 170
assimilation 8; of non-Han 12–14, 48, 58, 199; and Southeast Asia 179–80, 190
Association for Relations Across the Taiwan Straits (ARATS) 89, 91
atheism 11, 213; *see also* religion
Aung San Suu Kyi 131
Australia 167; and ASEAN 126, 148n32; and Indonesia 132, 134; and Trans-Pacific Partnership 127
authoritarianism; and China 12, 106, 205n106; "fragmented" 106; and Indonesia 131–2; and Russia 214; and Taiwan 85, 223; and Vietnam 138
autocracy 214
automobile industry 107–8, 131, 229
autonomy, regional 6, 42, 46–7, 51, 59–60, 62, 66, 77–80, 222–3; special administrative regions 79–80, 82–4; and Taiwan 88; and Tibet 26

balancing: of civilizations 216; of ideas 67; limited alignment 129, 138, 225; multipolarity vs. bipolarity 36n126, 45, 126, 129; of power 13, 21, 24–6,

35n118, 36n126, 37n137, 67, 69, 77, 122, 162, 172, 225; power transition 121–2; of practice 210, 217–18; soft-balancing 129, 135–6, 138, 22; *see also* bandwagoning; realism
Bandung Conference 202n34, 232
bandwagoning 21, 24–5, 36n126, 122, 129, 138–9, 162, 225; *see also* balancing; realism
Bangladesh 136
banking: Asian Development Bank 85, 131; British 19; China Development Bank 133; China Export-Import Bank 144–5, 149n68; Chinese banks 106, 141, 143–5, 149n66, 226; and German development 101; non-performing loans 106
Bank of China 144–5
barbarians 3, 11, 58, 70, 81, 196, 215; Eastern Europe 213
Barma, Naazneen 6
Barnett, Michael 2, 32n8, 237n17
Beijing consensus 12, 17
Bennett, Scott 24
Bernal, Martin 3, 240n102
biananxue see *border security studies*
bianjiang see *frontier*
bianjiangxue see *frontier studies*
bilateralism 20, 30–1, 122, 129; and India 137; and Japan 25, 139, 187; and Southeast Asia 130–1, 133, 135, 187; territorial disputes 125; of United States 25, 26, 130, 187
bipolarity 129
Bolshevism 186
borderlands 43–53, 111; *see also* frontiers
borders: ambiguity/fluidity of 11, 41, 42, 44, 50, 67, 69, 93; crossing 42, 50–1
border security studies (*biananxue*) 41, 53–7
Börzel, Tanja 218
boundaries *see* borders
Bourdieu, Pierre 220
brain drain: vs. "brain circulation" 16
brands: brand names 109, 112; China's "white brand" 17; Confucianism as 29
Brandt, Willy 66
Braudel, Fernand 217
Britain *see* England
brokerage 85; and compressed development 219, 224; cultural 153, 227; and Japan 25
Brunei 124, 125, 127
Buddhism 11, 13, 37n128, 202n41; Buddhist associations 16; as Indian import 45, 166, 168, 183; and Japan 229, 230
bureaucracy 101, 104–7, 114–15, 119n83; and Americanization 189; bureaucratic capitalism 147, 149n66; imperial 13; and regionalism 185, 187
Burlingame, Anson 161
Burma/Myanmar: ethnic composition 16; and regionalism 121, 123, 136–44, 146, 147, 225–6; and tribute system 201n14
Bush, George W. 1, 22, 135, 170
business alliances, transnational 141–7, 226; *see also* cooperation, economic; investment
Buzan, Barry 6, 55

Callahan, William 4, 6, 11, 198
Cambodia 130, 135, 187; Chinese language 15; economic factors 121, 136
Canton 164, 185, 188; Cantonese language 12, 185, 191, 192, 195–7, 203n69; 204n100, 205n121
capacity, state 15, 103–4, 164, 215
capitalism 5, 73–4, 153, 156, 174nn8,9; bureaucratic 147, 149n66; Chinese 12, 18–19, 21, 30, 99, 172; crony 149n66; and developmental state 18, 101; East Asian 11–12; "made in China" 18, 153; merchant 30; petty 112, 115; "Red Capitalist" 198
Carlson, Allen 6, 9, 25, 30, 41, 219, 221–3
Carter, Jimmy 77
CCP *see under* Communist Party
censorship 16
centralization 9, 30, 66–7, 71, 79–80; centralization/decentralization swings 105, 111–12, 114–15; *see also* decentralization
centrism 155, 158–63
Chen Shui-bian 67, 83, 85, 87–8, 223
Chiang Ching-kuo 83, 85–7, 89
Chiang Kai-shek 67, 74–6, 86–7, 202n34, 223
Chile 127
"Chimerica" 31
China: "China threat" 22, 35n118, 163; "cultural China" 11, 16, 197, 199, 228; as developing country 17; as floating signifier 177–8, 192, 200; as fragile 17, 49, 66, 106; Greater China 11, 16, 68, 82–5, 93, 169, 192, 198, 205n106, 228; as great power 1, 93; and misunderstanding 159–60; multiple traditions of 3, 12, 99–100, 113, 115,

117, 212, 224; "one China" 65, 67–8, 72–9, 87–92, 95n71, 224; as passive 49, 160, 198; as victim 17, 171; *Zhongguo* 69, 177
China Development Bank 133
China Export Import Bank 144–5, 149n68
Chinatowns 143, 190, 193
"Chindia" 167, 172, 173
Chinese (language) 15–16, 140–1, 154, 163, 175, 177, 184, 186, 196, 204n100, 205nn120,121; Cantonese 12, 185, 191, 192, 195–7, 203n69; 204n100, 205n121; Mandarin 4, 12, 15, 189–97, 203–4n69, 205n121; written 180, 184–5, 189, 194, 205n120; *see also* language
Chow, Rey 200
Christensen, Tom 5
Christianity 3, 16, 37n128, 179, 236; and Confucianism 11, 185; expansion of 213; as "Western Christendom" 212–13
Chua, Amy 204n88
Chu Shulong 34n97
citizenship 46, 82–4, 199, 205n121, 236; dual 82, 206n121; second class 188
civility 202n41, 216
civilizations: clash of 153–4, 166, 210–11, 215–17, 221, 236; civilizational analysis 211–18; convergence of 10; empathic 211; geo-civilizations 155, 166, 168, 173; global market civilization 27; and mechanisms 218–20; of modernity 11, 214–17, 230; processes and practices 218–37; and religion 100, 212–13, 215, 217; singular/unidirectional understandings 4–5, 10, 130, 138, 154, 176, 199, 210; and temporality 2, 117, 198, 211, 218, 222; and values 3, 100, 111, 172, 210, 213–16
civilized/uncivilized 3, 58, 74, 212, 215, 235; *see also* barbarians
civil war, Chinese 73–6, 86, 90, 181
clash: of civilizations 153–4, 166, 210–11, 215–17, 221, 236; of empires 177; of tradition and modernity 116
class, social 19, 136, 180; middle class 12, 15, 131, 180, 187
classification system, national 42, 46, 62, 222; *see also* nationalities
clientelism 104
Clinton, Bill 87
Clinton, Hillary 127, 132
coastal areas 109, 111, 113, 123, 195, 199
Cohen, Paul 5

Cold War 73, 162, 172, 190, 216, 223; early 73, 122; end of 89, 121, 124, 216, 221; and "Free Asia" 86, 122–3, 182, 187–8, 190–1; and India 232; and Japan 122; and Southeast Asia 132, 187, 190; and Taiwan 75, 89, 92, 181–2, 190
collectivization 102, 105, 112; collectively owned enterprises 108–10, 113
Collins, Randall 12
colonialism 198, 199 228; as concept 177; anticolonial struggles 187, 235; Han 228; in India 212, 235; Japanese 86, 223; postcolonial states 26, 86, 188, 190, 198, 199; in Southeast Asia 179–81, 184–5, 187; in Taiwan 86, 223; Western 19, 24, 168 203nn51,52; *see also* imperialism
commodity chains 112
commonwealth 79, 158, 167; Commonwealth of Nations 182, 232
communication 88, 182; facilities 141, 145; and language 183–5, 186, 194; micro-level 159; and technology 102, 217; *see also* language
communism 3, 28, 86, 122, 163; anti-communism 16, 165–6; and Eastern Europe 101; vs. "Free Asia" 86, 122–3, 182, 187–8,190–1; in Southeast Asia 165–6, 186–7, 198; as stereotype 175; *see also* Communist Party; socialism; Soviet Union
Communist Party: Chinese 28, 46, 73–4, 81–2, 116, 119n83, 120; policy toward Taiwan 78, 81, 86–91, 120, 178, 181; Thai 187; Vietnamese 134
competition (as mechanism) 219
compressed development 7, 9, 18, 99–117, 219, 223–4; *see also* development, economic
conceptualization (as mechanism) 219, 227
Confucianism 3, 10–13, 36n126, 37n130, 58, 119n83, 173n8, 182–3, 185–6, 188, 202n41; and Chinese nationalism 72; "Confucian culturalism" 199; Confucian order 27; Confucian studies 165; humanism 10–11, 28, 114; and Japan 11, 229, 230; New Confucianism 10, 17, 28–9; and self-restraint 23
Confucius 4, 29, 240n102; Confucius Peace Prize 16;
Confucius Institutes 15, 29, 205n121
conservatism 61, 123, 186; and civilizational clash 215; in Japan 169, 230–1; in Russia 214; in US 22, 169

constitution: China 74, 82; Japan 170
constitution, mutual: and Sinicization 155–7, 172–3; of united China 90, 95n71 224
consumerism 12, 229–30, 233; American overconsumption 31, 229; consumer goods 108, 229
containment 162, 188; of China 6, 26, 37n137, 122, 129, 188; "double containment" 122; of Japan 122; of jihadism 131; of Soviet Union 77, 122
Copenhagen School 54, 56
corporations, state *see* state-owned enterprises
corruption 86, 110, 116, 119n83, 144, 146, 226
cosmopolitanism 43, 214, 237
crime 137; organized 28, 35n113; transnational 130; wartime 169
crisis, financial 226; and bubbles 19, 102; in China 105–6; East Asian (1997–98): 114, 124, 128, 131, 133, 180, 192; global (2008) 1, 4, 121, 128, 133, 145; Indian (1991) 233; Chinese as "villains", 180
crisis, social 116; *see also* protests/unrest
cronies 133, 143, 146, 175; crony capitalism 149n66
cuisine *see* food
Cui Zhiyuan 12
cultural centers 14; *see also* Confucius Institutes
cultural imperialism 9, 210
culturalism 69, 197; "Confucian culturalism" 199
culturalization 57–60
cultural power 4, 28, 29; *see also* power
Cultural Revolution 47, 67, 113; *see also* revolution
"culture": as imported word 184
culture, popular 7, 14, 15, 175, 182, 181, 192, 200, 229–30; anime 191, 194, 204nn93,100; manga 191–2, 230; music 15, 158, 190–2, 204n100, 230; *see also* film; television
culture, strategic 36n126, 37n130
currency 1, 19, 124, 128; and India 232; and Myanmar 137; renminbi 4, 35n97

da-yitong see under *unity*
Dalai Lama 48; *see also* Tibet
Daoism 11, 202n41
Davidson, Jamie 197
de-Sinicization 9, 65, 67, 169, 176, 188, 227; and Taiwan 65, 67, 85–8, 223

decentralization: centralization/decentralization swings 105, 111–12, 114–15; economic 1, 100, 105, 107, 111–12; in Indonesia 132; in Japan 1; political 9, 181; *see also* centralization
defense budget, Chinese 121
demand, domestic (China) 128
democracy: and China 17, 92, 95n61, 123, 156–7, 163, 169; and Eastern Europe 123; and ethnic relations 60; and India 232; and Indonesia 131–2, 144; and Myanmar 136; and Russia 214; and Taiwan 7, 67, 85–9, 223; and Thailand 144; and Vietnam 135; and Washington Consensus 12
Democratic Progressive Party 86, 88, 91, 95n71; *see also* Taiwan
Deng Xiaoping: and economic reform 120, 122–3, 223; frontier policy 42, 47; pragmatism of 42, 85; and Taiwan 66, 77–82, 85, 87, 92–3, 95n49, 223; and US 77, 122
dependence, trade: in Asian region 22, 26, 29, 130, 131, 134, 140; of China 35n97, 116, 121
despotism 81, 111
deterrence 88, 126
developing countries 101–2, 111, 119n83, 212; China as 17; *see also* Third World
development, economic: compressed 7, 9, 18, 99–117, 219, 223–4; demand-led model 128; flying geese pattern 192; late development 9, 101–3, 115, 116; "peaceful development" 32n13, 54, 90–2, 94; regional 2, 19, 121–47, 180, 184, 192–3; under-development 102; and war 88
developmental state 18, 99–104, 116
dialect 19, 196, 204n69; *see also* language
dialectics 214; and "abduction" 220; globalization 116; of Sinicization 7, 65–8, 223
diaspora 11, 16, 20, 113–14, 153, 155–7, 165, 227; diasporic scholarship 153–7, 168–73, 197; Indian 229, 232; *see also specific individuals*; overseas Chinese
differentiation (vs. acculturation) 13, 27, 157, 211, 217, 226; and governance 66, 69, 78, 80, 106, 224; *see also* acculturation
diplomacy 25, 27, 45, 66, 88, 221, 223; banquet 7; cultural 203n68; diplomatic power 15; "kneeling down" 74; multilateral forum diplomacy 30–1; neighborhood 141; personal 158, 161,

170; public 14, 29–30; resource 226; and Taiwan 25, 67, 73–8, 86, 88, 91; and territorial disputes 127; *see also* normalization
diplomatic relations *see* normalization; recognition, diplomatic
discrimination 7, 188, 225
disease 102; *see also* health
diversity 198; and differentiated rules 43, 46–8, 80, 235; and "harmony" 209; linguistic 212, 234; religious 213; *see also* language; religion
drug trafficking 28, 130
Duan, Jinsheng 53
Duara, Prasenjit 71, 173n9, 233
Dumont, Louis 233
Dung, Nguyen Tan 134–5
Duvall, Raymond 2, 32n8, 237n17

East Asian Community 23, 128, 170
East Asian Institute 165–6, 170
East Asian Summit (EAS) 127–8, 135
East China Sea 127, 129, 202n39
education 12, 102, 110, 184, 186–9; and Anglo-Chinese 199, 203n51; Confucian 185; Education Ministry 15, 29; student exchanges 15, 34nn76,80, 184, 187, 192; *see also* language training
Egypt 214, 232, 237, 240n102
Eisenhower, Dwight 76
Eisenstadt, Shmuel 11–12, 229, 230, 239n93, 240n102
Elias, Norbert, 8, 27, 218, 235
Ellerman, David 104
empire 9, 11, 24, 210, 234; American 228; British 185, 203n52, 228, 232, 234; Chinese 13–14, 16, 24, 43–5, 58, 111–13, 115, 119n83, 179, 181, 183, 209; clash of empires 177, 211, 217; universal emperorship, 13, 36n126; *see also* colonialism; imperialism
energy 137, 140; coal 103, 143; oil and gas 125, 126, 132–3, 137–8, 141–2; pipelines 137–8, 141–2; power plants 126, 133, 135–8, 141–2, 144–5, 226
Engels, Friedrich 186
England 2, 22, 25, 183, 186, 226, 233, 234; British Council 29; culture 187; economic relations 19, 203n52, 229; education 12, 15, 167, 187, 188–9, 192, 203n51; imperialism 82, 176, 179, 181, 185, 187–9, 203nn51,52, 228, 232, 234–6; and India 167, 231–2, 234–6; industrialization 101, 234; and Taiwan 73
English (language) 4, 8, 12, 14, 95n71, 141, 182, 191–3; Anglo-Chinese 12, 70, 153–4, 169–70, 185–9, 199, 203nn51,52,53,69, 204n88, 205n121, 228; and diasporic scholarship 153–4, 163–6, 168–9, 171, 173, 227; and India 212, 232, 236; Sino-Japanese-English 183–7, 191–2, 195, 198, 204n100, 228; impact of translations 59, 67, 177
Enlightenment 71, 82, 213
enterprises: collectively owned 108–10, 113; small- and medium-sized 20, 30, 108–9, 112–13; state-owned 20, 109, 113, 116, 118n64, 137, 142, 226; township and village 108, 113
entrepreneurship 20, 191; cultural 193; political 211
environmentalism 17, 28, 116, 225; ecological security 56, 73
epistemology 159, 160, 168
equality 12, 17, 166; in international relations 24, 73, 75; *see also* inequality
ethnicity 57, 59, 180, 201n20; ethnic Chinese 16, 19–20, 119n78, 134, 176, 178, 180–2, 188–91, 193–200, 205n21; ethnic relations 57–8, 60, 87; ethnic tourism 47, 222
ethnocentrism 196, 199, 214
Eurocentrism 4, 6, 214
Europe: as civilization 8, 27, 186, 209, 212, 213, 215; Europeanization 210; geopolitics 22–5, 27, 36n126, 44, 114; integration 6, 123, 224; and non-traditional security 54; and Orientalism 234; perceptions of China 7–8; vs. Russia 213, 221; "white" Europe 179
Europe, Eastern 101, 123, 213
European Union 16, 30, 124, 126, 136
export-oriented development 128

Fairbank, John 37n130, 69–70, 160, 166, 167, 224
family 11, 114, 173, 175, 197; as Confucian metaphor 29; familial memories 182, 193; family-owned firms 30, 108; Japanese nation as 231; networks 30, 108, 112
Featherstone, Kevin 218
federation 79–80
feminization (of Chinese) 7
Feng, Yi 103
Feng, Youlan 70

feudalism 36n126, 71, 80–1, 177
film 14, 15–16, 29, 183, 190–2, 194–7, 205n121; Bollywood 232; Hollywood 15, 28–9, 187, 189, 190, 191, 197, 232; *see also* culture, popular
financial crisis *see* crisis, financial
Finnemore, Martha 220
flexible politics 7, 9, 103–8, 114–16; *see also* production, flexible
flexiblilty: and Chinese politics 47, 62, 66, 78, 93, 129, 222–4; and Chineseness 183, 199; and compressed development 7, 9–10, 21, 99–117, 119n83, 219, 224; conceptual 222; hyper-flexibility 82; and Japan 229, 231; temporal 51
food: Chinese 7–8, 47; fortune cookie 8; Indian 232–3
formal vs. informal sector 110–11, 225
Foucault, Michel 82
France 2, 111, 187; French language 163, 178, 185, 186, 204n100, 212
Frank, Andre Gunder 4
Freud, Sigmund 235
Friedberg, Aaron 23
frontier (*bianjiang*) 23, 41–64, 69, 75, 81, 86, 92, 176, 201n14, 219, 221–2, 224; borderland political studies 53; border security studies 41, 53–7; culturalizing the frontier 57–60; and Deng Xiaoping 47–50; frontier governance 52; frontier studies (*bianjiangxue*) 41, 50–6, 58, 62, 222; and nontraditional security 41, 53–6, 63, 125, 148n32, 219; and Qing dynasty 13, 23, 43–5, 49, 63n4, 81, 92; silence about 6, 41, 42, 43, 48, 222; and territorial integrity 44, 46–7, 49, 51, 53
frontier studies (*bianjiangxue*) 41, 50–6, 58, 62, 222; *see also* frontier; border security studies
Fujian Province 108, 182, 195, 201n20
Fujita, Koichi 136
Fukuda Yasuo 126, 170
Fukuyama, Francis 214
Fuqua, Antoine 15
Fu Ssu-nien (Fu Sinian) 195

Gandhi, Mahatma 234–5
gender 216, 237; feminization (of Chinese) 7
geography 23 202n39; geo-civilizations 155, 166, 168, 173; "historical geography" 52

Germany 1–2, 22, 111, 120, 235; development strategy of 100–1, 117; as divided nation 66, 123; German language 29, 177, 186, 212
Gerschenkron, Alexander 100
Gladney, Dru 59
globalization 4, 14, 18, 54, 73, 101–3, 115–16, 162, 197–8, 232–3
and China's rise 85–6, 91–2, 94, 99, 159, 197
global value chains 102, 116; *see also* networks
Goldstein, Avery 5
Golwalkar 233
Gramsci, Antonio 209
Great Britain *see* England
Great East Co-prosperity Sphere 159
Greater China 11, 16, 68, 169, 192, 198, 205n106, 228; and "unbundled territoriality" 82–5, 93
Great Leap Forward 115
great powers 93, 129; great power diplomacy 30
Great Wall 43–4, 194, 195, 222
Greece 232; ancient 213, 240n102
Group of Twenty 126
Guangdong Province 100, 108–9, 182, 194, 201n20
Guangzhou 195, 204n100

Haan, Arjan 103
Habermas, Jürgen 220
Hainan Province 127
Hamilton, Gary 100, 112, 211
Han Chinese: chauvinism 61; as civilization 3, 12–13; "Han imperialism" 178, 228; Hanization 13; as "nation" 46, 59; relations with non-Han 12–13, 45–6, 57, 62, 183
Han, Heng 106
harmony: in Chinese tradition 28, 55, 90–1, 116, 166; and "Chindia" 167, 172; and inter-group relations 58; as interesting diversity 209
Hatoyama, Yukio 128, 139, 170
Hau, Caroline 7, 10, 15, 17, 29, 175, 219, 223, 227–8
health 7, 85, 110, 233; nutrition 102
hedging, political 20, 26, 124, 128, 129, 138, 146 225, 227
Hedström, Peter 220
Hegel, G.W.F. 159
hegemony 6, 23, 177; American 68, 122, 176, 187, 189, 203n52, 205n121, 223; British 176, 188–9, 205n121;

Chinese 87, 146, 166; and Gramsci 209; Indian 166; Western 54, 75, 177
hierarchy 4, 107, 179; "all under heaven" 6, 69; in Asia 24, 37n131, 162; in Chinese tradition 6, 11, 28, 36n126, 69, 100, 223; civilizations and 215, 235; and Confucianism 11, 28; Han/non-Han 61; informal 24; international relations and 69; linguistic 185, 197; status 100
Hinduism 212, 240n102; Hindutva 232–5
Hirschmann, Albert 226
Ho, Ping-Ti 13
Hobson, John 4
Ho Chi Minh 186–7
Hokkien 12, 185, 192, 196, 201n20, 203–4n69
Holcombe, Charles 209
Hollywood see under film
home (vs. host) country 155–8, 169, 171
homogeneity 14, 231, 232, 234
Hong Kong 11–12, 20, 27, 30, 181, 236; and autonomy 66, 71, 79–80, 82–3, 85, 93, 173n10; and becoming Chinese 181–2, 184, 188, 190–8, 203n51, 204n100, 205–6nn106,121; diasporic scholarship 154, 157–8, 165; economic relations of 108, 110, 113, 119n78, 181; and language 184, 188, 205–6n121; and popular culture 16, 190–4, 196–7, 204n100, 205n106, 230; and tourism 195
Hopf, Ted 221
host (vs. home) country 155–8, 169, 171
household registration system 109–10
Howell, Jude 104
Huang, Philip 110, 116
huaqiao 178, 181, 190, 196; *huaqiao* syndrome 189; see also diaspora; overseas Chinese
Hu Haifeng 146
Hui, Victoria Tin-bor 36n126
Hu Jintao: and Confucianism 29; and Japan 126; and Southeast Asia 133, 141, 143–4, 146; and Taiwan 90–1; and US 127, 149n58
hukou see *household registration system*
humanism 10–11, 28, 114, 169
human rights 132, 135, 235; and China 16, 17, 48, 109, 156, 159, 163, 172; see also rights
human security 7, 54, 56–7
humiliation 12, 45; "century of humiliation" 23, 71, 74
Hunt, Michael 71

Huntington, Samuel 154, 166, 212–17, 236, 238n45; see also clash (of civilizations)
Hu Shih 228
hybridity 167, 176, 210; and Anglo-Chinese 12, 70, 153–4, 169–70, 185–9, 199, 203nn51,52,53,69, 204n88, 205n121, 228; "Chimerica" 31; and civilizational practices 220; and diasporic scholarship 157, 167; and Japan 230; "Sino-Japanese-English" 183–92, 195, 198–200; and Southeast Asia 176, 179–81, 183, 185–6, 188–92, 195, 198, 199–200, 201n8, 202n41, 203n51, 204n100, 227–8; and tourism 195

idealism 37n130, 157, 169–70, 173n8; see also liberalism
identities: civilizational 2, 8–9, 14, 65, 67, 214, 228, 235; collective 2, 19, 215–16; and contestation 14, 85, 92, 214–15, 223, 230; fragility of 56; home identity 155–9, 160; identity politics 56, 66, 68, 93; mutual constitution of 155–7; national 14, 56, 60, 65, 68, 72, 192, 223; ontological 155; self-identity 154, 156, 158
Ikenberry, John 5, 6, 121
illiberalism 4; see also liberalism
imitation/mimicking 29, 218; and Japan 229, 231
immigration 16, 165, 175, 177, 179–81, 185, 187, 194; see also migration
imperialism 19, 74, 160; anti-imperialism 167–71, 189; British 81, 236; Chinese 71, 166, 228; collective 183–4, 190; cultural 9, 190, 210; Han 228; and India 166, 212; Japanese 70, 86, 160, 186–7, 231; and language 9, 177–8; Western 5, 81, 167–71; see also colonialism
imports, cultural 230
independence: and frontier 45, 48, 181; Indian 232, 234, 236; Taiwanese 26, 30, 68, 72, 76, 79–80, 86–89, 91–3, 153, 223
India 18, 139, 212, 214, 216, 239n92; and Asian regionalism 127, 132, 134, 137–40, 149n58 and Buddhism 45, 166, 168, 183; "Chindia" 167, 172, 173; and Chung Tan 157–8, 166–73; Indianization 9, 210, 228–9, 231–7; as pluralist 60, 209; Sanskrit 212, 234; and secularism 233–5; and security issues 21, 37n137, 126–7, 132, 134, 137, 140

indirect rule 78, 80
individual 11, 15, 57, 114, 156–7, 166, 173, 219, 227–8; and consumerism 233; individual diplomacy 158; and rights, 235
Indochina 75, 173, 179, 203n5; *see also individual countries*
Indonesia: and ASEAN 121, 126–7, 130; and Asian regionalism 20, 113, 121, 124, 126–7, 130–4, 138, 140, 144–5, 226; and becoming Chinese 175, 179–81, 187–8, 191, 203n68; as Dutch East Indies 179–81, 185, 187, 203n52; East Timor 132; and ethnic division 131, 133–4, 138, 188, 225; *hitacis* 180; *peranakan* 179–80; security 126–7, 132–4; student exchanges 15
industrialization 5, 93, 101–3, 105, 116, 224, 234; and de-industrialization 101–2, 224
industrial policy 1, 103; national champions 20, 104, 224
industrial revolution 234; vs. industrious revolution 19
inequality 17, 35n97, 116, 229, 233; regional 104; *see also* equality
inflation 105
informalism: informal economy 110–11, 225; informal hierarchy 24; informal institutions 93; informal practices 99–100, 117; informal ties 19, 21
integration *see* globalization; regionalization
intellectual property: piracy 16, 175
interdependence 55, 121, 139; *see also* dependence, trade
internationalism 214
internet 168, 171, 194, 196, 204nn88,100; and censorship 16
intervention: China/Singapore 165; and human rights 159; non-interference 17, 44, 75; US interventions 73–5, 124, 129
interwar era 5
Inukai, Tsuyoshi 184, 187
investment, foreign 18, 20, 100; and Asian regionalism 122, 124, 127, 131, 133–4, 137, 141–3, 181, 190, 226; and compressed development 7, 108–11, 113–14, 119n78; by ethnic Chinese 181; and film industry 190; joint ventures 29, 108–9, 133, 141, 143
Iran 232, 240n102
Iraq 22, 232
Iriye Akira 153, 155, 157–63, 169–73, 227
Ishihara, Shintarō 216

Ishikawa, Yoshihiko 186
Islam 2, 11, 45, 173n8, 209–13, 217, 232–3, 235; Islamicization 210; jihad 131
isolation 236; of China 12, 71, 124, 194; of Myanmar 136–8, 140, 225; and Russia 221; of Taiwan 88

Jacques, Martin 4
Japan: anime 191, 194, 204nn93,100; anti-Japanese 126, 190; and Asian regionalism 120–40; Buddhism in 229, 230; colonialism/imperialism 70, 86, 160, 186–7, 223, 231; and Confucianism 11, 28, 229–30; conservatism 169, 230–1; industrialization strategy 1, 5, 18, 30, 99; Japan/China normalization 122, 124; Japanese market 132, 230; Japanization 2, 9, 189, 192, 210, 223, 228–31; Qing dynasty relations 45, 70, 181, 184, 190; Sino-Japanese-English 183–7, 191–2, 195, 198, 204n100, 22; Sino-Japanese war 184, 190; size of economy 120; US-Japan alliance 21, 25–7, 123, 124, 128, 139, 187; Yasukune Shrine 126, 197
Japanese (language) 141, 163, 177, 184–6, 192, 194–7, 204n100, 228
Jasanoff, Maya 215
Jia, Qingguo 5
Jiangsu Province 108, 112, 113
Jiang Zemin 89, 125–6, 141
ji mi see under *statecraft*
Jin, Canrong 30
Jin, Guantao 72
Jinmen and Mazu 76; *see also* Taiwan Straits
Johnston, Alastair Iain 5, 36nn118, 126, 37n130, 91, 218
Jutting, Johannes 107

Kalla, Jusuf 133, 144–5
Kan, Naoto 128, 139
Kang, David 10, 24, 37n130, 114, 157–8, 162
Kang, Xiaoguang 106
Katzenstein, Peter 1, 122, 155, 210
Khilnani, Sunil 233
Khouw Ah Soe 187
Kim Il Sung 66
Kim, Okgyun 184
Kim, Samuel 153, 155, 157–8, 161–3, 169–73, 227
kinship 108, 112, 199, 216
Kipling, Rudyard 209, 237

Kissinger, Henry 10
Kocka, Jürgen 218
Koguryo kingdom 28, 50
Koh, Tommy 216
Koizumi, Junichiro 126, 139, 197
Konuntakiet, Chitra 193
Korea: Koguryo kingdom 28, 50; reunification 66; *see also* North Korea; South Korea
Koyasu, Nobukuni 160
Krasner, Stephen 69, 71
Ku Chieh-kang 195
Ku Huang-ming 186, 203n53
Ku Hung-ming 186
Kukrit, Pramoj 175
Kunming 130, 137, 142
Kuomingtang 73–5, 81, 86, 88, 90–91, 95n71, 181
Kurth, James 213
Kyoto School of Philosophy 159–61

labor 178, 184; cost of 18, 109–10, 116; labor law 110, 116; migrant workers 35n97, 109–10; trade unions 106
Lake, David 69
land 110–11, 143, 149n66; cheap 110, 116, 225; rights 110
language: Chinese script 180, 184–5, 189, 194, 205n120; dialect 19, 196; language technology 204n100, 212; lingua franca 4, 184–6, 189, 197, 203n52, 205n121, 212; mother tongue 12, 203n69, 212; multilingualism 185, 205n121, 121; translation 59, 67, 184, 186–7, 203n53, 212, 221, 228; translingualism 184, 186, 187, 228; written 180, 185, 189, 194, 205n120, 212; *see also specific languages*
language programs 14–15, 140, 205n121; Confucius Institutes 15, 29
Laos: communism in 187; and regionalism 121, 130, 136, 142–4, 146–7, 149n66
Latin America 16; Chile 127; Latin American Forum 30; Trans-Pacific Partnership 127
law 27, 82, 99, 215; Anti-Secession 90; Basic Law of Hong Kong 80 82; commercial 100; international 95n41, 124–5, 132, 221; labor, 110; maritime 124–5, 132; martial 48, 86; regional autonomy 47
Lawrence, Bruce 212
Lee Kuan Yew 165–6, 216
Lee Teng-hui 67, 83, 85, 87–8, 186, 223
legitimation 66–8, 72, 86, 88, 92–3

Leheny, David 239n93
Leonard, Mark 12
Li, Hongzhang 70
Li, Keqiang 141
Li, Yizhou 89
Li, Zehou 71
Liang, Qichao 71, 178
liberalism 5–6, 17, 37n130, 79, 99, 103, 214–15; and Eurocentrism 214; illiberalism 4; liberal democracy 157; and markets 224; neoliberalism 104; and Russia 214
liberalization 27, 131, 233
liberation: peaceful 46, 81 223; of Taiwan 76, 78, 92; of Tibet 81
Lien, Chan 90–1
Lim Boon Keng 185–6
limited alignment 129, 138, 225
Liu, Lydia 184, 211
Liu, Qingfeng 72
Liu, Weiqiang 55
Liu, Xiaobo 16
loans 133, 149n66, 226; concessional 131, 137, 141–5; nonperforming 106; *see also* banking
local governments 89, 104–7, 110, 114, 116, 149n66, 225
Lu Xun 185

Ma, Dazheng 41, 50–3, 55, 57–8, 62
Ma, Eric 192
Ma, Rong 41, 50, 57–61, 63, 64n33
Ma, Ying-jeou 83, 85, 91
Macao 66, 79–85, 93, 108, 110, 113
Macapagal-Arroyo, Gloria 145
Maddison, Angus 34n97
Mahathir, Mohammad 216
Mahbubani, Kishore 216
Malaka, Tan 186
Malaysia 167, 175, 179–80, 188, 191, 193, 196; communism in 187, 198; as Malaya 179, 185, 187, 188, 198; and regionalism 121, 124–5, 130, 132–4, 145
Manchus 13, 37n128, 111, 176, 179, 183
Mandarin (language) 4, 12, 15, 189–97, 203–4n69, 205n121
Mandarinization 189, 193, 196
Mao Zedong 12, 28, 46–8, 57, 73–8, 235, 239n86; and economic development 112, 115; and Taiwan 67, 75–6, 78, 87, 92, 223; and Tibet 81
Marchetti, Gina 197
maritime issues 124–35, 202n39; maritime trade 113, 180, 195, 201n14

markets: Asian 5, 20–1, 190–1, 229–30, 232; Chinese 4, 14, 20, 24, 26, 109, 128, 131, 170; emigreé community 190–1; global 5, 20–1, 134, 184, 191, 217, 229; global market civilization 27; Japanese 132, 230; "mutual markets" 177; socialist market economy 123, 134; Thailand 137; US 16, 124, 128
Marx, Karl 186, 234
Marxism 6, 52, 67, 186; and minority policy 63; in Russia 214
materialism 22, 35n118, 211, 218
McNeil, William 217
mechanisms: of Siniciziation 156, 172, 218–20, 225, 227
merchant capitalism 30; *see also* capitalism
meritocracy 11, 36n126
Mertha, Andrew 106
Middle East 14, 137, 231; Forum on Cooperation between China and Arab States 31; *see also individual countries*
migrants/immigrants 16, 28, 113, 165, 180–1, 187–8, 194, 200; migrant workers 35n97, 109–10, 116, 225
migration 5, 21, 177, 179–80, 182, 185; to mainland 83; passport, Chinese 83, 205n21
military, Chinese: expanding capabilities of 21–3, 26–7, 31, 121, 124, 128, 133; and flexible politics 114; People's Liberation Army 76, 79, 81, 87, 124, 137
Mills, C. Wright 19
Ming dynasty 36n126, 37n128, 43, 81, 113–14, 181; fall of 13, 23; and tributary trade 177, 201n14
minorities 6, 13, 41, 46–9, 51–3, 56–64, 164, 188, 196, 222; and assimilation 12–14, 48, 58, 199; and culturalization 57–60; minority rights 59, 61, 235; orthodoxy 58–9; *see also* frontier; nationalities
minzu see *nationalities*
missiles 22, 121, 123, 127, 130; missile-firing exercises 87; *see also* military, Chinese; nuclear weapons
missionaries 161, 184–5, 188; Greek 213
misunderstanding 159, 160
Miyazaki Tōten 184–5
Mizoguchi, Yuzo 160
modernity 8, 11, 66, 71, 93, 122, 177, 239n93; alternative 29; "Chinese" 185, 198; global civilization of 11, 214–17, 230; postmodernity 93–4; Westphalian/western 86, 92, 195, 230

modernization 6, 20, 71, 79, 89, 122–3, 181, 185; of Japan 231; military 22, 121, 124, 128, 133; and state-owned enterprises 20; of Taiwan 192
Mongolia 45, 181
Mongols 13, 23, 111, 176, 181, 183, 202n39, 230
morality 67, 115; and Confucianism 11, 28, 36n126, 72, 114, 119n83, 185; vs. hegemony 23; and scholarship 161; *see also* Confucianism
Mori, Yoshiro 126
Morris, Ian 211, 215
multiculturalism 55, 57, 153, 185
multilateralism 23, 25–6, 30–1, 47, 127, 129–31, 139, 222; vs. bilateralism 20, 26, 125; forum diplomacy 30–1; *see also* bilateralism
multinational corporations 20, 111, 236
multipolarity 36n126, 45, 126
museums 14; Beijing National Museum 28; Dragon Descendents Museum 193
music 15, 158, 190–2, 204n100, 230
Myanmar see Burma/Myanmar

national champions 20, 104, 224
nationalism, cultural 183, 192, 234
nationalities: *minzu* label 46, 52, 59, 63; nationality policy 41, 46, 51, 52, 56, 59, 82, 222; orthodoxy 58–9; *see also* frontier; minorities
nationalization: of industry 102–3, 105; and minorities 188, 199
National People's Congress 82, 127
nation building 67, 71, 86–8, 176, 223
nation state 11; as actor 154, 228; China as 65–6, 92, 173, 189, 197; India as 233–4; postcolonial 188
NATO 123, 221
naturalism 177
natural resources 129, 132, 141–2; *see also* energy
Naughton, Barry 106–7
navy: China 22, 121, 124, 127; India and Mynamar 137; Japan 127; Vietnam 135; *see also* military, Chinese
Nehru, Jawaharlal 232–4
networks 1–2, 122, 183, 218; and British empire 232; economic 1–2, 5, 19–21, 30, 100, 104, 108–9, 112, 130–4, 136, 138, 140, 224–5; and film industry 191; intellectual 11, 16; and language 29, 184–5; regional production 130–4, 136, 138, 140; revolutionary 198; Sinicization as 13, 67; social 108; and

Taiwan 20, 88, 104, 224; and tipping points 218
Neumann, Iver 221
New Zealand 30, 126, 127
Nixon, Richard M. 77
Nobel Peace Prize 16
nomads 10, 44, 111, 115, 212
nongovernmental organizations 106, 236
non-intervention *see under* intervention
non-traditional security (NTS) 41, 53–6, 63, 125, 148n32, 219
normalization: CCP/KMT 90; Japan/China 122, 124; Philippines/China 188; and Southeast Asian countries 124; Thailand/China 193; US/China 73, 77, 122, 124; Vietnam/China 124, 135; *see also* diplomacy; recognition, diplomatic
North Korea 123, 162–3, 170–3
Noulens, Hilarie 186
nuclear technology: civilian 127, 135–6; weapons 23, 123, 130
Nye, Joseph 34n80

Obama, Barack 127
Occidentalism 216
Oksenberg, Michel 46, 71
Olympics 16, 62, 84–5
"One China" 65, 67–8, 72–9, 87–92, 95n71, 224
"one country, two systems" (*yiguo liangzhi*) 66, 72, 78–83, 85, 93, 95n49, 223
opium 5, 179; Opium War 13, 19, 113, 114, 177
order: regional 14, 68, 122; world 44, 51, 70, 72, 161–2, 169
Orientalism 213, 216, 234; "Orient" vs. "Occident" 159–61
orthodoxy 46, 50, 55, 71–2, 235; and Confucianism 186; and minority issues 58–9, 63; vs. orthopraxy 72–3, 78; Russian Orthodoxy 213–14; Westphalian 72
Osiander, Andreas 93
Ostler, Nicholas 212, 238n24
sugi, Sakae 186
"Other" (vs. "Self") 3, 6, 8–9, 36n118, 153, 176, 198, 199, 216–17, 221–2
overseas Chinese 11–12, 16–20, 165, 181–2, 196–7, 199–200; "alien Chinese" 180, 188; defined 19; economic role 11, 18–20, 27, 29–30, 108–9, 113–14, 225; and popular culture 190–1, 194, 200, 205n120; as *huaqiao* 178, 181, 189, 190, 196; and social power 27; and Taiwan 182, 202n34; *see also* diaspora

Pakistan 149n58, 232
Paracel Islands 124, 127, 132
passport, Chinese 83, 205n21
Pax Sinica 4, 121
peaceful coexistence 31, 75, 95n41
peaceful reunification 20, 78, 90
Pearl River Delta 12, 195
peasants 110, 112, 113, 131, 225; uprisings 37n128, 214
People's Liberation Army 76, 79, 81, 87, 124, 137
peripheries 2–3, 8–9, 11, 23, 41–63, 64n9, 66, 78, 80–1, 223–4; and becoming Chinese 181, 198–9; center/periphery studies 198; and compressed development 107; core-periphery relations 78, 80–1; and diasporic scholarship 155–8; Russia as 213, 221
Peru 127
Phan Boi Chau 185
Philippines: and "becoming Chinese 175, 179, 186–8, 190–2, 201n20; and colonialism 179, 187, 203n52; and language 212; *mestizos* 179; military 22; Mischief Reef 125; and regionalism 121, 123–5, 127, 134, 145, 226; *sangley* 179, 201n20; security issues 22
Pierce, Charles 220
pigtail 179
piracy 28; intellectual property 16, 175
planning, central 9, 103, 107–9, 112–13, 115; *see also* industrial policy
pluralism 10–11, 45, 209–17, 234–6
policy stretch 104, 224–5
Ponce, Mariano 185
popular culture *see* culture, popular
population 3, 109, 172, 217
populism 22
postmodernity 93–4, 102, 116; *see also* modernity
Pouliot, Vincent 220–1, 239n80
poverty 35n97, 62, 131, 137
power: as concept 2, 209; cultural 4, 28, 29; differentials 8; power transition 121–2, 209; social 14, 15, 17–18, 27, 29, 34n80, 226; soft 15
practicality, logic 220–1
pragmatism 49, 82, 198, 222–5; and Chinese nationalism 164–5; and Deng Xiaoping 42, 47, 85, 222; and IR theory 220; pragmatic accommodation 12; flexibility and 105

primordialism 216–17, 231
production, flexible 109, 112; *see also* compressed development; flexible politics
productivity: Chinese 35n97; Japanese 229; productivity politics 122, 131–2, 134, 138, 140
property rights 10, 99–100, 103, 116, 224
protectionism 229, 231; economic closure 9, 113
Protestantism 213; *see also* Christianity
protests/riots 204n100; anti-Japanese 126; Hong Kong 194; Tibet and Xinjiang 42, 48–9, 62
provincial governments *see* local governments
Purdue, Peter 44
Putonghua 189, 196–7, 204n100, 205n121
Pye, Lucian 92, 104, 114

Qiang, Shigong 80–2
Qin, Yaqing 6
Qin dynasty 36n126, 114
Qing dynasty 23, 70, 111, 113–14, 177–81, 186, 201n14; defeat of 6, 45, 49, 70, 181; economic relations 113, 177; and frontier 13, 23, 43–5, 49, 63n4, 81, 92; and Japan 45, 70, 181, 184
Qu Wanwen 107

race 57, 59–60, 179–80, 199, 215, 216; multiracialism 175; racism 146, 193; whiteness 179
rationalization 27, 36n126
Rawski, Evelyn 13
Reagan, Ronald 77
real estate 2, 141, 143, 149n66
realism 5, 68–9, 122, 162, 163, 164, 173n8, 231; classical 69; cultural 36n126, 37n130, 214; defensive 21, 23; neoclassical 23; neorealism/ structural realism 36n126, 37n130, 69; offensive 21–3, 35–6n118, 163; *realpolitik* 27, 37n130, 69
recognition, diplomatic: of PRC 73–5, 77–8; of Taiwan 67, 86–7, 91; *see also* diplomacy; normalization
recombination 2, 4–9, 117, 172; and diaspora 155; and global culture 14, 18, 192; and India 234; and international security 21, 25, 26, 35n113; regionalization 192; Sinicization as 12, 27–31

reform: and Deng Xiaoping 47, 78, 120, 122–3, 223; Doi Moi 123; economic 9, 12, 18, 21, 78, 103–7, 119n78, 120, 122–3, 191; and hukou system 109–10; in Myanmar 136, 138; and state capacity 103–5; tax reform 116
regional autonomy *see* autonomy, regional
regional disparities 104
regionalism: and economic development 2, 19, 121–47, 180, 184, 192–3; evolution of system 122–9; and infrastructural development 126, 133, 135–8, 141–2; linguistic 212; as mosaic 138–40; regional architecture 125, 133; transnational effects 140–7; *see also specific countries*
regulatory state 103–4, 224
Reid, Anthony 201n20
religion 11, 13, 45, 47, 132, 173n9, 185; as civilizational marker 100, 212–13, 215, 217; freedom of 81, 106, 135; fundamentalism 56; and India 212, 232–5, 240n102; and language 211–13; and Russia 213–14; Western 212–3
Renaissance: Chinese 4, 73, 85, 90, 92, 94; European 4
Renan, Ernest 2
renminbi *see under* currency
Republican era 44, 179, 181, 223
Republic of China 6, 41, 46, 73–5, 77, 83, 86–7, 89, 177, 95n71, 202n34
restaurants 7–8, 233; *see also* service industries
restraint 23, 27, 125, 224, 25
retailers/merchandisers 109, 112; *see also* consumerism
return (vs. recombination/rupture) 2, 4, 6–7, 9, 14, 18, 20–1, 23–8, 31, 117, 171–2
reunification, Chinese 7, 9, 72–3, 82, 87–94, 95n71, 219, 223–4; as "dialectics of Sinicization" 65–8 223; "one country, two systems" 66, 72, 78–83, 85, 93, 95n49, 223; peaceful 20, 78, 90, 223
revolution: anti-Manchu 179; Chinese 72–5, 78, 195, 233; Cultural 47, 67, 113; democratic 123; electronic 230; and *huaqiao* 181; industrial 19, 234; Republican 71; revolutionaries 178, 187; in Southeast Asia 176, 186–7, 198
Rice, Condoleezza 132
Rifkin, Jeremy 211, 236

rights 12, 153; citizen 82; human 16, 17, 48, 109, 132, 135, 156, 159, 163, 172, 235; individual 235; land use 110; minority 235; political, 46, 59, 61; property 10, 99–100, 103, 116, 224; of states 37n131
Risse, Thomas 218
ritual 72, 78
Rizal, Jose 185
Ross, Robert 5
Rudolph, Susanne Hoeber 212
Ruggie, John Gerard 71, 93, 220
rupture 2–14, 18, 21–23, 26–8, 31, 35n113, 117, 120, 155, 171, 221; economic 99; and minority framework 45–6,
rural areas 19, 102, 108–10, 112, 115–16; and collectivization 102, 105, 112; India as 234; vs. urban area 35n97, 109, 116, 199
Russia 25, 104, 108; as civilization 213–14; development strategy 100–1; language 163, 178, 228; and NATO 221; role in Asia 25, 128, 135; *see also* Soviet Union

sacredness 212, 216
sanctions: China 124, 169; Indonesia 132; Myanmar 136–9, 225
sangley 179, 201n20
Sanskrit 212, 234
scholarship: as cultural brokering 153, 227; diasporic scholarship 153–7, 168–73, 197; independent 157; *see also* Iriye, Akira; Kim, Samuel; Tan, Chung; Wong, John
Schwartz, Benjamin 71–2
science 137, 185, 218, 235; scientism 169
secession 181; Anti-Secession Law 90
secularism 11, 213, 217; and India 233–5
security: border security studies 41, 53–7; East Asian security system 25; frontier security 41, 53, 56, 63, 222; hub-and-spokes model 122, 182, 187 191; human security 7, 54, 56–7; nontraditional security 41, 53–6, 63, 125, 148n32, 219; securitization 54; security studies 30; Sinocentric order 3, 14, 21, 23, 25, 69–70, 122, 146, 199, 205n121; and "Western" concepts 54, 68–9, 222; *see also* Westphalian system
Segal, Adam 107
Sein, Thein 136–8
Selden, Mark 35n97, 110, 123

"Self" (vs. "Other") 3, 6, 8–9, 36n118, 153, 176, 198, 199, 216–17, 221–2
self-identity 154, 156, 158
self-knowledge/self-understanding 155, 157, 172–3, 230–1
self-restraint *see* restraint
Sen, Amartya 233
Sena, Shiv 233
September 11: 15, 22, 30, 215
service industries 7, 102–3, 109, 116, 212
Shambaugh, David 5, 34n80
Shanghai 4, 7, 112, 185–7, 188; and film 190–1; Shanghai Communiqué
Shanghai Cooperation Organization 23, 25, 31, 47, 125, 222
Shanghai Five 47, 222
Shen, Kuo 4
Shibata, Satoru 149n66
Shih, Chih-yu 7, 10, 15, 17, 29, 153, 189, 219, 223, 227
Shinawatra, Thaksin 131
Shintoism 231
Shiraishi, Takashi 7, 10, 12, 19, 29, 115, 120, 185, 219, 225–6
Shūsui, Kōtoku 186
Shwe, Than 136–7, 141–2
Singapore 15, 91, 167, 205n121; and anti-Western discourse 216; and Asianism 184, 186; and Chinese normalization 124; and Confucianism 28, 185; economic relations of 20, 27, 30, 113, 119n78, 121, 130, 133–4; and film 191, 192; and John Wong 154, 157–8, 164–6, 169–71; and language 12, 184, 186, 188, 203n69; and overseas Chinese 11, 19; and regionalism 126, 127, 130, 133–4
Sinicization: defined 9, 12–15, 65, 120, 153–4, 176, 209; Anglo-Sinicization 189, 198–200, 205n121; as border-crossing 42, 51, 54, 61, 219; in comparative perspective 209–11; cultural 156; dialectical 7, 65–8, 220, 223; as discursive 153–6, 178, 186, 194, 199–200, 222–3, 227; de-Sinicization 9, 65, 67, 85–8, 154, 169, 176, 188, 223, 227; as horizontal and vertical 99, 100, 111, 115, 117, 219; mechanisms of 218–20; as multidirectional 9–10, 44, 154–5, 157, 218–19, 227, 233; as multi-sited 9–10, 122, 154, 172–3, 179, 192–3, 199, 218–19, 227–8, 233; as mutual constitution 155–7, 172–3, 176; and non-linearity 9–10, 44, 170, 176, 179, 218, 219; partial 144, 226; as

recombination 27-31, 155, 172; unilinear/simplistic understandings 4–5, 10, 130, 138, 154, 176, 199, 210; re-Sinicization 9, 65, 67, 85–6, 92, 154, 169, 176, 188, 189, 192, 199, 223, 227; reversibility of 9–10, 45, 49, 176, 179, 218, 219, 222; self-Sinicization 154
Sinocentrism 3, 5, 10–11, 14, 66, 122, 146, 157–8, 164, 199, 205n121; Han-Sinocentrism 181, 196; and international security 21, 23, 25; neo-Sinocentrism 72; and Taiwanese nationalism 88; and the "West" 126, 176; and world unity 69-70
Sinosphere 176, 196
small- and medium-sized enterprises 20, 30, 108–9, 112–13
Smedley, Agnes 186
smuggling/trafficking 28, 130
So, Alvin 103
socialism 18, 74, 95n61, 123, 173n8, 176, 182, 186–7, 198, 232; and economy 122–23, 134; socialist revolution 176, 223; *see also* communism
Soe Hok Gie 175
solidarism 158–9
Song dynasty 36n126, 81, 112–13
South China Sea 125–7, 132, 135, 138
South Johnson Reef 124
South Korea 22–3, 28; and Asian regionalism 113, 121–6, 131–2, 134; cultural influence of 230; developmental strategy 18, 99, 101, 104, 224; film industry 191; industrialization 101, 104; *see also* Korea
sovereignty: and Asian regionalism 129; Chinese commitment to 6, 26, 41–2, 44–5, 48, 50, 61, 222; Chinese way of 78–80, 82–3, 85, 90, 93, 223–4; emergence of 68–9; and frontier, 41–2, 44–6, 48, 50–1, 54–6, 61; historical loss of 19; incomplete 92; and nontraditional security 54–6; and constraints for "One China" 65, 66–9, 71–3, 75, 77–80, 82–93; and "one country, two systems" 66, 72, 78–80, 82–3, 85, 93, 22; pooled 90, 224; popular sovereignty 198; versus *tianxia* 69, 82, 91–2
Soviet Union 73–7; and central planning 115; collapse of 42, 47, 59, 64n33, 123, 134, 214, 221, 222; containment of 122; ethnic relations 59; film industry 232; and Leninism 82; Soviet model 59; *see also* Russia
Spain 2, 24; Spanish Philippines 179, 203n52
spatiality 41, 50, 68, 106, 186, 194–5, 201n12, 218, 222, 227; compression of 66; "international space" 87; political space 54, 69, 71, 92; rhetorical space 42, 56, 222; symbolic space 211
special administrative regions 79–80, 82–4
splittism 56
sports 34n80, 85; baseball 230; cricket 233; *see also* Olympics
Spratley Islands 124, 127, 132
Stalin, Josef 57, 73; Stalinism 59, 214
Stam, Allan 24–5
state corporations *see* state-owned enterprises
statecraft 68, 78, 80–1, 92; "loose reign" (*ji mi*) 80–1, 219, 223–4
state-owned enterprises 20, 109, 113, 116, 118n64, 137, 142, 226; *see also under* collectivization
statism 4, 68, 71, 91, 93, 158, 224; and Russia 214
status quo powers 26, 216
stereotypes 175
Stokes, Gale 6
Straits Exchange Foundation 89, 91
student exchanges *see under* education
Sudarsono, Yuwono 134
Suehiro, Tetcho 185
Suganami Hedemi 157–9
Suharto 132–3, 203n68
Sukarno 132, 203n68
Sun Yat-sen 86, 95n61, 178, 181, 185, 187
suzerain states 23–4
Swedberg, Richard 100
Tagore, Rabindranath 166–8, 232, 234
Taiping rebellion 37n128, 177
Taiwan: '92 consensus 90–1; as "Chinese Taipei" 82, 85, 91; during Cold War 75, 89, 92, 181–2, 190; *dangwai movement* 86; de-Sinicization 65, 67, 85–8, 223; and democracy 7, 67, 85–9, 223; Democratic Progressive Party 86, 88, 91, 95n71; economic relations 18, 20, 99, 108, 110, 119n78, 122, 181–2; independence 26, 30, 68, 72, 76, 79–80, 86–89, 91–3, 153, 223; industrialization 101, 104; Kuomintang 73–5, 81, 86, 88, 90–91, 95n71, 181; liberation of 76, 78, 223; Mainland Affairs Council 83;

One China" 65, 67–8, 72–9, 87–92, 95n71, 224; one country, two systems 66, 72, 78–83, 85, 93, 95n49, 223; and peaceful development 90–2, 94; and pooled sovereignty 90; re-; popular culture 16, 189–95, 205n120, 230; Sinicization 9, 65, 67, 85–6, 192, 223; Taiwanization 67, 86–7, 89, 202n34, 223–4
Taiwanization 67, 86–7, 89, 202n34, 223–4; *see also* de-Sinicization
Taiwan Strait: crises 76, 87
Takeuchi, Yoshimi 160
Tan, Chung 153, 155, 157–8, 166–73, 174n38
Tan, Yun-shan 166, 168
Tang dynasty 43, 81, 196
tariffs *see* protectionism
taxes 20, 36n126, 85, 105, 179, 190; in SARs 79; tax reform 116
Taylor, A.J.P. 22
Tejapira, Kasian 179
television 14–6, 183, 193–5, 230; in India 232–3; in Southeast Asia 175, 205n120; Taiwanese 190, 193
temporality 154; and borders 42, 50; and civilizations 2, 117, 198, 211, 218, 222; and compressed development 99–102, 104, 117; and flexibility 50, 51
Teng, Teresa 191
territorial integrity 25; and frontier 44, 46–7, 49, 51, 53; China's historical loss of 71, 75; and Southeast Asia 132, 135; and Taiwan 67, 75, 77, 90
territoriality 6–7, 69, 71–3, 91–3, 222; de/reterritorialization 177–80, 182, 194, 195, 200, 201n12; and disputes 124–32, 134, 135, 138, 225; incomplete 71, 92; territorial sea 124–5; territorialization, 194, 201n12; unbundling of, 82–5, 93
terrorism 32n13, 56; September 11: 15, 22, 30, 215
Thailand 22, 225, 226; and Asian regionalism 113, 121, 124, 130–1, 133, 134, 137–8, 140–1, 144, 147, 148n32; becoming "Chinese" 175, 179, 187, 190–1, 193–4; democracy in 144; Dragon Descendant's Museum 193; and Myanmar 137–8; and popular culture 175, 191
Thayer, Carl 126, 129
Third World 101–2, 111, 162; Bandung Conference 232; *see also* developing countries
Thirty Years War 213

Thun, Eric 107
Thurow, Lester 34n97
Tiananmen Square 124, 163
tianxia see under *unity*
Tibet 13, 23, 26, 37n133, 43, 45, 71, 80–1, 181; Dalai Lama 48; Maoist policy 81; protests in 42, 48–9, 60, 62–3; tourism in 47
Tilly, Charles 114, 209, 218
Toer, Pramoedya Ananta 187
Too, Lillian 193
tourism: Chinese tourists 126, 131, 140; "ethnic tourism" 47, 195, 222; from Taiwan 83
township and village enterprises 108, 113
trade: dependence 22, 26, 29, 35n97, 116, 121, 130, 131, 134, 140; forced free trade 184; intra-Asian 5, 19, 29, 121, 120–41, 139, 147, 182, 184, 187, 226; total trade (China) 120; triangular 122, 124, 128–9, 139, 187; tributary 3, 24, 36n126, 37n130, 177, 183, 201n14; World Trade Organization 20, 85, 124, 135; *see also individual countries*; markets; protectionism
trafficking/smuggling 28, 130
transnationalism: analytical approaches 11–12, 29, 198, 228
Trans-Pacific Partnership 127
transparency 128, 142; vs. opaqueness 226
triangular trade 122, 124, 128–9, 139, 187; *see also* trade
tributary trade 3, 24, 36n126, 37n130, 177, 183, 201n14
Truman, Harry 75
trust 11, 169, 222 233
Tsui Kai-yuen 104,
Tu, Wei-ming 11, 87, 197
"two Chinas" 67–8, 76–7; *see also* reunification, Chinese

Uchimura, Hiroko 107
unemployment 103, 110
unification: as cultural value 70, 71m 92; German unification 1, 123; *see also* reunification, Chinese; unity
unions, trade 106
United States: American Creed 213; American Dream 17; Americanization 9, 99, 189, 210; Anglo-America 12, 189, 236; and arms sales 77–8, 132; and Asian regionalism 120–40; Congress 77, 231; consumption 31, 229; decline 4, 139, 170; defense cooperation 122, 127–8, 132, 134–5; ethnic relations in 60;

foreign interventions 73–5, 124, 129; Hollywood 15, 28–9, 187, 189, 190, 191, 197, 232; hub and spokes model 122, 182, 187 191; popular culture 7, 16, 187, 230; power of 4–6, 67–8, 122, 171, 183, 176, 187, 189, 203n52, 205n121, 223, 228; and religion 213; scholarship in, 5–7, 32n13, 167, 233; student exchanges 15; and unilateralism 26, 30; unilateralism 26, 30, 210; US/China normalization 73, 77, 122, 124; US-Japan alliance 21, 25–7, 123, 124, 128, 139, 187; US market 16, 124, 128; Washington consensus 12, 17
unity: all under heaven" (*tianxia yitong*) 6, 68–70, 82, 91–2, 154, 228; disunity 70–2; "great unity" (*da-yitong*) 10, 81, 228; ideology of world unity 69–70; *see also* reunification, Chinese; territorial integrity
universalism 155–61, 213, 215, 220, 224, 235; and Confucioniams 185; and universal emperorship 13, 36n126, 69, 72
urban areas 194, 236; compared to rural 35n97, 105, 109; 116; middle class 131, 180, 188, 197, 199; workforce 225
Uyghurs 80, 181

values: Asian 216; Chinese 99–100, 169; and civilizations 3, 100, 111, 172, 210, 213–16; universality of 155, 158–60
vassal states 24, 28
Vejjajiva, Abhisit 137
Vietnam 2, 11, 16, 26, 212; and Asian regionalism 113, 121, 123–5, 127, 130, 134–6, 138, 140–1, 147; and becoming Chinese 183, 185, 186, 187, 191, 202n41; security issues 36–7n128, 114, 123-5, 127, 135, 140, 225

wages 110, 116
Wahid, Abdurahman 175
Waldron, Arthur 43, 47
Wallerstein, Immanuel 56
Waltz, Kenneth 69
Wang Daohan 89, 91, 95n71
Wang, Edward 6
Wang, Gungwu 13, 70, 158, 167, 177, 182, 185, 189, 197, 202n41
Wang, Jisi 5
Wang, Shaoguang 103
Wang, Yizhou 54–5
Wang, Yong 55
Wang, Youqiang 104

Wang, Yuan-Kang 36
warring states period 23, 70, 114
Washington consensus 12, 17
Watson, James 72
Weber, Max 27
welfare, social 116; *see also* education; health; inequality; unemployment
Wen, Jiabao 29, 131, 136–7, 141, 149n58
West: anti-West sentiment 216; and binary thinking 2, 14, 184, 198, 209, 237, 239n93
Westphalian paradigm 5–7, 25, 30, 162, 223; and frontiers 42, 45, 50–1, 54; and "one China" 66–75, 84, 86, 88–93; predicament of 86, 88–93; as single lens 91; *see also* sovereignty
Wittfogel, Karl 111
Wolfe, Martin 31
Wolff, Larry 213
women 3, 7; *see also* women
Wong, Christine 104
Wong, John 153, 155, 157–8, 164–6, 169–73, 227
Wong, Kar-wai, 196–7
Woodside, Alexander 44
world order studies 161
World Trade Organization 20, 85, 124, 135
World War I 22
World War II 19, 30, 86, 158, 160, 182, 223, 231, 232
Wu Jieh-min 35n97, 110

xenophobia 212
Xiamen 195
Xi Jinping 136, 141
Xinhua News Agency 14
Xinjiang 13, 23, 42–3, 45, 47–9; protests in 42, 48–9, 60–3, 181
Xu, Lili 41, 50, 53, 55, 57
Xu Xin, 7, 9, 25, 30, 65, 219, 223–4

Yan, Xuetong 6
Yang, Dali 103
Yang, Lien-sheng 70, 80–1
Yellow River 111, 194, 195; Yellow River Capitalism 12
yiguo liangshi see *"one country, two systems"*
Yuan dynasty 43, 111, 113
Yudhoyono, Susilo Bambang 127, 132–3, 145
Yunnan Province 47, 138, 142; Kunming 130, 137, 142
Yu Xiaofeng 41, 50, 53–7, 63
Yu Ying-shih 71

Zeitlin, Jonathan 9
Zeng Guofan 70
Zhang, Feng 6, 36n126
Zhang, Guohua, 81
Zhang, Ruizhuang 23
Zhang, Yimou 196–7
Zhang, Zhidong 70
Zhao Tingyan 6, 91
Zhejiang Province 108, 112–13, 165
Zhejiang University 54–6

Zheng, Bijian 91
Zheng, He 4, 14, 24
Zheng, Yongnian 107, 158, 164–5
Zhou Enlai 74–6, 82
Zhou Ping 52–3
Zhu, Rongji 126
Zhu, Tianbiao 7, 9, 18, 20, 21, 29, 99, 219, 223–4
Zi Xun 23